The Growth of African
Civilisation

D0282067

The Making of Modern Africa

2 The Late Nineteenth Century to the Present Day

E. A. Ayandele B.A., Ph.D.
Professor of History, University of Ibadan

J. D. Omer-Cooper M.A.
Professor of History, University of Zambia

R. J. Gavin M.A., Ph.D.
Reader in History, Ahmadu Bello University

A. E. Afigbo B.A., Ph.D.
Lecturer in History, University of Nigeria

Longman

Longman Group Limited
London

Associated companies, branches and representatives
throughout the world

First published 1971
Third impression 1974

ISBN 0 582 60262 9

Filmset by Photoprint Plates Ltd., Rayleigh, Essex

Printed in Hong Kong by
Sheck Wah Tong Printing Press

Contents

Acknowledgements

The publishers are grateful to the following for permission to
reproduce photographs:

J. Allan Cash, pp. 71, 293; Associated Press Ltd., p. 297;
Barnaby's Picture Library, pp. 338, 355; Black Star (René
Groebli), p. 85; Camera Press, pp. 66, 172, 300; Clarendon
Press, p. 170; Collins, Publishers, from *Lugard, the years of
authority*, by Margery Perham, p. 156; De Beers, p. 202;
Edinburgh University Press, from *Independent Africa*, by
George Shepperson, p. 282; Ghana Information Service,
p. 169; The John Hillelson Agency Ltd., pp. 250, 265;
Histoire de l'Algerie Illustrée, p. 115; Historical Picture
Service, Chicago, pp. 205, 207, 215, 260; Institute of Ethiopian
Studies, Addis Ababa, p. 98; Keystone Press, pp. 77, 120, 186,
189, 298, 360, 366; Mansell Collection, pp. 217, 219, 223, 242,
311, 321; Nigeria Magazine, p. 143; Popperfoto, pp. 89, 96,
280, 285, 350, 369, 372, 374; Public Record Office, pp. 58, 138,
139, 140, 225, 226; Radio Times Hulton Picture Library,
pp. 54, 233, 240, 252, 273, 333; Rhodesian Information
Service, p. 302; Jean Ribière, p. 184; Universal Pictorial
Press and Agency Ltd., p. 62; University of Ibadan Library,
pp. 146, 165.

The photograph on the cover is reproduced from a painting
by Afewerk Teklé

iv

List of maps

The Growth of African Civilisation Series

This series is especially designed to provide students in Africa with books covering the new syllabuses for West African and Cambridge Overseas School Certificates and the East African Council for Examinations. Factually and in interpretation the books are in line with the most modern thinking on African history in universities and research institutes in Africa.

The following books are included in the series:

1. **A History of West Africa 1000–1800**
   New edition: by Basil Davidson, with F. K. Buah and the advice of Professor J. F. A. Ajayi

2. **The Revolutionary Years: West Africa since 1800**
   by Professor J. B. Webster and Professor A. A. Boahen, with a contribution by Dr. H. O. Idowu

3. **The Making of Modern Africa 1800–1960**
   (two volumes)
   by Professor J. D. Omer-Cooper, Professor E. A. Ayandele, Dr. A. E. Afigbo and Dr. R. J. Gavin

4. **East and Central Africa to the Late Nineteenth Century**
   by Basil Davidson, with J. E. F. Mhina and the advice of Professor B. A. Ogot

Other books are planned for this series.

Introduction   The invasion of Africa

Uninvaded Africa

For a great part of recorded history Africa has been in contact with peoples living outside the continent in Europe and in Asia. This contact was closest in the case of the peoples living north of the Sahara desert. North Africans, Egyptians and, to a lesser extent, Ethiopians discussed religion and trade and disputed power with neighbours beyond Africa's shores in southern Europe and the Middle East. As for the rest of the continent, contacts with non-Africans were mainly confined to the coasts and their immediate hinterland. Above all Africa was seldom successfully attacked by forces from outside. While conquering hordes and powerful states from time to time surged across the Eurasian land mass between China and India and the shores of the Atlantic and while every substantial state in that area had to calculate the strength or weakness of its neighbours, Africa south of the Sahara was very much a closed world of its own which made its own adjustments between rising and falling African empires without reference to the state of things in Europe or Asia. Apart from the Portuguese incursions into Angola in the seventeenth century, the Europeans, Arabs and Indians who traded on Africa's coasts did not venture far beyond their trading ships or forts at any time before the nineteenth century. The foreign traders on the coast could to some extent influence the politics of the hinterland especially by their encouragement of the slave trade. But the impact of the slave trade has often been grossly exaggerated by historians as have been the estimates of the number of slaves carried across the Atlantic. The political influence of foreign traders did not reach far inland and the traders themselves seldom secured more than a local dominance while many carried on their businesses by leave of the African rulers. The peoples of North Africa who were involved in power struggles with non-African states were, from the time of the seventh century Arab invasions onward, more or less able to hold their own. Between the eighth and tenth centuries they extended their empires to Spain and Syria. In the sixteenth century all North Africa up to Morocco fell under Ottoman rule but the local governments maintained a large measure of autonomy within the Ottoman system. Egypt in particular remained an important centre of power within the Empire and from time to time parts of western Arabia fell under the control of Cairo.

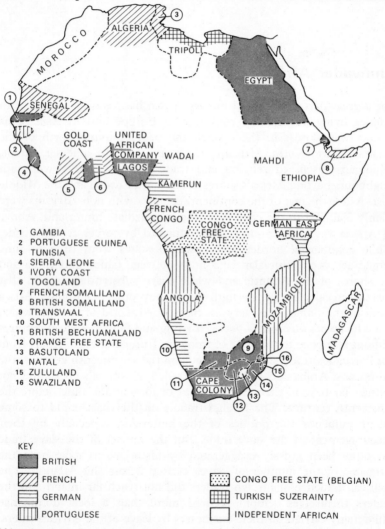

1 GAMBIA
2 PORTUGUESE GUINEA
3 TUNISIA
4 SIERRA LEONE
5 IVORY COAST
6 TOGOLAND
7 FRENCH SOMALILAND
8 BRITISH SOMALILAND
9 TRANSVAAL
10 SOUTH WEST AFRICA
11 BRITISH BECHUANALAND
12 ORANGE FREE STATE
13 BASUTOLAND
14 NATAL
15 ZULULAND
16 SWAZILAND

KEY

▓ BRITISH

▨ FRENCH

▤ GERMAN

▥ PORTUGUESE

▦ CONGO FREE STATE (BELGIAN)

▦ TURKISH SUZERAINTY

☐ INDEPENDENT AFRICAN

Africa showing colonial possessions by the end of the nineteenth century

It is easy to confuse Europe's subjection of people of African descent in the Americas with European dominance over Africa itself. Such a confusion existed in the minds of many people in Europe from the late eighteenth century onward. The fact that African rulers and traders sold prisoners of war, convicted criminals and others into European slavery did not of itself diminish the political independence of those who made such sales. The slaves once sold became a subject people but Africa remained as free as ever. The European trading posts on the African coasts were, until the nineteenth century, like flies on the back of an elephant. Africa went its own way, settling its own problems without having to take account of the pressure of invading forces from outside.

Why was Africa invaded in the late nineteenth century?

This situation began to change during the nineteenth century and had completely changed by 1900. By 1900 most of Africa had been invaded by outsiders for the first time in its history and had fallen into the possession of a number of European states. Egypt, which, despite invasion in 1798, had driven off a British attacking force as late as 1807, was occupied by Britain in 1882. Morocco, which had once ruled Spain, was partitioned between Spain and France in 1912. Everywhere throughout the continent the Europeans in the small trading forts along the coast had pushed out over the land and soldiers and administrators from European countries had fastened their rule upon the people of the continent. Why did all this come about? Why did Africa so suddenly fall, for the first time, and, as it turned out, for a very brief period of its history, under foreign rule?

A problem for historians

Many historians and others have tried to find answers to these questions. Much thought has been given to the question of why Europe *decided* to occupy Africa in the late nineteenth century. Somewhat less attention has been paid to the related question of why Europe *was able* to do so. It is easy to take it for granted that whenever Europe decided to occupy Africa it could do so and that therefore one need only look for European motives. We need not agree that Europe could have taken Africa whenever it liked. First let us investigate the question 'why did Europe decide to occupy Africa in the late nineteenth century?'

The forces of industrial capitalism

In the hundred years before the 1880s Europe had been steadily drawing ahead of the rest of the world in the fields of economic organisation and application of science and technology to production. The 'industrial revolution' began in central England in the eighteenth century as large cities grew and the numbers of those working in industry began to exceed those engaged in agriculture. From England, large-scale industry spread in the early nineteenth century across the channel to Belgium, north-east France and western Germany. Thence it extended further, reaching the Hapsburg Empire and northern Italy by the end of the century. Europe during the nineteenth century became the workshop of the world with an insatiable appetite for the raw materials to feed her industries and an ever vigilant eye on the growth of markets for her manufactures. By the late nineteenth century this concern about sources of raw materials and markets had become more serious in the different European countries than at any time hitherto. European industry in the 1890s was still producing more or less the same things as it had at the start of the industrial revolution. Textiles and iron and steel goods were still the main final products. The numbers of firms producing these goods had steadily multiplied. They competed vigorously with one another. Improved methods of production usually favoured larger firms with larger financial resources and so the smaller, weaker businesses were being increasingly driven into bankruptcy or eaten up by the larger. All were engaged in a race for survival. The smaller firms were trying desperately to maintain their positions, the larger were seeking to extend themselves to avoid being overtaken by their rivals. All were subject to the effect of periodical trade depressions when it became particularly difficult to sell goods, so that factories and men stood idle. At the time of the 'scramble', 1884–85, European industry was in a depressed condition and industrialists were especially anxious at that time to protect themselves. They turned to their governments to help them in this by hedging round the national market with high tariff barriers to keep out foreign manufactures. In 1880 Germany went over to a high tariff policy. Within twelve years, France, the United States and other European countries (except Britain) had followed suit. This ended the free trade period of the mid-nineteenth century. It ushered in a period when the idea that governments should protect their industries became one of the strongest economic ideas in Europe.

A new idea about colonies

It was a short step from the idea of protecting a market for industry at home to the idea of creating a new, protected market for industry by seizing colonies abroad. This was especially so in the late nineteenth century because the idea of what 'colonies' were was changing. In the early nineteenth century, 'colonies' had been thought of mainly as places where Europeans could go and settle—like Canada, Australia, New Zealand or Algeria. The setting up of this sort of 'colony' did not particularly interest industrialists. It was also the sort of 'colony' that men like Bismarck the Chancellor of Germany did not want. But at the very time that Bismarck was saying that he did not want 'colonies', some writers were changing the meaning of the word 'colony'. They spoke of 'colonies of exploitation' where Europeans would not settle but where European money could be used to increase production and create new markets and sources of raw materials. This sort of colony *did* interest industrialists. The idea of such colonies also became popular among people generally, apart from those directly connected with industry. As enthusiasm for such colonies grew, people began to press governments to establish them and create new markets for national industry which would, they expected, be protected from the competition of goods produced in other countries by high tariffs. Britain still stuck to free trade. But as other powers became interested in making colonies with high tariff barriers British industrialists became alarmed and called on the British government to set up colonies where British goods would not be kept out.

How important was Africa economically ?

The development of ideas of this sort and the background of industrial rivalry which gave rise to them in Europe produced a general disposition favourable to the acquisition of colonies. It strengthened the already prevailing belief that governments had a duty to use national power overseas to support national economic enterprise. But this general disposition favourable to the acquisition of colonies should not be confused with specific pressures placed upon government actually to seize territory in Africa. These broad ideas may have altered the level of national aggressiveness but they were not necessarily followed through in detail in all circumstances. For example, despite what was said of the necessity to secure exclusive markets, the goods and trade of other European countries were not in fact excluded from the great majority of colonial territories seized by particular European states in Africa up to 1914. Furthermore, Africa was not regarded as an area in which large commercial gains could be made. The existing trade between Europe and Africa was small in the 1880s by comparison with European trade with other parts of the world. In particular, industrialists in Britain, which was to acquire such a large number of African colonies, had a low opinion of Africa's commercial potential. Germany's trade with Africa was rising at the time of the 'scramble' but so was Germany's trade elsewhere and the African proportion of Germany's total foreign trade was extremely small. The competitive search for markets and sources of raw materials that was growing in Europe only affected European attitudes to Africa in a very general way. Few of the great producers of goods in Europe put direct pressure on their governments to occupy territory in Africa.

The economic interest groups

Direct pressure came rather from those in Europe who were already directly involved economically in Africa at the time the scramble began. It came from those who had invested money in trading establishments on the African coasts, those who had lent money or secured concessions of land in Egypt and North Africa, and those who were making money from South African diamond and gold mines and who hoped to make more by extending their operations north-ward. All of these groups had behind them the financial power of industrial Europe. To a greater or lesser extent they could draw upon the capital resources of the European money market which during the nineteenth century had become incomparably larger, better organised and wider spread in its ramifications than any money market the world had hitherto known. During the nineteenth century the European banker or money-lender could lend money more cheaply and in larger quantities than anyone else. The European trader who could more easily borrow from these sources could wait longer than his rivals for repayment for the goods he sold. The result of this was that wherever legal arrangements were favourable, European merchants, money-lenders and their local agents had penetrated African society and secured control of a large part of the economic life of particular countries. This was most outstandingly the case in Egypt and North Africa where the system of 'capitulations' which placed Europeans and their protégés under a special legal statute operated to their advantage. Had the amount of credit or capital available in North Africa and Europe been equal, these 'capitulations' would not have had this effect. The 'capitulations' were only meant to provide the sort of special arrangements that predominantly agricultural societies all over the world had frequently accorded to the small communities of foreign or cosmopolitan traders. But the amount of credit available in North Africa and Europe was not equal and the 'capitulations' opened the door to large European investment in trade and other branches of North African economic life. Not only this but North African governments who wanted loans to extend their activities had to turn to Europe which alone could provide finance on the scale required. Elsewhere in Africa there was not the same scope for the penetration of the economy by European finance. Along most of the West African coast, the inland movement of European economic enterprise was blocked by so-called 'middlemen'—these were states or groups who combined the control of politics and economics in the areas close to the coast and who would not permit the establishment of direct contact between European firms and those in the hinterland. The 'middlemen' themselves absorbed substantial amounts of credit from European sources but they made their own commercial links with the peoples neighbouring them and the economies of West Africa were full of economic, social and political discontinuities that hampered the free flow of credit. In East Africa European merchants were active and, in addition, the Indian merchants used the capital concentrated in the Indo-British money markets of western India to finance trade along the routes from Zanzibar to the Lakes. In South Africa English law prevailed although its form was modified in the case of the Boer Republics. Generally speaking, European capital could move in freely and it did so in the form of investment in diamond mines and railways and, after 1886, in the gold mines of the Transvaal. Those who had invested money in Africa were apt to turn from time to time to seek the assistance of European governments in protecting their investments or furthering their trade. They did not always do so. Before the late nineteenth century European merchants in West Africa were not very enthusiastic about getting European governments to interfere in Africa. When they were doing good business, as they had been at the middle of the century, government interference could sometimes be more of a hindrance than a help. Certainly they were happy to have government warships come and help them collect debts. But the actions of the government could often cause them inconvenience. For example, in the middle of the nineteenth century, the interference of the British government in the Niger Delta made it easier for new European and even African traders to start business in competition with the old established European merchants on the coast. The traders in Senegal quickly tired of the political interferences and consequent wars of the Colonial Government during the 1850s because the wars were too often paid for by taxes on their trade. But in the 1880s business for European traders in West Africa was bad. Trade was stagnant and the prices of palm oil and groundnuts in Europe were not rising as they had been thirty years before. The European merchants therefore had to find new ways of employing their capital or force the Africans they were trading with to accept lower prices. If not they had to reduce their own profits. A number of them sank into bankruptcy as a result. The rest anxiously sought ways out of their difficulties either by combining to force down producer prices or by forcing their way past the middlemen to employ their capital in organising the purchase of cash crops nearer the source. The twists and turns they made to achieve these ends brought them into conflict with African traders and rulers who were under similar pressure and as relations deteriorated the European traders turned to European governments for political and military assistance.

But which governments were to interfere? This question frequently produced divisions among the traders because each tended to fear that the government of some country other than their own would tend to discriminate against them. So, in most cases, each set of merchants appealed to its own government to interfere first before the other governments had a chance to act. And when it came to the question of breaking through to the interior markets, which interested merchants so much in the 1880s, another reason for international rivalry came up. The traders in each port feared that the land behind the port would be taken by a European colonial power which owned another port nearby. For example the French at Cotonou might take Abeokuta and divert all the trade of Egbaland away from Lagos. The Lagos merchants would thereby lose many of their customers and the valuable shops and warehouses they had built would become worth much less. The Germans in Duala similarly feared a British movement round Cameroon mountain and the French in Ivory Coast feared the British moving across from the Gold Coast. Merchants in all the ports of West Africa were very anxious that as much as possible of the country behind the ports should be brought under the same government as the port itself. So they urged their governments in Europe to take land in the interior and they could expect that in this they would be supported by the colonial officials in the West African colonies who feared that the diversion of trade would result in a fall in their revenues which came almost entirely from taxes on trade. European governments frequently received petitions from merchants trading in Africa during the late nineteenth century asking them to claim African land.

Such petitions from European merchants in West Africa carried less weight than the clamour of those who had money invested in Egypt and North Africa, either privately or in Egyptian or Tunisian government bonds. The Egyptian public debt amounted to 96 million Egyptian pounds in 1884 most of which was held in Europe. Much of the debt had been incurred during the middle 1860s when Egypt was exporting cotton heavily at attractive prices. When the American Civil War ended and American cotton began once more to compete, Egypt's economic boom came to an end. The Khedive was not able to find the money to repay debts he had contracted and to cover other commitments and so he had to borrow more at ruinous rates of interest. Egypt had scarcely the resources available to continue paying the interest on the debt but the European bond holders were determined to have their 'pound of flesh'. The bold holders were numerous and vociferous especially in France. They included more men of importance in European political society than the West African merchants could muster. The bond holders did not actually tell the governments of Europe to occupy Egypt but they insisted that the interests on their loans be repaid and it soon became clear that no Egyptian government which depended on the consent of the Egyptian people could afford to do that. Their demand for repayment was therefore tantamount to a demand that Egypt be brought under European control.

Traders in West Africa and bond holders in Egypt were trying to get government to protect investments which had gone sour. Investors in South Africa sought government sanction for new optimistic enterprises beyond the frontiers of Cape Colony in Zimbabwe and Zambia. The British South Africa Company had less difficulty in raising capital than any of the European chartered companies that operated in Africa in the 1880s. British investment in South Africa amounted to £34 million in 1884 and increased tenfold over the next twenty-seven years. The South African economy was booming in the 1880s as Transvaal gold was added to Kimberley diamonds. The imperialist entrepreneur Rhodes hoped to find new gold fields to the northward and so did other groups and individuals who scrambled across the Limpopo. When Rhodes asked the British government for a charter for his British South Africa Company and permission to bring new territories under the British flag, he was asking only that the government sanction a forward moving self-financing force which would thrust on northward until it exhausted itself—until its vision of new mineral riches had become faded. The British South Africa Company channelled a vital force; elsewhere in Africa European investors and traders during the 1880s were mostly asking governments to shoulder a political burden in order to save them from losses.

Merchants and investors, however, were not the only people who were pressing European governments into invading Africa. There were also adventurers and visionaries of various types who hoped to cut a figure for themselves and boost their own prestige by acquiring territory. There was King Leopold of the Belgians who hoped to endow his country with an Empire in Central Africa if nowhere else. There was Carl Peters who hoped to do likewise on behalf of Germany in East Africa. There was the ambitious Crispi who hoped to divert people's attention from his government's failure to solve Italy's internal problems by securing an Empire in Ethiopia. There were French army officers who wanted to win promotion by successful campaigns in Senegal and Mali. And then there were the missionaries who had become politically involved in such areas as the Lagos hinterland, Uganda and Nyasaland and who had come to see the intervention of European governments to protect them and the growing Christian communities as essential to the extension of Christianity.

With all these groups at various times demanding government intervention one could assume that the cause of Africa's invasion has been identified. But when we weigh up these various pressure groups and consider the government's responsiveness to them it will become apparent that their will that the government should intervene did not necessarily lead to government action. In the first place although the various investors and merchants interested in Africa carried weight in the politics of European countries, they were not as influential as some similar groups interested in trade and investment elsewhere. Europe's trade and investment in Africa was small by comparison with Europe's trade and investment in other continents. So long as what those urging government action in Africa asked for did not conflict with what others wanted the government to do—for example reduce taxation or provide protection for trade elsewhere—the comparative weakness of the pressure groups interested in Africa would not matter. But if it did, and the government had to make a choice between conciliating them or others the fact that they so often represented a minority even among the small class of capitalists who

exercised such great influence over late nineteenth century governments, would tell against them.

The concern of European governments

Most European governments recognised an obligation to protect
their nationals engaged in economic activity abroad and most especially
in the internationally competitive atmosphere of the late nineteenth
century already mentioned. But European governments would not
support their nationals in all cases. During the nineteenth century
European governments frequently ignored investors' protests at the
failure of various non-European governments and companies to repay
their debts. The governments of Europe would not intervene if it
were diplomatically inconvenient to do so. They would not undertake
a war with a major power in order to save a few speculators from ruin.
Nor would they take action which might weaken their position in the
general European power balance in order to protect a small branch of
national trade. If, on the other hand, a European government felt that
its national power would be increased by intervening on behalf of its
traders and investors and bullying another government into paying
them their due it would do so with alacrity, as Palmerston did in the
case of Don Pacifico in 1850. The response of European governments
to the pressure of the traders and investors was regulated by the state
of the relations between the various European powers themselves.
Each watched the other before moving. If a European government felt
it would weaken itself in relation to others by grabbing African territory it would hold back. If it felt that it could do so with impunity
because others were doing likewise it would be encouraged to go ahead.
In the early 1880s European governments were hesitant on this score;
as time went on they became less so because they were able to make
agreements with each other as to who should have what in Africa.

Calculating the factor of African defence

There was however one other important factor which all European
governments had to take into account and which, unlike the diplomatic
factor just mentioned, always stood against the political intervention
by European governments in Africa. This of course was the armed
force of the peoples and governments of Africa itself. The peoples
and governments of Africa were the major obstacle to the European

invasion of Africa. The European governments had to take the strength of African opposition into account because although the various groups in Europe, already mentioned, were telling governments to occupy, no government wanted to fight costly and diplomatically compromising wars in order to do so. It was extremely difficult to get European parliaments to provide men and money for wars in Africa. Governments feared to approach parliaments on such matters as they knew that they would be asked embarrassing and unpleasant questions and perhaps fail to secure the necessary money in the end. This was the case during the 1880s whether the country was Britain, France or Germany. The government could count on the support of those who had an interest in securing African territory in any particular instance but they had to contend with the opposition of the mass of members of parliament who did not want higher taxation. If the occupation of Africa meant costly wars and therefore higher taxes, most members of parliament would have been strongly prejudiced against any such idea. Some groups were pressing for occupation. Generally speaking, apart from a minority who worried about international morality, the peoples of Europe were prepared to welcome an extension of their national territory. But they did not want to pay for it. They would certainly have objected strongly if the governments had asked them to pay a very high price.

Hiding expenditure on invasion

This was why European governments at least in the early stages of the invasion sought for ways of occupying Africa without asking their parliaments to pay anything. For this reason the British government left the Royal Niger Company, the Imperial British East Africa Company, and the British South Africa Company to occupy various parts of the continent. This was why the German government persuaded the German East Africa Company to occupy East Africa and Herr Luderitz to occupy South West Africa. It had hoped to do the same in the Cameroons and Bismarck was much annoyed when he had to do it himself. King Leopold occupied the Congo through his own organisation, quite independent of the Belgian government and parliament. Another method used by governments to occupy Africa without recourse to parliament was to make existing colonies pay for expansion out of their own revenues. But this was difficult in the 1880s because most African colonies were short of revenue. Much use was made during the 1880s of naval vessels which could be despatched without consulting parliament, but they could only work on the coasts or in areas adjacent to navigable rivers. The British government employed contingents of Indian soldiers—an old method of avoiding parliamentary scrutiny. King Leopold got the Belgian army to second fully paid officers to the Congo. Various other means were used to find resources for small wars in Africa. Perhaps the worst case was the 1897 Benin expedition which was paid for by selling the looted art treasures of Benin to museums in Europe and the United States.

The cost of leaving the coast

This brings us again to the question 'why was Europe *able* to occupy Africa in the late nineteenth century?' European powers had seized colonies in Africa before the 1880s and had fought wars there but the colonies they held were small and close to the coast. Only in Algeria and South Africa had European powers occupied territory any distance inland. In both these cases, the wars resulting from moving inland had involved European governments in considerable expense. At the peak of its campaign to occupy Algeria in 1847, France had 100,000 soldiers in that country, the largest European army to stand on African soil before the end of the nineteenth century. The frontier wars fought by the British in South Africa were costly too. About one tenth of the British army had to be maintained there even in peace time. These examples were enough to discourage European powers from attempting to move inland in other parts of Africa during most of the nineteenth century. Interference by European warships on the coast was common enough but European governments feared moving away from the sea. They feared defeat by African armies. In many instances even victory would have been so costly as to be worthless.

An expensive military visit: Abyssinia 1867–8

European powers received some clear reminders of the dangers of meddling in African politics in the twenty years before the Berlin West Africa Conference of 1884 to 1885. In 1863 the British and French Consuls in Ethiopia had both been imprisoned by Emperor Theodore for disrespectful behaviour. The British government anxiously tried to get their man released, but failed. In 1867, after four years of unsuccessful negotiations the British government decided, after much hesitation, to send an expeditionary force to free the Consul. Since it was feared that Theodore, whose Empire was already crumbling, might still be strong enough to defeat any force sent, it was announced, to avoid angering the whole of the Ethiopian people, that there was no intention of occupying the country. The expedition was to go in, release the prisoners, and leave as fast as possible. To do this limited work the commander of the British army in India was told he could spend as much as he pleased to ensure victory. The force sent was the largest the British believed could be transported across the Ethiopian mountains. It succeeded: but at a cost of £9 million— at that time a very large sum. The government was severely criticised for spending so much of the taxpayers' money. After this Britain stopped meddling in Ethiopian affairs for some considerable time.

The balance begins to swing: Asante 1874

In 1874 another British expedition was sent to the interior of Africa, again after much hesitation, this time against the Asante. The Asante had already defeated one British army and killed its commander in 1826. In 1863 they had marched to the coast through British protected territory while the British watched powerless from their forts. The first episode had led ultimately to the British government's abandonment of the Gold Coast forts; the second brought about a general reappraisal of British West African policy in favour of caution. Fear of the Asante decided the British in 1863 not to strike back. In 1874, however, ambitious military men who had reorganised and re-equipped the British army with new weapons persuaded the government that they were strong enough to beat the Asante. Two thousand picked troops were sent and with the help of thousands of Fante allies the Asante were defeated and their capital, Kumasi, taken. The British commander maintained that he had proved at last that British soldiers could fight successfully in West Africa. But again the object was limited. After Kumasi had been taken and burned the British troops hurried back to the sea. The expedition was costly and the commander admitted that were it not for his superior weapons, the Asante would probably have won. The British government remained as impressed as before by the fighting qualities of the Asante and were anxious to avoid another war with them.

Africa strikes back: Isandhlwana 1878

In 1878 Britain fought another African power—the Zulus under Cetewayo. The British commander was over-confident. His army had superior weapons but the Zulu impis moved too swiftly. The result was a decisive victory and what was left of the British army struggled back to Natal after the battle at Isandhlwana. The British sent out reinforcements, raised men on all sides in South Africa, and the Zulus were finally defeated, but their courage became a legend in Britain and the war was regarded as a mistake. It had cost £4 million and the ministers responsible were violently attacked. These events in South Africa were one of the main reasons for the government's defeat at the subsequent election.

Defeat and victory: Egypt and the Sudan 1884–85

The next major battle between Britain and an African power came in 1882 when a British force of 40,000 men met an Egyptian army of much the same size and strength. The British won after a surprise attack on the main Egyptian fortress at Tel el Kebir. The British disembarked on the Suez Canal after a clever surprise manoeuvre and the final battle was fought along the short line of railway between the Canal and Cairo. Two years later a British force was sent to relieve General Gordon who was besieged in Khartum deep in the Sudan. The force never reached its objective and suffered severely at the hands of the Mahdi's army. This failure so impressed the British that they were prepared to risk leaving the Sudan an unoccupied threat to Egypt rather than try to defeat these Sudanese forces. A new expedition was not sent until 1896 and then it advanced to victory while taking the most careful precautions.

No easy victories in Africa before the 'scramble'

The French also had had some difficult experiences which made them reluctant to engage in military adventures. The French Assembly approved the establishment of a Protectorate in Tunisia in April 1881 but turned round and violently attacked the government in October when it had to gather together 50,000 soldiers to suppress the subsequent rising. The French Chamber also withdrew its support from the project for building a railway from the Senegal to the Niger in 1885 when four years of campaigns showed that military costs had absorbed the greater part of the funds voted for construction. At the time of the 'scramble for Africa' (1884–85) therefore, the European powers were hesitant about moving inland in force because they still had not found the means of fighting wars in the interior at an acceptable cost. They concerned themselves mainly with claims to the coast and the main navigable rivers.

Revolutionary weapons

But the means were rapidly becoming available. From the 1860s onward important improvements were made in all forms of weapons in Europe. Hand firearms were produced with rifled barrels making them more accurate than the smooth bore 'dane gun' type. The rate of fire was improved with the introduction of rifles which could be loaded at the breach instead of at the muzzle. Further improvements in this system in the 1870s made it possible to increase once again the accuracy of the shot, its range and killing power. In the 1870s the magazine or repeater rifle was invented. This most effective weapon came into general use in the middle 1880s. In the late 1860s the first machine guns were invented—the French 'mitrailleuse' and the American 'Gatling gun'. These fired shots rapidly from revolving barrels but they were heavy, difficult to handle and often broke down. In 1889 a far more effective machine gun was invented by Maxim. Its performance was not basically different from modern machine-guns. It had only one barrel but the recoil from each shot mechanically re-loaded the gun so that it could fire an almost continuous stream of bullets. This gun, one of the most deadly weapons man has ever invented, ultimately forced armies to change radically their methods of fighting.

Cannon come to Africa

Before the late nineteenth century most European weapons could not be used properly in Africa. Powerful cannon had been used for a long time on the battlefields of Europe but until the second half of the nineteenth century few cannon were seen in the interior of Africa. Poor, narrow roads made it difficult to wheel these guns inland and often there were no horses or mules to pull such heavy weapons. Ships at sea and on the rivers could carry them—many coastal African states were well equipped with cannon. But inland, especially in thick bush, heavy cast iron or cast bronze cannon were usually more trouble than they were worth. Even the early models of the Gatling gun were too heavy and cumbersome to use there. But the Maxim machine gun was not. And in the second half of the nineteenth century, better and lighter steel cannon were devised until it ultimately became possible for one of these guns of substantial calibre to be carried by two men. Between 1860 and 1890 one after another of these revolutionary weapons came out of the arms factories of Europe. After 1870 nearly every large expedition that went to Africa from Europe carried with it yet another new and more terrible weapon of war. When the French Assembly was becoming disgusted with the cost of wars in the Western Sudan in 1885, new magazine rifles were on their way to the French forces there which enabled them to win battles even with the restricted funds available.

The most modern weapons

Most European commanders insisted on having the latest and best weapons the arms factories could give them for expeditions to Africa. In fact some expeditions were used to try out the most modern systems of fighting. The British expedition against the Asante in 1874 was of this sort and the men carried the newest rifle just issued to the British army. They also had the new light cannon and Gatling guns. The deadly Maxim gun was first tried on a large scale against Ndebele warriors in 1893 though one had been used in Uganda in 1891. In 1896 it was still a very new weapon and the inventor Maxim himself helped to prepare the six machine guns for the Royal Niger Company's expedition against Bida in that year.

Technology wins the battles

Most invading armies used these newest guns in as large numbers as possible. The West African Frontier Force, for example, which the British government raised in 1897, was deliberately equipped with an abnormally large number of machine guns and cannon. No army unit in Europe at the time or for the next fifteen years had so large a proportion of machine guns to fighting men. The Royal Niger Company force which marched against Bida in 1896 was little more than an escort for its four small and one large cannon. It marched on Bida as a small square with the large twelve-pounder steel gun in the centre. And it was the twelve-pounder gun that defeated Bida by bombarding the city while machine guns and rifles kept the Nupe army at a distance. The European commanders had no intention of fighting it out man to man with the African armies if they could avoid it. They deliberately set modern European technology against African men. In fact the European armies that invaded Africa were predominantly African in composition. Almost all the soldiers were African; in the French armies some of the officers were Africans too. But the European controlled armies, although much smaller than the defending African armies, were incomparably better armed.

Victory upon victory, defeat upon defeat

As the power of the weapons increased so the cost to Europe of fighting wars in Africa fell. As victories became easier and cheaper for Europe, so European military men in Africa became anxious for further victories and higher promotion for themselves. The power of their weapons also boosted the morale of the invading armies and they became bolder and more daring. Although such boldness sometimes brought disaster it more frequently resulted in victories for the small powerful army over the much larger opposing forces. The boldness of the invading armies and the terrible effects of the new weapons contributed to widespread demoralisation among African states. Stories of the awful destructiveness of the white man's cannon and machine guns spread from town to town. One might say that some African armies were beaten in spirit before they ever reached the battlefield and resistance to invasion was thereby greatly weakened.

Divided we fall

The severe divisions that existed in African society at this time made things much easier for the foreign powers. The nineteenth century had seen a whole series of political, religious and military revolutions in Africa south of the Sahara which had produced sudden and severe changes in the political systems. The jihads in the western Sudan, from that of Usman dan Fodio and others at the start of the nineteenth century to that of Samori Toure and others in the latter half of the nineteenth century, had brought widespread and continuing political change throughout the valley of the Niger and beyond. In the eastern Sudan, the military incursions of Muhammad Ali Pasha and his successors followed by the Mahdist movement and the activity of such men as Zubayr and Rabih produced vast changes in that area also. From the southern confines of the continent the effects of the mfecane and the growth of new military empires spread northward almost reaching the area of jihadist turbulence in the north. Also, from the middle of the nineteenth century, an increasing flood of European firearms poured in from ports all round the continent, usually confirming, but also on occasion undermining what the African revolutions had effected. The number of new states multiplied at the expense of self-governing independent farming communities.

Weaknesses in Africa's international system

By the late nineteenth century a number of these 'new states' which had been set up earlier in the century had achieved a measure of internal stability. The Emirates in the north of present Nigeria, Ibadan in the west of Nigeria, al Hajj Umar's Tukulor Empire, the Hehe and other similar states in East Africa were fairly stable internally. But most of these states were so dynamic socially and politically that they were almost compelled to expand. Most of them were empires which did not recognise any clear limits to their growth since so many were based on a revolutionary challenge to the existing social and political order. Those which followed a policy of jihad were usually able to adjust their relations with each other within each Caliphate. The Sokoto Caliphate system was on the whole more successful in solving disputes among the Emirates than the 'Concert of Europe' was in maintaining peace among the governments of Europe. But the jihadist states did not properly recognise independent non-muslim communities. Thus although some states were internally strong and stable, the international system as a whole was weak and vulnerable. The new states often created wide areas of conflict around them and were feared and hated by neighbouring communities which believed they would be the next to be attacked.

The political price of purchasing arms

The European invaders were able to exploit these divisions in African society especially during the diplomatic phase of the invasion which preceded military conquest. The agents of the European governments were very short of money at this time but they had the advantage of having powerful guns to sell. Arms selling was a profitable business because, as European armies changed to new rifles, they sold their old guns cheaply and in large quantities. Therefore the European explorers and trading companies had a good supply of cheap weapons which African rulers and communities in most parts of the continent were anxious to buy. Even African rulers who fought from time to time against European colonial powers were often ready to make agreements with their European enemies in order to acquire guns for defence or attack. Indeed governments all over the world were trying to buy modern military equipment from Europe and were prepared to run the risk of falling under European control by asking for loans in order to do so. While the European powers were scrambling for other peoples' territory, other peoples were scrambling for European guns, railways and other items of military value.

Technological discoveries had changed the basis of military power. Modern rifles and cannon produced a revolution just as the discovery of iron, of war chariots and effective cavalry equipment had fundamentally altered the basis of military power in past periods of human history.

Diplomatic reservations

The new weapons that European forces could dispose of, by reducing military and other costs and weakening the effectiveness of African resistance, provided European governments with increasingly tempting opportunities. They produced a context in which the invasion of Africa became increasingly possible and likely. But each Power still had to consider the reactions of its European neighbours before undertaking schemes of African conquest. Changes in the diplomatic situation in Europe were of crucial importance in determining whether, when and how Africa would be invaded. In this respect, the British occupation of Egypt in 1882 represented an especially important turning point because it produced a set of diplomatic circumstances which favoured, and in the view of some European statesmen, required a forward movement by particular European powers in Africa.

Britain and France and Egypt

The British occupation of Egypt resulted from the breakdown of the system of informal control that Britain and France had been trying to exercise over Egypt with varying success since the beginning of the nineteenth century. Both Powers had important interests in that country. France had created strong commercial, financial and cultural links with Egypt and was concerned also about the distant threat it could possibly pose to French Algeria. Britain was interested in Egypt as one of several roads across the Middle East by which European forces might advance towards Britain's massive colony of India and her commercial preserves in the eastern seas. Egypt was part of the Ottoman Empire and while France had tried to secure her influence there by supporting Egyptian attempts to break the links with the rest of the Empire, Britain until the 1870s sought to control Egypt as well as the other Middle East routes by supporting the Ottoman Sultan's claim to suzerainty. During the 1870s Britain's policy altered. The Ottoman Sultan appeared to be too weak to defend the routes to the East effectively, his finances were in a bad state, his government seemed unprogressive, his European provinces were in revolt and his new Panislamic policy of claiming the allegiance of all Muslims threatened British positions in Muslim countries including India. Furthermore, the completion of the Suez Canal in 1869 had made the Egyptian route to India more vital than ever because now a European fleet as well as a European army could be passed through to India by that way. British eyes were focused more closely on Egypt and the purchase of the Suez Canal shares in 1875 from the Khedive gave Britain a financial lever to strengthen her influence there. Britain therefore swung towards the policy of supporting the Egyptian Khedive against his Turkish master and this made possible a deal with France which was pursuing a similar policy and which had also been upset about the possible disturbing effect of the Sultan's Panislamic ideas in Algeria. The two governments agreed to share influence in Egypt.

The failure of informal empire

The Khedive's bankruptcy helped the French and British Governments to exercise a joint control over the Egyptian government after 1876 and their determination to make Egypt pay the interest on its debts was only partly the result of solicitude for the interests of the French, British and other European bondholders. Insistence on financial rectitude was in this case also politically convenient. It enabled the French and British governments to force on the Khedive two of their nationals as controllers to supervise the Egyptian government's finances. But as Egypt was squeezed dry to satisfy its creditors, political disadvantages began to appear. The economies and severe taxes imposed alienated various sections of the Egyptian populace—the overtaxed peasants, the landowners, the retrenched army officers and civil servants. Traditionalists and modern nationalists rallied the people against the hated regime and the movement of protest found a leader in Colonel Urabi, one of the few native Egyptian officers in the mainly Turkish-officered army. The British and French governments were too suspicious of each other to adjust to this situation. They backed the Khedive against the nationalist movement and refused financial concessions. The result was a conflict between the two European governments and the nationalists and when Colonel Urabi threatened to seize the Canal the British government sent a force which defeated the Egyptian army in September 1882 and occupied Cairo.

The consequences of the British occupation of Egypt

The British government hoped that having removed Urabi from power they would be able to withdraw. But they soon found that the state of nationalist sentiment was such that they could not establish a government which would at the same time co-operate with Britain and be sufficiently popular to maintain itself without the backing of British arms. It appeared that the British troops would have to stay and Britain in effect became responsible for Egyptian affairs. Being placed in this position, the British government felt that it would have to have a free hand in trying to organise the Egyptian government. So it declared to France which had refused at the last minute to participate in the occupation, that the Anglo-French dual control in Egypt was at an end. This enraged French opinion and from then on France tried to upset the British position in Egypt and also began aggressively to acquire positions elsewhere in Africa in retaliation whenever opportunities offered. Britain had become responsible for a country which was encumbered with debt and with a complicated machinery of international financial control which could not be got rid of. France was still represented on the International Debt Commission which controlled sixty per cent of Egyptian revenue. So was Germany. With France hostile, Britain was dependent on German support and Bismarck was determined to secure the maximum benefit from this situation. Various people in Germany were pressing him to allow them to establish colonies in Africa. Luderitz wanted to collect guano in South West Africa. German merchants in West Africa wanted political support for their commercial ventures. Carl Peters hoped to build a great empire in East Africa. Bismarck himself may not have been very interested in seizing colonies, but for various reasons of domestic and international politics it became rather advantageous for him to do so in 1884 and 1885. And at that juncture it cost him little or nothing to stake claims in Africa. At the wave of his 'Egyptian stick' —the threat to vote against Britain in Egypt—Britain gave him what he wanted in Africa. The British government told the colonial government at the Cape to waive its claim to keep others out of South West Africa and let Luderitz in. The British Consul in Zanzibar was told to use the informal control Britain exercised over the Zanzibar Sultan to let Carl Peters make treaties of protection with the chiefs who feared the extension of the Sultan's power in the hinterland. The British attempt to screen the mouth of the Congo from the pushful French and others by extending inactive Portuguese rule over that area was stopped largely owing to Bismarck's intervention, and the way was laid open for Leopold to elaborate his Congo schemes. The large inroads made into areas where Britain had hitherto exercised informal control made it clear that the old system of informal control was no longer effective and Britain herself entered the race to claim the coastline. These changes in the diplomatic situation made it expedient for governments to pay more heed to the urgings of interested merchants and investors who had been asking them to take African territory.

The Horn of Africa and the Upper Nile

In addition to this, the financial weakness of Egypt and the rising of the Mahdi in the Sudan in 1884 led Britain to force the Egyptian government to cut its losses by abandoning control of the whole African coastline from the confines of Egypt to the borders of present day Kenya. This evacuation of Khedive Isma'il's African Empire in order to avoid financial and therefore diplomatic complications exposed another large part of the African coastline to European encroachment —an encroachment which was facilitated by the pre-existence of Egyptian establishments. The Italians moved into Eritrea and the French and British (and later, the Italians) established themselves in Somalia. The British occupation of Egypt had even wider spreading repercussions because, within seven years of the occupation, it became clear that the White Nile was vital to Egypt's irrigation. The headwaters of that river were beyond the Mahdist government's control and they and the Egyptian garrisons still established there became the object of a race primarily between Britain and France but in which Leopold and Carl Peters also participated. The prize was the control of a vital area which could closely affect the still unstable British position in Egypt. Investors and merchants did not have to encourage the British government to take interest in or occupy the area of present day Kenya and Uganda. When the occupation of the interior of Africa by various European Powers had got seriously under way, the British government decided on its own and for strategical reasons that the route to the Upper Nile had to be secured.

The invaders manoeuvre into position

In 1885 however, the inland rush had still not begun and for five years the Europeans advanced gradually from their positions on the coasts and navigable rivers, selling their guns, gathering information and making treaties. Sometimes they allied with the powerful new African states and sold guns to them; sometimes they sold guns to the older and smaller communities which the new states were trying to absorb or destroy; sometimes they allied with one new state against another. The French in Senegal for example, allied at different times with almost all the different states and groups—with the Tukulor Empire, with their Bambara enemies, with Samori Toure and with his enemies at Sikasso. The British at Lagos sought good relations with all the contending parties in Yorubaland at different times. The Royal Niger Company supplied arms both to the Emirates of Northern Nigeria and to those who fought them. King Leopold's agents in the Congo sometimes allied with Arab state builders like Tippu Tip and sometimes they supplied arms to their opponents. The Imperial British East African Company and Lugard joined Bugunda against Bunyoro, allied with the Christian Ganda chiefs against the Muslim Ganda chiefs, and with the Protestant faction against the Catholic faction in Buganda. And thus during this diplomatic phase of the invasion the European agents twisted and turned in several parts of Africa allying now with this, now with that African power, but always strengthening their own position and proving to their governments that the occupation of Africa was perhaps not so difficult as it had seemed.

War clouds gather

There was, however, a limit to what diplomacy could achieve and by the end of the 1880s that limit was being reached in several parts of the continent. African rulers were becoming increasingly suspicious of European intentions. Some began to launch serious attacks on European establishments and expeditions. There was a serious flare-up of opposition in the coastal areas of East Africa, 'the Bushiri rising', in 1888 and news of this spread quickly along the trade routes of middle Africa. On the other hand diplomatic successes were making the European agents bolder. They became impatient, wanting to rule and control rather than ally with the African states. This meant that in the first place they would have to strike at and defeat the powerful new African states and one after another, from the late 1880s onward, the various groups of European invaders in different parts of Africa decided to declare war on the nearest powerful African government.

Europe combines against Africa

Since Europe was able to exploit the divisions between the various African states, why did the African rulers not attempt to exploit the differences between the rival powers in Europe? In fact, Menelik of Ethiopia did succeed in making the European powers compete for his favour and this helped him maintain the independence of his state. But most African rulers had no chance to do this since before Europe launched its attack matters had been so arranged as to prevent them deriving any benefit from European rivalry.

The anti-slave-trade crusade

Although the various states in Europe in the nineteenth century each claimed to be sovereign, and not subject to any higher authority or other than purely national considerations, they could, at times, combine for some common purpose not necessarily connected with their own interest. As the agents of European invasion began to come into conflict with the new states in Africa, a movement of opinion developed in Europe which favoured an attack on the major African states. This movement began with a campaign, sometimes referred to as a 'crusade', against the slave trade. This campaign was led by religious figures and was supported by various humanitarian and missionary bodies, most of which had influence in more than one European country. Public meetings were held, and books, pamphlets and newspaper articles were published on the subject in France, Germany, Britain and several other European countries. They chiefly attacked the export slave trade, which was mostly carried on by Arabs on the east African coast, but attention was also drawn to the internal slave trade, and the powerful new states were soon singled out as the main culprits, for they were amassing wealth and power by enslaving and securing the labour of the communities around them. Previous anti-slave trade campaigns had aroused opinion in Britain but had not been effective in other parts of Europe. Now all over Europe people began to take an interest in stopping the slave trade. Even in Africa there were some echoes of the agitation amongst those who opposed the new states and others who saw that slave trading meant war and divisions which would weaken Africa.

From humanitarianism to ideas of conquest

Meanwhile another idea spread across Europe, that of Europe's 'civilising mission'—an idea which suggested that Europe had not only a right but a duty to occupy Africa. The troubles and many wars being waged in Africa in the late nineteenth century were taken in Europe as evidence that Africa was unable to rule itself. Also, the reports from European agents in various parts of Africa of how they were winning battles with their modern weapons helped the idea to develop that Europe could easily conquer Africa and impose its rule. The fear created by the military skill and courage of such people as the Asante was now forgotten as confidence in the overwhelming superiority of modern European arms grew, or rather confidence simply in European superiority over Africans. People in Europe easily confused the superiority of the weapons with the superiority of the men who handled them. Since the middle of the nineteenth century European writers, when speaking of 'race', gave the impression that man was imprisoned by the customs of his society, that the ideas of each 'racial' society were fixed in time and that there could be no flow of ideas between societies of different race. They also maintained that the 'races' of the world could be arranged in order of superiority, and of course they put themselves at the top. As these ideas spread Europeans became increasingly arrogant in their dealings with other peoples. When these ideas were first put forward Britain was involved in quarrels with Abeokuta, with the King of Asante and with Emperor Theodore of Ethiopia and, consequently, people were inclined to believe that the fewer dealings they had with Africa the better. Moreover, the racialist writers suggested that because of racial differences peaceful co-operation between Europe and Africa was impossible. But, in the late nineteenth century when Europe had the weapons to win wars in Africa, the idea of racial superiority spread fast and was given a new meaning. The supposed 'scientific' proof of European racial superiority was used to suggest that Europeans had some sort of natural right to conquer and rule Africans. The idea of racial difference which had earlier been used as an argument for leaving Africa to itself was now used as an argument for excluding Africans from the government of their own countries.

Africans begin to use modern arms against the invaders

All these ideas favourable to invasion provided a basis upon which the rival quarrelling governments could combine against the major powers in Africa. The European governments were pleased at the change in public opinion towards invading Africa because they too were favouring occupation of the interior. African resistance to European encroachment was growing and was threatening even the first European settlements on the coasts and rivers. The 'Bushiri rising' in 1888 and after, had made things difficult for the Germans and the British. The Arabised states in the Congo had begun to oppose King Leopold's agents. Samori Toure blocked the path of the French on the Upper Niger and various African rulers were opposing British agents around Lake Nyasa. Most of the African powers concerned were 'new states' which possessed some fairly modern weapons purchased from British, German, Belgian, Portuguese or French sources. The European invaders began to realise that by competing with one another they were enabling Africans to buy modern guns with which they could keep out all European forces. For example, in East Africa, those involved in the 'Bushiri rising' bought guns from the British to repel the Germans and guns from the Germans to push back the British.

The arms blockade of Africa

The anti-slave trade campaign provided the governments with a means of halting this situation in a comprehensive fashion. In 1889 to 1890 the European powers held a conference at Brussels on the slave trade and agreed on an arms blockade of Africa, particularly of modern arms. The import of the old dane guns, which were ineffective against well armed European forces, was permitted. Modern weapons were restricted to colonial governments who were only permitted to allow guns to pass through their territories if they were required by another colonial government. The blockade, although never fully effective, was gradually extended from East Africa to other parts of the continent and it spelt the doom of large scale African resistance. Two major African countries, however, avoided its effect. In particular, Ethiopia, through the skilful diplomacy of Emperor Menelik, was still able to buy modern arms since his country was

27

excluded from the effect of the Brussels agreement. Huge quantities of the latest rifles were purchased by the Emperor from French and Italian traders and with them the Ethiopian army was able to defeat a large Italian army at Adowa in 1896. Morocco was also unaffected since the Sultan continued to exploit European rivalries until the European powers combined against him at the Algeciras Conference of 1906. Morocco was by then well armed and when the French began to occupy the country in 1908 they had to send one of the largest armies ever sent to Africa in order to occupy just one section of the country. At that stage Germany was still opposed to the French invasion and modern arms from Germany enabled the Moroccans to put up a powerful resistance. But Germany was bought off by France in 1911 by a gift of land in the Cameroons and in 1912 a French Protectorate over Morocco was proclaimed. The Moroccans were still heavily armed and France was far from occupying the whole country when the First World War broke out in 1914. Elsewhere in Africa the European arms blockade was more effective and Africans were thus deprived of the means of successful resistance.

The anti-slave-trade campaign opens Europe's purses

As the European governments prepared to attack the new states in Africa they found they needed more money for their campaigns. The small groups with direct interests—merchants, investors and so on—pressed the governments to act but the public, the taxpayers, had to be persuaded to provide the money. The anti-slave trade campaign, widely publicised among sections of the public who had hardly even heard of Africa before, offered a means of doing this. People were told that the comparatively small sums needed to invade Africa were to be used to put down the slave trade and alleviate human misery. This helped to convince the German parliament to provide money in 1890 to take over Tanzania from the German East Africa Company and raise forces for conquest there. This was largely how the British Parliament was persuaded to provide money for building the Uganda railway and the occupation of Kenya and Uganda after 1893. King Leopold used the same argument to persuade the governments of Europe to allow the Congo Free State government to collect larger taxes on European trade in the Congo with which he could finance his military campaigns.

International misbehaviour

The movement of European public opinion in favour of conquest also removed any doubts there may have been about the morality of occupying Africa.

One may say that European powers took little note of morality in deciding what to do. But it would be wrong to suppose that there were no rules of international behaviour that could restrain the acts of European governments. The political system of Europe was multicentred and was accepted as being such. Most Europeans in the nineteenth century preferred power to be divided among many independent states rather than concentrated in the hands of any single government. Such a system was bound to have rules such that each state respected the independence and integrity of the others. Without some such rules the European international system would have been in constant danger of falling into chaos. A state interfering with another risked attack from all the other states combined. The growth of European colonial empires shows that this rule of non-interference was not observed outside Europe. Nevertheless when European powers seized territory outside Europe they had an uncomfortable feeling that their action was against the rules of international behaviour. The invaders of Africa in the late nineteenth century, however, had few doubts about the morality of their actions. The propaganda about the slave trade, about Europe's civilising mission, and about European racial superiority convinced most of those who took part in the invasion that what they were doing was right. Even states like Russia and the Habsburg Empire which occupied no territory in Africa themselves, were prepared to sign documents at international conferences, the provisions of which undermined the independence of African states. Only non-European powers—the United States with its own experience as a British colony, and the Ottoman Empire— asked embarrassing questions about the independent rights of African states, questions which were quickly brushed aside by European delegates who talked instead about 'civilisation'. Even those who made a profession of criticising transgressions of the rules of international behaviour by their governments were carried away by the propaganda and rather spent their time arguing about how the colonies should be run. Few questioned whether Europeans should be ruling Africans at all.

A condition of independence

This question of international morality is important because one of the great achievements of the African leaders of the independence movement in the 1940s and '50s was to reverse the flow of imperialist ideas which justified colonial rule. By uniting with other African leaders and with leaders of peoples in other parts of the world colonised by Europe, they re-established on a new basis the old rules of the European international system against one state imposing its rule on another, and made them apply on a world-wide scale. The battle for independence in Africa, apart from the cases of Ethiopia, Algeria and the south, was fought mainly on an intellectual and political rather than on a military level. Some of the most important victories were won in speeches, pamphlets and at international conferences. The nationalists' aim was to destroy the ideas of imperialism in world opinion and in European opinion itself and to establish a new international framework and a new set of rules of international morality and behaviour.

The assault in the west

These successes were far off in the late nineteenth century when the colonial powers were united in their determination to conquer a then divided Africa. They agreed which parts of the continent each should have and promised to help each other against African resisters. The great African states mostly stood alone, except for some attempts at co-operation between Muslim rulers in the Western Sudan and in East Africa. One after another the great African states were defeated in battle or forced into submission. In 1890 after a brief campaign, Segou, the principal city in the Tukulor Empire, fell to the French. Between 1891 and 1898 Samori Toure was driven back, skilfully fighting rearguard actions and seeking to maintain his supply of the precious modern arms and ammunition from European traders on the coast. In 1896 the European arms blockade became fully effective against him and two years later Samori was forced to surrender. The Mossi Empire of Ouagadougou was overthrown by the French in 1896 and a powerful British force occupied Asante in the same year.

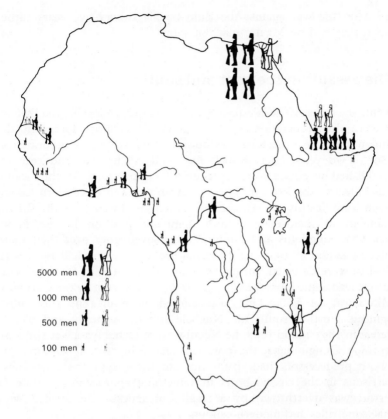

5000 men

1000 men

500 men

100 men

The forces of occupation, 1890. Colonial armies in Africa, excluding Algeria, Tunisia and South Africa

Between 1892 and 1894 Dahomey was occupied after strong resistance. In 1892 the power of the Ijebu kingdom was broken by the British. After the terrible effects of its new weapons had been shown, the colonial government at Lagos was able to penetrate the whole of Yorubaland, where it came first as a mediator helping to end the exhausting and apparently interminable Kiriji wars, and then, after further use of its cannon, as the superior authority controlling Yoruba politics. In 1896 the Royal Niger Company defeated the Nupe army and entered the city of Ilorin. In 1897 Benin fell. Between 1901 and 1903 a series of major battles around Kontagora, Yola, Kano and Sokoto left the great Emirates of Northern Nigeria under the control of the British. With the increased fire-power of the new weapons this Nigerian campaign cost the British about one tenth of what they had

31

spent on the war against the Zulu people twenty-five years earlier when they had no Maxim machine guns.

The assault in the east and south

While the states of the Western Sudan were thus collapsing the British, after careful preparation, sent a large Anglo-Egyptian force into the Sudan and broke the Khalifa's power at the battle of Omdurman in 1898. Two years later, Rabeh ibn Fadl Allah, who had recently established his power in Bornu using rifles imported across the Sahara, was killed by the French. The new Arab states in the eastern Congo basin were destroyed between 1892 and 1895. From 1891 the British manoeuvred themselves into a dominant position in the inter-lacustrine kingdoms and imposed their sovereignty over their main ally, Buganda, in 1901. In Tanzania the leaders who had risen with Bushiri were defeated during 1889 and 1890. In 1893 Siki the Nyamwezi leader and Meli the Chagga leader were beaten by the Germans. Mkwakwa, the Hehe king, was hunted down in 1898 after bitter fighting. Further south the Ndebele suffered a heavy and bloody defeat in 1893 and in 1898 the Ngoni west of Lake Nyasa were broken. In 1895 Gungunhana, the powerful leader in central Mozambique whose predecessors had, from time to time, kept the Portuguese garrisons in the coastal ports in something approaching a state of terror, was overthrown by a small Portuguese force armed with magazine rifles and modern cannon.

Europe seizes the commanding heights in Africa

It was the 1890s then that saw the rapid destruction of almost all the most powerful and dynamic states in Africa. But the small European forces were not capable of occupying all parts of Africa and were slow to enter the more remote lands and the territory of small self-governing communities whose complex social and political organisations often baffled them. Once paralysing blows had been struck to the major African states colonial officials went out with small escorts over a large part of the continent ordering chiefs great and small to do this or that, to arrest opponents of the new regime, to provide labour, collect taxes, change laws, or abolish tolls; to permit European mining or settlement, to admit missionaries, grow certain crops, give land for railways, or protect telegraph lines.

Introducing new technology and European control

Modern technology, in the form of advanced weapons, had been the key to the invaders' success and their first impulse was to bring modern technology in the form of railways, telegraphs and new methods of production into Africa at no matter what human cost in order to speed up production in Africa for the European market and generally to exploit the African economy. They betrayed a compulsive urge to brandish their technology in order to assert their new won superiority and to maintain their own self confidence. This was the substance of their 'civilising mission'. Earlier in the century some colonial powers had hoped to achieve their ends in Africa by encouraging reform within African society, by supporting cash crop producers against slave traders, Christian converts against traditionalists, by seeking alliances with reforming rulers, and encouraging the growth of the mercantile classes engaged in foreign trade. But these later invaders generally speaking were little interested in the internal reform of African society. The sort of rule they established varied in different parts of the continent. In some places old political arrangements were ruthlessly broken down; in others they were carefully preserved. But colonial rule at this stage was not really intended to lead African society in any particular direction. European co-operation with Africans was now more or less a dead idea. Conquest and white superiority had become the ruling ideas among the invaders. Their first aim was to keep themselves in power and their second to keep the peace in those areas where modern technology was to boost production. Most of the invaders doubted the ability of the Africans to grow even cash crops for export and the majority of colonial governments looked to European planters, miners and traders to develop the resources. They believed that European direction and capital would produce rapid economic results and a rapid growth in trade.

Africa's great leap forward

The result of all this was a vast mobilisation of labour all over the continent. Railways were started all round Africa south of the Sahara; on the west coast from Dakar, Freetown, Accra and Lagos; on the east coast from Mombasa and Tanga; in the south apart from strengthening the railway system in Cape Colony and the Transvaal, a railway was pushed northwards through Botswana to Zimbabwe. The large amount of labour required for the construction of these lines was found either by hiring or by force. Men were needed, too, for the construction of new harbours, government buildings and offices, bridges and roads. European planters and miners sought men to clear the bush, to dig for gold, tin or copper. During these years of feverish European activity, farmers in many parts of West Africa were setting out to make their own fortunes as prices for their crops like palm kernels, rubber and cocoa began to rise on the world market. The end of the wars, the weakening of the power of traditional rulers and chiefs, the breaking of powerful houses by anti-slavery legislation and so on led to a scramble for a new means of power—money. In Nigeria and the Congo whole villages rushed to the bush to cut rubber, although in the case of the Congo most villages did so because of government compulsion. In Ghana and Nigeria farmers cleared great new areas of bush for cocoa or kola farms. Others gathered larger quantities of palm oil and kernels for sale. In Uganda the great chiefs who, with British help, had escaped the authority of the Kabaka, set about adding wealth to their new power by growing cotton on their vast new estates. All over Africa there was a tremendous upsurge of economic activity which put a heavy strain upon Africa's manpower resources.

The growth of the colonial economy

This great post-invasion economic effort sketched out the main lines of the colonial economy in Africa. It created new concentrations of wealth rather than a widespread improvement in conditions. The few modernised ports benefited most; areas around railways and navigable rivers prospered as did cash crop producing areas; the areas beyond became reservoirs of labour providing migrant workers and cheap foodstuffs for European plantations or new African farms. The small 'new cities', where goods for export were collected, or where the colonial governments made their central or provincial capitals, secured the greatest share of the new amenities and opportunities for making money. A substantial proportion of the value of export crops flowing through the cities remained in the hands of traders and their employees. Fees, fines and bribes piled up in the administrative centres as new colonial laws raised some men and hurled others down. In all these 'new cities' Europeans presided. Africans could make money and have some power but most were forced to do so in a subordinate capacity, as agents of Europeans, as political officers, commercial clerks, soldiers or policemen, as court clerks or catechists. The old order where Africans had dealt with Europeans as equals or as superiors in business and politics in the ports and African state capitals was quickly changed as the invasion took place.

The popular revolts

The severity of conditions produced revolts in different parts of the continent. These revolts, mostly occurring after 1900, differed from the wars waged during the invasion in that they were more broadly popular in character and extended beyond the boundaries of existing African political organisations. Common suffering under colonial rule led to the spread of ideas of resistance across wide areas of formerly divided African society. The Ndebele and Shona, once enemies, rose together between 1896 and 1897. In 1900 the once divided Asante united in revolt. In 1904 the Hereros in South West Africa rose behind the formerly shadowy paramount chief. From 1905 to 1907 the great combined Maji Maji revolt in South Eastern Tanzania took place, given strength by the traditional spreaders of political ideas—the native doctors. In 1902 the tribes of Somalia began general resistance under the banner of revivalist Islam. These popular revolts occurred mainly where the colonial governments in their determination to push forward economic change were especially ruthless in demanding taxes or forced labour or where the invasion was followed by a natural disaster, such as the rinderpest epidemics which swept through Africa from Somalia to the Kalahari desert in the late 1890s destroying the cattle and therefore the main wealth of whole African communities. Taxation affected everyone from the chief to the smallest farmer and produced widespread and bitter grievances which the new political ideas were able to focus and turn into united revolt.

A second clash of arms and ideas

The popular revolts taxed the resources of the colonial regimes but most were put down with great bloodshed. More men were involved in the revolts than in all the battles of the invasion and more men were killed in the first decade of the twentieth century than in the dramatic decade of the 1890s. The revolts did not end with the first defeats but continued in the bush as a form of guerilla warfare. The breaking of popular resistance, what the colonial powers called 'pacification', was often a long and bloody affair. The will of the colonial powers to conquer and rule was not, however, undermined

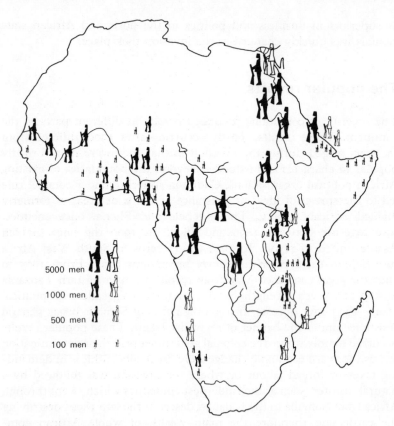

5000 men

1000 men

500 men

100 men

The forces of occupation, 1900. Colonial armies in Africa, excluding Algeria, Tunisia and South Africa. Police forces are not included, except in the Congo, where the police and army were one force

despite the strength of the revolts and the cost of their suppression. Arguments in Europe were chiefly concerned with how rule should be exercised, how much exploitation was possible, how fast change should be introduced and especially with the matter of forced labour which so closely resembled the slavery Europe reputedly had come to abolish. Only in Germany, the country hardest hit by the revolts, did opposition politicians seriously attempt to make the government abandon its colonies. But at the elections of 1907 the government's colonial policy was strongly supported by the majority of the German electorate. Some of the underlying ideas of imperialism were also shaken in Britain and in Europe by the Boer War (1899–1902) which was won at great cost. That event also raised doubts about the morality of extending colonial rule and produced violent arguments about who or what groups in Europe were responsible.

But its immediate effects did not benefit the Africans. The European colonial powers now began to fear white settlers in Africa and consequently became even more anxious than before to keep them happy and to do so were prepared to give greater help to the settlers in their exploitation of Africans.

The growing strength of the pressure groups

When most of the popular revolts occurred the colonial regimes had already acquired the means to maintain their positions. With the growth of African trade the strength of the pressure groups of investors and the like had increased and there were now powerful bodies in Europe who were determined not to allow the governments to abandon the colonies. Thus, although governments found the suppression of revolts costly, these powerful, interested agitators ensured that the governments found the money that was needed. Imperialism now had a solidity which it did not have when the invasion of Africa was merely a project.

Europe's grip on Africa tightens

At the time of the invasion the colonial powers had been able to exploit the divisions in African society, and had made alliances with states willing to fight other African states. But at the time of the popular revolts the colonial powers had very little voluntary help from Africans. Certainly some Africans fought for the Colonial governments in the army or police and some chiefs and African officials assisted the colonial forces. But they did so more in the hope of being on the winning side than with the enthusiasm of equal allies. However, the colonial powers had new advantages which they did not have before the invasion. They could use some of the newly established modern installations: the telegraph gave them better intelligence so that they could concentrate their efforts in the right places at the right times; forts and strong new buildings were used as well-defended bases; troops could be quickly moved along the new railways to threatened spots and from peaceful colonies to others where risings had occurred; the increasing revenues of Colonial governments paid at least some of the expenses of war. But, above all, the colonial powers still had vastly superior weapons. Nevertheless, the popular revolts were not all put down immediately. The rising in Somalia was largely successful and the colonial powers were not able to re-establish their rule there until after 1922 and then their victory resulted from the use of another and more revolutionary weapon—the bomb-carrying aircraft. This same weapon helped the French finally to fasten their rule on Morocco and the use of aircraft was the decisive factor in the last great battle of the invasion of Africa—that between Italy and Ethiopia from 1935 to 1936. From the bombing aircraft even the most inaccessible mountains and deserts offered no refuge.

1 SPANISH MOROCCO
2 GAMBIA
3 PORTUGUESE GUINEA
4 SIERRA LEONE
5 LIBERIA
6 TOGOLAND
7 SPANISH GUINEA
8 FRENCH SOMALILAND
9 BRITISH SOMALILAND
10 SWAZILAND
11 BASUTOLAND

KEY

███ BRITISH		░░░ CONGO FREE STATE (BELGIUM)
▓▓▓ PORTUGUESE		▦▦▦ ITALIAN
▨▨▨ FRENCH		▒▒▒ SPANISH
≡≡≡ GERMAN		☐ INDEPENDENT AFRICAN

Africa showing colonial possessions in 1914

The ultimate futility of localised revolt

The first post-invasion popular revolts achieved little or nothing. Their defeat left the Africans who took part in them disillusioned and more depressed than before by the apparent invincibility of the colonial rulers. The Colonial governments became more firmly entrenched than ever. Although the popular revolts had united society in quite an impressive manner they had only produced local unity. The ideas they produced were much too local in character to stop such a worldwide movement as European imperialism. Nor could the ideas be spread widely through the continent because the colonial powers themselves controlled the new means of effective and rapid communication such as posts, telegraphs and printing. The revolts, too, were essentially rural in character and failed to capture or win over the emergent 'new cities' with their arsenals, barracks and warehouses, their railheads and telegraph stations, their harbours and offices. The colonial powers remained secure in these seats of power and from them they went out steadily in the first half of the twentieth century completing the invasion of rural Africa.

Where the future lay

Perhaps more significant for the future of the struggle against colonial rule than any of these popular revolts of the post-invasion period, was the surrender of the Lagos government to the economic demands of striking labourers in 1897. For the liberation of Africa from colonial rule was to be organised from the 'new cities' when they had become larger, more complex and more dominant in the life of the continent. It was those who had acquired modern skills in these cities who were able finally to paralyse the machinery of Colonial government. They were able to organise the people in city and rural areas alike to combine against alien rule. Those who had been educated were able to produce and propagandise the ideas of African identity and independence which could appeal to their fellow countrymen, swing opinion throughout the world and force a change of mind in a Europe severely shaken by violent internecine strife and foreign invasion.

Part **one**

Northern Africa

1 Egypt since 1882

While the ring-leaders of the 'Egypt for the Egyptians' movement were being imprisoned or exiled the British began a re-organisation of Egypt's administration and constitution soon after their military occupation of the country. According to the constitution proclaimed in the Organic Law of 1883, under which Egypt was ruled until 1912, the Khedive was to continue to be the head of the administration and 'choose' ministers who were to be responsible to him. A Legislative Council and an Assembly were established to enable Egyptian people to participate in the running of their affairs. The British also asserted that in law and in theory Egypt was still a part of the Ottoman Empire and as such recognised the suzerainty of the Sultan of Constantinople.

But events revealed a situation different from the British declaration. The actual head of Egyptian administration was the British Agent and Consul-General, to whom the Khedive was no more than a puppet who should do the biddings of the British. The Egyptian ministers, exclusively people of Turkish origins, were no more than figure-heads, under the effective control of the British inspectors, the *muffatish*, who controlled all departments. The Turco-Egyptian 'ministers' constituted the Council of Ministers contemptuously described by a British official as 'this collection of supine nonentities and doddering old pantaloons'. The constitution was by no means liberal; it was a step backward, compared with the vocal, assertive and mainly elected Assembly that was abolished by the British. The Sultan of Turkey was given no voice in the affairs of Egypt which, in all but name, was an integral part of the British empire.

Lord Cromer

Of all the heads of the British administration in Egypt from 1883 to 1922 the best known is Evelyn Baring, 1st Earl of Cromer, whose tenure of office covered the years 1883 to 1907. In Cromer's book, *Modern Egypt* (London 1908), and in most of the works on Egypt by British writers, Cromer is regarded as a first-class administrator and financier who created modern Egypt by organising a highly efficient civil service, a judiciary that dispensed justice without fear or favour, and who conferred unexampled prosperity on Egyptians by his fiscal reforms and by the building of Aswan Dam, and who educated the Egyptians in a way that made it possible for them to manage their affairs successfully when Egypt became an independent territory.

This view of Cromer, and indeed of British administration in Egypt, is very one-sided. Cromer certainly deserves credit in many respects and none can doubt that he was an efficient financier. A member of the Baring family that had loaned money to Ismail Pasha, Cromer had had administrative experience in India before he assumed the control of Egypt. He combined commercial and financial ability in a useful fashion. He saw his task in Egypt as primarily financial. In this respect, from the view-point of British interests, his administration was a huge success. Foreign debt was largely disposed of during his reign and the Suez Canal was well run. Cromer organised the finances of Egypt so well that the country came to depend upon its own resources from 1888 onwards. In 1882 the Khedive could not pay interest on his loans; by 1906 Egypt was able to pay interest on her foreign loans and reduce her debts by ten million pounds. Cromer achieved this by reorganising the accountants section of the Finance Ministry so that money was not wasted and by increasing the productive capacity of Egypt. Between 1883 and 1906 the annual revenue available to the Egyptian Treasury rose from £4½ million to about £11½ million, in spite of the lowering of taxes.

Also to his credit Cromer made Egypt produce more crops by improving irrigation. He did this by building the Aswan dam, thus reconstructing Mohammed Ali's Mahmudiyeh canal. The work on the dam, through which water could be stored in large quantities for irrigation, began in 1898 and was completed in 1902. It was built at a total cost of £3½ million. Heightened from 1907 to 1912, during the '30s it proved of immeasurable benefit to Egyptians. Hitherto seasonal cropping was the order of the day; henceforth perennial cultivation began. Famine, which used to bring disaster to a large section of the population in years of the low Nile, was no longer a serious danger. Indeed the Aswan dam has been so crucial to the economic life of Egypt that after seizing power in the early '50s Gamal Abdel Nasser, late President of the United Arab Republic, undertook to heighten the dam further and employ it for Egypt's industrial programme, at a cost of £180 million. The results of Cromer's decision to build the dam appeared early: an area of 500,000 feddans in Upper Egypt was converted to perennial irrigation. The cultivated area rose from 4,800,000 feddans in 1877 to 7,500,000 feddans in 1906. The yield of cotton and sugar crops trebled in ten years. Henceforward Egypt depended upon the export of cotton, in the same way as Ghana and Western Nigeria came to depend on the export of cocoa.

Reassessment of Cromer's policies

But Cromer's achievements are being differently assessed today by Egyptians. His economic policy, they argue rightly, centred on agriculture, that is the production of specific crops for European manufacturers. They contend, with some justification, that the economic policy that would have been in the best interests of Egypt would have been encouragement of industrialisation as well, as Mohammed Ali had attempted to do and as independent Egypt has been doing since 1922. The best evidence for this criticism of Cromer's economic policy is clear from the encouragement given to the cultivation of cotton of which Egypt was producing one of the best varieties. By 1912 cotton accounted for 80·1 per cent of Egyptian exports. One would have thought that a textile industry would have been in the interest of Egyptians. Indeed in the 1890s a group of Englishmen attempted to establish local textile factories in Egypt. These factories would have competed with the Lancashire factories aimed at the Egyptian consumer market. But the Cromer administration killed the venture by imposing 8 per cent excise duties on locally manufactured goods, the tax being equivalent to the tariff on imported goods. Cromer imposed an 8 per cent customs duty on imported coal in order to prevent the industrialisation of Egypt and he killed the tobacco industry in the country with a threat of heavy fines. Many Egyptians argue further, that although Cromer made Egypt solvent, he did not pay off the entire debt of Egypt in his long period of rule, but when Egyptians resumed the control of their affairs they were able to pay off their country's debt at a much faster rate.

It is also argued that Cromer's successful running of the Suez Canal conferred no benefits upon Egypt. After the British occupation all revenue from the canal was drained out of Egypt; millions of pounds, one and a half millions annually to the British, went out every year as dividends to the foreign shareholders of the International Suez Company. It is important to note that throughout his rule

Cromer was silent about this. From 1880 to 1936 the government of Egypt did not receive a single penny for the use of its territory or in return for its original investment of £16 million in the canal.

Also, while Egyptians do not question the efficiency of Cromer's administration they argue that it was British, rather than Egyptian, in personnel and that Cromer wilfully neglected the education of Egyptians, who did not conceal their eagerness to learn. The ministries of finance, justice and education, the army and the police, were all staffed in the senior posts by British subjects. The number of British officials increased from 286 in 1896 to 662 in 1906. Egyptians were employed as junior clerks only, in spite of the existence of a corps of well-educated individuals who had received university education in Europe. The civil service policy came to be described as that of British heads and Egyptian hands.

It is true that Cromer did not want a western form of education to thrive in Egypt. He spent only $1\frac{1}{2}$ per cent of the total revenue of the country on education and health. Even the modest education programme that he planned was not properly carried out. It was left to the nationalists to organise schools at their own expense. Cromer argued that a western form of education would be bad for the British administration: it would create a band of disgruntled individuals who would wish to get rid of the British rulers. He believed that all that Egypt needed was vernacular education for the masses, with secondary education to produce a sufficient number of Egyptians to do the lower grade clerical and technical jobs and no more. He had an intense hatred for university institutions for Egyptians. There was no question of his encouraging the three higher institutions of learning that had been founded under Ismail to achieve university status by western standards. These institutions, which could easily have been turned to advantage, were the Law School, the School of Medicine and the Engineering School.

One must stress that Cromer believed that by not encouraging the development of higher education he was acting in the best interests of the Egyptian masses. It was his conviction that to foster the growth of a tiny minority, the educated élite—a group of people whose political and social aspirations were not necessarily identical with those of the masses—would be to throw the latter into the hands of demagogues incapable of ruling. Cromer believed that the administration of the country should not be left in the hands of the largely demuslimised élite who would misgovern the country. He held the view that for a long time British administration was best for Egyptians; that it was not only benevolent but enlightened and that it was only under the gradual tutorship of the British that Egyptians could learn the rules of administration of the modern state. He expected Egyptians to submit to British rule and tutorship with gratitude.

Reappearance of the nationalist movement

However the Egyptian masses never showed much gratitude towards the British. By 1891 the nationalist movement, stimulated and led by the minority élite for whom Cromer had unrelenting contempt, had reappeared. It should be remarked that Egyptian nationalism began in the '70s, but that it was driven underground by British suppression for the decade following the British occupation. In the '70s nationalism had expressed itself in several ways. There was the press which was largely under the control of exiles from Syria who found in Egypt a haven for journalists. Then there was the Chamber of Deputies established by the Khedive Ismail in 1866. By 1879 many of the elected members of the chamber had begun to criticise the Khedival authoritarian tendency and had begun to ask that the voice of the Egyptians should decide the destiny of the country, through their elected representatives. Two people also gave an intellectual stimulus to nationalism in these years. They were Jamal al-Din al-Afghani and Sheik Mohammed Abdu, both of whom were renowned scholars whose ideas influenced the later nationalists. The substance of their teaching was that all faithful Muslims should reject the polluting aspects of European civilisation and unite against foreign rule; and that Islam itself was not opposed to science and technology which, they argued, should be adopted by all Muslim countries in order that they might achieve technical marvels similar to those of European countries.

The 'Constitutionalists' and the Nationalist Party

The nationalists were divided into two distinct groups from the last decade of the nineteenth century. There were the 'Constitutionalists' who were made up of the ruling class of Turkish, Armenian and Circassian Egyptians with whom the British preferred to co-operate rather than with the pure Egyptian nationalists. They desired that the Khedive should rule 'constitutionally' through themselves, and wanted the British to withdraw from the country gradually. They took offices under Cromer and they hated the extremist nationalists, most of whom were pure Egyptians. They formed the *Umma* party and aired their views through their most important newspaper, *Moayyah*. The other group of nationalists were more radical in their demands and were led by lawyers, doctors, teachers and junior government officials. They were mainly of *fellah* origin and they hated the British. The racial and social differences between the two groups of nationalists became more marked after the attainment of independence by Egypt in 1922. The radicals were led by people like Mustapha Kamil and Sad Zaghlul. They formed the Nationalist Party. Two of their influential papers were *al-Liwa* and *al-Alam*. Through their newspapers they disseminated their ideas in French and Arabic, educating the masses about the evils of prolonged British occupation, the autocratic tendencies of the Khedive and the necessity of Arabic being taught in schools.

Reasons for revival of nationalist movements

The reasons for the resurgence of nationalist agitation in the last decade of the nineteenth century are not far to seek. Taking the statements by British politicians at their face value and the manner in which their country was occupied, the nationalists believed that British occupation would be of very short duration. Between 1882 and 1907 England made about 120 declarations and pledges of her intention to evacuate Egypt but with every year her hold upon the country became tighter and tighter. Those declarations and pledges were intended for France and other European powers who did not accept the suzerainty of England over Egypt until the first decade of the twentieth century. After 1888 it began to appear that the British would stay on in Egypt for an indefinite length of time. By 1906 Cromer was already urging the British Government to declare a Protectorate over Egypt. The nationalists were stung by the fact that the Egyptians were paying the cost of the army of occupation of their country as well as the cost of the alien administration forced upon their country. There was also the maintenance of Khedival authority by the British, a very bitter pill for the radical nationalists to swallow. To them Khedival authority symbolised oppression, tyranny and corruption. It meant putting in power the alien Turks, Armenians and Circassians at national and local levels. In the provinces, districts and villages it was these Turco-Egyptians who were appointed as rulers by the Ministry of Interior. These Turco-Egyptians despised the Egyptians, kept themselves socially apart, used the Turkish language, were self-indulgent and corrupt. The first ministry under British occupation was headed by Nubar Pasha (1883–87), a Christian Armenian who had been imported to Egypt as recently as the reign of Mohammed Ali. Educated in France, he spoke French and Turkish but not Arabic. An apostle of a British Protectorate, he was disliked by the Egyptians for being pro-western and a firm supporter of British rule in Egypt. Riaz Pasha, who was Prime Minister from 1887 to 1891, was no more liked by the Egyptians. Alleged to be a converted Jew who came from a family of goldsmiths he was, according to Cromer, 'a stupid, obstinate and violent (man who) has not the most elementary ideas of government by law.' Mustapha Fahmi, who succeeded Riaz Pasha in 1891 was a wealthy and vain Turk who was entirely committed to the service and interests of the British.

Nationalism revived also on the Sudan question. The nationalists had never liked the 1885 evacuation of the Sudan which, it will be remembered, had been a Turco-Egyptian appendage since 1821. In the early '90s when Menelik II of Ethiopia was threatening to divert the Nile from Egypt, many nationalists advocated a reconquest of the Sudan. In 1896 Lord Kitchener led an army, the bulk of which was Egyptian, into the Sudan. Out of the total cost of £2,354,000 entailed by the expedition Egypt provided £1,554,000 and Britain only £800,000. Nevertheless the condominium established in the Sudan in 1898, which in theory meant that both Britain and Egypt were to administer the Sudan, was no more than a British administration, a disguised form of British annexation of the Sudan. The Sudan was financially and administratively separated from Egypt, and when on 27 January 1906 the railway from Khartoum to Port Sudan was opened, it also acquired economic independence. This, which made it clear that the Sudan had not in any way come under Egyptian control, was described by the popular press in Cairo as 'the day of Egypt's funeral'. To add to the grievances of the Egyptians, the British made Egypt contribute financially to the administration of the Sudan from the date of its reconquest until 1936.

Many external developments strengthened Egyptian nationalism. Until the Anglo-French Agreement of 1904, according to which the French recognised Britain's claims to Egypt, the French welcomed nationalists, many of whom studied law in France, and strengthened their anti-British feelings. Leaders like Afghani, Abdu and Mustapha Kamil disseminated anti-British feelings through French journals, denouncing the British occupation and asking the British to withdraw from Egypt as well as from other Islamic countries. The success of Japan in the Russo–Japanese war in 1905 was an encouragement to the nationalists. They began to think that they too could defeat British imperialism as Japan had forestalled Russian imperialism. In the following year, to the surprise of British rulers in Egypt, the nationalists and the press indicated support for Turkey in the dispute over Taba in the Gulf of Aqaba which both Turkey and Britain claimed. The Sultan, who claimed ownership of the entire Sinai Peninsula, sent in troops and there was danger of war between Britain and Turkey. Edward Dicey, correspondent in Cairo of the *Daily Telegraph*, estimated that 90 per cent of the people of Egypt would have risen for the Sultan if that war had broken out.

The Suez Canal

By the beginning of the nineteenth century the Suez Canal had become a burning issue for the nationalists. In 1880 the 15 per cent of the net profit, which in the original contract with de Lesseps should have gone to Egypt for owning the territory through which the canal passed, had been senselessly and ruinously sold away by the French and English controllers for the meagre sum of £4 million. Henceforth millions of pounds flowed to England and France without a single penny going into Egypt's treasury. The nationalists could forget neither this diversion of money nor the trickery that led to the original contract. In 1910 Butros Ghali, the Coptic Prime Minister, acted against the national interests of Egypt when he agreed to, and put before the Legislative Assembly, a proposal by the International Suez Company which sought to extend the contract of the company by forty years for a sum of £4 millions and a profit of 5 per cent whenever the company realised in a year £100,000,000 net profit. The anger of the nationalists was unconcealed in the Assembly where the proposal was thrown out. So enraged were the Egyptians that a fanatic assassinated the Prime Minister, who could do nothing right in the eyes of the Egyptians. In 1899 he had signed the Condominium Agreement and had in 1906 presided over the Dinshawai incident, an incident that demands more than casual mention.

The Dinshawai incident

The Dinshawai incident of 1906 is an event which is remembered even today. In the small village bearing this name a party of Englishmen went pigeon-shooting. Contrary to tradition, the officers had not sought permission to shoot the pigeons, which were a means of liveli-hood. Incensed by this, and by the fact that a barn caught fire from the gun of one of the officers, the villagers flogged the latter and an Egyptian woman was seriously wounded. The officers managed to escape from the village to the camp but one of them, Bull, dropped dead. In spite of the fact that the medical report on Bull certified that he died of sunstroke, the British authorities decided to treat the case as one of premeditated murder. Very harsh measures were taken. A special tribunal tried the villagers for murder. Both the composition of this tribunal and its proceedings were a travesty of justice. All fifty-two accused were examined within half an hour, that is thirty-four seconds per man, time just enough for the accused to give his name and age. The charge of premeditated murder was upheld. Four of the men were condemned to death and were hanged in the presence of the other villagers; two were sentenced to penal servitude for life and others to various terms of imprisonment.

The Egyptians were outraged by this unblushing demonstration of injustice and riots broke out in Cairo and in the provinces. Anti-British feelings rose to fever heights, doing far more for the nationalist cause than the press and oratory had done for nationalist awakening since the British occupation. Secondary school boys and the *fellahin* became infected with the nationalist spirit. Indeed the *fellahin* composed a folk-ballad, reproduced by Dr. Afaf Lufti Al-Sayyid, *Egypt and Cromer* (London 1968), worth recording:

They fell upon Dinshawai
And spared neither man nor his brother,
Slowly they hanged the one and flogged the other,
It was a gloomy day when Zahran was killed,
His mother from the roof watched, while tears from her was spilled,
His brother, O you people, stood by him,
And gazed till his eyes grew dim.

The ghost of Dinshawai was haunting Cromer when he resigned as the British ruler in Egypt in 1907. The nationalists were delighted at his resignation. In the words of *Al-Ahram* of 12 April 1907, Cromer was 'a violent destroyer and a tyrant. He destroyed the Egyptian Sudan and built an English Sudan. He destroyed the Egyptian ministry and built an English advisory body . . .'

The nationalist movement gained in strength under Gorst, Cromer's successor. Like Cromer, Gorst treated the nationalists with contempt but allowed them free use of the spoken and written word. It was under Lord Kitchener, who succeeded Gorst in 1911, that the nationalists came under the sledge-hammer. Kitchener enacted measures designed to paralyse the nationalist movement. In this year he enacted the Criminal Conspiracy Act, the Press Censorship Act and the School Discipline Act. In the face of these severe measures some nationalists were imprisoned and others exiled. Nevertheless, nationalism increased rather than decreased. In 1913 Kitchener dismissed the General Assembly because it dared to ask for the establishment of a representative parliamentary system of government. However, he discovered that the nationalist movement could not be destroyed. Already since the death of Mustapha Kamil in 1908 national consciousness was being aroused through the writings of Ahmad Lufti al-Sayyid, the intellectual editor of the newspaper *al-Jaridah* from 1907 to 1915.

World War One

The outbreak of the First World War further poisoned Anglo–Egyptian relations. In December 1914 Egypt was formally proclaimed a British Protectorate. Sir Arthur MacMahon was appointed High Commissioner, the office of Agent and Consul-General being abolished. Britain placed the Egyptian Foreign Office under the new British High Commissioner, deposed Abbas II, abolished the Khedival title and chose Hussein Kamil, a member of the royal family, as Sultan of Egypt. Because Egyptians, religiously one with the Turks and like the latter intensely anti-British, were pro-Turkey, a power fighting on the side of Germany, the British proclaimed martial law and rounded up Egyptians whose tendencies appeared dangerous to them.

To Egyptians the word Protectorate, *Himaya*, had a very unpleasant meaning. According to the Koran it is the duty of Muslims, the true believers, to 'protect' Christians, 'people of the Book'. Now, to the horror of the Egyptians, 'Christian' British claimed that they would be 'protecting' Egyptian Muslims. To the Egyptians this was turning the world upside down, infidels 'protecting' the faithful.

Although the Egyptians did not feel that they had a stake in the issues that led to the outbreak of the war, they saw their country being turned into a military base for Britain's Mediterranean Force for the Gallipoli campaign. By 1916 no less than three General Headquarters had been established in Egypt. The army of occupation became in effect the government of the country. Moreover, the Egyptians suffered many hardships throughout the war. Much against their wish they were forced to contribute to British success. Egyptians were conscripted as porters, their foodstuffs were taken from them and their camels were seized at cheap prices. They were forced to build roads and barracks in Egypt and Syria. 135,000 Egyptians, who would never have wanted to reside in Syria, took part in the Syrian campaign, 8,500 men in Mesopotamia and 10,000 in France. Furthermore, a collection for 'Christian' Red Cross funds was somehow converted into a forced levy on a Muslim people.

The war had economic effects on the country. Cotton was cultivated at the expense of subsistence crops, thus making foodstuffs very expensive. Moreover the price being paid for cotton was the lowest in Egypt's experience; and yet this was the time when the British administration demanded higher taxes from the people.

Sad Zaghlul

The nationalist leader who spoke on behalf of the Egyptians in these years was Sad Zaghlul. Born in 1857 he had been a disciple of al-Afghani and Mohammed Abdu. He participated in the Arabi Pasha 'rebellion' and was jailed. He studied law and then took office in the British administration. In 1906 he was made minister in charge of education and in 1910 he was given control of the Ministry of Justice. In 1913 he resigned his ministerial appointment and became bitterly anti-British. He demanded the abolition of the privileges enshrined in the treaties known as Capitulations which European powers had signed with Turkey since the sixteenth century, constitutional reforms, improvements in education and agriculture, and above all, the independence of Egypt.

The behaviour of the British in the Middle East outraged the nationalists. In 1916 France, Britain and Russia signed the Sykes–Picot Agreement, according to which these powers would partition the Turkish Empire after the war. Egypt, Hijaz in the Arabian Peninsula and Iraq were embittered by the revelation of the secret agreement by Russia in the following year. Egyptians believed that Britain would not hesitate to absorb Egypt into her empire if this Agreement were to be put into effect. The nationalists also noted the fact that Britain was encouraging Sharif Hussein of the Hijaz to revolt against the Sultan of Constantinople, with the promise that independence would be given him after the war. The nationalists in Egypt could not see how Britain could give independence to Hijaz, the most backward country in the Middle East, and deny it to their country, the most advanced. Furthermore, the principle of self-determination, which meant the right of a people to decide for themselves how they

Sad Zaghlul

were to be ruled, which was being advocated by President Woodrow Wilson of the United States, was proclaimed by the British, through the High Commissioner in Egypt, in the *Declaration to the Seven*. Although Egypt was not specifically mentioned in this document it was stated that the self-determination principle would apply to the Ottoman Empire.

It is not surprising that after the war Sad Zaghlul led a delegation to the British High Commissioner, claiming the right to send delegates to the Peace Conference in Paris. To their shock the High Commissioner, Sir Reginald Wingate, did not recognise their claims and refused them permission to go to Paris. When the High Commissioner insisted that the three-man delegation of Sad Zaghlul was not really representative the Egyptian nationalist made his famous speech: 'Do we have to ask a nation whether it wants independence? Ours is the oldest of civilisations. Our ancestors have handed down to us indisputable social virtues. Our civic sense is there for everyone to see. One can see it in our respect for the rule of law, our even temper and identity of outlook. To ask a nation like this whether it is agreed on independence is an affront to it.' It is worth noting that the delegation —'Wafd'—gave its name to the most popular political party in Egypt from 1922 to 1950.

Zaghlul and other leaders were deported to Malta and as a result tension became very high. By 1920 Egyptian nationalism had grown much stronger than in 1881. The common man was now infected with the new fashion and women, both in the towns and the countryside, began to join the nationalist movement. They left their harems and participated in demonstrations with secondary school boys who left their classrooms. The *fellahin* felt that they had every cause to hate the British. Not only had the cost of living risen very high but the lowest price within their memory was being paid for cotton and taxation was crushingly heavy. The educated people were shocked that the British did not think they were mature enough to rule themselves. Thus the ground was prepared for Zaghlul to succeed where Arabi Pasha had failed. Zaghlul associated the *fellah* and the townsman with the nationalist movement and gave the country a party in the modern sense of the word.

Violence breaks out

The Egyptian people resorted to violence. Such severe riots broke out in the Delta towns and Upper Egypt that the British had to import special troops to restore law and order. The British government decided to send a commission to inquire into the situation in the country. The man who led this Commission was Sir Alfred Milner, by no means a liberal. He was instructed to suggest the best form of constitution by which Egypt could be ruled within the Protectorate system. It was expected that this constitution would have as its aim the promotion of peace, order, prosperity, the protection of foreign interests and the progressive development of self-governing institutions.

The Milner Commission

The Milner Commission was not well received by the nationalists. They had formed the Committee of Independence after Zaghlul's deportation and they boycotted the Commission completely. Having studied the charged atmosphere on the spot Milner came to the conclusion that the nationalist movement was not just an organisation of a few disgruntled educated Egyptians. He could not have been unaffected by the wave of terror which broke out again a few weeks before he arrived in Egypt. On 22 November a British officer was murdered; the following day four British soldiers were fired at and wounded; the following January Sirry Pasha, a member of the Egyptian Cabinet, was attacked with a bomb; the next month an attempt was made on the life of Shafiq Pasha, the Minister of Agriculture.

In the circumstances the British decided to release Zaghlul and his associates. Zaghlul was summoned to London for negotiation with Milner. Both sides found it difficult to reach an agreement. The British would not grant full independence to Egypt. Zaghlul was asked to give a guarantee to protect British interests in Egypt, to recognise Britain's right to station an army of occupation there, to approve clauses that would give Britain rights of protecting foreigners in Egypt and to leave Egypt's foreign policy in the hands of the British. Zaghlul refused to accept the British terms and the negotiations ended inconclusively. In 1921 disturbances broke out again. In the following year the British Government granted self-government to Egypt but retained control of foreign policy, the defence—both of Egypt and the Suez Canal—and of the protection of minorities, including the protection of the small but powerful minority of Europeans with business interests in Egypt, and retained their share in the government of the Sudan.

Egypt becomes self-governing

Obviously this was not a satisfactory declaration to the Egyptian nationalists. By it the British only gave with one hand what they took away with the other. In the circumstances, however, the nationalists could do nothing but accept the measure of independence that had been given to them. In the following year a constitution on the British pattern was established and Fuad, the Sultan, became King. He was expected to behave like a parliamentary monarch, choosing ministers from a popularly elected Parliament. Nevertheless between 1923 and 1952 the constitution never worked, simply because the kings, Fuad up to 1936 and Faruk from 1936 to 1952, did not intend to be constitutional rulers. They wished to be autocrats who would both reign and rule, irrespective of the wishes of the electorate as expressed in the parliamentary elections. The kings hated the Wafd, the most popular of the political parties that usually won the elections, a party that wished the kings to rule like their British counterparts. In the first year of the promulgation of the constitution King Fuad I violated it and he did so again in 1928; in 1930 he suspended it altogether. Between 1937 and 1952 King Faruk ruled by martial law for eleven years.

Then there was also the fact that the kings allowed their fear of the Wafd to drive them to adopt a pro-British attitude and thereby support British interests in the country. They hoped that in this way the British would become a counterforce to the Wafd who were intensely anti-British. The Wafd wanted full independence for Egypt and complete exclusion of British influence. As a result of the pro-British attitude of the kings the British High Commissioners became a decisive voice in the affairs of the country. In 1924, after the murder in Cairo of Sir Lee Stack, the Governor-General of the Sudan, the High Commissioner influenced King Fuad to force Zaghlul, the first Prime Minister of Independent Egypt, to resign. In his place was appointed Abdul Ziwar, a man who did not control a majority of votes in Parliament. The Egyptians felt humiliated when as late as February 1942 Sir Miles Lampson, the British ambassador in Cairo, forced King Faruk to appoint Mustapha Nahas Prime Minister. From 1925 to 1930 Parliament was dissolved because it would not support the measures favoured by the king. In 1930 the king dissolved Parliament permanently and used as his advisers the Palace Party, an organisation of conservative big landlords who exacted high rents from their peasant tenants and hated the Wafd. It is not surprising, then, that hostility began to build up against the king as a result of his

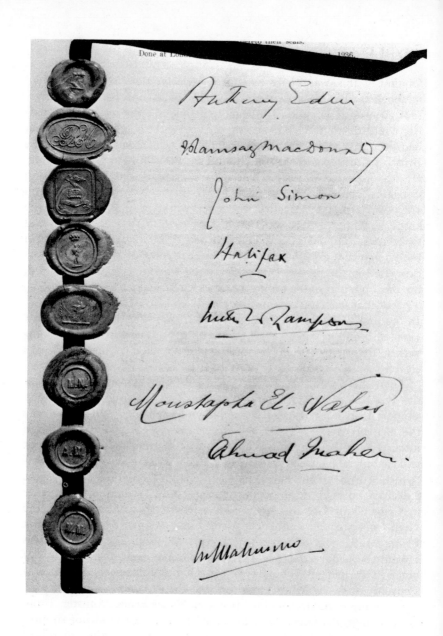

The signatures to the Anglo-Egyptian Treaty of 1936. Among those who signed were Sir Miles Lampson and Mustapha Nahas

autocratic tendencies. The feeling became strong that it was the British who continued to rule Egypt through the king and that the centre of power was London and not Cairo. By 1952, when a military *coup* ousted King Faruk from authority, the Egyptian people had lost faith in the monarchy and Faruk's enforced abdication evoked little sympathy.

In 1936 the Wafd, who in that year were swept into power in an election, succeeded in strengthening Egypt's position through negotiations with the British. What brought both sides to decide to iron out their differences in this year was the invasion of Ethiopia by Italy and Britain's need of Egypt's support. Britain feared that Italy might plan to revive the Roman Empire in Africa and in the process employ Egypt against Britain. Naturally the nationalists made reduction of Britain's control over Egypt the condition on which they would not ally with Italy against Britain. The 1936 Anglo–Egyptian Treaty confined British power to the Suez Canal zone. Also the number of British troops in the country was limited and provision for the treaty's revision was made. By the treaty of 1936 Egypt became an independent nation. She joined the League of Nations and the system of capitulations was brought to an end. Yet England still had a firm hold on Egypt for the treaty now gave her a legal right to protect the Suez Canal and to station British forces on Egyptian territory. In 1951 this treaty was formally abrogated by a *Wafdist* government. Negotiations continued from 1947 to 1952 but the British did not evacuate the canal zone until after the termination of the monarchy.

The Muslim brotherhood

In the meantime an organisation which started as a religious one was becoming a strong political body threatening both the king and the Wafd alike. This was the *Ikhwan al Muslimin* (Muslim Brotherhood), founded in 1927 by Hasan al-Banna. It advocated the establishment of an Islamic theocracy, based upon the Koran and the wise sayings of the Prophet known as the *Hadith*. The Brotherhood then began to advocate the social, economic and political betterment of the believers. It established schools, co-operatives, hospitals and textile factories. Soon after Faruk ascended the throne in 1936 the organisation began to advocate a re-establishment of the caliphate in preference to the king. The Brotherhood regarded the British as 'usurpers' and preached the doctrine that it was the duty of all Muslims to co-operate in a *jihad* against all infidel colonial powers. By 1946 the Brotherhood had about one million members who were already being trained in the art of fighting. They took an active part in the war against the Jews in Palestine in 1948, at the end of which both the king and the government began to fear that the Brotherhood would seize power by force. Therefore orders were sent out dissolving the organisation and its provincial branches, confiscating most of its property and arresting most of its members. In 1949 Hasan al-Banna, the leader of the organisation, was murdered.

King Faruk became increasingly unpopular. In 1945 and 1946 he met a number of Arab leaders without the previous knowledge, consultation, or presence of any member of his cabinet. He also acquired or transferred *Waqf* properties (religious trusts and bequests) to the Royal Domains at his pleasure. He interfered directly in political, cabinet and senate appointments and attempted to influence the proceedings of the courts. In 1946 his portraits were torn from university walls. In 1948 he ordered an unprepared army to invade Palestine with defective arms, against expert advice. The result was the humiliation of the Egyptian army by the Israelis.

Egypt becomes a Republic

The political situation was not improved by the pro-king behaviour of the Wafd government which was restored to power in 1950. The Wafd had become totally discredited. Corrupt to the core, the wealthy members of parliament and Cairo's privileged social élite would not support sweeping reforms that would herald social justice in the country. The Wafd protected the interests of landowners, businessmen and top ranking civil servants. In December 1951 there were violent demonstrations against the king in Cairo, Alexandria and all the provincial capitals. In the next seven months there were no less than six governments. It was clear that the monarchy and a parliamentary pattern of government had failed in Egypt. The confused situation was convenient for the army to take over the control of affairs on 23 July 1952. Faruk was forced to abdicate and Egypt was declared a Republic the following year.

The Muslim Brethren, who had been allowed to organise again, did not wish to co-operate with the soldiers for long and had a different political and social programme from that of the military officers. They did not believe that soldiers were competent to rule the country in which they felt a theocracy in the classical fashion should be established. The Brethren began to say that they would give the soldiers, who had formed the Revolutionary Council, ten years of life. They believed that during this period the Egyptians would have become the ardent Muslims of their imagination. In January 1953 the Revolutionary Council dissolved all political parties and the Brethren began to think of overthrowing the army regime. When on 26 October 1954 a member of the organisation made an attempt on Nasser's life the Brethren became discredited and their organisation was dissolved.

The army seizes power

The seizure of government by the army in 1952 has marked a new era in the history of Egypt. Henceforward the social differences began to be minimised, if not eliminated; a beginning was made to create an egalitarian society. The Wafd were discredited as a band of politicians who did not have the real interests of the country at heart. The titles of 'bey' and 'pasha' were abolished and corrupt officials removed from office. In the same year the Revolutionary Council enacted a law restricting the maximum land property of Egyptians to 300 acres; nine years later this maximum was further reduced to 200 acres. The aim of the military regime in regard to land was similar to Mohammed Ali's—distribution of impounded land to landless peasants. In order to stimulate further the country's agricultural production the military regime decided to build the High Dam, not far from Aswan, which is estimated to cost £180 million and make available 700,000 acres for perennial irrigation.

Egypt under Nasser

Since 1952, particularly since 1954 when he assumed power, events have revolved round the late Gamal Abdel Nasser, President of the United Arab Republic. One of the organisers of the coup of July 1952 Gamal Abdel Nasser was born in Alexandria on 15 January 1918 to an assistant postmaster's wife. In 1937 he entered the Military Academy which until the previous year had not opened its door to pure Egyptians. In 1943 he became a captain. He participated in the Palestine war in which he was wounded. In late 1949 he and eleven officers founded a secret organisation known as the Free Officers. It was this organisation that arranged the coup of July 1952, under the leadership of General Neguib. By 1952 Nasser nursed intense hatred against 'imperialism, monarchy and feudalism'. The incident of

Gamal Abdel Nasser

February 1942, in which the British encircled Faruk's palace with tanks and forced Mustapha Nahas upon Faruk, made a deep impression on him. By 1943 he had formed a secret organisation within the army pledged to seize government. His hopes for Egypt and the reasons behind his bid for power are clearly expounded in his book, *The Philosophy of the Revolution* (Cairo 1954).

The military regime lost no time in initiating profound social and economic reforms. Nasser himself led a very simple and austere life and succeeded in establishing himself as an exceptionally qualified leader. He certainly set Egypt on the path of development. Some of his achievements in social and economic affairs and in his fight against imperialism are worthy of note.

Fully aware that literary education is the key to the social development and strength of a nation, the leaders of the revolution initiated a big programme. For the first time in the history of Egypt a serious effort was made to provide primary schooling throughout the country. The ambition of the regime was to build 'a school a day' and it was hoped that between 1955 and 1964, 4,000 schools would be constructed. However, the challenge outstripped the resources available to the government. Consequently by 1958 only 848 schools had been constructed. In this year there were 2,104,000 pupils in the primary schools, that is nearly double the figure for 1952.

Notable achievements were also made in teacher training and technical education. The growth in university education is clear from the fact that the number of undergraduates in the three major universities rose from 30,641 in 1952 to 71,994 in 1958. Between 1952 and 1958 the Revolution government spent a total of £22 million on new school buildings alone.

Nor did the Nasser administration neglect the social conditions of the peasants and urban workers. Although the diseases of bilharzia and trachoma are still to be conquered, medical facilities expanded considerably. Low cost housing schemes were also inaugurated for workers earning less than £300 a year and birth control was introduced. The gap between the haves and have-nots was reduced by a law which limits the incomes of individuals to a maximum of £5,000 a year.

The social welfare ideal to which the Nasser administration dedicated itself is nothing peculiar to Egypt. Such an ideal is being preached, and in some measure is being practised, by the governments of Algeria and Ghana, and in a less spectacular manner in Nigeria and other independent African states.

The social welfare programme of the Revolution government has become a reality because of the conscious effort made to improve the economy of the country. Touching the *fellahin* most is the Agrarian Reform Law of 9 September 1952. By 1959 240,000 feddans had been requisitioned from private individuals and 180,000 feddans confiscated from the Mohammed Ali family. These were distributed among the *fellahin* on fair terms which enabled a hundred thousand families to receive up to twice their former income. Also to the advantage of the *fellahin* was the ceiling put by government on the rents chargeable by landlords. Henceforth the small farmer was given a sense of security and whether he owns or rents the land he cultivates he feels more attached to the land.

Economic reforms

With these agrarian reforms went an increase in productivity. Agricultural production has increased by 6 per cent every four years. Wheat and rice showed the most remarkable advances. Wheat productivity over the four-year period 1953–56 showed a 19 per cent higher productivity than over the 1949–52 period, while rice yields

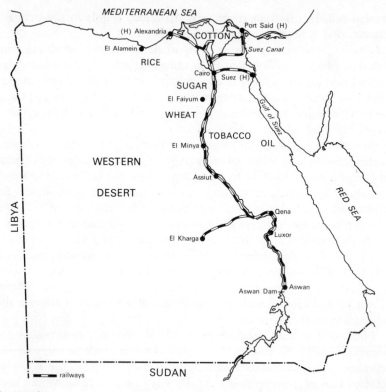

MEDITERRANEAN SEA

(H) Alexandria

Port Said (H)

COTTON

El Alamein

Suez Canal

RICE

Cairo   Suez (H)

SUGAR

El Faiyum

WHEAT

TOBACCO

El Minya

OIL

WESTERN

Assiut

DESERT

LIBYA

RED SEA

El Kharga

Qena

Luxor

Aswan Dam   Aswan

Gulf of Suez

railways

SUDAN

Egypt today

showed comparable gains. But it should be remarked that as long as the export economy of the country depends on one major crop, cotton, which in 1952 still accounted for 80 per cent of the country's total exports, Egypt must suffer the fate of producers of raw materials for the industries of Europe. If the world demand for cotton is high the farmer is wealthier and in a position to import greatly needed manufactured articles. However, as often happens, when demand is slack, prices fall and the farmer is badly hit. In order to stabilise prices for the *fellahin* the Revolution regime has since 1952 done what other ex-British territories have done; it has created the Egyptian Cotton Commission which performs a function similar to that of the Marketing Boards of Nigeria and Ghana.

Fully alive to the fact that a one-crop economy would see Egypt put all her eggs in one basket, the Nasser administration revived the dream of Mohammed Ali about industrialisation. By 1960 more than £150 million had been spent by the Government on expansion of the industrial sector. In 1954 an iron and steel complex was designed and it went into production in 1958. The Government also went into the petroleum industry in a big way, from prospecting to refinery and marketing. This industry is vested in the General Petroleum Authority. The hydro-electric plant at Aswan and its adjoining fertiliser plant are also big schemes, major strides in the march of Egypt towards becoming an industrial state. The state has also taken over or participated in various enterprises like banks, insurance companies and trading concerns, which up to 1962 were largely owned and controlled by alien investors whose interests were hardly identical with those of Egypt.

Nationalisation of the Suez Canal

Perhaps the most important single event since the 1952 Revolution was the forcible nationalisation of the Suez Canal Company by Nasser in 1956. Apart from his determination to efface all forms of imperialism from his country the need for funds to finance the development of the Egyptian economy prompted Nasser to adopt the measure which so infuriated the Western capitalists, to the point that France and Britain waged war on Egypt. It should be stressed here, again, that Egypt received no share whatsoever of the substantial profits of the Company from 1880 to 1936. It was not until August 1937 that an agreement was reached between the Suez Canal Company and the Egyptian Government, stipulating that Egypt would receive £300,000 per year. In 1949 the Company agreed to pay taxes to the Egyptian Government to the amount of £3 million a year. In 1951 the Company paid a total of £4 million, that is only 2 per cent of the total receipts of the Egyptian budget for that year.

It was clear to the Nasser administration that this absentee-owned enterprise, with its administrative headquarters in Paris and its French-dominated directorship, was not designed to reflect the interests of the Egyptian economy. The indirect contribution of the canal to the Egyptian economy before nationalisation was in the form of tolls which were credited to the Egyptian balance of payments. Although some Egyptians were employed, training measures were deliberately designed to restrict Egyptians to piloting and to senior posts in the Company. The benefit accruing to the economy through the tolls was sharply reduced by the fact that more than half of the canal's revenue was used for Company remittances in the form of profits and other payments. Moreover, rather than plough back its

The High Dam at Aswan, built with assistance from the Soviet Union. The Egyptian and Russian flags fly side by side over a section of the Dam

profits into Egyptian enterprise, the Company enhanced the financial prosperity of its shareholders by acting as an investment firm, placing its profits in European, French Saharan and American industrial and commercial firms.

Egyptian dissatisfaction with the Company's policies related also to its managerial performance. The canal badly needed widening and deepening to meet the growing volume of petroleum shipment and the world-wide construction of supertankers of deep draught. Aware that the ninety-nine year concession agreed upon in 1869 would expire in 1968 the Company was not interested in the long-term welfare of the Egyptian economy.

With the nationalisation of the Suez Canal enterprise Nasser was assured of enormous profits constituting on the average about 10 per cent of the country's revenue. The war which Egypt fought against the invading British, French and Israelis over the nationalisation issue enhanced Nasser's stature both in Egypt and in the Arab world. Henceforth he became the leading defender of the interests of the Arab world against the imperial threat of the western powers.

The military regime in Egypt has adopted what is now described as a policy of neutrality in foreign affairs. This means that the country is not committed to either of the two power-blocs—the western powers and the Soviet Union. Technical and financial aids are welcomed from any of these blocs, provided the aids given would not make Egypt subservient to the interests of the power giving them. Thus although the Soviet Union sponsored the High Dam project when the western powers had refused to grant the necessary loans Nasser refused to allow the existence of a communist party in his country. Egypt is the spokesman of the Arab League, a body of Arab countries founded in 1944 to promote the interests of the Arab peoples. Since attainment of power and until his death in September 1970 Nasser with his programme of 'positive neutrality' was the symbol of Arab nationalism.

To the western democracies Nasser was an autocrat. But it should be remembered that his people did not see him in this light. In 1957 he convened a National Assembly and since then elections have been taking place. On the whole they admired a man who assumed the administration of their country at a time of despair, a man who made them proud to be Egyptians, a man who in the final analysis did Egypt a great service.

2 The Sudan and Ethiopia since 1898

The 1899 Condominium Agreement

The status of the Sudan after its reconquest by Egyptian and British forces was put in precise legal terms in the Anglo-Egyptian Conventions of 1899 signed on behalf of Britain by Lord Cromer, and on behalf of Egypt by the Coptic Foreign Minister, Butros Ghali. Certain stipulations of this Condominium Agreement, as it is better known, should be noted. The Sudan, it was stated, was to be jointly administered by Britain and Egypt. The Governor-General, who was to head the armed forces and administration, was to be appointed and could be dismissed by the Khedive on the recommendation of the British government; the British and Egyptian flags were to be jointly hoisted throughout the territory; slave trading was henceforth abolished.

British domination of the Sudan

But from the start the British never intended to rule the Sudan with Egypt. Throughout the Condominium, 1899 to 1956, no Egyptian was ever appointed as Governor-General. Only in the early years were Egyptians appointed to junior positions in the civil service of the Sudan, the British monopolising the higher posts. As time went on, particularly after 1924, the Governor-General took decisions without prior consultation with the Khedive or without the Khedive being formally informed. The British accepted the Condominium principle in 1899 for purely diplomatic purposes—to sweeten the bitter pill to France, to ward off possible Ottoman interference in the Sudan and to obtain international approval for the disguised annexation of the Sudan to the British Empire. As time went on many British officers began to argue that Egyptians were unqualified to rule over the Sudan, partly because in the period of Turco–Egyptian administration, 1821–1885, the Sudanese were exploited and badly governed and partly because, as the British officers believed, contemporary Egyptian administration in Egypt was itself corrupt and would corrupt the Sudan administration if a free hand were given to Egyptians in the Sudan. Moreover the British began to declare that their mission in the Sudan was a disinterested one; to rule in the interests of the Sudanese, establish law and order, dispense justice, develop the economy of the territory and put the Sudanese peoples on to the path of progress.

Egypt's financial contribution to the Sudan

Ironically, however, from the year of the reconquest to 1912, when the resources of the Sudan were inadequate to meet the requirements of the administration, the British persuaded the Egyptian government to make financial grants to the Sudan. The series of advances made by Egypt enabled the railway to be built from Atbara on the Nile to the Red Sea, and the new port of Port Sudan, with deep-water quays, to be developed there. Later they enabled the Blue Nile to be bridged at Khartoum and the railway extended down the Gezira to Sennar and across the White Nile at Kosti. It was not until 1949 that the Sudan could pay back the loans Egypt had made to her in these earlier years. Before and after 1912 Egypt was constrained by the British to maintain an army for the internal and external defence of the country.

Throughout the Condominium, when Egypt's participation in the administration of the Sudan progressively diminished, the Sudanese witnessed the spectacle of two masters discussing and disputing with themselves the destiny of the Sudan without any consultation with the Sudanese peoples. The point must be stressed here that in these years of the Condominium neither the British nor the Egyptians considered primarily the interests of the Sudanese. They both looked upon the Sudan with imperial eyes with the sole aim of treating the territory as a mere projection of the economic, political and strategic interests of Britain or Egypt. However, it should be noted that the clash of interests of these two alien masters, which was prominently displayed on the international scene, contributed in no small measure to the nationalist awakening and termination of colonial rule in the Sudan.

Egypt felt towards the Sudanese a sense of belonging to the same geographical area—the Nile valley; they liked to think of the traditional historical and economic links that had held them together in the past. But, as historians of the Sudan have shown clearly, Egypt had economic reasons for desiring to exercise influence and control over the Sudan. It was a chief market for Egypt's exports, a potential field for Egypt's capital investment and for colonisation by emigrants from over-populated Egypt. Above all Egypt wanted to control the Sudan to prevent being strangled economically by Sudanese over-use of the Nile water.

The British, too, had commercial and strategic interests in the Sudan. Several British companies invested millions of pounds in various enterprises. Britain valued highly the long staple cotton of the Sudan and bought most of the Sudan's other products, including gum arabic, hides and skins, oil seeds, dates and vegetable oils. The strategic importance of the Sudan in the scramble for Africa has been mentioned in Volume One. Through her control of the Sudan Britain could, and many times did, curb the excesses of Egyptian nationalism by threatening to starve Egypt of the Nile water. Also by her occupation of the Sudan Britain was in a position to watch militarily over her interests in the Middle East countries of Egypt, Iraq, Syria, Palestine and the Transjordan and in Eastern and Central Africa.

Economic advantages to the Sudan

Economically there can be no doubt that the Condominium conferred advantages on the Sudan. Roads and railways were constructed to facilitate transportaion of products. By 1930 the Sudan had a railway system linking Wadi Halfa in the north to Sennar in the south, with a main branch to the east from Atbara to Port Said on the Red Sea coast. There is also a subsidiary branch which goes southwards from Port Said to Sennar and another line from Sennar to El Obeid in the west, the centre of the gum arabic and cattle trades of the western provinces. Port Said was modernised. But the greatest economic achievement of the Condominium was the irrigation programme launched and encouraged by the administration. As early as 1904 Leigh Hunt, an American financier, was given the concession of 10,000 feddans at Zeidab for the cultivation of cotton and wheat. In that year he founded the Sudan Experimental Plantations Syndicate, which three years later became the Plantations Syndicate. In 1911 the administration opened the first test pumping station on 600 acres of land rented from local native owners at Tayiba. In the Northern

Water stored by the Sennar Dam is fed into canals to irrigate the Gezira plain

Region the government established seven pumping schemes between 1917 and 1928, for the irrigation of areas varying in size from 2,000 to 4,000 acres. These were demonstration farms which willing individuals were expected to copy. By 1947 private irrigation schemes numbered 347. In the north dates, citrus and mango were extensively cultivated. On the White and Blue Niles there were in 1947 over

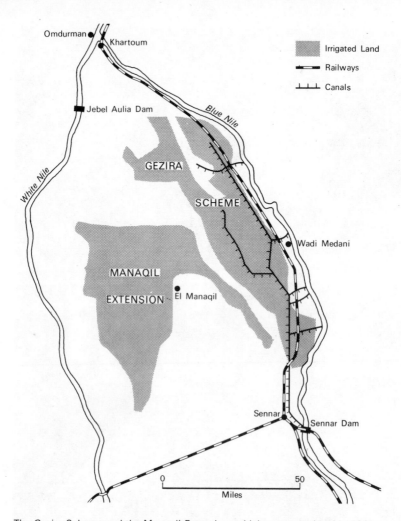

The Gezira Scheme and the Manaqil Extension, which was completed in 1961

twenty-four private pump-watered fields growing fruit, vegetables, grain, forage crops and cotton.

However, the greatest feat of the Condominium was the construction of the Sennar Dam which was completed in 1925. With its canal system the dam irrigates 900,000 acres of the Gezira plain, the triangular area between the White and Blue Niles. The crop which is grown here is cotton, the mainstay of Sudan's economy, amounting in value to 80 per cent of the country's total exports. In 1937 the Jebel Auiliya Dam, thirty miles south of Khartoum, work on which was begun in 1924, was completed.

It is usual for writers to praise the Gezira Scheme as the best illustration of partnership between foreign investors and Africans, illustrating in the words of Margery Perham 'how the wealthy and economically experienced nations can help the poorer peoples of the world to develop their own resources without either economic or political subordination'. There is no doubt that the Sudanese have had much to be grateful for in the Gezira scheme compared with Africans in East Africa, Southern Africa and the Maghreb, where white settlers dispossessed Africans of their lands and forced them to become labourers, and with Africans in the Belgian Congo whom the Belgians exploited as labourers on European plantations. For 25,000 Sudanese families derived livelihood from irrigated land. But it should be stressed that by the scheme the Sudanese, original owners of the land, became 'tenants' of the Syndicate. Each 'tenant' was given forty feddans, ten of which were used for cotton, five each for millet (the staple food grain) and fodder, the remaining twenty being left to fallow. Whatever profits were realised were shared as follows—the 'tenants' 40 per cent, the government (which invested £13 million in the Sennar Dam and the major canals) 40 per cent and the syndicate 20 per cent.

The point should also be made that the real gainers from the scheme were the British textile manufacturers of Lancashire who enjoyed virtual monopoly of the fine quality long-staple cotton grown in the Gezira. Moreover, the British financiers and directors were able to harness British interest by their control of the Gezira plains through two British companies—the Sudan Plantations Syndicate Ltd., and the Kassala Cotton Company. These two companies supervised the cultivation, the ginning and the marketing of cotton until 1950 when the extravagant concessions they were enjoying were terminated.

Distribution of the Nile water

It is not surprising that one point of dispute between the Condominium powers was the distribution of the Nile water between the Sudan and Egypt. It was clear that unless an agreement could be reached between the British and Egyptian governments the Sudan could starve Egypt economically. For, as Colonel Helmy, one-time Secretary-General of the High Dam authority, Egypt, was quoted as saying: 'From the dawn of history Egypt has depended on the flow of the waters of the Nile as the individual depends on the circulation of the blood'. It is not surprising, then, that Egyptian nationalists were alarmed at the efforts of the British to erect barrages in the Sudan. In 1920 an international commission looked into the matter. The commission was faced with the problem of how water should be allocated. Was it to be according to volume, or percentage of volume, or should it be according to need? The 1920 Commission agreed that allocation by volume was premature, as water was available for everybody. In 1925 another Commission, with English and Egyptian representatives, was appointed to allocate water in terms of volume. In 1929 negotiations were re-opened and an agreement was reached. It was agreed that no waterworks of any kind should be built in the Sudan without the consent of the Egyptian government and that the Egyptian government was not to set up any water scheme in the Upper Nile until after due consultation with the Sudan. Waterwork was defined as any scheme that would reduce the volume of water flowing into Egypt. An Organisation of Irrigation Department was set up in Egypt. Only one twenty-third of the Nile waters was allocated to the Sudan. There is no doubt that the 1929 Agreement favoured the Egyptians in the sense that it limited the development of irrigation in the Sudan while leaving Egypt free to develop her irrigation as fast as she pleased. Such an agreement could hardly have satisfied the Sudanese nationalists, who in later years lost no time in denouncing it. In 1955, when the Sudan was on the eve of independence, the Sudanese government denounced the 1929 Agreement, declaring that they needed more water for expansion of the Gezira cultivation. This was the time when Egypt also required more water for the High Dam project. It was not until 8 November 1959, when the Sudan was already an independent country, that a satisfactory agreement was concluded with Egypt. The Sudan was allocated a third of whatever volume of water was usable by Egypt, apart from £15 million compensation for the land in the neighbourhood of Wadi Halfa which would be flooded when the High Dam was completed.

The Condominium should be praised also for improving the health of the Sudanese. Small-pox was virtually wiped out through a vaccination campaign and sleeping sickness, bilharzia, cerebro-spinal meningitis and yaws were attacked with medical science.

The beginnings of a nationalist movement

A nationalist movement of the type led by a westernised élite began late in the Sudan compared to the rest of North Africa. There were several reasons for this. Perhaps the most important was the fact that internal division along racial and religious lines was very acute and made it impossible for the many peoples to think in terms of one Sudanese nation. Apart from the parochial and sectional outlook of the Arab tribes and their contempt for the non-Muslim non-Arab tribes, there was the division between the Ansar and the Khatmiyya tariqas, each with millions of followers. The Ansar were the followers and supporters of the Mahdi, the Khatmiyya the bitterest opponents of the Mahdi and his regime. In the early years the Condominium tried to play one faction against the other. Fearing that the Ansar were still looking for a return to the Mahdiyya the British began to support the Khatmiyya Brotherhood. In 1916 the head of the Brotherhood, Sayyid 'Ali al-Mirghani, was knighted. In later years when the Khatmiyya began to show pro-Egyptian leanings the British swung to supporting the Ansar under the at first pro-British posthumous son of the Mahdi, Abdel Rahman al-Mahdi.

Other factors that delayed the emergence of the nationalist movement in the Sudan included the establishment of different administrations for the north and south which perpetuated the cultural and racial differences between the two areas. Then there was the fact that the Condominium administration did very little to educate the people, thereby delaying the rise of an élite who in Colonial Africa were often the champions and spearhead of the nationalist struggle. Government schools were few and far between. Apart from the Gordon Memorial College, which began as a primary school in 1902 and became a secondary school in 1905, the government had no other secondary school until 1946, when a second was built at Hantub in the Blue Nile Province.

It was only after the First World War that nationalist sentiments were openly expressed. It was only to be expected that the anti-British agitation in Egypt should have effects on the small band of westernised educated Sudanese. In the towns, in the army and in the lower ranks of the civil service Sudanese nationals came in contact with their Egyptian counterparts. In 1921 'Ali 'Abd al-Latif, a man of Dinka origin, who envisaged an independent Sudanese nation, formed the Sudanese United Tribes Society. He was arrested and imprisoned in the following year. Soon after his release he began to co-operate with the Egyptians and formed the White Flag League, an organisation made up of young army officers, ex-students of Gordon College and government employees. This organisation inspired demonstrations between June and November 1924 and riots occurred in several towns. The White Flag League was dedicated to the establishment of a Nile Valley state under the King of Egypt. There was also a mutiny of Sudanese and Egyptian soldiers. It was in this tense atmosphere that on 19 November 1924 the Governor-General, Sir Lee Stack, was assassinated in Cairo. The British seized the occasion to compel Egypt to withdraw all Egyptian officers and troops from the Sudan. Troops of the 11th Sudanese battalion sympathised with the Egyptians by mutinying and establishing themselves in the military hospital in Khartoum.

In 1936 was founded the Graduates' General Congress, comprising ex-Gordon College students and other educated Sudanese. This body informed the Condominium government that henceforth they should be regarded as spokesmen for Sudanese interests. In 1942 the Congress submitted a memorandum in which they demanded from the Condominium administration recognition of the rights of self-determination for the Sudanese after the war, abolition of restrictions placed upon the Northern Sudanese intrusion into the south and creation of a Legislative Council. The negative response of the administration to these demands led to a split in the Congress in 1945.

From this year onwards the issue of achievement of independence by the Sudan was not the exclusive concern of the Sudanese. Thanks to the conflict of the interests of the British and the Egyptians, both alien masters began to patronise opposing factions, each claiming that they alone identified with and would defend the true interests and aspirations of the Sudanese. Indeed the two factions that emerged in the Sudan in the '40s were consciously encouraged by their alien patrons.

Ismail el Azhari

One faction in the 1945 split became the Ashigga (Blood Brothers) Party. This organisation was led by Ismail el Azhari, (who died in 1969), the most popular Sudanese leader both before and after achievement of independence. In 1939 Secretary of the Graduates' Congress, the following year its President, Azhari was one of the seven founders of Ashigga and a hater of the British colonial presence. He became committed to the 'Unity of the Nile Valley' slogan of those Egyptians who desired political and economic integration of Egypt and the Sudan. Until 1955, when Azhari began to perceive that the interests and aspirations of Egypt and the Sudan were not necessarily identical, he leaned heavily on two main props for his support—Egypt herself and the Khatmiyya *tariqa*. Since 1942 Egypt had recognised in

Ismail el Azhari on a visit to Cairo

the Graduates' Congress, and later in the Ashigga Party, a nationalist movement that would promote Egyptian-Sudan unity. Within the Sudan support came from the Khatmiyya *tariqa*, led by Ali El Mirghani, an unbending protagonist of union with Egypt. Educated in Egypt he did not speak a word of English and saw the British as infidels. But the pro-Egypt attitude of the Khatmiyya should be understood in another sense: with the memory of the sufferings which members of their sect had suffered under the original Mahdi, they feared the political ambitions of the Mahdi, who they believed wanted to turn the Sudan into another Mahdist State with Sayyid Abd al-Rahman al-Mahdi, the posthumous son of the original Mahdi, as king.

The Umma Party

The other faction, which developed into the Umma Party, consisted of those who still had faith in the British administration. They preferred co-operation with the British, who they hoped would grant their country independence within the Commonwealth. They did not wish to see the Sudan become an appendage of Egypt. The Umma

Party came to have as its patron Sayyid Abd al-Rahman al-Mahdi. Regarded at first by the British as a potential danger, in view of the large number of the Ansar in the three provinces of Darfur, Kordofan and the Blue Nile, the Condominium administration restricted his movement to the Gezira Province until after the First World War. By this time the Condominium administration began to see in him a possible ally and in 1926 he was knighted. In the meantime he had become wealthy through his cotton enterprise in the Gezira. His son, Siddik el Mahdi, was President of the Umma Party from its foundation in 1945 until 1958.

Moves towards independence

From 1948 the Sudan moved fairly rapidly towards independence. In this year was established a Legislative Assembly, to which the South sent thirteen members and the North fifty-two members. In 1951 the Egyptian government formally abrogated the Condominium Treaty of 1899 and the Anglo-Egyptian Agreement of 1936, whereby Egypt and Britain exercised joint sovereignty over the Sudan. In the same year Faruk was declared the King of the Sudan. As a result of these actions the British began to think of granting independence to the Sudan much earlier than had been contemplated. In the Anglo-Egyptian Agreement signed on 12 February 1953, Britain accepted the principle of self-determination for the Sudan and Egypt conceded sovereignty to the Sudanese, leaving them the choice between a link with Egypt and an independent Sudan. It was decided that the transitional period of self-government should not exceed three years after 'the Appointed Day' that would be announced after elections had been duly held. In the meantime the National Unionist Party, embracing the Ashigga and other pro-Egyptian groups, had been formed under Azhari. With the massive support of the Khatmiyya this party won the elections held in the course of the year. There is no doubt that events in Egypt influenced the results. The cause of a Sudan–Egypt union had an appeal for those Sudanese at a time when General Neguib, whose mother was a Sudanese, was at the head of the Egyptian Revolution administration. The 9th of January 1954, when Azhari was appointed Prime Minister, was declared 'the Appointed Day', and he appointed an all-Sudanese cabinet.

In the short period of its rule the Azhari administration made efforts to advance the Sudan in her path towards full independence. Barely a month after the cabinet had assumed office a Sudanisation

Committee was set up and before the end of the year the civil service was already being Sudanised. The Azhari government also desired a measure of economic independence for their country. It instructed the Gezira Board, the hitherto all-white directors of the Gezira cotton enterprise, to Sudanise its administration. Soon afterwards Mekki Abbas, a Sudanese, became Managing Director of the Board and Sayed Abdel Hafiz its Chairman.

The Sudan achieves independence

It was not long before the prospects of some form of union with Egypt began to fade. The Sudanese did not like the deposition of Neguib by Colonel Nasser before the end of 1954 and they also resented the brutal suppression of the Muslim Brotherhood with whom they felt they shared the same religion. Moreover many members of the Khatmiyya sect in the cabinet began to clamour for unfettered independence for the Sudan. By the end of 1955 Nasser and Azhari had become cold towards each other. The forces of independence became so strong in the Sudan that even Sir Sayyid Abdel Rahman had begun to ask for a Sudan completely independent of the British. Early in 1956 the Sudan became a sovereign state, a Republic and not a member of the British Commonwealth.

Post-independence problems

The period after independence has not been one of political calm in the Sudan. Political parties multiplied and by 1958 there were four principal parties—the Umma, the Southern Liberals, the People's Democratic Party and the National Unionist Party. The last but one party was formed in 1956 by the Khatmiyya sympathisers who broke away from the National Unionist Party of Azhari, on the grounds that his policy tended more and more to be secular. The Southern Liberals, as the name implies, was mainly based in the largely 'pagan' non-Arab South and had been formed on the eve of the 1953 elections. In the 1958 Elections the Umma Party had a majority of seats, but not an over-all majority over the other parties. The result was that the Umma Party had to continue the uneasy coalition that had been made in 1956 with the People's Democratic Party, in order to form the government. Neither of the two sects—the Ansar and the Khatmiyya —upon which the coalition was based, trusted each other. While they

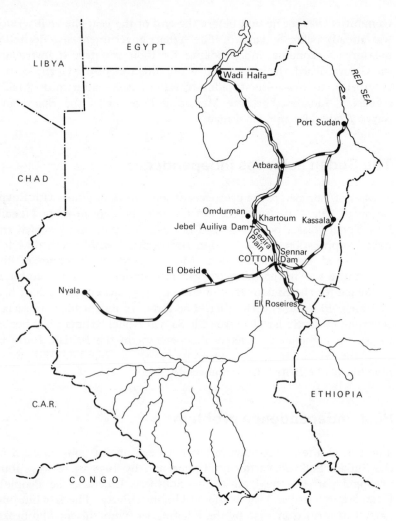

The Sudan today

were plotting against each other—the Umma members of the cabinet making a bid to ally with Azhari and the Khatmiyya with Abdel Nasser—the army believed that the time was ripe to seize control of affairs. On 17 November 1958 General Abboud, at the head of the army, seized power and dissolved the political parties. The army remained at the helm of affairs for the following six years. On 21 October 1964 the army regime was overthrown by a popular demonstration which wished a return to a civil and parliamentary system of government. However, the civilians were not to govern the country for long. In 1969, after nearly five years of factiousness among the politicians, the army struck again and seized control of government.

Civil war

The civil war now going on between the South and the North is topical in contemporary Africa. It should be noted that the revolt of the South against the North first took a violent form in 1955 and that its causes are rooted, in many respects, in the nineteenth century. It was not until the last century that the largely Arab Muslim North first came into contact with the predominantly 'pagan' heterogeneous Negro tribes of the South among whom may be mentioned the Dinka, the Azande, the Bari and the Shilluk. These contacts were unfortunately an unpleasant experience for the Southerners and not one likely to help to build a united country, for the Turco-Egyptians and Arab Northerners raided the South for slaves. This past enslavement of their ancestors by the Northerners has been used by many Southern politicans to prove their contention that the domination of the South by the North in the civil service and in the distribution of amenities since 1954 is only a matter of history repeating itself.

In a sense the Condominium administration added fuel to the flame of the traditional bitterness which the Southerners had for the Northerners. For the South was until 1948 administered as a separate territory and in the '40s some British officers toyed with the idea of merging the South with British East Africa. In 1930 what has been described as the 'Southern Policy' came to be defined and was rigidly applied. All Northerners in administrative, technical and clerical services in the South were transferred to the North; the Muslim Northerners were transferred to the North; Northerners who wished to trade in the South were refused permits; the Muslim religion was suppressed and Arabic as a school language was abolished in favour of English. Christian missions, which had been allowed to operate in the South, supported this policy. In the years that followed, it is being alleged, the missionaries emphasised to their votaries the danger of the North to the South.

This 'Southern Policy', which was applied for eighteen years, naturally increased the fears of the Southerners about their Northern countrymen. But after 1948, when the administrative union of the South and North began, the barriers that had existed began to be removed. Northerners resumed trading activities in the South,

Islam began to gain adherents and in government schools Arabic began to be taught. Had the North and South developed at the same rate during the period of separate administration the unification of the two areas would have been easier than it actually was. Unfortunately the South was much less developed than the North in local government, irrigation schemes, health, education and industrial development. In the circumstances, when unification came, most of the government positions in the South came to be held by Northerners. Feelings in the South ran high against the North when the result of the Sudanisation programme of the Azhari administration began to show itself. The bulk of promotions went to Northerners. Consequently by 1955 the Southerners, upon whose sectional feelings aggrieved Southern politicians (dismissed by the Azhari government from the posts they held in the government) played, were very much on edge. It was unfortunate that many Northern officers in the South were not discreet in their behaviour. Efforts of the Southern politicians to organise meetings and conferences were frustrated; a Southern politician was tried in a manner that gave the widespread impression that justice was not done; a demonstration by some dismissed Southern workers was met with force involving the killing of six of the demonstrators. The government did not assess the situation carefully and tactfully before issuing threats and making provocative broadcasts to people who felt that their grievances were real. The situation degenerated to the point that the Southerners in the army in the South began to sympathise with the grievances of their fellow Southerners. Revolt occurred in August 1955; it was bloody and government reprisals were bloodier.

There is no doubt that by abolishing the 'Southern Policy' in 1948 the British administration deliberately sacrificed the interests of the Southerners to those of the Northerners. Even before the British began to hand over government to the Azhari cabinet in 1954 the behaviour of the Northern politicians was calculated to arouse the fears of the Southerners. The Northern politicians were not keen to have Southerners take part in the negotiations from 1953 to 1956 preceding independence.

Since 1955 relations between the South and North have not improved. The impression is widespread that the North-controlled government has added to the grievances of the Southerners by encouraging the spread of Islam and the Arabic language, while discouraging missionary activity and the spread of Christianity. Many of the articulate groups in the South, some of whom are in exile, are demanding a separate state; others are agitating for a self-governing region within a Federal Republic. Up to the time this book goes to press there is no sign that the Sudan government would accept either of these proposals. Force is the only answer that has been given to the Southerners, thousands of whom have fled to the neighbouring countries of Uganda, Kenya and the Congo.

Ethiopia

Menelik II

So much attention was demanded by the necessity of warding off European aggression and extending the frontiers of his country that Emperor Menelik II had little time for internal reforms. More than any of his predecessors he unified Ethiopia and commanded the obedience of the local rulers throughout the country. Important, too, was the fact that he was master in his own house, dominating the European residents whom he taxed heavily. It was in his plan to abolish slavery, reform the laws of the country and introduce compulsory education. It was Menelik II who founded Addis Ababa and made it the capital of Ethiopia, which it remains until this day; he introduced electric light, telephone and the postal system with stamps; he established the first public school (1905) and ordered his subjects to be vaccinated in 1898 (he built a hospital staffed by Russian and French doctors); and it was during his reign that the Bank of Abyssinia was founded.

Haile Selassie

Unfortunately for his country Menelik's health began to fail in 1906 and for the rest of his reign—he died in 1913—he suffered from paralysis. The two strong men who might have succeeded him, Ras Mangasha, son of Emperor John IV and Ras Makonnen, the progressive and able ruler of Harar province and a man particularly trusted by Menelik, had died in 1906. Menelik's successor was a weakling, Lij Iyasu, a boy of seventeen who had little respect for the traditions of the Solomonian throne. He outraged his subjects by marrying Muslim women and ultimately declared himself a Muslim. At the outbreak of the First World War he favoured the Turks and thereby alienated the British, French and Italian representatives in Addis Ababa. Naturally the people withdrew their allegiance from their apostate Emperor and the rases seized the opportunity to reassert the independence they had lost under Menelik. In 1916 Lij Iyasu was formally deposed and Menelik's daughter, Zauditu, was crowned as Empress and Dejazmatch Tafari, later Emperor Haile Selassie, as Regent.

Although Tafari was Regent and did not have a free hand to direct the affairs of the country on the lines of progress and enlightenment until he ascended the throne in 1930, to a very great extent it might be said that the history of Ethiopia since 1916 has been largely that of this remarkable man. Therefore he merits some attention.

Tafari is a great grandson of King Sahela Selassie of Shoa and the son of Ras Makonnen who, as mentioned already, was Menelik's right hand man. Born in Harar on 23 July 1892 Tafari received his early education in a French missionary school and was for several years trained in the court of Menelik, who discerned his talents. By 1911, that is when he was still under twenty, he was already given the governorships of the provinces of Sidamo and Harar. In 1916 Tafari led the opposition to Lij Iyasu. Ras Mikhael, the deposed Emperor's father-in-law, incited the Wollo Galla against the Regency and heavy fighting took place outside Addis Ababa. The rases re-asserted their independence, the treasury was empty and there was no army to enforce the laws of the central government. Even after the rebels had been crushed, Tafari had to contend with the opposition of the Empress and the Church who deplored his progressive outlook and modernising tendencies. In 1928 an attempt was made to depose him as Regent. But his position became so much stronger after the crisis that he assumed the title of Negus. Two years later he survived the last major crisis at home in his bid for ultimate control of affairs when he defeated Ras Gugsa, Governor of Begemder. Soon afterwards the reactionary Empress died. He was crowned Emperor in St. George's Cathedral, Addis Ababa, and he took the name of Haile Selassie— 'Might of the Trinity'.

The monarchy in Ethiopia

The point to note about Haile Selassie is that not only has he been attempting to transform Ethiopia from a medieval isolated country but he has made the monarchy continue to be essential to the stability and progress of Ethiopia. This is a vital point, in view of the discredit

Emperor Haile Selassie

or decline or disappearance of the monarchical institution in many
parts of Africa, for example in Egypt and Tunisia. The monarchy in
Ethiopia, far more than the monarchy of Morocco in the reign of
Mohammed V, became the spearhead of constitutional, social,
economic and political changes. Haile Selassie realised that Ethiopia
could no longer be isolated from the rest of the world; that European

powers who had economic interests in the country were so powerful, militarily, that they could not be ejected; that all over Africa European intrusion in the guise of commercial activities, missionary propaganda and technical marvels had come to stay in emergent African states, irrespective of the predilections of the traditional rulers. Shrewdly he decided to harness these various intruding forces to the progress of the State.

His enlightenment in this respect began in his Regency years. He inspired the founding of the Ras Tafari school, and sent graduates of this school abroad for higher education. He attached so much importance to education that its control from the beginning has remained in his hands. After he fought back into his country in 1941, he built other secondary schools, including the Haile Selassie I and Orde Wingate secondary schools. In 1957 there were over 600 primary schools and twenty-four secondary schools in Ethiopia, apart from commercial, technical, agricultural and teacher-training establishments. At the apex of his educational programme is the University College of Addis Ababa, now the Haile Selassie University, inaugurated in 1951 with the Emperor as the Chancellor.

Knowing that it would be a long time before the country would be able to produce the much-needed trained men to direct the various departments of administration and development of the country, Haile Selassie has for a long time chosen skilled foreigners as his advisers— not in the way Ismail Pasha did in the nineteenth century. These foreigners, mainly Europeans, were expected to advise and train and not to be political agents or a law unto themselves. In 1931 his foreign advisers belonged to various nationalities. His Legal Adviser was a Swiss; the head of Foreign Affairs was a Swede, the Adviser in the Ministry of Interior was an Englishman, the Adviser on finance an American. Nor has he looked to the western powers alone for financial and technical aid. In 1959 he went to Moscow, obtained an honorary LL.D degree of the University of Moscow and secured promise of financial and technical aid, which Russia has begun to give. But as late as 1960 an American was the Emperor's chief adviser on foreign affairs.

Constitutional reforms

While embarking on development of education at all levels Haile Selassie was also aware of the fact that the traditional, unmitigated absolutism of the Ethiopian monarchy would become out of date as people became educated and informed of the growth of democratic institutions in most parts of the world. The Emperor himself took the initiative in 1931 by proclaiming a constitution which, for the first time in the country's history, took the people into partnership in the government of the country. The constitution was by no means democratic to the extent of giving the people the franchise. The Emperor was fully aware of the necessity and wisdom of moving gradually in the alteration of the system of government of the country. The constitution established two chambers—the Senate and the Chamber of Deputies. Members of the former were to be appointed by the Emperor from the rases and notables while members of the Senate in turn were to choose members of the lower chamber. But the Emperor remained very powerful; he was to appoint, promote, transfer, suspend and dismiss his own ministers. Under the constitution all the officers of the ministries and departments, as well as the mayors of municipalities, were responsible to him. Christianity was declared the State religion, the Emperor assuming the title of the 'Defender of the Holy Orthodox Faith based on the doctrines of St. Mark of Alexandria'. The Constitution also attempted to stabilise the monarchy by regularising the succession. Henceforward the throne was vested in the Haile Selassie family's male line. This would have the effect of saving Ethiopia from the traditional chaos following succession disputes by numerous claimants to the throne.

In 1955 Haile Selassie granted another constitution which gave greater powers to the Ethiopian people, through their representatives. Members of the Chamber of Deputies were now to be elected by direct franchise by all Ethiopians of twenty-one years and above, while the Emperor retained the power to choose all senators for a period of six years. The Lower Chamber in this constitution had the power to approve yearly budgets submitted by the various ministries, to initiate legislative proposals and constitutional amendments, to adopt various international agreements concluded by the government and to impeach government officials. However the Emperor still had veto powers over legislation passed by Parliament, initiated legislative proposals and reserved the right to determine the size, organisation and responsibilities of the armed forces. The Emperor also exercised certain administrative controls over Ethiopia's Christian Orthodox Church. Nevertheless there is no organised opposition against the Emperor by people who are, on the whole, satisfied with his progressive measures. Freedom of religion is allowed; the press is free, although the constitution has no provision for political parties. Amharic was made the official language.

One criticism that people who have a first-hand knowledge of Ethiopia level at the Emperor is that for all practical purposes the parliamentary form of government he has attempted to establish is a sham. They emphasise the point that he is the supreme authority who not only reigns but rules; that he bestrides the country like a colossus and that there are no rights of free speech, press and assembly. There can be no doubt that democracy in the sense of a government of the people by the people and for the people has no place in present-day Ethiopia and that Haile Selassie is an enlightened despot. But the difficult position in which he has found himself should be clearly understood. Though he is fully aware that a number of the young élite exposed to the parliamentary notions of the western world are impatient that he is not a constitutional monarch, he knows very well that they are a very tiny minority; that the bulk of the population do not want revolutionary changes and that the landed aristocracy and the powerful Church on whom he has to depend for maintenance of law and order would not relish radical changes. On the necessity of recognising the force and restraints of customs in the operation of the 1955 constitution he observed in the Speech from the Throne to Parliament on 4 November 1955: 'No single document, however profound and persuasive can, of itself, bring about far-reaching and fundamental constitutional progress. No constitutional progress can take effect unless it is rooted in the fundamental traditions, customs, habits, and predilections, as well as the legal customs, of the society upon which it is based.'

Because of its physical features Ethiopia is not a rich country. No minerals in commercial quantities have been located and roads are not easy to construct. Nevertheless Haile Selassie has made appreciable efforts to develop communications and has thereby stimulated the economy. Between 1930 and 1949 Ethiopia's trade increased more than sixfold. Since 1949 the value of the country's exports has risen greatly, mainly because of the boom in coffee, most of which is produced in the sparsely populated west and south-west of the country. Coffee remains the country's main export, followed by hides and skins, pulses and oil seeds.

Another way in which Haile Selassie completed the sovereignty of his country was in the appointment of an Ethiopian national as the Abuna (Archbishop) of the Ethiopian Church. Ever since Christianity was introduced into Ethiopia the Ethiopian Church had been subject to the Coptic Church in Egypt, the head of which appointed the Abuna. This head of the Ethiopian Church had invariably been a foreigner, consecrated in Alexandria, in Egypt. In 1926 when the Egyptian national, Abuna Mattheos, died, and another Egyptian national was appointed as usual, the Emperor, then Regent, pressed that four Ethiopian monks be consecrated Bishops by the Patriarch in Alexandria. In 1944 the demand was made that an Ethiopian be made Archbishop and that the Ethiopian Archbishop should be vested with the power to appoint bishops. In 1950 an Ethiopian was consecrated Archbishop with power to consecrate Bishops on the sole condition that he gave the Patriarch in Alexandria prior notification.

Abolition of slavery

One important reform carried out by the Emperor was the gradual abolition of slavery, an institution of basic importance in the social system and economy of traditional African society. Slaves were used in Ethiopia, as in other parts of Africa, for domestic purposes and for the cultivation of land. Even the priests of the Church and the Abuna had slaves. But it should be noted that slaves were, on the whole, well treated, often regarded as members of the family, and they often rose to positions of trust and confidence in the service of the nobility.

Pupils at the School for Freed Slaves

In 1924 and 1931 measures for the gradual abolition of slavery were announced. In 1932 a Slavery Bureau was established under an Ethiopian director assisted by an English adviser and a council composed of all the rases of the country. In the next two years there were established sixty-two local offices of the Slavery Bureau, where cases affecting the emancipation of slaves might be tried before the judges who were authorised to free children born to slave parents, as well as slaves whose former masters had died. By 1934 nearly 4,000 slaves had been set free. Haile Selassie decreed the death penalty for slave traders and fines for the rases in whose territory the traffic occurred. In 1932 he expressed the hope that the institution of slavery would die out in Ethiopia in a matter of twenty years.

External affairs

Since the last years of Menelik's reign Ethiopia realised that the European powers were not prepared to respect her sovereignty if this went against their own interests. The independence that she was enjoying was an eye-sore to various European powers, particularly Britain and Italy. Britain, France and Italy would not scruple to undermine Ethiopia's sovereignty to further their economic interests. In 1894 France had obtained a concession for the building of a railway between Jibuti in French Somaliland and Addis Ababa. The British were concerned about their possible utilisation of the Blue Nile water and Lake Tsana and the River Sobat—important sources of the Nile flood so vital to the Sudan and Egypt. The Italians, who never forgot the humiliation of Adowa until it was avenged in 1935–36, still nursed political and territorial ambitions and wanted in particular to control a strip of land in Ethiopian territory linking Eritrea and Italian Somaliland and running through the fertile highlands 'to the west of Addis Ababa'. In 1906, without consultation with Menelik II, these three Powers signed the Tripartite Treaty in which they paid lip service to the independence of Ethiopia but also pledged themselves to recognise one another's 'sphere of influence' and interfere in Ethiopia's affairs by 'protecting' their nationals 'in the event of rivalries or internal changes in Ethiopia'. In the circumstances Menelik II had to reply in the following words: 'We have received the arrangement made by the three powers. We thank them for their communication and their desire to keep and maintain the independence of our government. But let it be understood that this arrangement in no way limits what we consider our sovereign rights.' In the same decade these three powers defined their boundaries in a number of treaties in a way that gave Ethiopia no access to the Red Sea coast, an area Ethiopia regarded as traditionally belonging to her.

Haile Selassie perceived during his Regency the imperialist intentions of the powers. In order to safeguard his country's sovereignty he pressed for the admission of his country to the international body of the League of Nations in 1923. He hoped that by becoming a member of this organisation, which had been formed after the First World War to maintain peace and prevent aggression by one member state against another, Ethiopia would become immune to the dangerous ambitions of Britain, France and Italy, themselves members of the League. Italy was very hostile to the African state's application on the grounds that slavery and the slave-trade still existed in the country.

The Italian threat to Ethiopia

Two years later it became clear that Ras Tafari had judged rightly about the imperialist threat to his country when Britain and Italy discussed how best the two powers could promote their interests in Ethiopia, at the expense of Ethiopia's sovereignty and territorial integrity. Britain demanded Italian support for irrigation proposals she wanted to undertake on Lake Tsana inside Ethiopia. In return the Italians wished to obtain British support, or recognition, for the construction of a railway through Ethiopia, west of Addis Ababa, to link up Eritrea and Somaliland; for exclusive Italian economic control in the west of Ethiopia and in the whole territory crossed by the proposed railway and for economic concessions throughout the territory. In other words the Italians would constitute themselves into a state within the State of Ethiopia. It is significant to note that Italian interests were made known by Benito Mussolini, Premier and Foreign Secretary of Italy. Following Ras Tafari's vigorous protest to the League of Nations the British and Italians denied that they had any designs against the sovereignty of Ethiopia.

After 1925 Ethiopia's concern in foreign affairs was the persisting Italian threat. However Ras Tafari left no stone unturned to give Italy no pretext to attack his country. In order to reduce the tension of 1925 he began to stretch hands of fellowship and friendship to Italy. The result was the Treaty of Perpetual Friendship which Ethiopia and Italy signed in 1928. It was expected to last twenty years. This treaty also provided that any disputes that might arise between the two countries should be settled by arbitration. It was not long, however, before one clause of the treaty began to strain their relations. It was agreed that Ethiopia should use the Italian port of Assab, to be connected by a road to Dessye inside Ethiopia; the Italians were to construct the road up to the frontier and Ethiopia the rest of the road, inside the country. The Italians constructed their own part of the road but began to complain about how Ethiopia was constructing her own part. Fearing the intentions of the Italians Haile Selassie decided that the road should continue to the capital, Addis Ababa. The Italians objected to any extension—a situation that would have denied them a military advantage over Ethiopia—and demanded that Italy should have control over the entire road from Assab to Dessye, that is including the stretch inside Ethiopia. The Ethiopians would not have a razor applied to their throat in this way, fearing that Italian control over the road would make their country vulnerable. The Ethiopians decided to employ Dutch engineers in the construction of their own part of the road. The Italians, however, took offence at this, claiming that there were qualified Italian engineers to build the road.

The Italians took offence at the concern of the Emperor about the independence of his country. Military officers in Eritrea and Italian Somaliland, who were already strengthening the defences of these two territories and preparing for war against Ethiopia, lied that Ethiopia had broken the 1928 treaty. As one of them spoke of the Ethiopian Emperor in bitterness: 'He negotiated treaties and then broke his word, or opposed them with the most tenacious obstructionism; he did not conceal the anti-Italian spirit that animated his action; he lulled himself—he, at the head of an arrogant, proud, presumptuous race that traced its origins to the remote civilization of Solomon and boasted that it had never known defeat—he lulled himself, I say with the memory of Adowa'.

It is now known that as early as 1932 the Fascist ruler of Italy, Benito Mussolini, had decided to attack Ethiopia. For in that year he sent one of his principal military officers, De Bono, to Eritrea with the object of surveying the military situation there. This military officer also spied on the state of affairs in Ethiopia and in the following year submitted to Mussolini a memorandum. In this document De Bono described the political condition of Ethiopia as a 'deplorable' one and declared that it would not be difficult for Italy 'to effect the disintegration of the (Ethiopian) Empire'; it was hoped that some rases would rebel against the Emperor and thereby 'give us an opportunity to intervene'. Although Mussolini continued to deceive the world that Italy had no intention of 'territorial conquests' he had made up his mind that Ethiopia would be invaded by Italy in 1936 at the latest.

The Wal Wal incident

It is clear that all that Italy needed was a pretext to attack and annex Ethiopia. One came in November 1934 in the Wal Wal incident. Wal Wal was a well, about sixty miles inside Ethiopia. Up till 1931 this and other wells in the Ogaden desert of Ethiopia were used by the British, Italian and Ethiopian Somalis for their camels. In 1930 a troop of Italian Somalis had occupied Wal Wal, but they never interfered with the tribes from all directions using the well. In 1931 Haile Selassie, who since his governorship of Harar had regarded the area as part of Ethiopia, sent a force of Ethiopian troops to clear off the area and expel intruders. For some reason, however, the troops omitted Wal Wal. The Italians therefore began to think that Wal Wal belonged to them. When in November 1934 the Anglo-Ethiopian Grazing and Boundary Commission, which had set out to demarcate the frontier between Ethiopia and British Somaliland, came to Wal Wal, they were surprised to find there an Italian encampment. The British withdrew, leaving about 600 Ethiopian troops to face the much larger Italian forces. As was to be expected in such an explosive situation, shooting began, both parties accusing each other of firing first. The Ethiopians suffered the greater loss and withdrew, followed by Italian aeroplanes which, the Ethiopians claimed, bombed the villages of Ado and Gheriogubi.

The Wal Wal incident provided Mussolini with the opportunity he had been hoping for since his seizure of power in 1922. By 1934 he had whipped up to fever heights the nationalist feelings of Italians. It was believed by many Italians that Italy was a great power which should imitate the other great powers by acquiring colonies. Ethiopia, it was believed, held out bright economic prosperity for Italy. It was argued that the country might even be richer than the highlands of Kenya which white settlers had occupied. It was believed that Ethiopia had offended Italy by refusing to allow Italian economic activities to develop freely, and by not appointing a certain number of Italian experts in the various technical and public services. They pointed out that after 1928 only one Italian, an electrical engineer, was appointed, whereas an Englishman was selected as adviser for internal administration, a Frenchman for public works, another for archaeological research, and a third for foreign affairs.

Mussolini exploited the Wal Wal incident to the full. He decided to humiliate Ethiopia in a way that would enable Italy to remove 'the scar, yes, the shameful scar of Adowa'. The demand in Italy that the humiliation of Adowa be avenged had been made for years and many

Italians had been dismayed that Ethiopia began to be modernised along European lines in matters of communications, education, administration and military reforms, and that Ethiopia had begun to organise and arm its troops 'in an up-to-date European manner', as an Italian military spokesman said. Indeed it was believed by many that the aim of Ethiopia was to expel Italy from Eritrea and Italian Somaliland along the coast, which were the only gains Italy made in the Horn of Africa during the Scramble.

Mussolini made it clear that he would not allow himself to be bound by the provision of the 1928 treaty which, as Ethiopia pointed out, bound the two countries to refer the Wal Wal dispute to an independent arbitration. He hated to think that Ethiopia should be regarded as a state with equal rights with Italy in international affairs; he would not have Italy put in the same class as Ethiopia. Mussolini dictated terms which he knew Ethiopia would never accept. Ethiopia was asked to pay to Italy a compensation of £20,000 and send an Ethiopian delegation to Wal Wal to salute the Italian flag there. Of course no nation would submit to a humiliation of this sort.

Failure of the League of Nations

It was in these circumstances that Haile Selassie turned to the League of Nations to help prevent the outbreak of conflicts. But Ethiopia was to be rudely disappointed by Britain and France, the two powers in whom Haile Selassie had reposed much confidence. In fact the British tried to dissuade the Emperor from resorting to the League. This was a time when both Britain and France were bent on conciliating Mussolini in order to prevent him from becoming a supporter of Germany's Hitler. In January 1935, that is about two months after the Wal Wal incident, the French signed a treaty with Italy, giving the latter some areas in Africa and also 25,000 out of the 34,000 shares in the Jibuti–Addis Ababa Railway. Three months later Macdonald and Flandin, Prime Ministers of Britain and France respectively, met Mussolini in Stressa and agreed to collaborate for peace. Britain and France were absolutely silent over the Ethiopian crisis and Italy had the impression that when the actual time of invasion came she would not face any opposition worth speaking of from the two powers.

In the meantime the League of Nations went on prevaricating. A conciliation committee was set up but made little progress before it was overtaken by events. Later in 1935 Britain and France drew up the Zeila Agreement, according to which the signatories of the

Tripartite Treaty were to supervise economic, financial and political 'reforms' in Ethiopia, 'particular account being taken of the special interests of Italy'. Although this Agreement was humiliating for Ethiopia she accepted it. Mussolini, however, refused to have any dealing with Ethiopia on terms of equality, the same reason for his rejection of the peace efforts of the League. In his view Ethiopia was a backward territory where slavery still persisted and where a proper form of government had not been organised.

Arms embargo on Ethiopia and Italy

In 1935 Haile Selassie placed an order for arms from Belgium, Czechoslovakia, Britain and France. This was the time the two last powers announced an embargo on arms for both Italy and Ethiopia. However it was only Ethiopia that was really hit by this decision. Italy could supply her own arms, which she was already pouring into Eritrea and Somaliland through the Suez Canal, still at that time under the control of the British. Haile Selassie kept on hoping that the British would not allow Italy to attack her and that in the last resort Britain would fight for her against Italy, an impression given to him by Sir Samuel Hoare, Britain's minister in Addis Ababa. The Ethiopian Emperor also believed that the League would intervene effectively, according to its Charter, and prevent a member state from committing an act of agression against another member state. In both respects his hopes were destined to cruel disappointment. The British government, headed by Stanley Baldwin, decided to appease Mussolini and would not even allow British nationals to represent the League in keeping watch over the border between Ethiopia and Italian East Africa. Britain and France signed the Hoare–Laval Agreement which would eventually have turned Ethiopia into an Italian dependency. The League then decided on economic sanctions, denying Italy products and materials she did not really consider of crucial importance.

Italy invades Ethiopia

In the meantime the Italian war machine was fully geared for a complete invasion of Ethiopia. In the view of Pietro Badoglio, the Marshal of Italy who commanded the Italian forces of invasion, the objectives of the invasion were 'the utter destruction of the Abyssinian armed forces and the complete conquest of Ethiopia'. In October 1935, after inciting a number of local governors in Ethiopia to rise up

Ethiopian chieftains preparing to fight the invading Italians

against the rule of Haile Selassie, Italian forces began the invasion.

In a matter of seven months Ethiopia was occupied and brutalities were committed. Most of the educated élite who were being raised by the Emperor were put to the sword; planes, batteries and poisonous gas were used to crush Ethiopian resistance. On 9 May 1936 Italy formally announced the annexation of Ethiopia and King Victor Emmanuel of Italy was named Emperor of Ethiopia. Haile Selassie fled his country and lived in exile until 1941.

One important thing to note before concluding this chapter is that the League of Nations failed signally to fulfil its obligations by Ethiopia and thereby became discredited. Not long after the Italian occupation of Ethiopia member states began to recognise the new régime and the ineffectual economic sanctions that had been announced against Italy were removed. This was in spite of the prophetic speech made before the League in Geneva by Haile Selassie on 30 June 1936, in which he warned that if the League did not stand by its Charter, then 'the very existence' of the League was in danger. He declared that what the League should settle was 'the confidence that each state is to place in international treaties . . . the value of promises made to small states, that their integrity and their independence be respected and ensured . . .'.

The Italians did not find their occupation of Ethiopia easy. Revolts against them were common and Italy's control was limited to the

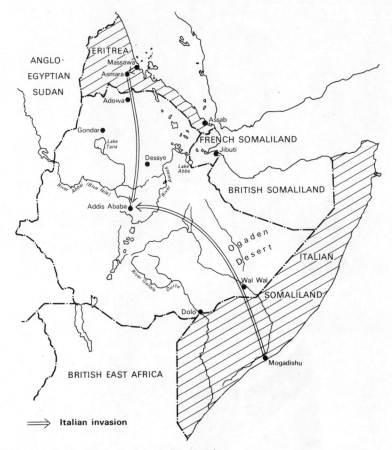

ANGLO-
EGYPTIAN
SUDAN

ERITREA
Massawa
Asmara
Adowa

Gondar
Lake
Tana

Dessye

Assab

FRENCH SOMALILAND
Jibuti

Lake
Abbe

BRITISH SOMALILAND

River Abbai (Blue Nile)

River Awash

Addis Ababa

Ogaden
Desert

ITALIAN

River Gandle

Dorya

Wal Wal

SOMALILAND

Dolo

BRITISH EAST AFRICA

Mogadishu

⟹ Italian invasion

Ethiopia, showing the lines of the Italian invasion

cities and villages where there were garrisons; there were many
provinces over which the invaders had no control. In 1937 an attempt
was made on the life of the Italian viceroy. The Italians seized the
occasion to put to death about 3,000 Ethiopians, mostly the educated,
including over 100 priests. Another problem was that there were no
resources in Italy to sustain the Italians' heavy expenditure on roads
and public works. By 1940 the Italians had lost their grip on Ethiopia.

Italian forces expelled

In the meantime the Second World War had broken out and Italy
decided to fight with Germany against France and Britain. It was this

97

A painting dating from the Italian-Ethiopian war, depicting Saint Michael, representing Ethiopia trampling on the faces of Hitler and Mussolini

situation, rather than genuine concern for Ethiopia's independence, that made the British government decide to give military help to Haile Selassie to fight his way back to his country. Even then many British administrative officers in the Sudan, who believed that Italy would be victorious in the war, were opposed to the idea of Haile Selassie being helped back into the country, believing that Italy would annex the Sudan. In June 1940 Haile Selassie arrived in Egypt and was taken to the Sudan where he organised Ethiopian refugees into the patriot Army armed by the British and officered by British, French, Kenyan, South African and Australian volunteers. In January 1941 Selassie crossed the frontier into Ethiopia. By the end of the year Italy's rule in Ethiopia had come to an end.

Since his restoration to his throne and country in 1941 Haile Selassie has devoted his resourcefulness to the modernisation of Ethiopia in directions indicated earlier. Excepting for the unsuccessful attempt made in December 1960 to topple him, while he was on a State visit to Brazil, his control over the State has been effective and there can be no doubt of his popularity with his subjects.

In foreign affairs Haile Selassie has succeeded in enlarging the stature of Ethiopia by showing himself as an apostle of Pan-Africanism. While examination of the Pan-African movement is left to the last chapter of this book it should be remarked here that in three ways Ethiopia has in the last fifty years been an inspiration to African patriots. Firstly the references to the territory in the Bible were seen as a testimony to its long existence, its wealth and the brilliant future that awaited her. In this respect many early nationalists in different parts of Africa used to quote Psalm 68: 31 'And Ethiopia shall soon stretch forth her hands to God'. Secondly African patriots admired the fact that Ethiopia was able to expand her frontiers, retain her sovereignty and territorial integrity and make herself acceptable as an equal by the European powers during the scramble. And lastly African patriots recall with pride the resounding victory which Ethiopia achieved over Italy at Adowa on 1 March 1896.

3   The Maghreb from the scramble to independence

The background to the nationalist struggle

It will be remembered that most of the Maghreb fell to the French —Algeria in 1830, Tunisia in 1881 and Morocco in 1912; that Northern Morocco became a Spanish Protectorate and that Libya was occupied by Italy. However, in none of these territories did the Muslim population willingly accept the forcible occupation by the European infidels. In the conception of the Maghrebians it was illegal that infidels should rule over the Faithful. However, although in their hearts the Maghrebians were never reconciled to infidel rule, the military might of the colonial powers was not to be trifled with. In Algeria the last attempt of Berbers in the nineteenth century against the French, which occurred in Kabylia in 1871, was crushed mercilessly; in Spanish Morocco the rebellion led by Abdel Karim from 1921 to 1926 failed disastrously; by 1933 Italian forces had put an end to the resistance organised by the Senussiya of Libya; in 1934 the last pocket of Moroccan resistance to the French was removed. The stiffness of the opposition of the Maghrebians to infidel rule has justification in the Koranic injunction on what the attitude of the Faithful to infidels should be. For instance verse 4 of Chapter 47 of the Holy Koran says: 'And when you meet those who disbelieve— then strike off heads until ye have massacred them, and bind fast the bonds!'

It was infidels who bound fast the bonds imposed on Muslim Maghrebians. Indeed in no part of Africa, the Republic of South Africa excepted, was there to be found such a rapid build-up of settler populations as farmers, industrialists, small retail merchants, middle grade civil servants, teachers and even workers who organised trade unions. In Algeria the European population formed 10 per cent of the total population; in Morocco and Tunisia the European population formed between 6 per cent and 8 per cent of the total during the last decades before independence. Even in Libya Italian workers numbered almost 10 per cent of the population. Also far more than in any other part of colonial Africa the European rulers, particularly the French, imposed their culture and created an African élite who aspired to be assimilated to French civilisation. It was in the Maghreb that the French colonial policy of assimilation was most emphatically established.

Indirect rule in Morocco

But since in comparison with the British, whose policy of indirect rule in West Africa has always been lauded, the French have more or less been criticised for desiring to Frenchify their African subjects, it is essential to stress that between 1912 and 1925 there was an indirect ruler in the Maghreb. He was Hubert Lyautey. In the light of his career in Morocco where he was Governor-General from 1912 to 1925 it should be remarked that in two important ways this shrewd and statesmanlike French administrator was a better indirect ruler than Lord Frederick Lugard and C. L. Temple, both of Northern Nigeria, who are usually given the credit for the inauguration and consolidation of this philosophy of administration in colonial Africa. Firstly, for Lyautey, unlike Lugard for whom indirect rule was really an expedient, it was an article of faith. He believed that the best interests of Moroccans would be served by respecting their culture and institutions, by preserving and ruling through the Sultan and the Caids, by making no attempt to Frenchify them. Secondly, unlike C. L. Temple who believed that the culture of Africans was inferior to that of white men, Lyautey declared that French civilisation was not necessarily superior to that of Morocco. In other words Lyautey recognised what social anthropologists were to recognise in later years, that civilisation is relative not absolute.

In his conviction that the Moroccans had their religion, customs, traditions, institutions and philosophy of life which they considered were best for them, Lyautey issued instructions to his lieutenants that the first condition for the success of their administrative missions was 'minutest knowledge of the natives, their chiefs, their traditions, and their needs, and constant and direct co-operation with them'. He encouraged the traditional Moorish arts, native music and dance, old customs and observances. He encouraged the rebuilding of the

Mosques of Moulay Idris and of Kairwan, which, with its university and koranic colleges, had formerly been a centre of learning and beauty, but which had fallen into decay. He also created a special institution where research into the past of Morocco was to be carried on—the *Institut des Hautes Etudes Marocaines*, at Rabat. Lyautey would not assault the Islamic religion, nor would he allow any white man to do so, hence the law that no Christian must put a foot into the mosques.

Lyautey, who since 1881 had begun to learn Arabic, knew the importance of the Sherifian dynasty in the minds of the Moroccans. Therefore he ruled indirectly through the Sultan whose prestige he raised. He consulted always with the Sultan and in every way associated him with what had to be done. Lyautey caused to be revived ancient traditions of Court ceremony, thereby making the monarchy's existence of a greater interest to a people who appreciated pomp and show.

As part of his conviction that the interest of Moroccans must be given priority over that of the French, Lyautey was strongly opposed to the idea of *colons* (white settlers) flooding Morocco. However, he could not have his way in this matter. All he could do was to discourage their influx and to pass laws that foreigners should live several miles away from the indigenous inhabitants in places like Fez, Rabat, Meknes and Marrakesh.

It should be remarked that although the French government hated Lyautey for the indirect rule policy he established, and reversed it after his removal in 1925, the Moroccan peoples appreciated the work of this extraordinary man. In 1928 the African Society of Britain, composed of people who desired that colonial rulers should work in the interest of Africans, awarded him a gold medal. Finally, Lyautey's vision and statesmanship may be judged from the fact that as early as 1925 he spoke out on behalf of sovereignty for the Maghreb and on the wisdom of France cultivating the friendship of the Maghrebians so that when the latter achieved independence excellent relations with France might continue. As he declared in Rabat on 14 April 1925: 'It is to be foreseen—and indeed I regard it as a historic truth—that in the more or less distant future North Africa—modernised, civilised, living its own autonomous life—will detach itself from metropolitan France. When this occurs—and it must be our supreme political goal—the parting must occur without pains and the nations must be able to continue to view France without fear. The African peoples must not turn against her. For this reason, we must from today, as a starting point, make ourselves loved'.

Official French policy in the Maghreb

Unfortunately the French government in Paris and the *colons* in Morocco, Algeria and Tunisia lacked the prophetic insight and understanding of Lyautey. They had no thought that the Maghrebians would become independent some day; no thought that Morocco, Algeria and Tunisia constituted 'nations'. It was their belief that French laws, customs and institutions should flourish throughout the Maghreb and efface the traditional culture and institutions of the Maghrebians. In the view of policy-makers in France and the *colons* in the Maghreb Lyautey was preaching a heresy which by 1925, when Lyautey was forced out of Morocco, had begun to yield results in the nationalist movement.

One contrast between the nationalist struggle in the Maghreb and that in Egypt is worth emphasising. Compared with Egypt, where nationalism began only in the nineteenth century, the struggle for the preservation of their country and sovereignty began among the Berber inhabitants of the Maghreb from the time of the Roman intrusion into North Africa. Unlike the Egyptians who accepted one invader after the other, the Berbers organised stiff resistance against all intruders—the Romans, the Vandals, the Arabs, the Portuguese and the Turks. Consequently none of the invaders ever succeeded in administering the interior of the Maghreb outside the coastal areas. For the Berbers were traditionally passionate lovers of their independence. It is not surprising, then, that the French paid dearly in men and money before they could establish their rule over Algeria, Tunisia and Morocco.

The roots of the nationalist struggle

Two observations are called for by the point made above. First, it reveals the error of the view usually expressed by writers, that African nationalism was the exclusive creation of those who received a western form of education and through it came to know about the Parliamentary system of government which they asked the colonial powers to establish in their territories. According to such writers the nationalist struggle in the Maghreb was initiated by members of a westernised élite like Ferhat Abbas of Algeria, Habib Bourguiba of Tunisia and Ahmed Balafrej of Morocco. But the history of the nationalist struggle in the Maghreb indicates that credit should be given to the illiterate

Berbers and their rulers, who though they did not advocate a parliamentary system of government, fought against all invaders. It was they, and not the westernised élite, who initiated nationalism in the Maghreb. Both the illiterate traditionalist resisters and the westernised élite fought for some common ideals, including the preservation of territorial integrity and sovereignty of their fatherland, customs and institutions, particularly Islam and Islamic institutions.

However, there was a difference between the two classes of nationalists. The traditionalists wanted the Maghreb to remain administratively divided into semi-independent villages and tribes without any strong administration. They also wished authority to remain in the hands of the traditional rulers—village heads and religious leaders known as marabouts. On the other hand the westernised élite wanted authority to be transferred to themselves under a central administration. They wished to adopt the railways and the industrialisation of the territory. The clash of interests of the two classes of nationalists is a prominent feature of the history of the Maghreb.

The second observation on the point made in a previous paragraph about the long existence of nationalism in the Maghreb is that it reveals the fact that the French cannot justifiably claim that they created the Algerian nation, the Tunisian nation and the Moroccan nation. The inhabitants of these areas had always had a sense of national identity, a sense of being one people different from others, before the French came. The concept of nationality had always been present among these people and this was why they had resisted all peoples they believed were different from them. What the French did, and what contributed to the consolidation of nationhood, was to create a centralised form of administration, develop a modern system of communication that facilitated mobility and inter-mingling of people and develop the mineral and agricultural resources of the three states to a high level, thereby making them into modern states.

Policy of assimilation in the Maghreb

In fact the French never consciously encouraged national consciousness in any of the three territories of the Maghreb where they ruled. This is clear from their colonial policy which, as mentioned already, is generally described as one of assimilation. According to this theory French laws, French judiciary, French language, French education and French customs were held to be not only the best in the world but the ones which every people in the world should adopt. To this end, at least in the early years of French administration in the Maghreb, French customs and institutions were introduced to replace the Berber customs and institutions, which were regarded as uncivilised. In Algeria the *code Napoléon*, the legal code which Napoleon I introduced into France in early nineteenth century, was put into effect in place of Islamic law and courts. For the French there could not exist any concept or feeling that could be described as African. Therefore they laid down the conditions which the natives of the Maghreb must satisfy before they could be offered French citizenship. And although until after the First World War many natives of the Maghreb who had French education praised the policy of assimilation in the hope that they would be accepted as equals of French-born people, the majority of the people were not prepared to forgo their customs and institutions. The masses did not covet French customs and institutions, for which they had contempt. They also hated the French infidels. They wished to remain Muslims and preferred Arabic to the French language.

It was the logical result of the so-called policy of assimilation that the French should wish to crush what they regarded as the heresy of nationalism. It seemed to the French that the nationalists were opposing civilisation and did not have the interests of their people at heart. Moreover, since the number of educated natives was small, the French began to argue that the westernised élite did not represent the will of the majority of Berbers, who the French affected to believe wished to become Frenchmen. The policy of the French on the nationalist movement differed from that of the British. It was not until after the Second World War that the French established anything like a parliamentary form of government. What made the French most strongly anti-nationalist was the presence of French *colons* in their North African territories. These settlers rejected the so-called policy of assimilation in order to protect their privileges as tillers of the most fertile lands, controllers of banking, shipping and mining interests, holders of the best positions in the administration and the real beneficiaries of western education and medical facilities. They came to hate the natives whom, they contended, it was futile to educate and civilise. There can be no doubt that had the French policy of assimilation been fully carried out there would have come a time when the westernised Africans would have outnumbered the *colons* and would have controlled, logically, the governments of the three territories. The self-preservation behaviour of the *colons* in French Mediterranean Africa compares essentially with that of the British settlers in present-day Rhodesia and the white minority in the Republic of South Africa.

The Berber *Dahir*

One important point about nationalism in North Africa as a whole, but particularly in the Maghreb, was that it assumed a religious character. In Volume I we have seen that the jihad was proclaimed against the French in Algeria, Tunisia and Morocco. Europeans were looked upon as 'Christians', that is infidels, people inferior to the true believers according to the Holy Koran. In pre-colonial days European infidels had been treated like slaves and efforts were made by the Maghreb rulers to convert them to Islam. The establishment of government over the true believers by infidels was regarded by the population as a backward step. Nor did the French show discretion when they paraded themselves as Christians and ridiculed Islam as an inferior religion which, they said, was responsible for the technological backwardness and primitiveness of the Maghreb peoples. In Morocco, having discovered that the Berbers remained unreconciled to the occupation of their country, the French picked upon Islam as the cause of their troubles. This was why the French issued in 1930 the notorious Berber *Dahir*. On the assumption that the Berbers were not in their heart of hearts Muslims, but had for centuries professed this faith out of fear of the Arab elements of the Moroccan population, the French, by the *Dahir*, attempted to secularise the judiciary. This decree was also intended to arouse exclusively Berber nationalism on the side of the French administration against the Arab sections of the population. The Berber *Dahir* implied that all laws were to emanate from infidel France, and no longer from the Sultan in his capacity as the descendant of Prophet Mohammed. The *Sharia* (that is Muslim Law) was no longer to apply to the Berbers; French criminal law was to replace the Sharifian law.

Contrary to French expectations the Berbers did not thank them. Rather, believing that the greatest harm had been done to them, they joined hands with their Arab brothers in protesting against the *Dahir*. This was the time chosen by the French administration to add one indiscretion to another, by encouraging the Roman Catholic missionaries to intensify their activities in Morocco. Crowds surged into the mosques to pray for deliverance from 'the time of peril'. In Fez the Moroccans performed pilgrimages to the shrine of Moulay Idris, founder and patron saint of the city, invoking his help and protection against the French infidels. Outside Morocco Muslim communities prayed for the Moroccan people who, it was rumoured, were in danger of being forced by infidels to renounce Islam.

Algeria: the Society of the Reforming Ulema

In Algeria there was also a strong Islamic strand in the nationalist movement. Sheik Abdel Hamid ben Badis, a descendant of a very ancient family of the eleventh century who had overthrown the Fatimids, began a reformist nationalist movement in 1928, the aim of which was the restoration of Islam to its pristine purity. In 1931 he founded the Society of the Reforming Ulema, a religious, cultural and political organisation. He proscribed smoking, drinking and dancing, denounced as polytheistic the cult of saints and of marabouts and viewed science with suspicion. In 1938 he issued a proclamation labelling any Algerian who coveted French citizenship as an apostate. The Society became very powerful in the field of education. Since the French refused to give compulsory and Muslim education this Society founded community schools in which Arabic, arithmetic, history and geography were taught. They were schools with a nationalist message for the rising generation and the pupils were taught the slogan 'Islam is my religion, Arabic is my language, Algeria is my fatherland'. This Society published many journals which supported political parties, including the National Liberation Front which won independence for Algeria in 1962.

Tunisia: the religious character of the nationalist movement

In Tunisia the nationalist movement assumed a predominantly religious form until the outbreak of the First World War. This was due to the violation of the Muslim tradition of government by the French against the Articles of the Protectorate. Gradually the Resident General and his lieutenants in the provinces began to supplant the beylik government. In the name of efficiency the French began to seize control of *waqf* lands, religious endowments, the proceeds of which were traditionally used by Muslims for schools, hospitals and mosques. Their preservation was essential in a Muslim community. In 1906 the *Ulema*, whose religious centre was the Zamtuna Mosque, attacked the French concept of land ownership. In the following year the Muslim people of the country were embittered by the action of the French in persuading the Jews, objects of hatred by Maghrebians, to accept French citizenship. Also while the Berber *Dahir* was arousing discontent in Morocco the French administration in Tunisia encouraged Christian Missions to attempt conversion of the Muslims. In 1931 the administration made a grant of two million francs to the Eucharistic Conference which had been convened to meet in Tunis to mark the fiftieth anniversary of French occupation of the country. The Bishop of Tunis described the proposed conference as a crusade against Islam. The people became so enraged that they demonstrated and protested against the conference being held at all. Dockworkers went on strike on the date delegates were to arrive in Tunisia and they were joined by cotton merchants and their employees. The national press joined in the protest and the conference had to be abandoned.

Tunisia

It was in the Protectorate of Tunisia that the westernised élite first began to express nationalist aspirations. Under the leadership of a French-trained lawyer, 'Ali Bash Hamba, the Young Tunisian Party was founded in 1908. A prominent member of this organisation was Shaik al Aziz al Thaalbi who became its leader from 1911 to 1923. The party's ideas were similar to those of the Young Turks of Turkey and they expressed the wish to see Tunisia become part of a re-organised Ottoman Empire again. In 1911 Hamba was deported by the Resident-General when the Young Tunisian Party presented him with a demand for constitutional reforms. In Constantinople, whither he had fled, Hamba disseminated anti-French feelings but died in 1918 on the point of leading an expedition to liberate North Africa from European rule.

The effects of the First World War

The First World War, in which the Tunisians had been compelled to fight on the side of the infidels, had effects on the thinking of the westernised élite as in other parts of Africa. Particularly attractive to them was the Wilsonian principle of self-determination, proclaimed by President Woodrow Wilson of America.

Like Sad Zaghlul, Thaalbi demanded the right to send a mission to Paris, where the Versailles Conference that ended the war was taking place, but was refused. In 1920 the Young Tunisian Party was transformed into *Hizb al Dastur al Hurr* (Destour) or the Liberal Constitutional Party. The nationalists put moderate demands before the Resident-General; they accused the French of violating the Protectorate Treaty of 1881 and asked for the establishment of a parliamentary form of government; they declared that confiscation of land and immigration of *colons* should stop and requested the encouragement of Islamic education, admission of Tunisians to the higher positions in the civil service and an end to the bogus policy of assimilation.

The Resident-General, Lucien Saint, treated these demands with indifference. In 1921 the French President visited Tunisia and announced that Tunisia would always remain linked with France. In the following year an attempt was made to deport the Destour leaders. When the Resident-General presented the Bey, Mohammed al-Nasir, with a list of proposed deportees, the Bey was reported as asking the Resident-General why his name had not been included and threatened to abdicate if the nationalists were exiled. However, he soon died and a pro-French Bey, Abdel Karim al Khattabi, succeeded him. Thaalbi was deported in 1923 and he remained in exile until 1937. For the next ten years the Destour Party was in disarray under the sledge-hammer of the French authorities. Moreover the westernised élite did not see eye to eye with the *Ulema*.

Habib Bourguiba

It was during this time that the French-trained barrister, Habib Abu Ruqayba (Habib Bourguiba) entered into the nationalist struggle. Born in Tunisia in 1903 he was educated at primary and secondary schools in Tunis. In 1924, like many members of the North African westernised élite, he went to Paris for further studies and obtained a law degree and a diploma in Political Science. While there he married a Frenchwoman. In 1927 he returned to Tunisia as a legal practitioner and three years later joined the staff of *The Voice of Tunisia*, organ of the Destour Party. When he observed that the party, as then constituted, lacked strong leadership and a programme that could attract the masses to the nationalist struggle he started his own newspaper, *L'Action Tunisienne*, and began to campaign in the villages. In 1934 he obtained the support of the radicals and formed the Neo-Destour Party, still the ruling party in independent Tunisia and perhaps the best organised political party in Africa.

Henceforward the nationalist struggle in Tunisia centred around this man, who is gifted with plenty of common sense. His watchword is realism. He has the rare gift of perceiving the best the nationalists could achieve in a given situation; he has never been an idealist or a doctrinaire. He realised that the French could not be forced out of Tunisia by violence and he refused to be involved in anti-French propaganda for its own sake. He asked for co-operation with the French in the granting of independence by stages. He did not expect the French to withdraw, realising that French capital and technological skill would be required for the rapid development of the country. At home his policy was also based on realism. In religion he refused to be a fanatical Muslim, recognising the fact that Islam has to be modified if Tunisia is to be modernised. It is not surprising then that he has abolished polygamy in order that the Tunisian population may be restricted and the children educated. Nor does he see any sense in veiling women, whose resourcefulness in the development of the state he recognises. Therefore he allows them to participate in politics. Appreciating the part the Tunisian Jews are playing in the economy of their country, Bourguiba has refused to be pan-Arabist to the extent of hating and discriminating against the Jews in Tunisia. Bourguiba does not want his subjects to fight among themselves over ideology. Rather he wishes all parties to unite and contribute their effort to the achievement of independence and modernisation of the Tunisian state.

But his moderation and willingness to co-operate with them notwithstanding, the French administration regarded Bourguiba and his followers as dangerous agitators and disturbers of the peace. The lot of these nationalists was either imprisonment or deportation. But they had the support of the masses and in 1945 the French administration at last decided to establish a Legislative Assembly, half of the members of which would be Frenchmen, who constituted a small minority in the country. Supported by the masses, the Neo-Destourians, whose party had been banned, successfully boycotted the elections. The *colons*, a quarter of a million strong, opposed any further concession to the Tunisians. It became clear to the latter that the French would not yield to argument and reason until power had spoken. By 1954 the Tunisians felt they had no alternative but to use force. In the meantime both in Morocco and Algeria the natives were being driven to the same conclusion.

Morocco

In Morocco, which the French had occupied in 1912, the nationalist movement of the westernised élite type began at the time when Abdel Karim organised the Berbers of the Rif area against the Spaniards. The westernised élite in Morocco could not have been uninfluenced by the self-government won by Middle East countries like Egypt, Syria and the Hijaz. Two members of the élite, independent of each other, almost simultaneously founded nationalist organisations. One was Ahmed Balafrej, a well-educated man who had university training in Morocco, Egypt and at the Sorbonne and consequently became well-informed about Islam, French poetry, philosophy and classics. In 1926 he summoned a group of men to Rabat and formed the 'Moroccan League' which, in order to escape oppression by the administration, was called 'Supporters of Truth'. The other was Mohammed Allal el Fassi who summoned another group of people to Fez. Son of a Professor in the University of Qarawiyyin and a poet of some ability he was in his student days an agitator and he wrote many nationalist songs. His organisation soon merged with the Moroccan League, ancestor of the Istiqlal Party founded in December 1943.

Abdel Karim, symbol of Moroccan resistance to foreign rule

Mohammed V

As in other parts of their Maghreb possessions the French lost no time in oppressing the élite nationalists who were either jailed or exiled. They were not given freedom of association or of speech. Fortunately for the Moroccan people their Sultan, Sidi Mohammed, rose to the occasion by identifying himself with the aspirations of his people for independence from French rule.

Mohammed V, as Sidi Mohammed became on accession to the throne in 1927, was a shrewd ruler who contrasted with many of his contemporaries in Africa who made themselves a tool in the hands of the colonial rulers. In fact he had been preferred to a better claimant to the Sherifian throne precisely because the French believed that he would be a dependable puppet to carry out French wishes in Morocco. For many years the French believed that they had judged him rightly. He co-operated with the French infidels, obeyed the orders of the Resident General and showed no favourable disposition toward the westernised élite nationalists.

But both the French and the nationalists misjudged him. He was only being realistic, biding his time until he would be able to join in the nationalist struggle most effectively. In fact he was already showing qualities which marked him as the greatest Moroccan ruler in modern times. Knowing the deep chord which Islam struck in the hearts of his subjects Mohammed V never outraged the principles of the Muslim faith. In public he performed the religious functions demanded of an Imam, regularly paid his official visit to the mosque on Friday, kept the fast of Ramadan as strictly as most of his subjects and never appeared in public except in traditional robes. He kept his two wives in seclusion and refused to drink alcohol. In private, however, he drove his own car, played tennis and wore European dress.

It was his chief desire to see his people enjoy an education that would combine the best of European and traditional systems. In order that the traditional morality might not suffer he advocated Islamic education for the children. In later years they were to learn the techniques of western education. His eldest son, Moulay Hassan, now the Sultan of Morocco, obtained a degree in French law.

Mohammed V began to show the stern stuff of which he was made during the Second World War. Morocco ranged herself behind the Allies and France against the Vichy regime established by the Germans when they occupied France in 1940. Moroccan blood drenched the soil of North Africa, Corsica, Elba, Sicily and France. On the whole about 300,000 Moroccans helped to liberate France, in recognition of which General de Gaulle, in the name of France, honoured Mohammed V with the Cross of Liberation. The Sultan and the westernised élite, however, had helped the French in the hope that in return France would recognise Morocco's right to independence. President Roosevelt of the United States encouraged the Sultan in this belief at their meeting in January 1943, in which he promised to do all he could to hasten Morocco's independence. Unfortunately he died not long afterwards.

Mohammed V clashes with the French administration

The French administrators in Morocco thought otherwise. They had no desire to evacuate Morocco, which they regarded as part of France. The inevitable clash between the Sultan and the French administration reached a crisis during the tenure of office of General Juin, Resident General from 1947 to 1952. He encouraged the Kittaniya brotherhood and Thami el Glaoui, the overmighty Pasha of Marrakesh, in their anti-Sultan propaganda. Both the Kittaniya brotherhood and the Glaoui family had been supporters of French administration from the beginning. Thami was actually aiming at the Sherifian throne for which he did not qualify. They were both against the nationalist aspirations of the Moroccan people. General Juin encouraged Thami to organise propaganda against the Sultan in order to present to the outside world a picture that the Sultan was unpopular. Illiterate tribal leaders were compelled to sign petitions, the content of which they did not know. These petitions were 'signed' in the presence of French administrators, who had summoned the leaders to Fez and Rabat on the pretext that they would be given anti-tuberculosis vaccinations or entertained to a great feast. When at last they came to know what had happened, that they had been duped to sign anti-Sultan documents, the Moroccan people began to protest in a way that bewildered General Juin himself. *Le Monde*, a French newspaper, described what was happening in the following manner: 'We are witnessing an inverse and new phase of the Moroccan crisis. Since the middle of last week, groups of natives have been assembling quietly at the borders of the Berber country, south of Meknes. Without any noise or any kind of disturbance they are spending long hours outside the French administrative offices. When asked what their purpose is, they say that they want their pasha and caids to be dismissed, since these recently set themselves to oppose the Sultan. All this is done with such calm, such politeness, that the authorities are at a loss to know how to intervene'.

Mohammed V deposed

Sultan Mohammed V was unmoved by the hostility of the French administrators. He refused the demands that he should openly de-nounce the Istiqlal, eliminate from his entourage all persons of nationalist persuasion, nominate a large number of French candidates for posts of pashas and caids and punish all those who had shown opposition to Glaoui. He also refused to sign decrees which sought to increase further the French hold over Morocco. In 1952 the Sultan communicated directly with Paris, demanding the abolition of the Protectorate Treaty and martial law and the right to form a govern-ment of his own, composed of persons competent to negotiate in his name in France. He declared that he wished to establish without delay a parliamentary system of government. The following year he was deposed and a puppet, Moulay Arafa, a member of the Filali family, was put on the throne.

The deposition of Mohammed V enhanced his prestige among his people, most of whom began to treasure his photograph. Although he was away in Madagascar his people believed that his eyes were on them and that he had become part of the moon watching over them. The Moroccans were beginning to think, like their Tunisian counter-parts, that violence was the only language the French would under-stand.

Algeria

Nationalist articulation of the westernised élite type began latest in Algeria in French North Africa. This was due to many factors. Algeria was conquered in detail and was administered as part of France. The *colons*, numbering about one million in 1960, looked upon Algeria as belonging to themselves only. Unlike the Moroccan and Tunisian Protectorates which, legally, were held in trust for the natives until they were able to rule themselves, Algeria was a colony, a prolongation of France. So powerful did the *colons* become that they were able to compel the French government in Paris to carry out their wishes.

Hadj Messali

The First World War had an impact on the westernised Africans in Algeria. In fact during the war thousands of Algerian Berbers showed their hatred for the French by defecting to the Turks. In 1919 a grandson of Abdel Kader, Amir Khalid, demanded application of the Wilsonian principle of self-determination in Algeria and formed the *Bloc of Algerian Elected Muslims*. He was deported in 1924. The best

Hadj Messali

known Algerian nationalist until the outbreak of the 'Rebellion' in 1954 was Hadj Messali. Born in Tlemcen in Algeria in 1898, he was educated locally up to secondary school level and then served, just after the First World War, in the French army in Southern France. He then went to Paris where he worked in the Renault car factory and joined others there in the formation of the *Etoile Nord Africaine*, a sociopolitical organisation of North African workers in France. Under Messali this organisation became until 1936 associated with the Communist Party in France. In 1926 Messali attended the Anti-Imperialist Congress in Brussels where he campaigned actively against French occupation of the Maghreb. The important thing to note about Messali, who in 1937 founded the *Parti Populaire Algerien* (P.P.A.), is that from the beginning he denounced the so-called policy of assimilation and declared as his objective independence for a Berber-controlled Algeria.

Ferhat Abbas

Opposed to the concept of the Algerian nation were the pro-French Berbers usually described as the *beni oui oui* (yes men) who were enchanted by French education and culture in which they had shared and who were Muslim councillors in the local assemblies in Algeria. They were mainly doctors, lawyers and businessmen. They believed that Algeria was part of France. Perhaps the best of this pro-assimilation Berber westernised élite was Ferhat Abbas. Born on 24 October 1899 to a caid who was later decorated with the French Legion of Honour, Ferhat Abbas received French education and qualified as a pharmacist. He considered himself as a Frenchman of the Muslim faith, on one occasion saying: 'La France, c'est moi.' He knew more of French than Arabic. It was only in later years that Ferhat Abbas learned Arabic and Islamic culture. Like many of the Maghrebian westernised élite he married a French girl. Ferhat Abbas loved to read Anatole France, Victor Hugo, Michelet's *History of France* and the Declarations of the Rights of Man. In 1936 he denied the existence of an Algerian nation in language that should be noted. 'If I had discovered the Algerian Nation I would be a Nationalist and I would not be ashamed of it as if it were a crime. . . . I will not die for the Algerian fatherland because it does not exist. I have not found it. I have searched history, I have questioned both the dead and the living, I have visited the grave yards: no one mentioned it, not even once'.

Events soon opened the eyes of Ferhat Abbas and other assimila-

Ferhat Abbas

tionists among the westernised élite to the fact that an Algerian nation had existed and should be restored to the Algerian people. Having discovered that the so-called policy of assimilation was no more than a myth they began to sing a different song and in 1943 Ferhat Abbas in a manifesto denounced the bogus policy and demanded a separate Algerian constitution, equal political rights for all races in Algeria, large-scale land reforms and measures of social improvement, the recognition of Arabic as an official language side by side with French, freedom of the press, the right of the natives to form political parties and trade unions and free and compulsory education.

French attempts at conciliation

In March 1944 an ordinance was promulgated in an effort to conciliate the nationalists and Muslims. The latter were to be given the right to vote and were offered French citizenship. This ordinance also announced a new system of representation, to come into effect in 1945. Three fifths of the members of the Assemblies were to be elected by French citizens (including a number of the westernised Africans), the other two fifths by Muslims who were not French citizens. The inadequacy of the proposals from the Muslim viewpoint is clear from the fact that the Muslims, most of whom refused French citizenship, constituted seven-eighths of the population. Moreover the Algerian people had already lost confidence in the so-called policy of assimilation which the ordinance attempted to put into effect. The three groups of nationalists—the Reformist Ulema, the Abbas' 'Friends of the Manifesto' and the Messalists—formed a union, the declared aim of which was 'to make familiar the idea of an Algerian nation, and spread the desire for the constitution in Algeria of a new autonomous republic federated to a renewed anti-colonial anti-imperialist French republic'.

Disorders which broke out in 1945 and the bloody repressive measures taken by the French disunited the nationalists. In the meantime the *colons* exercised their strong influence by 'arranging' elections so that the true representatives of the people were not elected, but only the *beni oui oui*. Naturally the people became distrustful of the constitution and began to question the wisdom of peaceful methods. The Messalists were either thrown into prison or sent into exile. The anti-French feeling of the people was driven underground and went unperceived by the French until the 'rebellion' which broke out in November 1954.

Violence breaks out: Morocco and Tunisia granted independence

By 1954 the nationalists in French North Africa had begun to resort to violence in a form and on a scale greater than the French could cope with. Moreover the French were also busy putting down a 'rebellion' in Indo-China. Mendès-France, the new Premier of France, realistically decided to grant concessions in Morocco and Tunisia. In the former the *colons* were attacked, attempts were made on the puppet Sultan, French shops, cars and farms were burned down and French goods boycotted. Natives who were believed to be in favour of the French were murdered. To the surprise of the French, Thami el Glauoi, the overmighty pasha of Marrakesh who had contributed to the forcible dethronement and exile of Mohammed V, requested that the French bring back the rightful Sultan to his throne. The French had no alternative. Ben Arafa was removed, Mohammed V was reinstated and independence was granted to Morocco early in 1956. In Tunisia freedom fighters known as *fellaghas* made things difficult for the French. Independence was in the same year handed over to Tunisia under the leadership of Habib Bourguiba.

The Algerian War

In Algeria the French would not give in until an actual war, the bloodiest in colonial Africa, was fought against the French administration and settlers by Algerian freedom fighters. The war in Algeria affected the military reputation of France, led to the seizure of power in France by General de Gaulle and dragged France before the tribunal of world opinion.

The organisers of the bloody war that began in November 1954 were a different set of men from Messali, Ferhat Abbas and the like. They were not well-educated; they were mainly soldiers, trained for the French army. They were of peasant origin and many in their youth had worked in factories in France; they were born after the First World War and did not perceive in France a great power but a country divided into bitter factions, a country easily overrun by Germany in 1940. They had no time for the battle of words; all they wanted was to fight for independence for Algeria—independence not by stages, but immediate and complete. Although they appealed throughout the war to the *ulemas* and the Muslim feelings of the masses they were not ardent Muslims themselves. Perhaps the best known among them is Ben Bella, the first President of independent Algeria who was removed by the army in June 1965. Born in Oran in western Algeria of Moroccan parents, he fought in the French army in the Italian and North African campaigns and was decorated for his bravery. In 1946 he returned to Algeria and was elected to the Munici-

Ben Bella, first President of independent Algeria

pal Council of Oran. By 1950 he was a member of the anti-French Secret Organisation and he fled to Cairo before he was apprehended by the French administration. Under the inspiration of Nasser's Egypt Ben Bella and other revolutionary exiles planned the 'rebellion', constituting themselves into the Revolutionary Committee for Unity and Action. The name was later changed to the National Liberation Front.

The F.L.N. received the moral and financial backing of Egypt, Morocco, Tunisia and the Arab League. Soldiers were trained in

Tunisia, Morocco, Egypt and East Germany. By 1956 the F.L.N. had become superbly organised in Algeria which was divided into six *wilayas*; each *wilaya* was divided into zones; each zone into regions and each region into sectors. They received the moral and positive support of the majority of the population, without which the 'rebellion' would not have been successful.

One important thing to note about the F.L.N. is that by 1960 they were already advocating the kind of social welfare they would wish to establish in Algeria whenever they came to power. As one of them declared early in 1960: 'The Algerian revolution is not and cannot be a mere fight for the conquest of political power. It is an economic and social, as well as a political revolution. Independence cannot be an end in itself. . . . The Algerian workers are . . . fighting in order to guarantee land for the peasant, work for the worker and better living conditions'.

Independence for Algeria

So serious was the armed revolt of the F.L.N. that the French government, the Fourth Republic, collapsed, partly over the Algerian problem. The result was that General Charles de Gaulle came to power in May 1958. At Constantine General de Gaulle announced his plan to speed up the development of Algeria in all spheres. The new government in France also declared that all Algerians were equal in all respects. On 16 September 1959 General de Gaulle promised 'self-determination' to Algeria. He offered the Algerians three choices: integration, absolute independence, or independence in co-operation with France. As far as the F.L.N. were concerned there could be no question of compromising on the issue of absolute independence. Faced with the prospects of Algeria becoming independent of France the *colons* and some French generals attempted in 1960 and 1961 to overthrow General de Gaulle. In Algeria and in France they organised the terrorist organisation of the Secret Army.

Nevertheless General de Gaulle was undeterred by the armed opposition of the *colons*. His visit to Algeria from 9 to 13 December 1960 convinced him that the F.L.N. represented the bulk of the Algerian people. Moreover in spite of the fact that the F.L.N. were outclassed in terms of the quality of weapons, their tactics were costing the French a lot in men and money. The F.L.N. planted bombs in public places, raided isolated *colon* farms and burnt down newly-built French schools. The Muslim populations were terrorised into boy-cotting alcohol and tobacco, thereby hitting French businessmen.

On 18 March 1962 the Evian Agreement was signed by France and the F.L.N., according to which a cease-fire came into force at noon on 19 March and Algeria voted for its independence on 1 July 1962.

Libya

The huge territory of Libya with its small population had an experience in several ways different from that of the three French-controlled territories we have examined. Firstly, Italian hold on the territory continued to be precarious until 1933, after heavy loss of life by the civilian population. Secondly, the Italians did not seek to create a westernised élite who, as in the French Maghreb, could aspire to ruling their country some day. Rather the Italians looked at Libya as an extension of Italy to be exploited in the economic interest of Italy. Hence the programme sponsored by Benito Mussolini which sought to relieve the most densely populated rural areas of Italy by sending large numbers of peasant proprietors to Libya. In 1938 20,000 and in the following year 10,000 Italian peasants were thus settled in Libya. Like the French, however, the Italians denied all political rights and economic advancement to native Libyans.

Thirdly, while there was no westernised élite of the type of the French Maghreb and therefore no nationalist movement to agitate for independence, it was Libya that first obtained independence in the Maghreb, in 1951. In a sense the Italians unwittingly created the Libyan nation-state. For by uniting Tripolitania, Cyrenaica and Fezzan under one administration the way was prepared for the emergence of the United Kingdom of Libya. One cannot overstress the factor of division that made Cyrenaica and Tripolitania bitter foes and one ethnic group the eternal enemy of the other group. Cyrenaica, the chief centre of the Senussi *tariqa*, was inhabited by semi-nomads and people of Arab descent who continued to hate the agriculturist and more settled Arab-Berber population of Tripoli.

The United Nations grants independence to Libya

The Second World War in which Italy fought with Germany against France, Britain and the United States became a godsend to the Libyans.

The Senussi, under the leadership of Idris el-Senussi, later King of Libya, gave support to the Allied Powers. The British were able to drive out the Italian forces from the country. Thus at the end of the war Libya became a problem for the United Nations. And thanks to the conflicting interests of the various powers—Britain, France, America and Italy—the Political Committee of the United Nations resolved in 1949 to give Libya independence 'as soon as possible and in any case not later than 1 January 1952'. Cyrenaica, Tripolitania, and the Fezzan were granted full freedom to decide on the form of their union. Under the supervision of a United Nations' Commissioner, Dr. Adrian Pelt of Holland, the three territories agreed on a constitution and formed the United Kingdom of Libya under the hereditary kingship of Sayiid Mohammed Idris el-Senussi, a grandson of the founder of the Senussiya *tariqa*.

The Maghreb after independence

Since attainment of independence three major events have occurred in the Maghreb. Firstly, the French cultural, social and economic presence has remained. Secondly, all the states have been making rapid economic strides, particularly with the booming oil discoveries. Thirdly, the monarchical institution has disappeared from Tunisia and Libya.

As in other parts of ex-colonial Africa the cultural and economic presence of the ex-colonial power has remained very strong in the Maghreb. Although Arabic is being encouraged, the French language is still supreme, French teachers at the primary and secondary schools run into thousands and the curricula are still French-oriented. In 1962 1,000,000 hectares of the best land in Morocco was in French hands; in Tunisia French landholders produced 40 per cent, in value, of all Tunisian cereals; 10 per cent of olives and 95 per cent of vintage. In 1960 there were 200,000 Frenchmen in Morocco and 65,000 Frenchmen in Tunisia. In 1961 France remained the leading export market for Moroccan phosphates and Frenchmen controlled the major part of the modern economy of the State and most of its foreign trade. The French were in control of Tunisian mining, 72 per cent of its banking and the industries of fertilising liquid air, perfumes, paper, glass and brewing.

However, it is the discovery of oil in the Maghreb in vast quantities between 1956 and 1966 that may be described as the greatest economic event in this part of Africa in modern times. It was in Algeria that oil

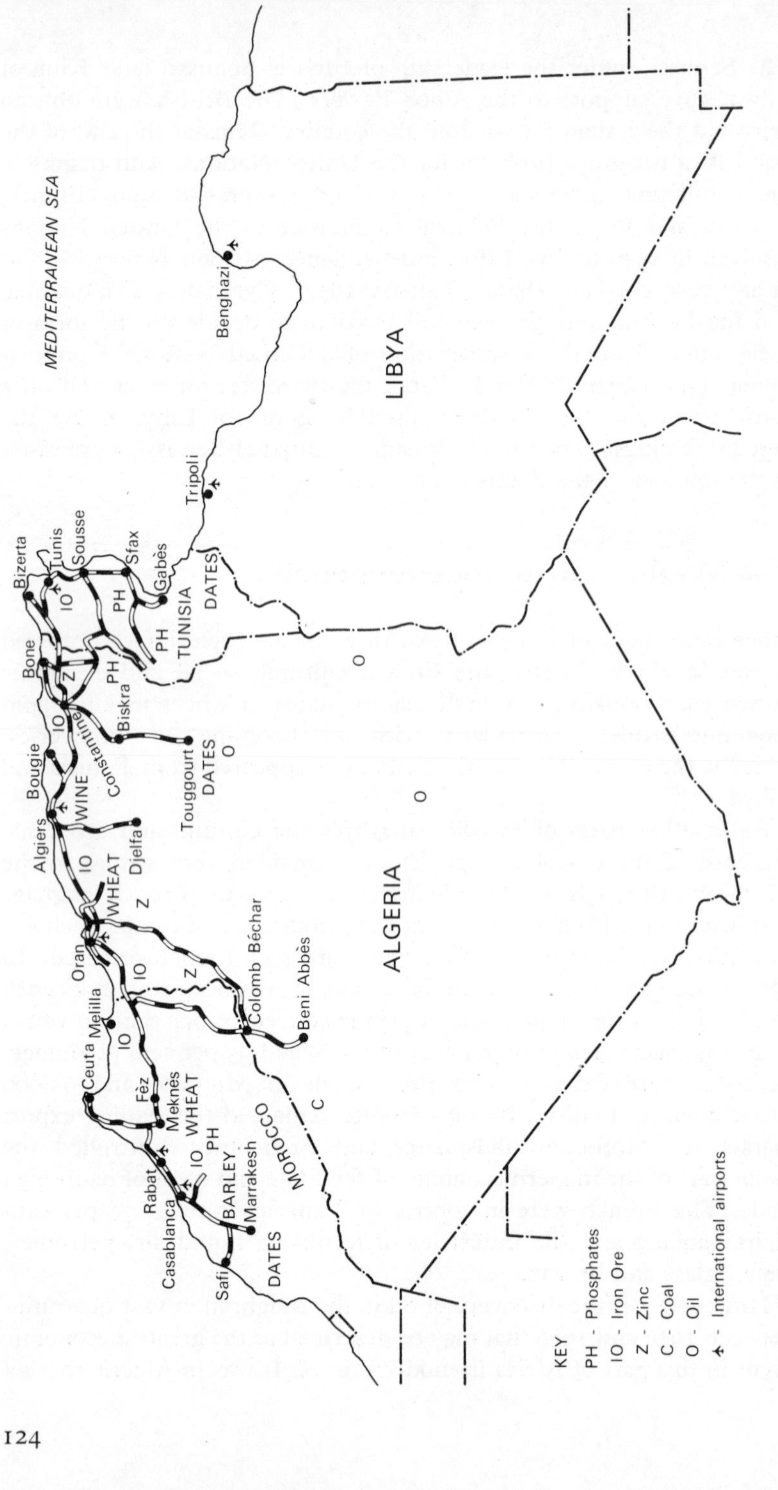

MEDITERRANEAN SEA

Benghazi

Tripoli

LIBYA

Bizerta
Tunis
Sousse
IO
Sfax
PH
Gabès
PH
TUNISIA
DATES

Bone
Z
PH
Constantine
Biskra
IO
Touggourt
DATES
O

Bougie
WINE
Algiers
IO
WHEAT
Djelfa
Z

ALGERIA

O

O

Oran
IO
Z
Colomb Béchar
IO
Beni Abbès

Ceuta Melilla
IO
Fèz
Meknès
WHEAT
IO
PH
MOROCCO
C
Rabat
BARLEY
IO
Casablanca
Marrakesh
Safi
DATES
PH

KEY

PH - Phosphates

IO - Iron Ore

Z - Zinc

C - Coal

O - Oil

✈ - International airports

The Maghreb: communications, minerals and crops

was first discovered and it became particularly important at the time of the Suez crisis. Between 1960 and 1964 revenue from oil and gas to the Algerian government rose from £7·5 million to £24 million. Oil production and refining is today Algeria's largest single industry and oil exports are worth more than £150 million, that is, more than half of Algeria's total exports.

The fortune of Libya has been even more signally changed for the better by oil. Until 1963 Libya depended for its revenue on £15 million 'aid' by Britain and the United States for their military installations and incomes from the local expenditures of the base personnel. Hitherto exports were limited to hides, olive oil and esparto grass. By 1964 the country's earnings from oil had risen to £80 million. By 1965 oil exports accounted for 98 per cent of total exports. As a result Libya's balance of trade from a £55 million deficit in 1961 has changed to a large and growing surplus since 1963. Production of oil has grown from 23,000 barrels a day in 1961 to over 1,000,000 barrels a day. There are over twenty oil companies in the country.

On the internal political front the elimination of the monarchy from Tunisia and Libya deserves some comment. It will be remembered that the *coup* of July 1952 swept the monarchy away from Egypt. In Tunisia where the Husseinid dynasty proved irrelevant to the political and social aspirations of the people the Neo-Destourians lost no time in dealing a decisive blow at the dynasty. In a rather quiet way and without much sympathy being expressed in favour of the monarchy, Sidi Lamine Bey, the Husseinid ruler, was deposed on 25 July 1957. The monarchy was abolished and a Republic proclaimed.

Twelve years later the monarchy was abolished in Libya, a country where this institution used to be regarded as the cement of the nation. For as a great grandson of the founder of the Senussi *tariqa* whose contribution to the modern history of Libya has been examined in Volume One, and as the leader of the resistance against Italian rule, Sayyid Idris el-Senussi was popular with his people. However, two events endangered the throne he was occupying. Firstly, largely because there was no strong westernised élite who would have provided a parliamentary democratic system of government King Idris was too powerful. Not only did he have the power to appoint and dismiss his Prime Minister but he also appointed directly all the provincial governors and senior civil servants. Secondly, King Idris could not produce a direct heir. Although he married his cousin, Emira Fatima, in 1933, he had no son. Consequently the question of a successor produced palace intrigues in the royal family. Around September 1969 while he was away in Turkey to seek cure for his ailing health the army took over the government of the country and deposed the seventy-nine year old monarch.

Thus it is only in Morocco that the monarchy is still preserved. At the death of Mohammed V on 27 February 1961 he was succeeded by his son, Hassan II. As is clear from the analysis of Sultan Mohammed V, the monarchy remains not only the fulcrum upon which the constitution of Morocco rests but it continues to be relevant to the spiritual, social, economic and national aspirations of the Moroccan peoples.

Part **two**

West Africa

4 The establishment of European rule in West Africa (*c.* 1880-1900)

The origins of European rule in West Africa

As their interests and influence changed in character and expanded in scope in the course of the nineteenth century, European nations, especially Britain and France, began to develop outright political ambitions in West Africa. Britain was the first European nation to acquire a West African territory over which she exercised direct political control. British interest in the campaign against the slave trade and in the protection of legitimate commerce necessitated her seizure of some territories along the West African coast from where to supervise these interests effectively. In 1808 she took over the Sierra Leone colony as a base from which the West African Squadron would carry on the campaign against the slave trade, while in 1843 she finally took over control of certain forts on the coast of Ghana in order to give effective protection to her commerce and her Fante friends against what was considered the Asante menace. For the same reason she bought off the Danes (1850) and the Dutch (1870) from the coast of Ghana. In 1874 she sought to consolidate her control of the Ghanaian coast by annexing the Fante states.

It was the same desire to protect her interests that led Britain to assume political control in one or two areas along the coast of what later became Nigeria. In this region she took the first step towards political power in 1849 when she appointed John Beecroft as consul for the Bights of Benin and Biafra. Supported by the then much dreaded British gunboats this official started meddling in the politics of the coastal states. In 1851 he interfered in a succession dispute in Lagos, an act which helped to prepare the way for British rule. In 1861 Britain seized this little Yoruba kingdom as a means of controlling the activities of Brazilian slave traders there and the overland trade route which ran from Lagos, through the heart of Yorubaland to Hausaland *via* Jebba on the Niger. Meanwhile the new developments in the trade and politics of nineteenth century West Africa had weakened the city states of the Bight of Biafra with the result that these states became increasingly unable to maintain order between the European and African traders as effectively as they had done in centuries past. The white traders immediately seized the opportunity of the new development to usurp part of this waning political control. In 1854 those of them in Bonny formed the Court of Equity which assigned itself the duty of regulating relations between African and European traders. This court, which was presided over by Europeans, was soon brought under the control of the British Consul. From Bonny the institution spread to the other states of the Niger delta and the Cross River estuary. Though this method of political control in the Bight of Biafra remained informal for a very long time, it was nonetheless real. The consul, the gunboat and the Court of Equity became very important factors in the politics of the region throughout the rest of the century.

With the French, political activity was concentrated in the region of the river Senegal, an area in which they had shown great interest even in the days of the slave trade. If in the course of the eighteenth century she had lost the greater part of her colonial empire to Britain, France now sought to build a new empire in Africa. Thus in 1817 she occupied the mouth of the Senegal where she established an administration and sought to encourage the cultivation of export crops like cotton and groundnut. By 1865 French rule had reached the upper Senegal, while her influence covered an even wider area.

The limitations of European rule

In spite of these early political developments, however, European rule in West Africa remained severely limited in its territorial extent and up to about 1880 most West African states and peoples knew nothing of European rule. There were many reasons for this. For the greater part of the nineteenth century, indeed up to about 1879, French governments were very unstable and throughout that period France could not think of a vigorous extension of the area in West Africa over which she exercised political rule. Britain, which had a stable government, was busy colonising Australia and New Zealand which she found more attractive than West Africa. Also at this same time British economic thinkers, known as the free traders, preached against colonisation. They argued that colonies were very expensive to maintain and that disputes over them often led to unprofitable international wars. They were confident that given a fair chance Britain would be able to dominate any market through peaceful competition with other nations. What was more, until about 1854, Europe had no answer to the problems presented by malaria in West Africa. In these circumstances European rivalries in West Africa declined. The Dutch and the Danes were even prepared to withdraw, and no other European power rose to challenge the West African interests of either the French or the British. For all these reasons therefore, though European political ambitions in West Africa were born early in the nineteenth century, they did not achieve an appreciable growth for nearly eighty years.

The scramble in West Africa

However, from about 1880 the European attitude to colonies in Africa changed remarkably and as a result within a space of only twenty years nearly the whole of the African continent was under European rule. The factors which caused European nations to scramble for colonial possessions in Africa have already been discussed elsewhere. Here we are concerned only with the form which that scramble took in West Africa.

To a large extent the scramble in West Africa was a straight fight between the French and the British. As we have already seen, Denmark and Holland had withdrawn from West Africa in the period when colonial possessions in Africa were not very much in favour with European powers. Portugal, which preceded all the other European nations in West Africa, showed very little interest in expansion there. In consequence she was confined to the small enclave of Portuguese Guinea. It was only the intervention of Germany that tended to make the scramble in West Africa a three cornered fight. Except on the coast of Togoland German interest in West Africa was very negligible by 1880. But in 1884 Germany quickly seized not only Togoland but also the Cameroons, the latter being an area where British interests had been clearly dominant for some time. After this swift move Germany did not attempt to acquire more territories in West Africa but settled down to giving precise definition to the boundaries of these two protectorates, an exercise that involved long negotiations with Britain and France.

The French in West Africa

The two latter powers thus had the rest of West Africa between them. Each not only held what she already had along the coast but from there sought to expand into the interior. Thus French expansion was directed largely from Senegal. This, however, does not mean that the French were not active elsewhere along the West African coast. On the contrary, from the beginning of the scramble they reasserted their control over all their forts along the coast which they had tended to neglect in the previous decade. In 1878 they formally took possession of Cotonou. Four years later they declared a protectorate over Porto Novo. In 1886 they reoccupied their forts on the Ivory Coast which they had abandoned in 1871. From these forts they extended their control over the whole coast between Liberia and Ghana through treaties with the local chiefs. Higher up the coast they occupied Conakry and from there claimed the whole region between Sierra Leone and Portuguese Guinea. In 1893 they formally proclaimed the Ivory Coast and French Guinea their colonies and undertook the conquest of Dahomey, a task which they completed in 1894.

French aspirations

But in spite of all these Senegal was the main base for French expansion in West Africa. Since the 1850s the French had entertained the ambition of obtaining the undisputed control of western and central Sudan whose ancient fame and glory as a region rich in commerce attracted them very much. To them Timbuktu was still the centre of this trade which they greatly wanted to capture. In consequence they regarded their stations elsewhere along the coast as merely providing alternative routes to the Sudan rather than as bases from which independent expansion could be made. Even their colony of Algeria in North Africa was seen as providing a gateway into the Sudan. From 1880 the French started sending out from Senegal a series of military and exploratory expeditions into the heart of the Sudan with the object of seizing the whole Sudan and linking it with other French bases along the West Coast. By 1883 the French had gone as far as Bamako. In 1890 they started the conquest of the empire of Sheikh Ahmadu, the son and successor of Alhaji Umar. By 1893 they had succeeded in overrunning the whole of this empire. Then they launched an attack on the empire of Samoury in the region of Upper Guinea and upper Ivory Coast. They drove this Mandingo

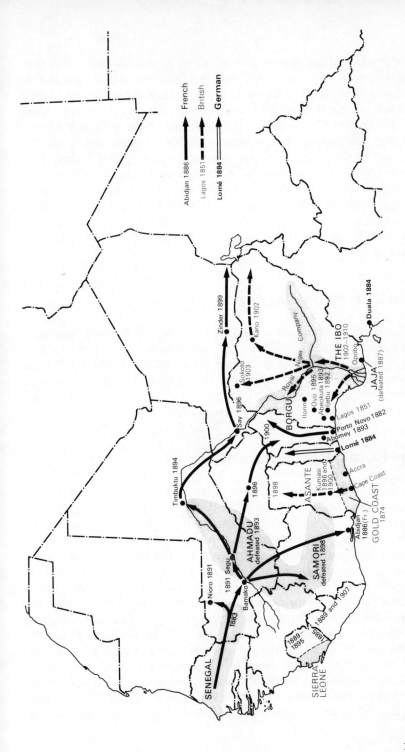

French — Abidjan 1886
British — Lagos 1851
German — Lomé 1884

Zinder 1899
Kano 1902
Sokoto 1903
Say 1896
Royal Niger Company
Timbuktu 1894
1900
Oyo 1895
Ilorin
Abeokuta 1893
Ijebu 1892
Lagos 1851
Porto Novo 1882
Abomey 1893
Lomé 1884
BORGU
THE IBO 1902–1910
Opobo
JAJA (defeated 1887)
Duala 1884
1896
1898
Accra
Kumasi 1896 and 1900
Cape Coast
ASANTE
GOLD COAST 1874
Abidjan 1886(Fr.)
AHMADU defeated 1893
SAMORI defeated 1898
Nioro 1891
1891 Segu
Bamako
1883
1889 1895
1886 1889 and 1907
SIERRA LEONE
SENEGAL

West Africa, showing the progress of European penetration

135

adventurer and nationalist from pillar to post until 1898 when they captured and exiled him. In 1894 the French occupied the ancient and romantic city of Timbuktu. In 1896 they occupied Say. As the French advanced they developed even wider territorial ambitions. At one stage they had plans for a great and glorious French African empire that would stretch across the whole continent from the Senegal to the Nile, thus embracing the whole of the Sudan. This empire was to be continuous with Algeria in North Africa, with French Guinea, the Ivory Coast and Dahomey on the West Coast as well as with French possessions in Equatorial Africa. It was to be served by a network of modern railways which would tap the resources of this whole region to the everlasting benefit and glory of Metropolitan France.

The British in West Africa

The British on their side concentrated mainly on the forest region of West Africa since they did not fall victim to the ancient romance of the Sudan. They set out to expand their holdings in the forest zone where they could create very profitable markets for their goods and at the same time obtain cotton, indigo, vegetable oil, timber and many of the other products needed by their industries.

The Royal Niger Company

There was another great difference between the French and British approach to the scramble in West Africa. To a great extent France extended her influence and rule mainly through the activities of men who were state officials. But the British relied partly on government officials and partly on private traders for the purpose of extending their rule and influence in West Africa. For instance the region of modern Northern Nigeria was secured for Britain by a commercial company. In the 1870s the trade on the Niger beyond the delta was dominated by four British companies: James Pinnock and Company of Liverpool, the West African Company of Manchester, Alexander Miller and Brothers of Glasgow and Holland Jacques and Company of London. The intense competition between these companies made the Niger trade less profitable than it would otherwise have been. To put an end to this unprofitable competition George Taubman Goldie, who had an interest in Holland Jacques and Company in

1879 persuaded the four companies to form the United African Company. But no sooner was this done than competition was faced from the French who by 1882 had at least seven trading stations south of Nupe. However, Goldie dealt with this new threat to British interest and influence by buying off the French. By 1884 British interests and influence were once again supreme on the lower Niger. What was more, Goldie's company collected a large number of treaties from the communities and states all along the rivers Niger and Benue which purported to give the company a measure of political power in the region. The area was therefore easily recognised by the other European powers as falling properly within the sphere of British influence. Goldie himself was present at the so-called Berlin West African Conference where this recognition was given, and he was very useful in helping to present the British case. When later it became necessary to establish an administration in the region in order to convince other powers that Britain was in effective control of the area, the British made use of Goldie's company. To this end, in 1886 the company was granted a royal charter which gave it the right to undertake the government and defence of the region. In that same year the company's name was changed to the Royal Niger Company. For many years the Royal Niger Company was able to keep the French out of Northern Nigeria by giving the false impression that it had an effective administration throughout the region. Later, however, the French discovered the trick. In 1890 a French expedition sailed up the rivers Niger and Benue only to find out that the Royal Niger Company had no administration or influence whatever in a place like the emirate of Yola. Immediately a struggle for the control of this region ensued. The Royal Niger Company, however, successfully met the challenge and secured for Britain not only Yola but also the extensive Bornu empire. But the company was not able to meet successfully all such challenges. Thus after the conquest of Dahomey in 1894 the French started moving up towards the Niger, and in the process discovered that the company had no influence or establishment whatsoever in Borgu and much of the area beyond. The French again made a determined effort to seize the region. In the course of the ensuing struggle for Borgu the British government realised that the Royal Niger Company had not the resources with which to meet this fresh and more serious challenge. The Borgu question brought Britain and France to the brink of war and Britain was forced to create the West African Frontier Force under the command of Frederick Lugard in 1897. It was this direct intervention of the British government that resolved the Borgu crisis and kept the region under British rule. On 1 January 1900 the Royal Niger Company was deprived of its charter and Northern Nigeria declared a British Protectorate. Nevertheless it can be said that the Royal Niger Company served Britain well in winning for her the extensive area of Northern Nigeria.

TREATY with King and Chiefs of *Opobo*

Signed at *Opobo*

HER Majesty the Queen of the United Kingdom of Great Britain and Ireland, Empress of India, &c., and the Kings and Chiefs of *Opobo* being desirous of maintaining and strengthening the relations of peace and friendship which have for so long existed between them;

Her Britannic Majesty has named and appointed E. H. Hewett, Esq., Her Consul for the Bights of Benin and Biafra, to conclude a Treaty for this purpose.

The said E. H. Hewett, Esq., and the said Kings and Chiefs of *Opobo* have agreed upon and concluded the following Articles:—

ARTICLE I.

Her Majesty the Queen of Great Britain and Ireland, &c., in compliance with the request of the Kings, Chiefs, and people of *Opobo*, hereby undertakes to extend to them, and to the territory under their authority and jurisdiction, Her gracious favour and protection.

ARTICLE II.

The Kings and Chiefs of *Opobo* agree and promise to refrain from entering into any

A copy of the treaty between Hewett and Jaja of Opobo

138

correspondence, Agreement, or Treaty with any foreign nation or Power, except with the knowledge and sanction of Her Britannic Majesty's Government.

ARTICLE III.

It is agreed that full and exclusive jurisdiction, civil and criminal, over British subjects and their property in the territory of *Opobo* is reserved to Her Britannic Majesty, to be exercised by such Consular or other officers as Her Majesty shall appoint for that purpose.

The same jurisdiction is likewise reserved to Her Majesty in the said territory of *Opobo* over foreign subjects enjoying British protection, who shall be deemed to be included in the expression "British subject" throughout this Treaty.

ARTICLE IV.

All disputes between the Kings and Chiefs of *Opobo* , or between them and British or foreign traders, or between the aforesaid Kings and Chiefs and neighbouring tribes, which cannot be settled amicably between the two parties, shall be submitted to the British Consular or other officers appointed by Her Britannic Majesty to exercise jurisdiction in *Opobo* territories for arbitration and decision, or for arrangement.

ARTICLE V.

The Kings and Chiefs of *Opobo* hereby engage to assist the British Consular or other officers in the execution of such duties as may be assigned to them; and, further, to act upon their advice in matters relating to the administration of justice, the development of the resources of the country, the interests of commerce, or in any other matter in relation to peace, order, and good government, and the general progress of civilization.

ARTICLE VI.

The subjects and citizens of all countries may freely carry on trade in every part of the territories of the Kings and Chiefs parties hereto, and may have houses and factories therein.

3

White

ARTICLE VII.

All ministers of the Christian religion shall be permitted to reside and exercise their calling within the territories of the aforesaid Kings and Chiefs, who hereby guarantee to them full protection.

All forms of religious worship and religious ordinances may be exercised within the territories of the aforesaid Kings and Chiefs, and no hindrance shall be offered thereto.

ARTICLE VIII.

If any vessels should be wrecked within the *Opobo* territories, the Kings and Chiefs will give them all the assistance in their power, will secure them from plunder, and also recover and deliver to the owners or agents all the property which can be saved.

If there are no such owners or agents on the spot, then the said property shall be delivered to the British Consular or other officer.

The Kings and Chiefs further engage to do all in their power to protect the persons and property of the officers, crew, and others on board such wrecked vessels.

All claims for salvage dues in such cases shall, if disputed, be referred to the British Consular or other officer for arbitration and decision.

ARTICLE IX.

This Treaty shall come into operation, so far as may be practicable, from the date of its signature, *Article VI. as herein printed being expunged.*

Done in Duplicate at Opobo this nineteenth day of December in the year one thousand eight-hundred and eighty-four

Edward Hyde Hewett

Cookey Gam
Prince Saturday Ja Ja
Firebourne   His X Mark

Official British Action

Elsewhere in West Africa the establishment and expansion of British rule was in the main the result of official action. As soon as Germany seized the Cameroons the British consul in the Niger Delta, Mr. Hewett, took steps to ensure that Britain was not pushed out of the Oil Rivers. He collected treaties of protection from various chiefs and villages on the basis of which Britain proclaimed the whole region between Lagos and the Cameroons the Oil River Protectorate in June 1885. This protectorate which extended as far inland as Lokoja on the Niger and Ibi on the Benue had no real administration until 1891, the year when its name was changed to the Niger Coast Protectorate. British acquisition of Yorubaland was the work of the Lagos government which since the 1860s had been deeply involved in Yoruba politics. In 1888 the Lagos authorities went into a treaty with the Alafin of Oyo who is said to have placed all Yorubaland under British protection. In the region of modern Ghana, Asante was occupied in 1896 and forced to admit a British resident to Kumasi. From there the authorities of the colony proceeded in 1898 to annex the Northern Territories of Ghana to Britain. In 1896 the Freetown government extended British rule to the Sierra Leone hinterland. British expansion on the Gambia was in like manner the work of British officials rather than of private businessmen.

After the scramble

By 1900 the scramble was virtually over, and all West Africa, except the small Republic of Liberia, was now under European rule. Even then Liberia was not unaffected by the scramble for she lost a considerable portion of the coast to which she had laid claim since the 1830s. Furthermore she lost every opportunity for expansion into the interior. Of all the powers involved France emerged from the scramble with the lion's share of territory. Whereas Britain, her nearest rival in West Africa, acquired a total area of 480,000 square miles, France's empire in West Africa measured about 1,800,000 square miles. Germany came third with Togoland which measured 33,0000 square miles and the Cameroons which had an area of 200,000 square miles. Portugal came last with a colony measuring 14,000 square miles in area. To some extent France achieved her ambition which at first appeared visionary. She secured most of the Sudan and linked this up with all her territories on the coast. Further-

more she was able to link her West African empire with her posses-
sions in North Africa. But she failed to link all this up with the Nile.
The Anglo-Egyptian Sudan stood in her way. The main rivers of
West Africa fell into French and British hands. Britain controlled the
lower Gambia, the lower Niger and the navigable portions of the
Benue, while France controlled the whole of the Senegal, upper
Gambia, the upper and the middle Niger. These rivers were useful
as gateways into the areas of West Africa which they drain. Though
Britain's four colonies, Gambia, Sierra Leone, Ghana, and Nigeria
were all widely separated, each of them enjoyed the advantage of
having direct access to the sea. But whereas the French could travel
from one end of their West African possession to the other without
passing through any other power's colony or entering the sea, the
British could not.

The Berlin West Africa Conference

The ease with which the European powers partitioned West Africa
without fighting among themselves should be explained. In the first
place before the scramble had started in earnest the European nations
held the Berlin West Africa Conference (1884–85) to set down the
rules of the game. This conference did not partition West Africa, or
any other part of Africa, as is often popularly believed. Among other
things it declared the Niger and the Congo international waterways,
which meant that these rivers were to be free for navigation by all
nations of the world. Though this principle was soon infringed on
both the Niger and the Congo, no international crisis resulted because
no nation seriously took it upon herself to challenge the action of
those who controlled the two rivers. The conference also set down the
conditions under which the occupation of a territory by one power
would gain the recognition of the others. An occupying power was
not only required to notify the others of the fact of her occupation
but also was to set up an administration as a visible evidence of her
effective presence. By and large this principle was adhered to. As a
result no power deliberately trespassed against the established rights
of her neighbour. Germany, who had offended the British by her
seizure of the Cameroons, soon withdrew from, and lost interest in,
further territorial expansion in West Africa. There was therefore no
opportunity for them to clash again in West Africa. Britain and
France seemed most likely to clash but did not actually do so because
their interests were not really in conflict except perhaps in one place.

France for the most part wanted the savanna belt, Britain the forest region. It was only the British 'intrusion' into the Sudan by way of her interest in Northern Nigeria that nearly brought the two countries to war over Borgu. There would have been a crisis over the *imamate* of Futa Jalon in which the French had shown interest since 1860, but the French suspicion between 1880 and 1882, that Britain wanted to annex Futa Jalon to Sierra Leone, turned out to be unfounded.

European 'diplomacy'

European rule was imposed on West Africans by 'diplomacy' and war. What is described as 'diplomacy' here, would be better described as 'trickery'. Britain, France and Germany claimed to base their rule in many areas on treaties of protection which they said they signed with the local chiefs. In these treaties the chiefs are said to have signed away

Jaja of Opobo

for ever their territories and peoples. Since no West African ruler ever had the right to give away his people and their land, it is doubtful whether these so-called treaties were treaties in fact. If any chief ever

143

signed such a treaty it was invalid in traditional law. A critical study of some of these treaties seems to reveal that many of them were fake. In 1880 a French Officer, Gallieni, visited the empire of Sheikh Ahmadu of Segu and came out with a treaty which claimed that the Sheikh had agreed to place under 'the exclusive protection of France' the basin of the Niger passing through his empire. This copy of the treaty did not carry the Sheikh's signature or the seal of his empire. The Arabic copy of the same treaty which bore the Sheikh's signature and imperial seal did not mention that Ahmadu had made any such grants to the French. The Arabic copy merely reveals that Gallieni and Sheikh Ahmadu signed only a treaty of peace and friendship. But in order to keep off possible European rivals Gallieni must have tampered with the contents of the original treaty. This is perhaps a good example of how many of the so-called treaties of protection were obtained.

If some of these treaties were actually signed by African chiefs, there is reason to believe that such chiefs did not know the full implications of what they were asked to do. When Consul Hewett was touring the Niger, 'hunting' for treaties with African chiefs, he came to Opobo which was then under King Jaja. He asked this delta chief to sign a treaty of 'protection' and 'free trade' with Britain. Jaja, who was a very intelligent man, asked him to explain what he meant by 'free trade'. When the explanation which Hewett gave did not satisfy him, Jaja refused to sign the treaty unless the section referring to trade was removed. This section was duly removed before Jaja signed the treaty. It is unlikely that, if the Europeans had explained the full meaning of these treaties to the people, most West African chiefs would have signed them.

Attempts to impose European rule by force

In most places, however, sometimes even in places where they claimed to have obtained the so-called treaties of cession, Europeans had to impose their rule by force. Though West Africans often clamoured for European goods, they did not clamour for European rule, and never trusted Europeans. One of Sheikh Ahmadu's lieutenants told Gallieni in 1880: 'We like the French but do not trust them, they trust us but do not like us'. Most West Africans knew that their way of life was different from that of Europeans, and that European rule would tamper with this way of life. They also did not want to lose the right to govern themselves. For these reasons they could not accept European rule with enthusiasm. The Europeans therefore had to conquer them in order to rule. It was by force that the French established themselves in Dahomey, Futa Jalon, Upper Guinea, Upper Ivory Coast, Kaarta, Segu and Masina. The British also had to fight many wars in order to subject the people in their West African colonies to their rule. They fought the people of Sierra Leone Protectorate (1898); fought the Asante throughout the nineteenth century; in Nigeria they fought Ijebu (1892), Brass (1895), Ilorin and Bida (1897), Benin (1897), Arochukwu (1901–02) and Northern Nigeria (1900–04). In certain parts of West Africa armed resistance lasted till the second decade of this century. By 1919 the British were still fighting to subdue certain villages in the Ibo and Ibibio areas for the first time. Military resistance in the French colony of Niger lasted until 1922. Thus the first problem which the Europeans faced in ruling West Africa was to get the West Africans to accept their rule. In this they never wholly succeeded. West Africans never accepted European rule with all their heart.

Reasons for the European success

Though the opposition to European rule was widespread in West Africa, the Europeans succeeded all the same in bringing West Africans under their rule. This was so for two reasons. Firstly the Europeans were better armed and had better trained soldiers than any West African people. The Maxim gun which played a major part in these wars was a weapon the like of which no West African people had ever seen or heard of before. They therefore had no answer to it. Secondly West African opposition was not co-ordinated. Each king-dom, and sometimes each village, fought its own battle and suffered defeat without any help from its neighbours. Even the Muslim states of the Sudan which had many common ties failed to combine against the European invaders. Samoury of Guinea and Sheikh Ahmadu of Segu were so opposed to each other, that Ahmadu sometimes pre-ferred co-operation with the French to co-operation with Samoury. Furthermore, many of the better organised African states were in decline at the time. Bornu started to decline again after al Kanemi. After the death of Muhammed Bello in 1837 the Fulani empire lost its vigour. The empire of Sheikh Ahmadu of Segu was never properly organised and properly governed, as a result of which the provinces were already breaking away when the scramble started. The French exploited this situation by pretending to be the liberators of the rebellious provinces and in so doing weakened Sheikh Ahmadu. The empire of Samoury was still rising and therefore unorganised when the scramble started. The Asante state had been severely weakened by a century of continuous warfare. The Oyo empire was already in disarray by the second decade of the century while the states which rose after its fall were engaged in mutual destruction. The kingdom of

The Maxim gun in action

Dahomey was probably the strongest and best organised West African state on the eve of the scramble. But then it had been very much weakened by its wars with the Egba, and in any case fought without any help from its neighbours.

5 European administration and the growth of nationalism in West Africa (*c.* 1900-1939)

German rule in West Africa did not last more than a few years for in the course of the First World War Britain and France seized Togoland (1914) and the Cameroons (1916). Germany had spent part of the peaceful years between 1884 and 1914 defining the boundaries of these two colonies and imposing her rule on their peoples. Thus proper German civil administration had little time to leave permanent impressions in West Africa. In 1919 the League of Nations divided each of the two former German West African colonies into two. The eastern half of each went to France while the western halves went to Britain. The latter's share of Togoland was administered as part of the Gold Coast, while her share of the Cameroons was administered as part of Nigeria. France administered her own sections separate from her other colonies in West and Equatorial Africa. By and large, however, Britain and France extended to these mandated territories the same basic policies as they applied in their West African colonies. The main differences were that their administration of these mandates was under the general supervision of the League of Nations and that France could not extend to them some of the more obnoxious aspects of her policy such as forced labour. Just as in the case of the scramble, therefore, the history of European administration in West Africa is largely the history of French and British administrations.

The patterns of French and British administration

Senegal was France's first colony in West Africa. In 1893 the Ivory Coast and Guinea, in 1900 Dahomey and in 1904 Sudan were created as separate colonies. The interior regions of French West Africa continued under military occupation until after the First World War when the colonies of Niger, Upper Volta and Mauretania were created. (In 1932 Upper Volta was 'partitioned' between Sudan, the Ivory Coast and Niger, but was restored as a separate colony in 1948.) France thus carved up her vast West African empire into eight colonies. In spite of this, however, she applied to all of them virtually the same administrative and economic policies. To understand properly the pattern of French administration in West Africa it is necessary to analyse the theories which lay behind it.

The French policy of assimilation

Up to the beginning of the the general European scramble for colonies in Africa French administration in West Africa was based entirely on the theory of assimilation. As a result of the famous French Revolution which started in 1789 Frenchmen had come to believe that all men were equal. They had also made a declaration which conferred the right of French citizenship on every inhabitant of a French colony. This latter measure derived from the fact that France believed that her culture and civilisation were the best in the world and that it was her mission to admit her colonial peoples into this rich heritage of her culture. This end, France believed, was to be attained by teaching the colonial peoples the French language, by subjecting them to French law and by giving them French civil and political rights. Throughout French West Africa the French applied this theory in full only in Senegal, her only West African colony at the time when this theory enjoyed unchallenged ascendancy. Thus in 1848 France conferred French citizenship on the Senegalese and also gave them the right to elect a representative, called a deputy, to the French National Assembly (the Lower House of the French Parliament) in Paris. The first Senegalese deputy to enjoy this distinguished position was Blaise Diagne in 1914. Also in accordance with the policy of assimilation Senegal was given the French system of local government based on *Communes*. In 1872 there were only two communes in Senegal— St. Louis and Gorée. In 1880 the commune of Rufisque, and in 1887 the commune of Dakar, were created. Each commune was endowed with a council which was elected by all its adult males, and a mayor who was the president of the council. In 1879 another council was created, the *Conseil du Sénégal*, which was made up of representatives from all the communes of Senegal and had the duty to levy taxation and to regulate the use of public property.

The communes of Senegal

The four communes of Senegal remained peculiar in French West Africa. All their indigenous inhabitants were French citizens and enjoyed the same civil and political rights as Frenchmen. Whereas people born in other parts of French West Africa could become French citizens only if they could read, write and speak the French language well, were known to be very loyal to France and had worked for a number of years in the civil service, those who were born in these four communes automatically became French citizens. They were called the *originaires,* that is, those who became French citizens by virtue of their birth. Also while French citizens from elsewhere in West Africa came under French law, the citizens of the four communes remained under Muslim law, a very special concession.

The doctrine of association

From the 1880s, however, the theory of assimilation came under vehement attack. As French rule and influence expanded in West Africa and elsewhere, France came into contact with very strongly organised African states whose cultures were still intact since they had not been influenced by centuries of contact with Europe. The French found it difficult to sidetrack completely the traditional authorities in these areas as they had done in Senegal where the people had been very greatly influenced by centuries of intercourse with France. Also in this period French expansion in West Africa was primarily for economic purposes, to find markets for her goods and raw materials for her industries. French businessmen therefore came to attack the policy of assimilation because it disorganised indigenous society and thus hampered the rapid economic exploitation of tribal areas. They also feared that assimilated colonists could become serious economic rivals. They doubted how possible it was to assimilate all the inhabitants of French West Africa. In any case, they argued, Africans were a different branch of the human family and therefore could not be properly absorbed into French culture. As a result of all this vigorous opposition, by 1905 France ceased to be completely committed to the policy of assimilation, though its influence remained strong. In its place the French people developed the doctrine of *association.* According to the advocates of this doctrine French colonial policy would respect the culture of her dependent peoples and allow each group to develop in their own way, rather than force them to adopt French civilisation and culture. To achieve this aim France would as much as possible govern each group through their traditional political institutions. Though *association* influenced later French colonial policy it never completely dominated it.

It was however largely as a result of this theory that the rest of French West Africa came to have local government institutions which were markedly different from those of Senegal. There was no longer any question of proclaiming all French West Africans French citizens and giving them French local government institutions. Outside Senegal therefore the French made an attempt to govern their subjects through local chiefs. They recognised three grades of chiefs. Firstly there were those they called *chefs de province* (we could call them paramount chiefs) who were usually the successors of the more prominent and influential chiefs of the pre-colonial days. Secondly there were the *chefs de canton* (district heads) who were in most places ordinary people of ability whom the French appointed to that position. To start with, the canton was an artificial administrative unit created by the French; it did not correspond to any ethnic boundary. Lastly there was the *chef de village* or the village head who was often the traditional head of his community. The village chief was responsible for collecting the taxes imposed by the government and was expected to maintain law and order, arrest criminals and organise relief in times of disaster, for instance during floods or locust invasions. It also was his duty to ensure that surplus food was stored up for use in times of scarcity, and to maintain the roads in his area of authority. The district head or *chef de canton* kept the register of tax payers in his canton, said how much each village paid, helped the government in conscripting people for the army and in recruiting forced labour for the road or for any other public work. This was the system of local government in the rest of French West Africa outside Senegal which some people have described as 'direct rule' in order to distinguish it from indirect rule which is said to be the British system. This description is not very accurate but we cannot go into the complicated controversy about it here. Later in the chapter we shall bring out the main differences between the French and British systems.

Centralised French administration

French administration in West Africa had one other distinguishing characteristic. It was highly centralised. The French believed in a strong and centralised government. As a result of bitter experiences some time in their history they had come to the conclusion that strong local government bodies constituted a danger to a state. The French also believed in efficiency and uniformity and if these two ideals were to be achieved, then government must be run from a common centre. In West Africa the French were lucky in that their territories formed one continuous block for this meant the colonies could easily be administered from one capital. The passion for centralisation visibly affected French administration of their territories in West Africa.

Every French colony in West Africa was divided into units called *cercles* (provinces) each of which was under a political officer called the *commandant*. A big *cercle* was usually further split into units called *sub-divisions* each of which was under an officer called a *chef de sub-division* (this officer corresponded to the district officer in British territories). The latter officer was responsible to the *commandant* who in turn was responsible to the Lieutenant-Governor who was the head of the administration in a colony. Each Lieutenant-Governor was assisted in his work by a council which he was expected to consult on certain issues touching the colony, especially on questions of fixing the income and expenditure of the colony. A decree of 1920 created another council, called the *privy council*, which advised the Lieutenant-Governor. All Lieutenant-Governors were responsible to the Governor-General in Dakar who was the administrative head of all French West Africa. It was the duty of this officer to see that all decrees issued by the French Ministry of Colonies and all laws passed by the French parliament which touched West Africa were carried out. He alone had the right to go into correspondence with the Ministry of Colonies, and for this reason all other officers in West Africa had to work according to his direction. Sometimes, however, owing to the difficulties of communication the Lieutenant-Governors and the officers under them enjoyed more initiative and powers in practice than they were allowed in theory. At one time the Governor-General was the same person as the Lieutenant-Governor of Senegal, but in 1904 the two offices were separated, and the headquarters of the Governor-General moved from St. Louis to Dakar. The Governor-General had a body called the *Conseil de Gouvernement* which advised him. This council met once a year to hear government policy from the Governor-General and to discuss the federal budget as well as the budget of each colony in turn. French West Africa was thus a federation of territories linked together through the Governor-General to the government of metropolitan France.

Generally speaking these were the main features of French government in West Africa until the end of the Second World War. The changes which came after that will be discussed in another chapter. Senegal had another local government body given to her in 1920. The *Conseil du Sénégal* dealt only with the affairs of the four communes. A body which would deal with matters affecting the communes and the hinterland later became necessary. It was to meet this need that in 1920 the French Ministry of Colonies authorised the creation of a *colonial council* comprising *citizens* from the four communes and *subjects* from the hinterland. This council had the duty of approving the budget of the Lieutenant-Governor of Senegal, of legislating on the control of public property and of making recommendations in matters of taxation. In 1929 Gorée ceased to be an independent commune and became part of Dakar.

Citizens and subjects

In the last paragraph we talked of French *citizens* and *subjects*. French *subjects* could be called second class 'citizens'. They were not culturally assimilated to France, French civil and criminal law did not apply to them, they could be polygamists which *citizens* could not be, they came under the system known as the *indigénat* which did not apply to French *citizens*. Under this system, for instance, a *subject* could suffer arbitrary arrest and summary trial at the hands of an administrative officer. Whereas a *citizen* was exempt from compulsory labour, a *subject* was not. A *subject* could be forced to serve for a longer period in the army than a *citizen*. This division of French West Africans into first and second class human beings continued until after the Second World War.

British indirect rule

The British, like the French, believed that their culture and social institutions were the best in the world. But unlike the French they also believed that their African subjects were so backward that they could not benefit from the introduction of these 'highly' developed institutions amongst them. In fact they held that any attempt to force Africans to adopt British political system and practices would only lead to disintegration and disaster. But at the same time the British believed that Africans should be introduced to what they called modern ideas of government, by which they meant British ideas of government. The question was how to do this without causing African culture and society to break up completely. Somehow the British convinced themselves that the best method was to 'purify' African institutions and govern Africans through them. Practices like human sacrifice, slave dealing and slavery, twin murder and secret societies were to be suppressed. After this reform had been carried out new ideas of government and development were to be gradually introduced into African society through what remained of the traditional system.

The above was not the only reason why the British chose to govern their African subjects through local African political institutions. On most occasions the British found that they had not enough men to control effectively the areas they brought under their rule. This situation arose partly because the British government was not prepared to spend much money on the colonies, and partly because the climate of West Africa made service there unpopular among the British people. Also the latter did not forget that they came to West Africa mainly to satisfy their economic needs. They wanted to create markets for their goods and to encourage West Africans to produce those raw materials which they needed. In order to do this it was not necessary to abolish everything African. The British therefore decided not to involve themselves more than was necessary in the business of governing their West African colonies.

For these reasons they governed these colonies by means of a system popularly known as indirect rule. The British claimed that under this system they did not rule their West African subjects directly, but through those local chiefs and elders by whom the people were being governed in the days before the colonial era. There was no single British officer who introduced this system throughout British West Africa. We have already seen how George Maclean co-operated with Fante chiefs in maintaining law and order on the Gold Coast. His example was continued by those who succeeded him. In 1878 the authorities of the Gold Coast colony passed an ordinance which authorised the chiefs of the colony and their councillors to make bye-laws on local matters, and to form courts in which they would try those who broke any of these bye-laws. The chiefs and their councils were also given the right to try civil and criminal cases which were not of a very serious nature. Though the British exiled Prempeh of Asante and his leading chiefs in 1896 they recognised the minor chiefs and tried to use them in local government.

Warrant Chiefs

In the region of Nigeria the same policy was being carried out. Here it was traders who started it all. We have already seen how along the

Niger Delta they co-operated with the local chiefs through the Court of Equity. When the Royal Niger Company was made to rule Northern Nigeria, it attempted to do so by not undermining the authority of the Emirs of the region. Under the Niger Coast Protectorate the example of the Court of Equity was continued. Institutions called Native Councils and Minor Courts were formed and given the power to make bye-laws, to regulate local matters and to try certain classes of cases. The members were all supposed to be traditional chiefs, but in the region later known as Eastern Nigeria they were not. This area had no prominent chiefs, but somehow the British managed to select some people whom they compelled to become chiefs. They gave these people 'certificates of recognition' which were called Warrants. For this reason these men were popularly known as Warrant Chiefs. Apart from trying cases and passing bye-laws the Warrant Chiefs also recruited and supervised the men who built the main roads and government stations. In the same way the Lagos government in the 1890s created in Yorubaland Native Councils which comprised local chiefs and carried out duties very much like those which chiefs in other parts of British West Africa carried out. In the Sierra Leone and Gambia Protectorates British political officers were also doing their best to make use of indigenous chiefs in local government.

Lugard in Nigeria

Thus by 1900 the policy of using African chiefs in local government was already well established in British West Africa. In that year Sir Frederick Lugard became the High Commissioner of the Protectorate of Northern Nigeria. Like other British Governors and High Commissioners in West Africa he found that he had not enough European officers to administer the region effectively. The Protectorate was not only very extensive, but also there were no good roads. Lugard was therefore happy to find that the Emirs had centralised governments which he could use easily and cheaply. And since the Fulani Emirs did not resist British conquest very vigorously Lugard had no fears in using them. The Emirs on their side were happy to find that the British did not intend to displace them completely and so co-operated with Lugard who told them plainly that he would respect their rules of succession as well as their religion. He also allowed them to impose and collect taxes as before and to try cases in their Muslim Courts. He issued the Native Courts Proclamation to legalise and define their judicial powers; and allowed them to have their own prisons where those convicted in the Native Courts served their terms. In each province he created what he called a Protectorate Court to serve as a court of appeal from the Native Courts. The Protectorate Court was presided over by the Resident and was the highest court to which the case of an indigenous Northerner could go. In this way Lugard sought to prevent the application of English law to Northern Nigerians. In 1904 he got the chiefs to pay a quarter of the revenue they collected from taxation to the central government while using the remainder for their private purposes.

Lugard left Northern Nigeria in 1906. Between 1906 and 1911 those who succeeded him went further in developing his particular method of using chiefs in local government. They got the chiefs to agree to the formation of what were called Native Treasuries into which they paid a part of the remaining three quarters of the sum they collected from direct taxation. The revenue which came through the Native Courts in the form of fees and fines also went into the Native Treasuries. All this money was to be used in providing local amenities and in paying those employed by the local government. Under the Emir was the District Head and under the latter the Village Head. If the British wanted something done they told the Emir who told the District Heads who passed this on to the Village Heads who in turn got their people to carry out the orders.

By means of this system Britain succeeded in bringing the large area of Northern Nigeria under control very quickly and cheaply. It was largely because of this success that the British concluded that of all attempts at ruling Africans through their chiefs, Lugard's was the best. In this however they forgot that this so-called success was owed to the nature of the political system then existing in Northern Nigeria. In 1912 Lugard came back to Nigeria. In 1914 he brought the northern and southern portions of the country under one administration. At once he condemned the other attempts which had been made in Southern Nigeria to rule through local chiefs. Because the approach in Southern Nigeria differed from that in Northern Nigeria he concluded that it was not indirect rule and that therefore it was pernicious. He then tried to impose his northern system on Southern Nigeria. Among the Yoruba people this meant that he gave the Obas more powers than they had in traditional law and custom. His attempt to levy taxation after the fashion in Northern Nigeria caused much resentment and led to a riot among the Egba in 1918 in which lives were lost. In the area east of the Niger he singled out some Warrant Chiefs and made them paramount chiefs overnight. This led to great confusion. He also wanted to introduce direct taxation there but

Frederick Lugard

failed. The confused situation which Lugard left behind east of the Niger later led to the Women's Riot of 1929 in which many women were shot down by government forces.

Lugard retired from Nigeria in 1919 and in 1922 published his famous book *The Dual Mandate in Tropical Africa* in which he discussed in great detail the theory of his particular method of ruling Africans through their chiefs. By this time Lugard had become very famous as a great colonial administrator. Even the League of Nations invited him to give advice on how dependent peoples should best be governed. The British concluded that many of their administrative problems in West Africa would be solved if all their West African colonies adopted Lugard's own principles of indirect rule. From 1931 local government legislations in the Gold Coast Colony sought to apply these principles to the Fante. From 1935 they were applied to the Asante, from 1939 to the Sierra Leone Protectorate, from 1933 to the Gambia Protectorate. In this way Lugard's own particular method of using chiefs in local government became more famous than those of the other administrators who long before him had also in their own different ways used chiefs in local government. As we shall see later all the hopes which the British placed on Lugard's type of indirect rule were to be sadly disappointed.

Differences between French and British administration policies

There were two major differences between the British and French methods of using African chiefs in local government. The first was that the British tried as much as possible to see that all the chiefs they used were traditional rulers, whereas the French were not particular on this point. As we have already seen the canton chief was usually not a traditional chief. However, this does not mean that the British did not sometimes make the mistake of using people who were not chiefs. We have already seen that in what later became Eastern Nigeria they created artificial Warrant and Paramount Chiefs to whom they gave excessive powers. In the non-Muslim parts of Northern Nigeria they created artificial District Heads and in this way caused much resentment among the people. In Western Nigeria they gave the Obas more powers than they usually had and since this made the Obas independent of their traditional councils it tended also to make them artificial. The second main difference between the British and French methods was that the British were more inclined to respect the chiefs under them and to give them more powers than the French did. This did not mean that where the British found a chief difficult to control they did not discipline him. The result of this second difference between the French and British systems was that the French system led to more efficient government. The French officer looked into everything a chief under him did, while the British officer left too much in the hands of the local chief, believing that a certain amount of inefficiency, corruption and even oppression must be tolerated if African chiefs must be used at all. It is, however, noteworthy that ultimately the French and British methods virtually led to the same result. They caused African chiefs to lose their traditional character. African chiefs became independent of their people and instead came to depend on their colonial masters. They also ceased to perform many traditional functions which the French and the British regarded as uncivilised. Since it was through them that changes were introduced into African society, the chiefs too became greatly changed in the process.

The British pattern of central government in their West African colonies also differed from that of the French. The British administered each of their four colonies separately from the others. This was partly because the British colonies were so widely separated that they could not be efficiently administered from one centre. Earlier attempts to do so had failed. In the 1820s the British had attempted to administer the Gold Coast and Gambia from Freetown, but this was soon abandoned as unsatisfactory. After 1865 they had also tried to administer Lagos, the Gold Coast, Sierra Leone and Gambia from a common capital. This too had failed. But the fact that Britain administered each of her West African colonies independently did not prevent her from applying to them the same kind of governmental system. We have already seen how in each colony an attempt was made to rule the Africans through their chiefs. Later still Lugard's particular method of indirect rule was applied to all of them. In the same way Britain divided each of her West African territories into two main sections. The first was the coastal region in which European influence had been present for a long time. To this region she first applied the so-called crown colony system of government. The main feature of this system was that the Governor passed laws for the colony with the advice of a legislative council dominated by government officials. Behind the colony, that is in the interior, was the section usually known as the protectorate which was inhabited by people who had not been under European influence for a long time. For these people the Governor legislated by proclamation, that is without the advice of any group of people supposed to represent the inhabitants of the protectorate. It was only after many years that the colony and the protectorate areas in each British West African territory were brought under the same legislature. One or two examples could be given.

In 1874 a legislative council was established for the Gold Coast colony. It had the power to pass laws for the colony, to set up local government bodies, to levy taxation and to encourage the provision of amenities. But it was not until 1946 that the Asante protectorate and the Gold Coast colony came under the same legislative council. The Northern Territories of the Gold Coast continued to be outside the area of authority of this body until much later in 1951. In Nigeria the colony of Lagos got a legislative council in 1862. In 1914 Lugard modified this body, renamed it the Nigerian Council and gave it the power to discuss matters affecting the whole country. Eight years later, however, Governor Clifford removed Northern Nigeria from the area of authority of this body which he reconstituted and renamed a legislative council. It was not until 1946 that the whole country was again brought under the authority of a central legislative body.

The British, unlike the French, did not attempt to pass laws in London for all their West African colonies. On the contrary the Governor of each territory drew up laws according to the needs of the area under his authority. But before these laws were applied they were sent to the Secretary of State for the Colonies in London for his approval and if he found anything he did not like in any law, he could order it to be removed or cancel the law altogether. It is therefore not surprising that many of the laws of British West African colonies tended to be based on the same principles. In a later section in this chapter we shall examine the reactions of West Africans to these two patterns of European rule.

Economic policies and developments

British and French attitudes towards the economic development of their West African colonies were very similar. Each of the two powers was concerned with encouraging West Africans to produce raw materials for her home industries. Both knew very well that the export of these raw products would bring more money into the hands of West Africans, and that with this money the latter would become increasingly able to buy more and more European manufactured goods. French and British economic policies in West Africa were thus very selfish; they were designed to benefit mainly the colonial powers. Throughout their years of rule in West Africa these powers spent their time promoting the production of export crops, but never attempted to encourage the increased production of locally consumed staple foods. There were research centres which sought to improve the yield of rubber, palm trees, cocoa, cotton and other cash crops, but none which tried to discover cheaper and better ways of growing and storing yams, cassava, millet and other local foodstuffs. For the same reason neither of these powers was interested in establishing industries in their West African colonies. Attempts which were made by local French officials to create industries in territories under their charge were vehemently opposed by French businessmen who feared that colonial industries would rival the home industries of France. Consequently cocoa, timber, palm oil, groundnut, leather, cotton and rubber were grown in West Africa and sold to European businessmen at very cheap rates. They took these crops home, processed them and brought the finished products back to West Africa to sell at a great profit.

From the beginning of their rule, therefore, these powers took such steps as they believed would help them realise their economic aims. They abolished trade by barter as well as indigenous currencies because they said these did not make for quick business. Trade by barter was slow while indigenous currencies were too cumbersome to be carried about easily and conveniently. In place of these the colonial

Laying railways in the Gold Coast

powers introduced their own currencies which helped to increase the speed of economic transactions. If trade was to flourish it was necessary to have efficient means of communication. West African rivers were not all navigable for long distances nor all the year round. The Niger and the Senegal, for instance, could be navigated by fairly big steamers up to certain points for only three months in the year. The rivers of the Gold Coast, the Volta and the Pra, were even more useless for purposes of communication. France and Britain therefore decided early on to build railways and modern motor roads in their West African possessions as a means of solving the communication problem. Between 1882 and 1906 the French built a railway line, 320 miles long, from Kayes on the Senegal to Bamako on the Niger to link the upper Niger and the Senegal. As the port of St. Louis did not prove very suitable for modern ocean-going vessels, the French built a railway to link it with Dakar which had a better harbour. By 1923 the French had built another line connecting this Dakar–St. Louis line to the Kayes–Bamako line. From their other stations along the coast they also built other lines to promote easy access to the Sudan. These lines, which started from Conakry in Guinea, Abidjan in the Ivory Coast and Cotonou in Dahomey sought to reach the Niger, but only the one from Guinea succeeded in getting to one of the tributaries of this great river.

The British were equally vigorous in building railways in their West African colonies. Gambia, a small country, needed no railway line since it was satisfactorily served by the river from which it derives its name. The British therefore merely built roads to feed the river. Gambia was also lucky in having a good natural harbour in Bathurst. Railway construction began in Sierra Leone in March 1896, in the Gold Coast in 1898, and in Nigeria in 1896. By 1932 there were about 311 miles of railway in Sierra Leone, 510 miles in the Gold Coast and 1,905 miles in Nigeria. Like the railways of French territories those of British West Africa were built to serve specific purposes. The Y-shaped railway system of Sierra Leone tapped the palm oil producing regions of the country. In the Gold Coast the line from Takoradi to Kumasi passed through the gold mines and was useful for transporting the heavy equipment needed for mining gold at great depths. The eastern line from Accra to Kumasi passed through the cocoa producing regions. In Nigeria the lines from Lagos and Port Harcourt not only passed through the palm belts of the south but also traversed Northern Nigeria from which the British got groundnut as well as hides and skins. Roads were also built to supplement these railways, while ports and harbours were improved. This revolution in communications did not serve only economic purposes. It enabled the French and the British to move soldiers and policemen easily to any region where their rule was challenged by force of arms. It also made it possible for a political officer to supervise the administration of a large district.

Colonial development funds

Apart from helping to build railways, roads and harbours Britain and France did little else of permanent significance to promote economic development in West Africa. For a long time France had no money to spend on her colonies, while her businessmen were reluctant to invest their capital in West Africa. British businessmen were better than their French counterparts in this respect but their half-hearted efforts did not produce any remarkable change. From 1929 the British government started to set aside a sum of one million pounds annually for the purpose of supplementing the scanty resources of all her colonies. But this sum turned out to be too small to serve any great purpose. The result was that the colonies continued to depend on money raised locally. However, 1940 brought a great change in British policy for in that year Britain passed the Colonial Development and Welfare Act which enabled her to set aside £5,000,000 annually for the development of her dependent territories. Another sum of £500,000 was set aside to promote research. In 1945 another act was passed which authorised the British government to spend the sum of £120,000,000 on her colonies in the period 1945–55. To enable this sum to be distributed according to need, the colonies were asked to submit their development plans for that ten-year period. Nigeria proposed to spend £53,000,000 in the period and of this sum £23,000,000 was to come from the Colonial Development and Welfare Fund. Sierra Leone planned to spend £5,250,000 of which £2,900,000 was to come from Britain; Gambia £2,000,000 of which £1,300,000 was to come from Britain and the Gold Coast £75,000,000 of which £3,000,000 was to come from Britain. The Gold Coast was at the time the richest British West African territory and so received proportionally least of all. In 1946 the French followed the British example by passing a law which enabled their government to set up its own colonial development fund from which grants were made to French West Africa. It has been estimated that under this arrangement French West Africa got from France four times the sum of money which Britain spent on her West African territories in the years after the war.

Results of colonial economic policies

On the whole British and French economic policy in West Africa produced similar results. In the first place the chief source of revenue for either the French or British colonies remained the export of raw materials. In the second place the greater part of the foreign trade of these colonies was in the hands of their metropolitan countries. The French were the worse offenders in this matter. To discourage other European nations from entering into direct trade with their dependencies they imposed very high tariffs on non-French goods. Britain did not adopt exactly the same method, but somehow her businessmen dominated the trade of her West African colonies. Also somehow the inhabitants of British West Africa came to believe that only British goods could be of good quality. Goods from other places were indiscriminately despised as cheap and inferior. In the third place developments in both French and British West Africa were concentrated in the forest or coastal areas. The rich regions of French West Africa were the Ivory Coast, Senegal, Guinea and Dahomey in that order. The other four colonies remained very poor. In British West Africa the Gold Coast was the richest owing to her cocoa and gold which came from the Asante and Fante regions respectively. The greater part of Nigeria's revenue came from cocoa, palm produce, timber and rubber which are all southern products. The chief export of Northern Nigeria was, and is, groundnut which in 1950 amounted to about one-sixth of Nigeria's total export.

This difference in the economic development of the Sudanic and forest regions is not surprising. The Sudan is not thickly populated, and thus lacks man-power. Its soil is also drier and poorer than that of the forest zone. Since the colonial powers were not prepared or able to undertake extensive development schemes the region with the natural advantages of thicker population density and richer soil remained economically in advance. This explains why British West Africa was relatively richer than French West Africa. As we have already seen, French West Africa lay mainly in the drier and poorer Sudan, while British West Africa lay mainly in the wetter and more fertile forest zone. Another important result of French and British economic policy in West Africa is the fact that the economic development of the region has depended entirely on peasant enterprise. Though Europeans were the first to grow coffee and bananas in a place like the Ivory Coast, the growth and export of cash crops in West Africa lies entirely in the hands of West Africans. They own the plantations and they supply the labour. It was once thought that Africans were very lazy but the continued increase of export crops from West Africa produced by Africans themselves without forced labour has proved this assumption false. Europeans found the West African climate very trying. They also discovered that almost all the land was occupied. For these reasons they made no attempt to seize the land from the people as they did in places like Algeria, East and South Africa. In this situation they had no alternative but to allow the people to occupy and cultivate their land and export their products. The last important result of the French and British attitude to the economic development of West Africa is the fact that the industrialisation of the region had to wait till after independence. Independent West African nations have been struggling to build local industries in which they would process their own raw materials, because this would not only provide jobs for their peoples but would also enable them to make more money from their own labour by selling the goods at increased prices in the world market. Industrialisation would also make it possible to pay lower prices for the manufactured goods.

Since for a long time neither Britain nor France was ready to spend much money on the development of her West African territories, the colonial governments remained too poor to provide adequate social services. Hospitals and schools remained few in number and ill-equipped, most of them having been built and maintained by missionary societies. Many areas lacked roads, while many of the roads which were built were not properly maintained. The British in West Africa were noted for narrow and winding roads. Proposed railway schemes were not carried out in full owing to shortage of funds. It is true that the colonial powers brought a number of improvements to West Africa yet one can say that if they had been less selfish and grudging in their economic and social policies they would have brought about even more rapid development.

Nationalism in West Africa

In the period of colonial rule nationalism in West Africa meant almost entirely a refusal to submit to foreign rule, and it took different forms at different times. We have already seen how West African peoples and their rulers tried at first to prevent by force of arms the imposition of European rule. In this they failed for reasons we have already discussed. But the story did not end there. The colonial powers soon adopted the trick of dividing the ranks of their African opponents by persuading or forcing West African chiefs to co-operate with them in the work of ruling the region. In areas where the chiefs were easy to discover the strategy succeeded to a great extent. But in those places where it was not easy to say who was a chief the traditional rulers, who were usually suspicious of the newcomers, successfully avoided co-operating with them. The ordinary people, who were thus in many places left leaderless, continued the resistance to foreign rule in different ways. Many of them refused to have anything to do with the new ways of the colonial powers and instead tried to live their lives as their fathers had done. From time to time this group of people rose in open rebellion either against taxation or the Native Courts or oppressive road work, but they were usually easily suppressed by the colonial army and police. What was more it was impossible to boycott the new ways completely. Some might refuse to go to church, or to take cases to the new and alien courts or to send their children to school or even to dress in the new fashions, but they could not refuse to use the new currencies or the new roads, or even to hear or see new things which they would normally not want to hear or see. The other section of the people reacted in a different way. They felt that the colonial powers were able to defeat them because of the many new and wonderful feats which they could perform. This group therefore concluded that the best thing to do was to send their children to school and workshops to learn these new ways and techniques in order to be able to meet the white man on equal grounds. Unfortunately, however, many of those who were sent to

Chiefs in Nigeria 'agreeing' to submit to British rule

learn the white man's ways came back to want things which their fathers did not quite like. This, however, is a different story and cannot be told here. The relevant aspect from our standpoint here is that they came back well-equipped to fight the white man. It is how this group fought and defeated their colonial masters that we are concerned with here and in much of the chapter that follows.

We have already seen how European activity, especially missionary enterprise, along the coast of West Africa led to the rise of a group of West Africans who were educated along European lines. As European rule expanded and as the missions spread their influence into the interior this class grew in number. Somehow British West Africa produced more people educated according to European tradition than French West Africa. At first this is surprising since the French tried to assimilate their subjects to French culture while the British did not. The explanation lies in the fact that the French did not give enough encouragement to missionaries working in their colonies. Ever since the Revolution of 1789 the French people had come to distrust the church. From 1903 the French government refused to give financial assistance to mission schools in their colonies and in her West Africa territories allowed education to be taken over by the colonial government. Since the French had not enough money to spend on their colonies this meant that many French West Africans had a limited chance of receiving western education. In British West Africa the situation was different. The British gave the missionaries a free hand, except perhaps in the Muslim areas where the colonial government did not want to offend the Muslims. Since various missionary bodies competed with one another in the establishment of schools, many British West Africans had a chance of receiving western education. This was one of the reasons why the struggle for political power between the new West African élite and the colonial powers started earlier in British than in French West Africa.

Also the élite in French West Africa were better treated by their colonial masters than their counterparts in British West Africa. They got well-paid jobs in the administration, and as civil servants could not criticise the government. Those of them who were not employed in West Africa even found employment in France itself. Thus they did not experience racial discrimination. In fact those of them who attained a certain level of education and showed loyalty to France were, as we have already seen, given French citizenship and enjoyed the same civil and political rights as Frenchmen. In Senegal the élite enjoyed the honour of being represented in the French National Assembly. This sometimes meant that protests against the colonial régime were heard in Paris rather than in West Africa. Furthermore, for the few who were not happy under the French régime there was no scope for political agitation which was banned until 1946. French political officers had at their disposal the *indigénat* which gave them wide powers over those labelled as troublesome subjects. As a result of all this, opposition to French rule was very limited. A few African journalists in Paris or Senegal or Cotonou asked for the abolition of the *indigénat* and for the removal of the difference between citizens and subjects. Some of those who were qualified to become citizens refused to do so in order to retain their African status. Some of these also developed an interest in African history and culture to show that Africa had a civilisation of her own. But there was no serious political agitation in French West Africa for a very long time, not in fact until after the Second World War.

The élite in British West Africa had every reason to protest against British rule. British officers treated them with contempt and often referred to them insultingly as 'black Englishmen' or 'apes in trousers'. The British argued that because of their western education the new African élite were not qualified to lead their people or to speak for them. The British said that Britain would prepare her African subjects for self-government through the system of indirect rule, because it was the chiefs rather than the new élite who were the true leaders of the masses. This policy offended the educated elements for various reasons. In the first place it meant that they would not find employment in local government since it was believed that indirect rule had no need for educated men. The lawyers were not allowed to practise in the Native Courts, and the Protectorate Courts took the place of Magistrates' Courts in many places. In the second place the new élite felt that indirect rule was a very slow method of preparing Africans for self-government. The chiefs were generally illiterate, conservative and ignorant of the modern methods of government which the new élite wanted to introduce. The latter soon came to the conclusion that the British ruled indirectly because they wanted to rule their West African subjects for ever.

The legislative councils were another source of trouble between the new élite and the British colonial administration. These bodies were expected to advise the Governors on how to govern Africans yet the majority of the members were European political officers. The few Africans who were members were nominated by the Governors, and generally the Governors chose those whom they felt would not criticise violently their administration. The new élite accused the British of hypocrisy. If the government were honest, they argued, it should allow Africans to choose those who should represent them, and furthermore Africans should form a majority in the body that helped to decide about their future. Since the British refused to employ the élite in large numbers in the central government or at all in the local government, many British West Africans who went to the universities took to professions like law, medicine and engineering which they could practise on their own. As these men did not depend on the government for their livelihood they could criticise and abuse the government as much as they liked. And as many of them were lawyers who liked argument they found fault with everything the government said or did and sometimes with what the government did not say or did not do.

The National Congress of British West Africa

We have already seen how early in this struggle with the colonial powers the Sierra Leone élite adopted the tactics of grouping themselves together as a means of achieving their ends. The practice grew in strength as the struggle spread from Sierra Leone to the rest of British West Africa. In 1897 the educated elements in the Gold Coast colony and their chiefs formed the Aborigines' Rights Protection Society led by J. W. Sey, the President. The purpose of this society was to protest against a law which the government wanted to pass to control the rate at which people sold their lands to foreign companies. Some people thought that the British wanted to seize their land, while some of the lawyers knew very well that if the law were passed they would not have enough land cases. Yet land cases were, and are, very lucrative. This was a time when the new élite and the chiefs could agree as indirect rule had not yet succeeded in creating a misunderstanding between the two groups. The Aborigines' Rights Protection Society succeeded in preventing the passage of the obnoxious law. In 1917 many educated elements from the different parts of British West Africa came together and formed the National Congress of British West Africa under the leadership of J. E. Casely Hayford, a Gold Coast lawyer and journalist. The Congress insisted that Britain should give each of her West African colonies a legislative council in which half the members would be elected Africans. It also demanded that the African members of the council should alone have the power to impose taxation, that chiefs should be left under the control of their peoples as in days gone by, that Britain should give Europeans and Africans equal chances in the civil service and that a university

J. E. Casely Hayford

should be established in British West Africa. In 1920 the Congress
sent a delegation to London to persuade the Secretary of State for the
colonies to grant these points, but the requests were refused. The
Governors of the Gold Coast and Nigeria refused to listen to the
Congress because, they claimed, the members had no right to speak

for their fellow Africans. By this time the new élite and the chiefs no longer agreed. The chiefs of the Gold Coast even sent a delegation to London to tell the Colonial Secretary that the Congress did not speak for them. Sir Hugh Clifford, the Governor of Nigeria, left nothing unsaid to make the Congress look ridiculous. He made fun of the idea that either West Africa or Nigeria could be a nation.

After attacking the Congress very bitterly Sir Hugh Clifford in Nigeria and Sir Gordon Guggisberg in the Gold Coast came round to grant the educated elements of the coastal cities the right to elect

J. E. Casely Hayford in London with members of the delegation from the National Congress

some of the African members of the legislative councils. In 1922 Clifford abolished Lugard's Nigerian Council which had proved useless and in its place created a legislative council for Lagos and Southern Nigeria. Of the ten African members four were to be elected, three from Lagos and one from Calabar. The Gold Coast constitution was likewise revised in 1925, and Accra, Cape Coast and Sekondi were given the right to elect their representatives to the council. However the legislative councils continued to be dominated by European officials. In Nigeria out of forty-six members of the council twenty-seven were government officials and only ten were Africans while the other nine were Europeans representing various interests. The Gold Coast council contained sixteen officials, nine Africans and five other Europeans representing different interests. In the Gold Coast there was another feature of the council which offended the new élite. Six out of the nine Africans were chiefs who by this time had come to be regarded as stooges.

With the coming of these revised constitutions the National Congress of British West Africa started to decline. The educated elements in Nigeria and the Gold Coast concentrated their attention on fighting the election to their respective legislative councils. For this purpose Herbert Macaulay formed in 1923 the Nigerian Democratic Party which from then on dominated Lagos politics until 1938 when it was eclipsed by the Nigerian Youth Movement whose origin goes back to 1934.

Thus by the time the Second World War came in 1939 the educated élite in British West Africa had not achieved much in their fight against colonial rule. They were handicapped by many things. The British were still convinced that the new élite had neither the ability to govern nor the right to speak for their fellow Africans and so held them in contempt. To some extent these men were responsible for the way they were treated. They confined their activities to the highly westernised urban cities of the coast—Calabar, Lagos, Accra, Cape Coast, Freetown and Bathurst and thus failed to make any attempt to rouse their countrymen in the interior. Also their demands made them appear self-seeking. Rights to be employed in the civil service, representation in the legislative council, employment of Africans in the judiciary, the establishment of a university—these were all demands which benefited members of their class and which the majority of the people in the interior could not understand. None of them called for the end of alien rule. It was not until 1938 that the Nigerian Youth Movement asked that Nigeria be granted complete autonomy within the British Empire'. Then the nationalist leaders of these years were mostly moderates. Since they did not ask or press for much they received even more limited concessions. Furthermore the political groups which fought the nationalist battles of these years were not really modern political parties. The Aborigines' Rights Protection Society of the Gold Coast, the National Congress of British West Africa, the Nigerian Democratic Party: each was a loose collection of gentlemen dominated by a single personality. They all lacked proper organisation and discipline. However, they prepared the way for the rise later of modern political parties.

Nnamdi Azikiwe

Radical nationalism

But even before the Second World War came there were signs of change in the tactics of the new élite, as seen in the activities of an American-educated Ibo, Nnamdi Azikiwe. This remarkable man came back from the United States in 1934, and after failing to get a job under the Nigerian government went to the Gold Coast where from 1935 to 1937 he edited the newspaper known as *African Morning Post*. In 1937 he came back to Lagos and established his most influencial newspaper, the *West African Pilot*. Azikiwe differed from the politicians who preceded him in two things. He was radical and inclined to use violent language against the Europeans and thus won the admiration of his fellow Africans who were happy to see one of themselves who could speak plainly to the white masters. In the second place he was the first to attempt to get the people in the interior to take part in the modern political struggle. To this end he made his newspapers cheap and established dailies at Ibadan, Onitsha, Port Harcourt and Kano and in this way got many more people to know what the fight between the new élite and the British was all about. After the Second World War another American-educated West African, Kwame Nkrumah, did precisely the same thing in the Gold Coast. However the fact remains that when the Second World War came the colonial powers in West Africa still felt as secure as ever. In the then British West Africa there were still educated men who enjoyed humming the song *British Empire Shall Never Perish*. But the war brought about a complete change in the situation. How this change came about and its consequences will be dealt with in the next chapter.

6 West Africa since 1940

The triumph of nationalism

The Second World War affected the nationalist movement in West Africa in two main ways. Firstly, by the end of it many more people had started to take part in the nationalist struggle than had done so in the years before 1939. Secondly, the agitation became more vigorous and continuous than before. Even in the French territories the outlook of the élite became greatly changed, largely as a result of political developments in neighbouring British colonies which soon made the French-speaking West African élite ask first for internal self-government and then for independence.

Effects of World War Two on West Africa

In the course of their conflict with Hitler the Allied Powers had framed their propaganda in such a way as to rouse peoples in different parts of the world against Germany. For instance in article three of the Atlantic Charter the Allies promised to 'respect the rights of all peoples to choose the form of government under which they will live'. This declaration was welcome to all colonial nationalists as they believed it to mean that at the end of the war they would have the right to ask for, and be granted, self-government and independence. At the same time the Americans gave much encouragement to colonial nationalists by openly attacking imperialism and supporting the demands of oppressed peoples for justice and self-government. Whereas the British Prime Minister, Sir Winston Churchill, wanted article three of the Atlantic Charter to be applied only to European peoples, the Americans said it applied to all peoples throughout the world. Even within Britain there were men and women who raised their voices against imperialism. The Labour Party, for instance, came out in favour of granting all dependent peoples the right of self-determination. Also the activities of the West African Students' Union in London strengthened the demands of the nationalists at home. Through the union (the W.A.S.U.) which was formed in 1925, West African students pressed their demands for political reform through public lectures and lobbying for the support of sympathetic statesmen and members of parliament. Apart from helping to intensify the nationalist agitation the West African Students' Union provided training in political organisation and leadership for many of their members. Some of these came back later to become leading statesmen in their different countries.

Economic expansion

The war also caused a certain amount of economic expansion in West Africa for after the Allied Powers had lost control of the Far East in 1941 they came to depend on Africa to a greater extent than before for much of the raw materials which they needed either in industry or for feeding their peoples. This changed economic situation caused a rapid increase in the export and import trade of West Africa and brought much money to her peoples. The population expanded, new urban centres sprang up and more people were sent to school. Part of the end result was that a large section of West African peoples came under unsettling influences which made them more difficult to control than before, and more ready to listen to the propaganda of the new élite against alien rule. As the war drew to a close thousands of West African ex-servicemen came back with new ideas and attitudes as well as with stories which showed that Europeans were ordinary flesh and blood, some of whom worked as stewards, cooks, cleaners or even lived by begging. Much of the respect and fear which European administrators excited before 1939 had disappeared by the end of the war.

Formation of trade unions

The nationalists used this new and favourable situation to great advantage. They did not forget that because they had so far paid attention only to the coastal towns their right to speak for the people in the interior had been challenged. They therefore campaigned for, and secured, increasing support from the masses both along the coast and in the interior. The élite were further favoured by the fact that many trade unions had come into existence during the war years. As the cost of living rose in those years the workers formed unions to enable them to help each other and agitate for increased wages without being victimised individually. These unions became ready and formidable instruments in the hands of the nationalists for bringing pressure on Colonial governments. To strengthen their hands further, the élite formed properly organised political parties which had branches all over the country and newspapers in the urban centres for making their points of view known to the people. The roads and railways which the Colonial governments had built to serve economic and administrative needs were now put to nationalist advantage. Improved communication made it easy for a political party to maintain continuous contact with its many branches and to plan and carry out extensive campaigns.

Changing attitudes of France and Britain

We can therefore say that by 1945 the ground had been well prepared for the final stages of the political struggle between the nationalists and the colonial administrations. Even before the war ended there were signs that the latter, especially the British, had become aware of the need to grant more political rights to their dependent subjects. This change of attitude on the part of the colonial powers helps to explain why the nationalists were able to secure one concession after another without having to use physical coercion. Britain led the way in the business of admitting her colonial élite to the heritage of political power in her West African territories. In 1942, for instance, some unofficial members of the legislative councils of the Gold Coast and Nigeria were given seats on the Governors' executive councils which formerly contained officials only. The same development took place in Sierra Leone in 1943 but not until 1947 in Gambia. As a result of this concession Africans got a chance of taking some part in the discussion of government measures and proposals before they came to the legislative council. But this concession did not satisfy the nationalists for the unofficial elements in the executive council were too few to influence official policy appreciably. Furthermore, since they were made to take an oath not to reveal what was discussed in the executive council, these men could not give their fellow African unofficial members the benefit of their inside knowledge of government policy.

Constitutional revisions in British West Africa

Immediately after the war the constitutions of the Gold Coast and of Nigeria were further revised. The most important concession in these new constitutions introduced in 1946 was the fact that Africans were given an elected majority in the legislative council. Sierra Leone and Gambia reached the same stage in 1951 and 1954 respectively. However, this constitution aroused much criticism from the nationalists in the Gold Coast and Nigeria. In the first place the new élite bitterly attacked the fact that only a small fraction of the African unofficials were directly elected while the larger fraction were elected indirectly by the Native Authorities which the élite neither liked nor trusted. In the second place the executive council was not reformed: African membership was not increased and the unofficials in it were not given any specific functions to perform. The constitutional revisions of 1946 in the Gold Coast and Nigeria therefore merely gave Africans an increased opportunity of taking part in the discussion of government business, rather than the right to help in framing and carrying out policy which was the very thing the nationalists wanted. In Nigeria there were two other reasons why the constitution was vehemently attacked. One of these was that the Governor, Sir Arthur Richards, introduced the new constitution without consulting the political leaders of the nation, let alone the common people. The nationalists regarded this as a slight. In the second place the fact that under the constitution Nigeria was divided into three regions each of which had its own house of assembly and an executive council offended those nationalists who felt that Britain was deliberately trying to weaken the country by dividing it into three semi-autonomous units.

In 1951 the constitution was further revised in the Gold Coast and Nigeria, in 1953 in Sierra Leone and in 1954 in Gambia. The aim of this revision was to give the nationalists some responsibility for taking official decisions and for carrying them out; in short it was the first real step towards transforming the Governor's executive council into a modern cabinet. The African members of the executive council were increased in number and given ministerial positions though not all of them were attached to specific departments. In the Gold Coast, for instance, the executive was made to consist of the Governor who was president, Kwame Nkrumah who was Leader of Government Business, eight other African ministers, six of whom had portfolios, and three European officials who also held ministerial positions. The legislative assembly was reconstituted to comprise thirty-eight members elected directly by the people and thirty-seven elected indirectly by the Native Authorities. There were four aspects of this revised constitution which failed to satisfy the nationalists. The first was the presence in the executive council of European officials who did not in any way represent the people. The second was the fact that the executive was not responsible to the legislative, that is that the members of the legislature could not force all the members of the executive to resign at once, though they could force an individual minister to resign. The executive remained responsible to the Governor who could sack it. The third shortcoming of the constitution was that the ministers who had portfolios did not enjoy the right to make policies for their departments; policy-making remained the responsibility of the European heads of those departments. The duty of the African ministers was to answer questions about their departments in the legislature, to introduce matters touching their departments in the council of ministers and to co-operate with the European heads of their departments in carrying out policies approved by the government. The fourth complaint against this constitution was that the members of the legislature were not all directly elected.

However, slowly but steadily, these shortcomings were removed. In the Gold Coast the constitution was revised again in 1954. In the first place the executive became an all-African cabinet presided over by a Prime Minister who chose from his supporters in the legislature those who were to work with him. The Prime Minister had the right to dismiss or replace any of his ministers and the whole cabinet remained in office for as long as it had the support of the majority in the legislature. The ministers became directly responsible for their departments, though owing to lack of experience they tended to depend a great deal on the European permanent secretaries. Nigeria attained the same position in 1957, Sierra Leone and Gambia in 1958 and 1962 respectively.

The remaining complaint which the nationalists had against the legislature was removed in 1954 in the Gold Coast and Nigeria when it was conceded that all members of the legislature in each of these two countries had to come in by direct election. This concession was a major victory for the élite. We have already seen that there was a time when Britain thought that it was to the traditional rulers and not to the new élite that she would eventually hand over political power in West Africa. Even after the war Britain had entertained the idea of making the chiefs share in political power at the centre as shown in the constitutions she granted the Gold Coast and Nigeria in 1946 and 1951. This 1954 concession, therefore, was a confession by

Britain that she had hoped for too much from indirect rule and that her previous policy towards the new élite was unwise. Even in Sierra Leone and Gambia where the chiefs continued to be directly represented in the legislature, political power passed into the hands of the new élite with the granting of internal self-government.

British colonies gain independence

From internal self-government the next, and the last, stage in the victory of the new élite over the British was full independence with which each of these four territories got absolute control over its own internal and external affairs. On 6 March 1957 the Gold Coast attained this stage under the name of Ghana. Nigeria followed on 1 October 1960, Sierra Leone on 27 April 1961 and Gambia on 18 February 1964.

Since British policy after the Second World War was in favour of granting political power to the nationals of her West African colonies, on the surface it seems strange that the conflict between the nationalists and Britain not only continued but in fact became more bitter than in the years before 1939. There were two reasons for this. The first was that both groups could not agree on how soon self-government and independence should come. Britain believed that it would take some time since she felt she still had to train the nationalists in the business of running a modern state. The nationalists on their side were impatient of the official approach and accused the British of hyprocrisy. They refused to accept the view that they were not already well-equipped to exercise political power. In the second place, as we have just seen, Britain still believed that the native authorities which she had nurtured with so much care must be made to take an important part in central government. This, again, was unacceptable to the new élite who felt that the chiefs were too ignorant and too conservative to play any useful rôle in the political and economic development of a modern state. They accused the British of adopting this policy in order to prolong their rule in West Africa. These were the issues at the root of the bitter clashes between the British and the nationalists which took place in the period 1945 to 1954 in the Gold Coast and Nigeria. Constitutional progress in Sierra Leone and Gambia took place not necessarily as a result of the efforts of the nationalists there, but at times in response to developments in the other two British West African territories.

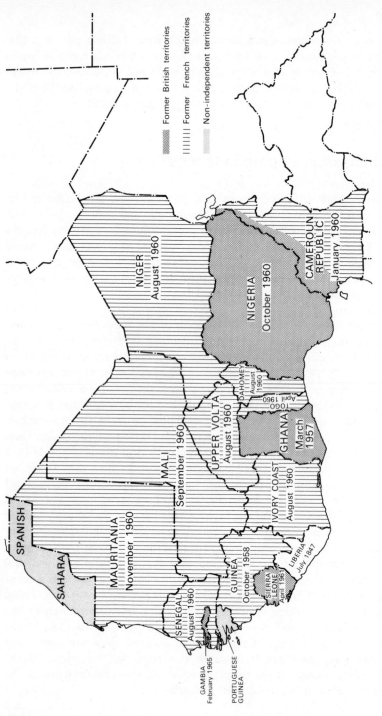

Independent West Africa

Legend:
- Former British territories
- Former French territories
- Non-independent territories

NIGER
August 1960

NIGERIA
October 1960

CAMEROUN
REPUBLIC
January 1960

DAHOMEY
August
1960

TOGO
April 1960

UPPER VOLTA
August 1960

GHANA
March
1957

MALI
September 1960

IVORY COAST
August 1960

SPANISH
SAHARA

MAURITANIA
November 1960

GUINEA
October 1958

LIBERIA
July 1847

SIERRA
LEONE
April 1961

SENEGAL
August 1960

GAMBIA
February 1965

PORTUGUESE
GUINEA

France grants political rights to her colonies

In less than two decades after the Second World War French rule in West Africa was likewise at an end. The French, like the British, showed themselves prepared to grant their colonies in West Africa more and more political rights after 1945. But whereas self-government and independence in English-speaking West Africa came as a result of pressure from the nationalists, in French-speaking West Africa the initiative came from the French themselves. In 1944, for instance, General de Gaulle called a meeting of France's colonial governors at Brazzaville to recommend what French colonial policy should be after the war. Though the conference denied that France could ever grant self-government to her colonies in Africa, it made important recommendations on how to reform French colonial administration. It advised the abolition of forced labour and of the *indigénat*. It also recommended that the powers of the Governor-General be reduced in order to give more powers to the administration in each territory. It suggested the setting up of an elected assembly in each colony to help the Lieutenant-Governor, and of a central council (Grand Conseil) to which all territories in French West Africa would send representatives. The conference also recommended that French West Africa should be represented in the constituent assembly which would draw up a new constitution for France after the war. The goal of post-war French colonial policy was the implementation of these suggested reforms.

French West Africa participated in the constituent assembly which met after the war. In the constitution which the assembly drew up the French empire was reorganised and renamed the French Union consisting of Metropolitan France, the Overseas Department and the Overseas territories in the latter of which French West Africa was included. All French West Africans were declared citizens and in this way the distinction between citizens and subjects disappeared. Forced labour was abolished, while a later decree abolished the *indigénat*. Also an elected assembly, known from 1952 as the Territorial Assembly, was set up for each colony. This assembly had more extensive powers in French Togoland and the Cameroun than in the rest of French West Africa. In 1947 a federal council known as *Grand Conseil* was set up under the High Commissioner (the former Governor-General) at Dakar. In addition to all these concessions at the local level French West African colonies were given the right to elect deputies to represent them in the French National Assembly and the Senate as well as in the Assembly of the French Union.

Inadequacies of French reforms

These reforms soon turned out to be inadequate. The French Ministry of Colonies continued to legislate for French West Africa and in doing so was not bound to take the advice of the deputies from there. The social reforms which were decreed were not carried out quickly: for instance the *indigénat* took time to disappear. Though all West Africans were declared French citizens, a new distinction was made between *French citizens of French status* and *French citizens of local status*. The former were subject to French law and so were considered superior to the latter who remained subject to their indigenous law. What was more, the Territorial Assemblies had only limited powers especially outside Togoland and the Cameroun. The élite in French West Africa in this period thus asked for increased powers for the assemblies, the introduction of democratic practices into the administration and for equality of social and political rights with Frenchmen. They did not, however, ask for self-government, nor were they ready to attack the administration as vigorously as their counterparts in British West Africa did. Therefore after 1946 France paid little attention to the question of political development in her West African territories for nearly a decade.

The *loi cadre*

It was largely due to happenings in British West Africa that France came to grant a further instalment of political rights to her colonies in 1956. In that year Félix Houphouet-Boigny, an Ivory Coast deputy to the National Assembly, who was given a cabinet post, helped France in framing the *loi cadre* (Enabling Law) which gave the French government extensive powers for carrying out political reforms in West Africa. A series of decrees issued under this law by the French Ministry of Colonies granted a form of internal self-government to each territory. Each Territorial Assembly was granted the power to elect, from among its members, a council of ministers which under the presidency of the Governor (the former Lieutenant-Governor) constituted the executive for the territory. The minister who had the largest vote in the assembly was made the vice-president. The council of ministers resigned if it was defeated in the assembly. Each Territorial Assembly was given the right to pass laws for its area of authority on such subjects as agriculture, health, primary and secondary education, internal trade and civil service, each of which came under a minister. Subjects like defence, foreign affairs, currency and economic development remained in the hands of the metropolitan government, and laws passed on them were carried out under the direction of the High Commissioner. In Togoland and Cameroun the reforms went a little further. The former became an autonomous republic within the French Union in 1956. But though it was given a Prime Minister its assembly had the same powers as those of other French West Africa territories. Cameroun attained the same status as Togoland in 1957.

De Gaulle's referendum

The above changes satisfied a large section of the new élite in French West Africa, but a few radicals insisted on full independence. Then in 1958 General Charles de Gaulle became French President, and in the new constitution which he published in July that year he decided to transform the French Union into the French Community. He saw the community as a sort of French Commonwealth of Nations, but unlike the British Commonwealth it was to be under the effective control of France. It was to have an executive council which would be made up of de Gaulle (president), a number of French cabinet ministers and the prime minister of each of the member states. This council would deal with issues of common interest to the community like defence, foreign affairs and economic policy. This constitution was to go for a referendum in September and the French West African territories had to choose between voting 'Yes' and becoming autonomous republics within the community, or voting 'No' and attaining immediate independence outside it. De Gaulle made it clear that any territory which chose the latter course would at once lose French economic and technical aid. Since the economy of the French West African territories was closely tied to that of France this threat succeeded in forcing nearly all of them to vote in favour of the con- stitution. Only Guinea voted 'No' to become independent overnight. For this France withdrew all assistance to her and even refused to accord her diplomatic recognition. In November 1958 the other territories became autonomous states within the community. But by this time complete independence had become the ultimate end which the new élite in these states had in view. Thus in 1959 Senegal and Soudan, which had meanwhile formed the Mali Republic, asked for an amendment of the constitution of the community in such a way as to allow them to achieve full independence without losing their

A poster from the French West African referendum of 1958. Only Guinea voted
against the referendum for immediate independence. France withdrew all aid

membership of the Community. This amendment was made and
by November 1960 all the former French West African colonies
had become fully independent states. With the exception of Guinea,
all the erstwhile French West African colonies remained closely

linked with France through agreements on such subjects as technical assistance, defence, currency and economic aid. Togoland and Cameroun also attained independent status about the same time as the other French Territories. In 1960 when the United Nations decided to end its trusteeship of these two territories, Togoland immediately became independent. Cameroun followed suit in 1961 after uniting to form the Cameroun Republic with the Southern Cameroons which had voted to remain outside the Federation of Nigeria.

Disagreement within post-war governments

An interesting feature of the politics of the post-war years in West Africa was the tendency for members of the élite to fight among themselves almost as bitterly as they fought their colonial masters. The reasons for this development varied from place to place and can be best understood by a study of the relationship which existed among the various political parties which came into existence within each territory at this time. We can start with the Gold Coast which was the first West African colony to attain independence.

Political parties in the Gold Coast

From the days of the Mankessin constitution to those of the Aborigines' Rights Protection Society and of the National Congress of British West Africa, the new élite in the Gold Coast had seemed to present a united front against the British. But with the coming of the post-war political concessions disagreements set in. In 1947 the new élite had formed the United Gold Coast Convention (U.G.C.C.) in response to the challenge of the Burns Constitution of the previous year. This party aimed at using all constitutional and legal means to press for self-government for the Gold Coast 'within the shortest time possible'. In 1948 Dr. Kwame Nkrumah was invited to become its Secretary-General. But it soon became clear that his attitude to political agitation was quite different from that of the foundation members of the U.G.C.C. The latter wanted to carry on in the leisurely manner which had characterised nationalist politics before 1939. They wanted to concern themselves with the colony and perhaps with Asante, but certainly not with the Northern Territories or the region beyond the Volta or with British Togoland. In short they had no plans for making politics an affair of the whole country and of the masses. Nkrumah on the other hand had contrary ideas. He wanted to call up the masses and to make the nationalist movement nationwide. For this purpose he sought the support of the trade unions and established newspapers at Sekondi, Cape Coast and Accra to inform the people. He also undertook tours of different parts of the country

Kwame Nkrumah, President of Ghana until the coup in 1966

during which he gave public lectures to educate the masses. Because he believed in militant politics he set up the 'Committee on Youth Organisation' which mobilised the youths of the country and affiliated them to the party. What was more, Nkrumah believed in achieving 'self-government now' rather than 'within the shortest time possible'. This radicalism proved too much for the leisurely gentlemen who founded the U.G.C.C. and they started planning to expel its author. But on 12 June 1949, a day before that on which he was to be expelled, Nkrumah took the radical elements out of the U.G.C.C. and formed the Convention People's Party (C.P.P.).

In 1954 the Gold Coast attained full internal self-government under the C.P.P. which derived most of its support from the colony area. As soon as it appeared that the British were about to hand over political power to the C.P.P. government, parties sprang up from various parts of the country to protect local ethnic interests. Already by 1954, there were about four such sectional parties in existence in the Gold Coast. The Northern People's Party rose to defend the Northern Territories against southern domination. The Togoland Congress Party wanted British Togoland separated from the Gold Coast and united with French Togoland. The National Liberation Movement which was based in Asante fought for Asante 'national' interests. In particular it was opposed to the C.P.P.'s policy of using the national income derived mainly from Asante cocoa for the development of the whole country. A Muslim Association Party which derived its support from Kumasi and the colony area was formed to protect the interests of the Muslims. The most important result of this rise of mutually opposed parties in the Gold Coast was that the new élite became divided on whether the country should have a federal or a unitary government. Those from Asante and the Northern Territories wanted a federation because they thought it would give them protection against the colony area. It was the C.P.P. alone that stood for a unitary constitution. The conflict between these two aims was in fact responsible for the fact that the Gold Coast did not become independent before 1957. And even when independence came in 1957 Regional Assemblies had to be set up for regions which wanted them as a means of allaying ethnic group fears. The bitterness which this disagreement bred among the nationalists still bedevils Ghana politics. As we shall see later it forced the C.P.P. government to take extraordinary measures in order to preserve the unity of the nation for which it had fought dearly.

Rival parties in Nigeria

Similar things happened in the rest of British West Africa. In Nigeria the Nigerian Youth Movement (N.Y.M.) broke into two factions in 1941 as a result of conflicts between its Ibo and Yoruba members. In 1944 one of the factions formed the National Council of Nigeria and Cameroons (N.C.N.C.) under the leadership of Herbert Macaulay. When the latter died in 1946 the party came to be led by Nnamdi Azikiwe. By the time of the Macpherson constitution in 1951 the N.C.N.C. derived its greatest following from among the Ibo. The Yoruba therefore felt that if they were to be saved from Ibo domination they must have a party that could speak for them. It was largely this fear that brought the Action Group into being in 1951. In the same way the Fulani and Hausa élite of Northern

Nigeria feared that if they did not organise their own party, independence would merely transform British rule into 'southern rule'. Their answer to this supposed threat was the formation of the Northern Peoples Congress (N.P.C.). At one stage, in 1953, the enmity between the southern parties and the N.P.C. nearly split Nigeria into two nations. The three parties came to agree on a federal constitution for the country as the best means of preserving the unity and ensuring that no single ethnic group dominated the others. This arrangement does not seem to have solved these problems as subsequent Nigerian politics clearly showed. Not all Northern Nigerians, however, belonged to the N.P.C. There were a few radical elements who regarded the N.P.C. as the party of backward-looking conservatives and autocrats. It was such men who formed the Northern Elements Progressive Union under Mallam Aminu Kano to press for democracy and rapid economic development in Northern Nigeria.

In Sierra Leone, and to a less extent in Gambia, the conflict was mainly between the more westernised coastal colony and the conservative and more backward inland Protectorate. The Sierra Leone People's Party (S.L.P.P.) which became the dominant party in Sierra Leone derived its main support from the more populous but less enlightened Protectorate.

The *Rassemblement Democratic Africain*

In French West Africa there were two main sources of disagreement amongst the élite and these are clearly brought out in the history of the *Rassemblement Democratic Africain* (R.D.A.) which was the most powerful political party in French West and Equatorial Africa. The R.D.A. was formed in October 1946 at Bamako under the leadership of Félix Houphouet-Boigny of the Ivory Coast. The African delegates to the French National Constituent Assembly had felt that they would be in a better position to exert a strong influence on French politics if they acted as a group. What was more, they wanted to fight the conservatives in the National Constituent Assembly who were not enthusiastic about colonial reform. Therefore they summoned a congress of political, trade union and youth leaders at Bamako in 1946. The French government, fearing that the Communist party would gain undue control over the Bamako congress, used its influence to keep some of the deputies away from it. For instance the Senegalese deputies—Lamine Gueye and Léopold Senghor—were prevailed upon not to attend. When the R.D.A. allied with the

Communist Party Léopold Senghor and the other African deputies who refused to join it came together and formed the parliamentary party known as the *Indépendants d'Outre-Mer* (I.O.M.: Overseas Independents). This was the party of moderates and was allied to the French Socialist Party. Thus after the Second World War the élite of French West Africa came to be openly split into radical and moderate groups.

Up to 1950 the R.D.A. enjoyed a measure of internal harmony and stability, but after that date it started to experience severe strains

Houphouet-Boigny, President of the Ivory Coast, with President de Gaulle

first because of ideological differences and then because of conflicting attitudes to the issue of federation in French West Africa. After 1950 Houphouet-Boigny came to favour compromise with the French government in place of the alliance with the French Communist Party. This policy of compromise was not acceptable to the Secretary-General of the R.D.A., Gabriel d'Arboussier, who led the radical wing of the party which favoured open defiance of France. The ensuing conflict soon led to the expulsion of the radicals. A further split among the élite followed as a result of the *loi cadre* of 1956.

Houphouet-Boigny was in favour of breaking up the federation of French West Africa. The Ivory Coast, as the richest French territory in West Africa, understandably did not like the way revenue derived from her crops was used for the development of the whole federation. Senegal was the second richest but she benefited from the fact that Dakar was the federal capital and so favoured maintaining the federation intact. Houphouet-Boigny supported the *loi cadre* because it weakened federal authority by giving each territory self-government. His ideal was independence for each territory and then federation with France. But other R.D.A. leaders, especially Sekou Touré of Guinea, wanted the federation maintained and strengthened and then granted complete independence of France. Léopold Senghor also favoured federal unity because he hoped that a united French-speaking West Africa would be in a stronger position than any individual territory to negotiate with France. France on her side wanted to break up the federation as she preferred dealing with each territory separately to dealing with the federation as a unit. An attempt in 1958 to bring all political parties in French West Africa together failed owing to this disagreement on the federal issue. When the R.D.A. refused to accept any compromise the small territorial parties came together and formed the *Parti Regroupement Africain* (P.R.A.). Before the internal conflicts in the R.D.A. could be resolved De Gaulle introduced his famous constitution for the French Community in 1958. This turned out to be the parting of the ways. The R.D.A. leaders in Guinea opted for immediate independence. The other territories in voting for the status of autonomous republic within the community helped in breaking up the federation. Still after 1958 federation remained a burning question in the politics of the former French territories. In December 1958 the P.R.A., which strongly continued to support the idea of federation, succeeded in getting Senegal, Soudan, Dahomey and Upper Volta to agree to the formation of a Mali federation. But before this verbal agreement could become practical politics Houphouet-Boigny and France brought pressure to bear on Dahomey and Upper Volta to stay out of the proposed union. In spite of this setback Senegal and Soudan went ahead to form the Mali federation in April 1959. In May the Ivory Coast sought to counter-balance the influence of this new bloc by forming the *Council of Understanding*, a loose economic union, with Upper Volta, Niger and Dahomey. In August 1960 the Mali federation broke up, Senegal withdrew leaving the name 'Mali' for the former Soudan. The idea of a French-speaking West African federation thus eluded its enthusiasts. Like their English-speaking counterparts the French-speaking élite found themselves uncompromisingly divided as the prospect for enjoying political power became brighter.

Post-independence trends and tendencies

Among the main problems which have confronted the new nations of West Africa since independence the most important are those of maintaining internal unity and of bringing about an economic revolution within the shortest time possible in order to raise the living standards of the masses. To some extent West African nations have tended to tackle these problems in the same way.

Each nation in West Africa is an artificial creation of the colonising powers with the result that the peoples who make it up are still too aware of their ethnic differences and peculiarities. The common experience of less than a hundred years of foreign rule has done little to lessen the centrifugal force of these differences. The truth of this opinion was clearly illustrated in the politics of these states just before independence as sketched above. West African statesmen have adopted two main methods of maintaining the unity of the states which they inherited at independence. Firstly, they have emphasised the separate identity of the nation to which they belong, even at the expense of alienating neighbouring African states. Under the colonial régime it was usual for a man from one colonial territory to work in another in West Africa under the same colonial power. For instance Sierra Leoneans worked and felt at home in the rest of British West Africa. In French West Africa which was administered as a unit this practice was even more developed. A large proportion of the Africans who worked in the administrative service of French West Africa came from Senegal and Dahomey. But since independence the tendency has been for non-nationals to be expelled and discriminated against in the recruitment of civil servants. In 1959 so many Dahomeans were expelled from Senegal that President Hubert Maga of Dahomey had to visit Senegal in connection with the matter. When in 1961 the Southern Cameroons became independent Nigerian civil servants and businessmen were forced to leave the country. This practice has attained ridiculous proportions in Nigeria where since 1957 Southern Nigerians have been forced out of jobs in Northern Nigeria under the 'Northernisation' policy. When the Mid-West Region was created in 1963 out of Western Nigeria, the government of the latter region gave all peoples from the new region a few days' notice to leave its service.

West African statesmen have also sought to maintain unity within each state by trying to form what might be called a united front of all peoples and groups within the state. Firstly all political parties and other groups—trade unions, youth organisations and so on—are encouraged to merge into central organisations in order to eliminate rival passions and competing interests. This tendency has been most pronounced in French-speaking West Africa where these different groups have since 1956 been merging to form nationwide organisations. In the field of politics the dominant parties have absorbed the smaller ones. This was the case in Guinea, Mali and Ivory Coast. In Ghana, though the trade unions had for long been closely allied to the C.P.P., steps were taken in 1963 to form them into one central body able to speak for all workers throughout the nation and co-operating with the C.P.P. in the work of building up Ghana. In Nigeria efforts were also made to form one central labour organisation but these failed.

Where persuasion and mild pressure have failed to produce a closing of the ranks, some nations have gone a step further and used government authority against rival parties and groups. Here the C.P.P. government of Ghana led the way. Immediately after independence it took strong measures against all those who were considered a threat to the unity and peace of the state. Foreigners suspected of meddling in the politics of Ghana were deported; parties based on sectional interests were declared illegal while uncooperative chiefs were destooled. When these measures failed to eliminate all forces tending to promote disunity the government passed the famous Preventive Detention Act of 1958. By this measure the government had the power to keep anybody suspected of subverting the state in detention for up to five years without bringing him to trial. The C.P.P. government used this power with such effect that Ghana became in practice, though not in law, a single-party state. In Upper Volta, Niger, Cameroun, Togo, Dahomey and Mauretania rival political parties have been officially banned. The Sierra Leone People's Party also showed itself unprepared to tolerate vigorous opposition in politics. In Nigeria, though the opposition was weak both at the federal and regional levels, there was nothing to show that the tendency was towards a one party system. Each of the major parties was firmly rooted in one region.

Economic development

The problem of maintaining the unity of the nation is closely linked with the problem of bringing about an economic revolution in West

Africa. All West African governments are fully aware of the economic backwardness of their countries. Also they all believe that in order to bring about a much needed economic revolution everyone in the state must make a positive contribution. In this programme there is no place for opposition for its own sake. If all the élite closed their ranks energy would be conserved and there would be no unnecessary waste of resources in election campaigns. The struggle for economic progress is regarded as a continuation of the struggle against alien rule. It is believed that if any nation is to be truly independent it must have a sound enough economy to maintain its own in this highly competitive world; it must also ensure that its economic life is not in foreign hands. It is these objectives that the economic programmes and development plans of West African governments have been struggling to achieve.

The problem here is twofold. The first is to convey the urgency of this economic revolution to the masses, a very difficult problem which different governments have tackled in different ways. In places like the Ivory Coast and Upper Volta laws have been passed authorising the government to draft men and women of over eighteen years of age into specified jobs for two years. Those who are discovered obstructing this drive could be placed under house arrest. In a place like Senegal units of the army have been used to push through urgent development projects. In other places where such striking measures have not been adopted statesmen have spoken again and again of the need for hard work and thrift.

The second aspect of the problem is to promote industrialisation. West African economy remained predominantly agricultural throughout the period of colonial rule. West African governments are now struggling to set up industries for processing local agricultural products. But this does not mean that agriculture is being neglected. On the contrary it is clearly realised that for a long time to come West African countries will derive the greater part of their revenue from the export of raw materials. Thus an effort is being made not only to increase the production of already established crops but also to experiment with new ones. Negotiations are also being conducted to secure better and more stable prices for these raw materials. In 1962, for instance, Ghana, Ivory Coast, Cameroun, Nigeria and Brazil formed an alliance designed to reduce competition in the cocoa market. Nigeria and Senegal have also set up a body to do the same thing for groundnuts.

West African economic development has tended to be more socialistic than capitalistic, that is, it has tended to depend more on state than on private enterprise. This is more so in certain countries than in others. In countries like Guinea and Mali the state has a monopoly of all large-scale economic enterprises. In Senegal it is the state that is responsible for buying and exporting groundnuts, the main cash crop of the country. In Ghana the C.P.P. government divided the economy into five sectors, in three of which the state was to bear the main burden of development. In Nigeria state participation in economic enterprise varies from combining with foreign firms to set up industries to the financing of major development projects like the Kainji dam.

There are many reasons for the socialistic trend in West African economic development. In the first place there are no private businessmen with sufficient capital and experience to play the part which the state is playing. In the second place large-scale private enterprise is distrusted, thanks to the part which foreign firms have played in the economic life of West Africans. In the third place many West African leaders have been influenced by Marxist and socialist thought, the French-speaking élite by the French Communist Party, the English-speaking élite by the British Labour Party. In spite of this, however, foreign companies still play a very important part in the economic life of West African nations. Hence statesmen have sought to limit the harm which they can do. The Ivory Coast has imposed extra taxes on the profits of the foreign companies, while Ghana in 1962 passed a law forcing foreign businessmen to reinvest at least sixty per cent of their profits in Ghana every year.

In spite of all this effort West African economic development has not been as rapid as envisaged in the various national development plans. The difficulties in the way have been many but only three main ones will be noted here. The greatest of these is the shortage of manpower of the right quality. The educational system of the colonial era was not designed to prepare West Africans for such a period of feverish economic development as we are now witnessing. Not only was the number of those who received any education severely limited, but many of the educated lacked the technical knowledge and skill to carry through the type of development programmes which are now being put forward. For the most part statesmen have had to rely on administrators who were trained only for routine administration rather than for planning and executing schemes which require high-level technical knowledge. Though attempts have been made to remedy this deficiency through a policy of vigorous expansion in education, the result still falls far short of the needs of the time. Secondly there is a shortage of capital. West African cash crops have not been fetching as much money as the makers of the development plans hoped. Nor has foreign aid been as liberal as was expected. Thirdly the politicians have not all proved themselves equal to the tasks facing them. Some of them have not given such dynamic and imaginative leadership as would inspire their peoples. Some have scared away foreign investors by the frequency with which they have 'discovered' plots to overthrow their régimes. Some have not had sufficient honesty to insist on efficiency and merit in the choice of the personnel whose work it is to carry out the development programmes. Others have allowed themselves to be guided by selfish sectional interests. Thus some of the key industries have either been sited in the wrong places or have not been built at all as a result of petty squabbles among the leading politicians. The desired economic revolution will begin to come as soon as West African statesmen are able to find solutions to these problems.

Part **three**

Southern and Central Africa

7 The consolidation of white rule in southern Africa

Soon after the rebellion of the Transvaal farmers and the re-establishment of virtual independence for the Transvaal Republic, the history of southern Africa began to undergo important changes.

As the industrial revolution spread from Britain to other countries in Europe, hitherto undreamt of power was placed in the hands of the new industrial nations. The world shrank as railways, steamships and the telegraph revolutionised communication and the search for raw materials and new markets for exports increased in intensity. Power struggles grew and soon the whole world was involved. Southern Africa now became immersed in the wider movement of the Partition of Africa, described in the Introduction.

The discovery of diamonds had already begun to turn southern Africa from a poor farming country into a relatively rich industrial one. Within five years of the Pretoria Convention, gold was discovered on the Witwatersrand and the whole economic position of the Transvaal and South Africa was transformed. The old quest for new farming land for white farmers continued but was now linked with the search for minerals, the financial resources of mighty capitalist organisations and international competition for territory in Africa. The racial attitudes of the old farming society were transferred to the new world of mines and industry, the battleground gradually shifting from the country to the towns. The process by which Africans had been brought under white rule was greatly speeded up and extended out of South Africa into modern Rhodesia, Zambia and Malawi. The Portuguese, after centuries spent holding a few isolated ports, suddenly woke up and established their authority over the vast areas of modern Portuguese East Africa. The Germans arrived in South West Africa. The struggle between the Boer desire for complete independence in their Republics and the British determination to maintain their paramount position in South Africa led to a major war which was to solve little and leave the deepest problems of South Africa untouched. However, it did prepare for the political unification of the country. By the end of the first decade of the twentieth century, white rule had consolidated itself in southern Africa.

Territorial expansion of the Transvaal after the First World War

Immediately following British withdrawal from the Transvaal, the republic began to expand vigorously. White farmers and adventurers took advantage of squabbles between chiefs to grab land and cattle. They supported one side and claimed huge areas in return and in 1882 they were able to set up two small Republics on the western border of the Transvaal, Stellaland and Goshen, with the passive support of the Transvaal authorities. The British Government was supposed to have overriding authority on questions of native policy in the Transvaal but the British Resident was treated with contempt and would do nothing to prevent the activities of the white adventurers. Similarly, a group of whites helped Dinizulu defeat contenders for the Zulu throne in return for which he was forced to surrender nearly half the remaining area of Zululand to the east of the Transvaal. A republic, the New Republic, was set up here in 1884.

This affected British interests: Stellaland and Goshen cut across the road to the interior that had been opened by the missionaries, Moffat and Livingstone, thus threatening British traders' access to the far interior. Britain first tried negotiating and in 1883 in London the British agreed to abandon the power of veto on native policy, to reduce the British Resident to Consul and to drop the word 'suzerainty' from the new convention. In return the borders of the new republics were altered so as to leave the road to the north outside them. The British retained control of the Transvaal's foreign policy and the Republic was not to make treaties with any state except the Orange Free State or with any tribes to the east or west without British approval. This 'London Convention' was ratified by the Transvaal Volksraad in 1884.

The rush for territory in southern Africa

As long as Britain did nothing to occupy areas supposedly outside the Transvaal, the danger of their eventually joining that state would still remain. Moreover, a new danger threatened British interests from 1883 when the German flag was hoisted at Angra Pequena Bay in South West Africa and the following year Britain was forced to recognise a German protectorate over the territory. It seemed Germany might try to link this new possession with the Transvaal thus severing the Cape from the interior and threatening the security of the Cape itself. To prevent this, a British expedition under Charles Warren annexed Stellaland and Goshen as British Bechuanaland. In 1895 a protectorate was declared over the lands of the chiefs Sechele and Khama and their area became the Bechuanaland Protectorate.

The eastward expansion of the Transvaal also seemed a danger. The Boers might gain control of a possible port at St Lucia Bay in Zululand and thus make contact with a foreign power, a fear heightened by the fact that the area round the bay was acquired from Dinizulu on behalf of the Transvaal by a German agent. As a precaution Britain annexed the area by virtue of an old treaty made with the Zulu king, Mpande. The leaders of the New Republic were forced to renounce their authority over the Zulu kingdom and the boundaries of their state were redrawn to keep them well back from the coast. In return Britain recognised the New Republic which later became part of the Transvaal. In 1887 the remains of Zululand were annexed and placed under the governer of Natal. In 1884 the Cape annexed the lands of the Gcaleka, the Xhoxa and the Thembu. In 1886 a show of force ensured the annexation of the Xesibe lands. The Pondo were still left with internal independence but their coastal area was declared a British Protectorate. (They were finally annexed by the Cape in 1894.)

Thus in the years after the British withdrawal from the Transvaal European authority over the African peoples of Southern Africa was enormously extended. The Germans established claims to the vast area of South West Africa. Britain took British Bechuanaland and the huge Bechuanaland Protectorate thus driving a wedge of British territory between the Germans and the Transvaal as far north as the Zambesi River. On the east coast the Zulu Kingdom and all the peoples between Natal and the Cape with the exception of the Pondo were brought under European rule. The only substantial area in South Africa in which South African chiefs still ruled in independence was the Swazi Kingdom and a short stretch of coast occupied by the Thonga people between Zululand and the borders of Mozambique.

The reasons for this sudden very rapid extension of European authority were firstly that economic developments in Europe and in South Africa itself, particularly the development of new more efficient weapons and means of transport and communications, had shifted the balance of military power decisively to the advantage of the whites. Growing competition between European powers and their jealousy of one another was one more reason for an accelerated drive to establish white control over African peoples. Another was the fact that African peoples outside the borders of white controlled

Cecil Rhodes (in the centre of the front row) with officials of De Beers Consolidated Mines. Barney Barnato is sitting to the right of Rhodes

areas were becoming an increasingly important element in the labour force of the white areas. It was vital to the whites to be able to control these African areas so as to exploit their labour resources more effectively. At the same time they would be able to prevent Africans in the areas from using money earned in white employment to purchase modern weapons and so endanger white supremacy.

The rise of Cecil Rhodes—the amalgamation of diamond diggings

Cecil Rhodes was destined to play a major part in the history of southern Africa. Born in England as the son of a parson, he came to South Africa for health reasons settling first with an elder brother on a farm in Natal and then, as the rush to the diamond fields began, trekking to Griqualand West to seize advantage of the new opportunities.

At first each prospector was allowed to dig in a square patch of ground but as they tunnelled deeper the area became a vast honeycomb. Everyone wanted to dig as much of his claim as possible so the walls between the shafts were very thin and it became increasingly difficult to manoeuvre the diamond soil laden wheelbarrows along them. Earth at the side of the diggings began caving in, often burying miners alive. When the shafts became very deep, water began to seep in and it was difficult and expensive to remove it. Costs thus grew greater and greater and the profits consequently dropped. Rhodes realised that if an individual could obtain several patches alongside each other and work this area as a single unit the mining would be more efficient and therefore more profitable. He began buying the claims of bankrupt and disillusioned miners and he was soon making a great deal of money and pressing on with his policy of buying more claims and forming larger units. While studying for a degree at Oxford, he continued his financial business through agents, travelling out to South Africa during each long vacation. He had a powerful rival in Barney Barnato, a Jew from London. By 1889 these two men virtually controlled the diamond fields and it remained to be seen which one would absorb the other. Although Barnato held the richer areas, Rhodes had obtained the financial backing of powerful capitalists in Britain such as Alfred Beit and Lord Rothschild. Through them Rhodes was able to force Barnato to amalgamate the two enterprises into one vast company, called De Beers Consolidated. Barnato remained immensely rich and was one of the directors of the new company but the greatest power in the organisation was in Rhodes' hands. By 1891 the company controlled most of the remaining mines in South Africa and thus dominated the largest source of diamonds in the world.

Rhodes' dreams for Africa and the world

Rhodes was never interested in making money for its own sake. Money meant power, power to fulfil his own fantastic dreams. He believed fervently in the destiny of the British and other racially related people such as the Dutch and Germans to dominate the world in the interest of mankind. He saw the extension of the British Empire throughout Africa, a vast block of British territory linked together by a transcontinental railway and telegraph running from the Cape to

Cairo. This block would form part of an imperial federation economically united by a customs union. Britain would ally with the United States and Germany to dominate the world and ensure peace and prosperity. But Rhodes had little confidence in the ability or willingness of the British Government to fulfil his dream.

During his years in South Africa, he had absorbed the attitudes of the white settlers, British and Boer, together with their contempt for Whitehall. Rhodes therefore believed that the extension of British rule throughout Africa should be undertaken from the Cape with assistance of British capital but without direct interference from the British Government. The two white South African peoples should be brought together to partake in the venture. His attitude towards the Africans was thoroughly paternalistic. Though at times he mentioned racial equality, he fundamentally saw Africans as destined to be under white rule for their own good. They would supply the physical labour in combination with European brains and capital. Rhodes considered himself as the central figure in this grand scheme since he alone could provide the leadership and drive to bring about the new world order.

Naturally, the road north must remain open and Rhodes played an active part in the agitation which eventually led to the annexation of British Bechuanaland. And in the constitution for De Beers Consolidated he ensured that a clause was included allowing profits to be used for purposes other than diamond mining. Thus he obtained the essential financial basis for his schemes.

The Transvaal and President Kruger

In 1886 gold was discovered in the Transvaal and the whole economic and political situation in South Africa was transformed. Until that time, a poor farming republic, it had been economically dependent on the Cape and it seemed that the Transvaal might eventually be absorbed by her rich southern neighbour, together with Orange Free State. It was so poverty stricken that in 1885 it had been forced to ask the Cape to agree to a customs union but the Cape was too selfish to agree and the following year the chance had gone, gold deposits had been found and the gold rush was on.

Suddenly, the Transvaal became the richest state in South Africa and soon the other states became dependent on the profits from the supply of goods to their wealthy neighbour. It now looked as if the Transvaal would be in a position to absorb the other white states.

President Kruger

Certainly, it had the means to maintain its independence and frustrate Rhodes' ambitions.

The Transvaal was led by President Kruger, a Boer with the characteristic Boer spirit of independence. Though he had had little formal education, he was an astute, capable politician with a fierce determination to be rid of British rule. His experiences of British policy up to the Pretoria Convention had given him a deep suspicion of British hypocrisy and deception. He wanted an independent sovereign state with the right to make treaties with foreign powers without interference from Britain.

British reaction to Transvaal's prosperity

The British Government did not share Rhodes' ideas of a British Africa and continued to regard the acquisition of territory in the continent as an unjustified expense. But powerful factions supported Rhodes and the Government still regarded the possession of the Cape as essential for the protection of the route to India in spite of the rapid increase in traffic via the Suez Canal. Now, alarmed at Transvaal's wealth and aware of Kruger's determination to escape from British control, the British saw their strategic position in the area threatened and this led to an alliance with Rhodes against Kruger.

Rhodes now prepared for his grand scheme of expansion northward. While he set about consolidating his base in the Cape by attempting to bring about an alliance between the British and the Boers, he sent his agents into the areas of modern Rhodesia and Zambia to secure treaties to provide a legal justification for his intended occupation of the area. Finally, he sought British government approval for the formation of a chartered company which would undertake the occupation and administer the new areas.

Meanwhile, in South Africa the successful uprising by the Transvaal farmers against the British government had roused very strong nationalist feelings amongst the Boers. A Boer nationalist organisation, the Afrikaner Bond, had been formed dedicated to encourage the use of the Afrikaans language and to protect the interest of the Boer farmers. The society spread rapidly after the rebellion but it died down again in the two Boer Republics maintaining its strength in the Cape only. Soon the character of the society changed since Afrikaans-speaking whites in the Cape were long accustomed to being part of the British Empire. The organisation's new leader, 'Onze Jan' Hofmeyer, believed, like Rhodes, in cooperation between the white peoples and a firm alliance grew between the two men which finally resulted in Rhodes becoming Premier of the Cape with the support of the Afrikaner Bond in 1890. Rhodes consolidated his hold over the white electorate by introducing measures to restrict the numbers of African voters.

The Ndebele kingdom and the whites

The kingdom of the Ndebele (Matabele), held a key position north of the Zambesi river. Under their first king, Mzilikazi, they had built up a Zulu type state with a society organised on military lines. Each

Lobengula

able-bodied man was a member of various regiments accommodated in a series of military towns.

Even before Mzilikazi died white infiltration had begun. The king had established a close friendship with the white missionary, Robert Moffat, and even after the Ndebele had been driven out of the Transvaal in 1837 Mzilikazi retained his feeling for his white friend. Moffat persuaded him to allow white men into his country so that his capital was crowded with white hunters even before his death in 1868.

The heir to the throne was believed to have been killed on his father's orders but others said that he was still alive somewhere in South Africa. This gave Sir Theophilus Shepstone, an officer of the Natal government, an opportunity to establish his influence over the Ndebele kingdom. He let it be known that one of his servants was Nkulumane, the missing heir, and tried to ensure that he would be chosen as king. The majority, however, were not convinced and supported Lobengula, a rival contender. After a minor civil war, the latter was secure in his position.

But the end of the succession dispute did not end white interference in the area. Europeans clamoured for a written treaty. Lobengula's position was difficult. Aware that his people could not defeat the whites in battle, he needed to re-equip his army with new weapons but this would take time and he had therefore to be careful not to offend the whites too deeply. On the other hand, he knew the whites would take advantage of his ignorance of writing to get him to agree to documents that he did not really understand. He described the position as like a chameleon creeping nearer and nearer the fly: 'He darts his tongue and the fly disappears; England is the chameleon and I am the fly.'

Lobengula tricked by Rhodes

The first treaty to which Lobengula agreed, with the Transvaal, was arranged by Peter Grobler and gave special rights to Transvaal citizens in the Ndbele Kingdom. Grobler was appointed consul for the citizens. Britain immediately took counter action and Robert Moffat's son, John Smith Moffat, obtained a treaty forbidding the giving away of territory without permission from the British High Commissioner in South Africa. Then Rhodes' three agents, Rudd, Maguire and Francis 'Matabele' Thompson, persuaded Lobengula to sign the 'Rudd Concession' which gave Rhodes exclusive prospecting rights in the area. In return, the king was given rifles and ammunition, and promised an annual subsidy and a steamboat for use on the Zambesi river.

Soon, Lobengula regretted signing this last treaty and sought assurance that Rhodes had the right to dig only for minerals. He even sent envoys to Britain for assurance. His suspicion was justified for Rhodes interpreted his rights to mean that he could occupy the Shona parts of Rhodesia. He formed a company, the British South Africa Company, to occupy Mashonaland and persuaded the British

NOTICE

I hear it is published in the newspapers that I have granted a Concession of the Minerals in *all* my Country to CHARLES DUNELL RUDD, ROCHFORD MAGUIRE, AND FRANCIS ROBERT THOMPSON.

As there is a great misunderstanding about this, all action in respect of said Concession is hereby suspended pending an investigation to be made by me in my country.

(Signed) LOBENGULA.

Royal Kraal,
  Matabeleland,
    18th January, 1889.

11. Facsimile of the Notice of Lobengula as it appeared in the *Bechuanaland News* and of the original Notice

A notice issued by Lobengula while he was attempting to clarify the terms of the Rudd Concession

Government to give him a charter giving the company administrative powers in the area.

Rhodes hastened to extend his influence further by encouraging his agents to sign treaties with chiefs far into the interior. He found an able ally in Harry Johnston, another believer in a grand British Africa. Johnston, British Consul in Mozambique, was particularly interested in modern Malawi. This area had been thrown into a state of confusion by the activities of Arab, Yao and Portuguese traders. Small Makololo kingdoms succeeded in holding the Portuguese back from the south of the region. Dr Livingstone's example had attracted many missionaries and this angered the Arab traders who knew that they were determined to end the slave trade. To help the missions, the African Lakes Company was formed but its resources were too small to be of effective assistance. The Portuguese now realised that they must act quickly to protect their claims in Africa. They planned to seize a wide corridor linking Angola to Mozambique and prepared an expedition to acquire rights in the south of modern Malawi and Zambia. Rhodes retaliated by giving Johnston money and assistance to make treaties with the chiefs in these areas.

Whatever their real worth, these pieces of paper were used to establish the British South Africa Company's rights to Zambia. However, Rhodes' agents were beaten by King Leopold of the Congo in the race to make treaties with the rulers of the Katanga area. Thus the copperbelt was split between two colonial powers.

Rhodes' and Johnston's plans were almost frustrated by the Portuguese when Serpa Pinto began to force his way through the resistance of the Makololo but the British Government intervened and the Portuguese plans were abandoned. The area of modern Malawi came directly under the Imperial Government. Rhodes paid Johnston £10,000 annually to establish British rule there and to act as administrator on behalf of the British South Africa Company in Zambia.

The British South Africa Company's charter, October 1889

Rhodes' quest for official backing in London for his policies faced many difficulties. He wanted the extension of British territory to be undertaken by colonists like himself with minimum interference from Whitehall. London's distrust was increased by Rhodes' association with the Afrikaner Bond and his far-reaching schemes were the dread of more conventional spirits who feared the responsibility and expense. People like the missionaries strongly supported the view that newly acquired areas should be administered from Whitehall in the interests of the indigenous peoples. But in spite of all this opposition, Rhodes had his way with the backing of powerful financial interests.

Rhodes argued that gold in Mashonaland was richer than that of the Transvaal and that a rich, dominant northern region would reverse the economic and political situation brought about by the rise of the Transvaal. The latter could be absorbed into the vastly expanded British sphere without the British government having to pay for it. Rhodes was finally granted a Royal Charter for the British South Africa Company in October, 1889. In return, Whitehall insisted on putting powerful, independently-minded men on to the Board to watch Rhodes' activities though Rhodes retained his right to act as sole authority for his company in South Africa. Thus, for all practical purposes he had an almost completely free hand.

Rhodes at the height of his power

Back in South Africa Rhodes prepared his pioneer column to occupy Mashonaland. The majority of recruits were English speaking but a deliberate effort was made to include Afrikaners. Volunteers were attracted by the promise of prospecting rights and farming land though the Rudd Concession did not give Rhodes' company the right to make such offers. The column set out to the north at the end of June 1890 carrying with it the traditional South African idea of farming with large areas of land worked by non-European labourers and all the racial prejudices this system produced.

Deeply concerned, Lobengula sent a message to the British High Commissioner at the Cape denying Rhodes' right to enter his kingdom in force but the High Commissioner would do nothing. By September the Union Jack was hoisted at Fort Salisbury and Mashonaland was declared occupied in the name of the Queen.

Rhodes was now a man of gigantic stature: master of the largest diamond mining complex in the world; controller of an important gold mining company in Johannesburg; Premier of the Cape, the largest if not the richest white state; head of the British South Africa Company and therefore the uncrowned king of the newly acquired territories.

Transvaal-British competition over Swaziland

Meanwhile, in the Transvaal Kruger was seeking to preserve and strengthen the state's independence and the Transvaalers, like the British and Boer settlers at the Cape, saw modern Rhodesia as a possible area for expansion. The Grobler treaty had been the first step in this direction. But Transvaal's main interest was expansion eastward into the independent Swazi kingdom and a strip of coastline occupied by the Thonga. This strip contained a possible port at Kosi Bay. Swaziland was organised on similar lines to the Zulu and Ndebele kingdoms but was not so highly militarised. Having witnessed the defeat of powerful African peoples by the whites, the Swazis were determined not to be drawn into any quarrel with Europeans. Moreover, Shepstone, the Natal officer responsible for relations with the tribes, had protected them from the Zulus on several occasions. Thus white settlers in the kingdom were well-received. These settlers were of two kinds; Boer farmers in search of new grazing land and a host of concession hunters, mainly British, looking for mining rights and other commercial privileges. These two groups naturally opposed each other since prospectors wanted mining rights on land sought for farming by the Boers. The Swazis found this situation very difficult to deal with since the whites despised the tribunals of the chiefs and ignored Swazi custom. The king summoned Shepstone's son to help control the affairs of the European population but the scramble continued. The king was bribed or tricked into signing more and more pieces of paper until he had given away all his land more than once over. Kruger was anxious to take advantage of the situation to win his access to the sea and was even prepared to threaten intervention in the Ndebele kingdom as a bargaining counter with Rhodes. But his intentions were strongly resented by powerful commercial groups in Britain.

A stalemate was reached which lasted for a number of years. In 1890 and again in 1894, Britain and the Transvaal jointly agreed to respect the independence of the Swazi kingdom but as Transvaal pressure increased Britain agreed that the kingdom could be taken over if the Swazi authorities consented. However, the authorities flatly refused and asked for British protection. This was refused and finally in December 1894 the Transvaal was permitted to take over the region whether the people were willing or not. But Kruger's successful occupation of Swaziland was countered by British occupation of the coastal Thonga area and the Transvaal lost its route to the sea. The offer of a railway strip to Kosi Bay was promised but never granted.

Rhodes tries to seize Mozambique

With the successful occupation of Mashonaland, it seemed Rhodes' dreams would be fulfilled. A new powerful British southern African state seemed about to be born which could eventually absorb the land-locked Boer states further south. But these hopes were not fulfilled. Linked with the occupation of Mashonaland was the intention to seize Portuguese claims to territory and thereby obtain a route to the sea. The Transvaal would then be completely surrounded by British territory.

Although the Portuguese claimed wide areas of land, for hundreds of years they had done little more than occupy a few ports along the coast and the Zambesi river. The greater part of Mozambique south of the Zambesi was dominated by the Gaza Empire, ruled at this time by Gungunyana who had established friendly relations with the Ndebele; his daughter had married Lobengula. Denying Portuguese claims to his kingdom, Gungunyana sought British protection but this was refused since it was contrary to British treaties with Portugal.

Rhodes believed that if he could obtain concessions from Gungunyana along the lines of the Rudd Concession, he could exploit the region, occupy Mozambique and then squeeze Portugal out of the rest of the area. In 1891 these plans were set in motion and agents were sent to the Gaza capital. But Portugal's position was beginning to undergo a change since trade with the Transvaal was increasing their wealth and Lourenço Marques was steadily growing from a fever-ridden port into a prosperous settlement. Public opinion in Portugal was waking up to the potential value of the colony and imperialist feeling supported the retention and expansion of Portugal's empire. Governmental authority was re-established along the Zambesi and the independence of Portuguese *prazo* (estate) owners destroyed. Rhodes' activities roused Portuguese imperial feelings further and Whitehall realised that if Portugal was humiliated again her present government might fall to a strongly anti-British regime. Rhodes therefore lost backing from Whitehall. His plans to occupy Mozambique were frustrated and Delagoa Bay, which was the key to much subsequent history, remained in Portuguese hands.

The struggle with Gungunyana

Portugal was now determined to establish effective control of the area but, being one of the weakest and poorest European states, she was racked with bitter divisions at home and it took some time before she could summon up the strength to grapple with Gungunyana and the forces of the Gaza empire. Only in 1895 did the Portuguese feel ready to commence hostilities. Gungunyana had long seen that sooner or later Portugal would try to destroy him and he made repeated efforts to obtain British protection. However, all his overtures were rejected and he was left to his fate. At last, the Portuguese found an opportunity for a quarrel and hostilities began. For some time it seemed they might be defeated after all but in the end the bravery of Gungunyana's people was no match for modern European weapons. Gungunyana was captured and exiled and the fabric of his kingdom systematically destroyed.

Lobengula's kingdom destroyed

Rhodes' failure in Mozambique was less disastrous than another disappointment. Far less gold was found in Mashonaland than Rhodes and his backers had hoped. There was a real danger that the Company would go bankrupt and the settlement would collapse. Rhodes therefore turned his attention to lands occupied by Lobengula and the Ndebele. It was rumoured that a ridge of gold-bearing rock ran through Lobengula's capital, Bulawayo, which could rescue the Company's finances and provide for the building up of a prosperous British colony. And even if the gold did not exist, the area contained some of the best grazing land between the Limpopo and the Zambesi.

Logengula did all he could to prevent a quarrel with the whites but his fate was also sealed. A party of Ndebele came near to Salisbury in pursuit of royal cattle stolen by the Shona. Rhodes' Company ordered them to withdraw but, since this retreat was not as swift as was demanded, the Company's patrol opened fire and the Ndebele retaliated. The incident was used as a pretext for war. A large section of the Ndebele army were in quarantine for smallpox and, though Lobengula possessed a considerable quantity of firearms, his people were not yet skilled in their use. The whites had the new and deadly Maxim guns and opposition to them was suicidal. Lobengula fled with a small group of devoted followers to make contact with the Ngoni to the north in modern Zambia. He died of fever on the way.

A sketch of a battle between the British and the Ndebele

The British-Transvaal conflict comes to a head

News of the Company's victory restored the investors' confidence and the price of its shares rose to unprecedented heights. But the longed for gold was not found and it soon became apparent that the new settlement would be more of a liability than an asset for many years. The plan to maintain British paramountcy in southern Africa by creating a richer British state to the north of the Transvaal had failed and inevitably the struggle between Kruger's desire for Boer independence and the British determination to maintain overall control became sharper.

This struggle had many aspects. Transvaal's new-found wealth gave the republic the need for a greatly expanded and more efficient means of communication with the outside world. It was to Britain's and Rhodes' advantage if the Transvaal could be linked with the railway systems of the Cape as this would entail drawing her into the British orbit. It was also vital to the British and Boer in the Cape who were increasingly dependent on trade with the Transvaal. Natal shared this dependency and the Orange Free State also had a strong interest in trade with the Transvaal. Both the Cape and Natal were anxious to build railway lines to the Transvaal and the Orange Free State willingly allowed the line to pass through her territory. However, the Transvaal sought an alternative route to the sea and the Portuguese possession of Delagoa Bay provided the opportunity. Even before the British annexation of the Transvaal in 1877, a railway had been planned to the Bay. This had ended in disastrous failure, but now that the Transvaal was so rich the project could begin again.

Kruger resisted the extension of the lines to the south until the Delagoa Bay line was near completion. Rhodes therefore decided that his railway link to the north to Cairo must go through Bechuanaland instead of the Transvaal. Kruger finally allowed the southern lines in but only after the completion of the link with Delagoa Bay which placed his state in a stronger position than ever thus threatening British interests in southern Africa. It could set the Cape against Natal by favouring one against the other and could blackmail the southern states by threatening to close their lines and send all traffic via Delagoa Bay. Nothing would prevent the Transvaal, with an independent access to the sea, from establishing relations with foreign powers like Germany and breaking free from British control over her foreign policy.

The Uitlanders in the Transvaal

But Transvaal's wealth gave her grave internal problems. Capitalists and white mineworkers flocked to Johannesburg. The majority were British but they also came from many parts of the world and Kruger was determined not to allow them the vote. The new settlers' culture and attitudes were very different from the conservative, Transvaal Boers. What is more, these Uitlanders (foreigners), had no permanent stake in the country. It was expected that as soon as the gold ran out they would depart leaving deserted mines behind them. Finally, the Uitlanders' vote might bring British influence back to the state and destroy the independence for which the Boers had fought so hard.

On the other hand many of the Uitlanders were discontented with the situation in the Transvaal; they had little in common with government officials many of whom could speak no English and they resented the lack of English-medium education for their children. The larger capitalists resented the preference given to the Dutch in awarding contracts and most of all that, though they provided the greater part of the finances of the state, they had no control over how it was

A general view of Johannesburg at the end of the nineteenth century

spent. They felt they would prosper better under the British flag and that African labour could be obtained more cheaply. This was all revealed in heated mass meetings, petitions and violent newspaper articles. It gave the impression that the Rand was simmering on the point of revolution though most Uitlanders were doing too well to risk their lives and property in any real fighting.

Rhodes saw this situation as the ideal means to force the Transvaal into union with British South Africa. He believed that the Uitlanders could easily overthrow the Boer government and that they should be supported lest they established a republic of their own as anti-British as the former Boer one. Thus an elaborate conspiracy was hatched involving Chamberlain, the imperialist-minded Colonial Secretary, Sir Hercules Robinson, British High Commissioner in South Africa, and Flora Shaw (later Lady Lugard), the imperialist-minded Colonial Editor of *The Times*. Rhodes' plan was to smuggle arms to the Uitlanders who would rise in revolt on a fixed day with the assistance of a column of the British South Africa Company's forces from Bechuanaland. Robinson would announce the annexation of the Transvaal on a pretext of British duty to maintain peace in the area and *The Times* would justify the action to the British public. The attraction of the plan was that it would provide a means of solving Britain's strategic problems in southern Africa without the direct aid of Whitehall.

The Jameson raid fiasco

Rhodes began to concentrate his troops in Bechuanaland on a strip of land that had theoretically been given him to protect the railroad against the 'ferocious Bechuana' tribes. But as the date for the revolt drew near the Uitlanders began to weaken. Many of the capitalists did not intend to fight but to use the situation to create rumours of war so that the price of gold shares would fall temporarily on the London Stock Exchange. They would make their fortunes when the prices went up again. Rhodes was sent a telegram suggesting that the revolt be postponed. He realised that his scheme was going to collapse but Dr. Jameson, his lieutenant in charge of the column in Bechuanaland, had other ideas. He was even more confident than Rhodes that the Boer government would collapse and his successful war against the Ndebele had given him tremendous confidence. He therefore decided to lead his troops into the Transvaal and force the Uitlanders into action. Rhodes was thunderstruck when he heard the news, for he thought it was an unjustified gamble with terrible consequences if Jameson's action failed. However, by the time he had sent a telegram to Jameson telling him to stop, the column was already on its way to the Transvaal, the telegraph wires being cut behind them.

The Uitlanders were horrified when they heard that Jameson was coming to rescue them uninvited. A half-hearted uprising took place and if Jameson had reached Johannesburg the plot might have succeeded but the column lost its way. A Boer guide led them into a perfect trap in a shallow bowl with Boers up in the hills surrounding

Jameson's men cutting the telegraph wires

them where the column's Maxim guns were useless. Jameson was forced to surrender and the rebellion collapsed. This was a bitter blow to Rhodes who had to resign as Premier of the Cape and his friendly alliance with the Afrikaner Bond was succeeded by bitterness and mistrust. There was even a danger that Rhodes would lose his control of the British South Africa Company. Kruger, on the other hand, seemed to have emerged triumphant and in his hour of victory he acted with extraordinary magnanimity. The captive raiders were handed back to the British for punishment and even the Uitlanders were treated leniently.

But the collapse of the Jameson raid could not alter the basic situation; it merely ensured that the conflict must come into the open and be settled by war. It also emphasised the Transvaal's strength and a wave of sympathy swept through the whole of southern Africa indicating the possibility that the Cape might join the Transvaal in an anti-British federation. Even the Kaiser sent a congratulatory telegram to Kruger and a German warship was rumoured to have landed marines at Delagoa Bay. War between Britain and Germany seemed likely until the Kaiser offered his apologies to Queen Victoria.

Rebellions in southern Rhodesia

The Jameson raid fiasco provided the opportunity for a massive African uprising in modern Rhodesia. White farmers had introduced a rigid colour discrimination into the lands between the Limpopo and the Zambesi. No sooner was the settlement in Mashonaland established than the Shona lands began to be confiscated to form cattle ranches for the whites and chiefs were forced to send their men to the mines and the farms. The arrogance of the invaders shocked the African sense of personal dignity and provoked a rapidly growing resentment. After the conquest of the Ndebele kingdom royal cattle were confiscated and the Ndebele left with the poorest farming lands. Finally, an epidemic of rinderpest decimated their cattle and naturally even this calamity was associated with the whites.

With most of the Company's forces away on the Jameson raid, an opportunity was offered for striking back. In March 1896 the Ndebele rose in massive rebellion. Isolated whites were killed on their farms and the forts were beseiged. In June, the Shona also rose and succeeded in killing a substantial number of whites in their area. The rebellion proved long and costly to suppress for the Africans had learnt not to expose themselves to the Maxim guns. In spite of heavy losses, the Ndebele held out in the Matoppos mountains. They were in a desperate condition but the Company was also in difficulties. Its debts were mounting without there being a sign of it being able to pay them let alone give its shareholders a dividend. Another costly campaign would be difficult to mount.

At this point Rhodes took the bold step of going into the mountains to negotiate with the Ndebele and in October he persuaded them to surrender in return for concessions and thereby salvaged his personal reputation in white southern Africa. The Shona resistance continued for a further year but was finally decisively crushed.

Aftermath of the Jameson raid

The raid was followed by a period of calm in which it looked as if the differences between Britain and the Transvaal would be settled peacefully. But this impression was deceptive. Chamberlain was more than ever determined to maintain British paramountcy and Kruger was confirmed in his worst suspicions of British policy by the raid and what followed. He had expected Rhodes to be tried and publicly disgraced but the Committee of Enquiry was first postponed and then, when it finally met, did everything to hush up the affair. Rhodes, in possession of telegrams implicating Chamberlain, was able to have him make a statement in the Commons that Rhodes had done nothing contrary to his personal honour. Kruger now despaired of reaching any agreement with such a dishonest opponent and the Transvaal entered into a close military alliance with the Orange Free State and both states began to arm themselves with German weapons.

The second Anglo-Boer war

Chamberlain came increasingly to believe that there was nothing to be done except to force the Transvaal to submit and he was strongly supported by the British High Commissioner in South Africa, Alfred Milner, another dedicated imperialist. At the same time, anti-republican Uitlanders in the Transvaal used every occasion to stir up trouble and a continual stream of propaganda appeared in the Johannesburg *Star* and British papers. Milner at last prepared to force a showdown. In May, 1899 he prepared a despatch comparing the lot of the British in the Transvaal with that of the helots (serfs), in ancient Sparta claiming that this situation was undermining British

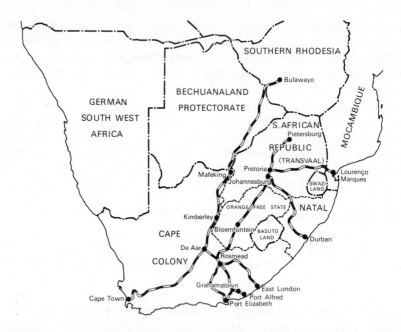

South Africa at the time of the second Anglo-Boer War, showing main railway lines

prestige throughout the Empire. Kruger realised the danger and offered large concessions. In August, he agreed that the Uitlanders could vote after five years' residence provided that Britain would leave his republic alone and not interfere in its affairs. But Britain was still determined to prevent the republic from consolidating its independence and rejected the offer. British troops moved to the borders of the two republics. Kruger and the Orange Free State decided to act before all the British forces arrived. An ultimatum was issued demanding the withdrawal of British forces from the frontiers and when this was not complied with the Cape and Natal were invaded in September, 1899.

In spite of overwhelming odds, the little Boer republics had a considerable advantage at the beginning. The British forces were vastly scattered and in southern Africa the Boers' fighting men outnumbered them. Also, the British generals had little conception of the military problem they faced and seriously underestimated their enemy. The war thus began with a series of British defeats and, had the Boers taken full advantage of their victories, the British forces would have been at their mercy. But the Boer generals made the serious mistake of wasting their strength blockading the British strongpoints at Ladysmith and Mafeking giving Britain time to reinforce her troops in South Africa. Two first-class generals, Lord Roberts and Lord Kitchener, were sent out to command them and the initiative passed on to the British. British troops invaded the Orange Free State, a whole Boer army was captured almost intact and Mafeking was relieved. The news gave rise to wild rejoicing in England. Then the troops marched on Pretoria. During 1900 the annexation of the two states as Crown colonies of Transvaal and the Orange River was announced and Kruger retired down the Delagoa railway line to die in exile. The war seemed over and Milner began to prepare the administration of the new colonies but many Boers refused to surrender. They began a guerilla struggle which lasted for another year and a half and their commandos even invaded the Cape. But some Boers felt that continued hostilities would destroy the prosperity of the country and joined the British side as a body called the National Scouts. They were naturally regarded as traitors by those who continued the struggle.

Impatient to end the war, Britain was baffled by those Boers who sat quietly at home one day and fired at British troops the next. In

A pound note used by the British forces during the siege of Mafeking

retaliation they burned Boer farms in the neighbourhood of guerilla activity and took women and children into concentration camps. They also began to run barbed wire fences across the country to hem in the Boers but these measures still did not bring about an end to the war. The tough measures increased the bitterness and many women and children died from diseases which spread through the camps. Gradually the Boers' fighting spirit was undermined and they were ready to compromise. The British, too, were ready to make concessions and end the war.

Treaty of Vereeniging

In May 1902 the Boer and British leaders met at Vereeniging where the Boers agreed to lose their independence in return for vital concessions from the British, the most important of which concerned African political rights. Britain had an opportunity of fulfilling her obligation to the Africans by securing their right to vote, perhaps on the same terms as in the Cape. This might have created a peaceful constitutional advance towards majority rule. But the Boers made it clear that they would rather continue fighting than accept such conditions and Britain capitulated. The question of African voting rights would be set aside until the two ex-republics had returned to responsible government. Britain also agreed to release all prisoners of war, to pardon all those still under arms and to provide massive financial aid to get the southern African economy back on its feet.

Reconstruction—Chinese workers

To help Milner with his immense task of reconstruction, he brought out a number of young administrative officers from Oxford and Cambridge who, because of their youth, became known as 'Milner's kindergarten'. Determined that southern Africa would remain firmly under the British flag, he planned to settle large numbers of Britons on farms in the two new Crown colonies and to anglicise the Boer population through education. This education had begun in the concentration camps and was now continued in the establishing of numerous government schools where the medium was English and where Dutch was taught during only a few lessons.

To succeed in his reconstruction and to provide a buoyant economy to attract British settlers, Milner had to bring the Johannesburg

ARMY HEADQUARTERS, SOUTH AFRICA.

General Lord Kitchener of Khartoum
             Commanding in Chief

   AND

His Excellency Lord Milner
             High Commissioner

   on behalf of the BRITISH GOVERNMENT

AND

   Messrs S.W.Burger, F.W.Reitz, Louis Botha, J.H.de la Rey,
             L.J.Meyer and J.C.Krogh

acting as the GOVERNMENT of the SOUTH AFRICAN REPUBLIC

AND

   Messrs W.J.C.Brebner, C.R.de Wet, J.B.M.Herzog
             and C.H.Olivier

acting as the GOVERNMENT of the ORANGE FREE STATE

             on behalf of their respective BURGHERS

Desirous to terminate the present hostilities, agree on the
following Articles.

1.   The BURGHER Forces in the Field will forthwith lay down
their Arms, handing over all Guns, Rifles, and Munitions of War,
in their possession or under their control, and desist from any
further resistance to the Authority of HIS MAJESTY KING EDWARD
Vll whom they recognise as their lawful SOVEREIGN.

      The manner and details of this Surrender will be arranged
between Lord Kitchener and Commandant General Botha, Assistant
Commandant General De la Rey, and Chief Commandant De Wet.

2.   Burghers in the field outside the limits of the TRANSVAAL
and ORANGE RIVER COLONY, and all Prisoners of War at present
outside South Africa, who are burghers, will, on duly declaring
their acceptance of the position of subjects of HIS MAJESTY
KING EDWARD Vll, be gradually brought back to their homes as
soon as transport can be provided and their means of subsistence

Part of the Treaty of Vereeniging (for signatures see next page)

a period of years with 3 per cent interest. No foreigner or
rebel will be entitled to the benefit of this Clause.

Signed at Pretoria this thirty first day of May in the
Year of Our Lord One Thousand Nine Hundred and Two.

Signatures on the Treaty of Vereeniging

mines back into full operation as soon as possible. But this was not
easy due to a shortage of labour. With the reconstruction of roads and
railways, the rebuilding of farmhouses and other repairs due to the
ravages of war, there was sufficient employment for Africans above
ground. Moreover, African wages in the mines had been cut during
the war and were slow to rise again. To solve this problem, Milner

entered into an arrangement in 1901, called the *modus vivendi*, with the Portuguese. Under this arrangement, the Transvaal mines could recruit labour in Mozambique in return for a percentage payment to the Mozambique authorities and a fixed proportion of the traffic was to go via Delagoa Bay. But this measure still did not bring the mines back into full production.

Milner then thought of recruiting Chinese labour and, in spite of considerable opposition, during 1904 and 1905 the Chinese were brought in and the mines reached full production. But the Chinese were very unpopular and the whites were afraid of these possibly dangerous non-Europeans. The Chinese were well known to have a long record of advanced civilisation and whites feared their arrival might undermine the whole idea of a social structure based on colour. This led to the introduction of colour bar regulations debarring non-whites from certain categories of employment. These regulations continued to be applied to the Africans after the Chinese had left. The Chinese labour question increased agitation for a return to representative government and in Britain the conditions under which the Chinese were made to live became a national scandal exploited by the Liberal Party to drive the Conservatives from office.

Growth of Afrikaner nationalism

At the end of the Boer war, Britain and pro-British groups seemed to occupy an unchallenged position throughout southern Africa. In the Cape, large numbers of Afrikaans-speaking citizens had been deprived of the vote for joining the Boer side and as a result power was in the hands of a pro-British group, the Progressive Party. The Premier was none other than Jameson, the leader of the notorious raid. Natal presented a similar picture where the Progressive Party controlled the administration. The Boers were deeply divided into hostile factions. The greatest bitterness was between those who had fought to the end of the war, the *Bitter-einders*, and those who had accepted British rule at an early stage, the *Hans-oppers*. The National Scouts were particularly hated by the Bitter-einders.

However, appearances proved deceptive for Milner's policy of Anglicisation was seen as a threat to the very existence of the Afrikaners and an upsurge of Afrikaner nationalism spread throughout the area bringing the warring factions together to form a common front. This opposition first took the form of a cultural and educational movement. A society for Christelike Nasionale Onderwys was formed to promote Christian national education and large numbers of schools were founded from collected finances to oppose the government schools. But they could not afford to recruit good teachers and were comparatively unsuccessful. They did however help to rouse Afrikaner nationalist feelings.

Nationalism moved from the cultural to the political front. In 1905 in the Transvaal, Botha, with the support of Jan Smuts, two of the most important Transvaal generals of the war period, formed a party, the Het Volk, which campaigned for the restoration of representative government. In the Orange River colony, the Orangia Unie Party, led by Steyn with the support of Fischer and Herzog, took a similar line. In the Cape, the Afrikaner Bond was recovering confidence and when the ban on ex-rebels expired, it would be in a good position to win a majority. Many English-speaking settlers shared the Boers' outlook, regarding themselves as South Africans first and believing in self government for the South African whites.

Faced with this opposition, the Conservative government at Whitehall decided upon a compromise. Milner left and was replaced by Lyttelton who was charged with introducing constitutional reforms in the two new colonies which would provide an element of self-government. But this was never introduced because the Conservatives were heavily defeated at the polls by the Liberal Party which had used the slogan of 'Chinese Slavery' as its election battle-cry.

Responsible government restored

During its years in opposition the Liberal Party had adopted a more or less pro-Boer attitude arguing that war was wrong and that the Boers were unjustifiably deprived of their freedom. It had particularly opposed the concentration camps. When it came to power it proceeded to restore self-government to the two ex-republics. The Transvaal obtained responsible government in February 1907 and the Orange River colony in June 1907. In both colonies the Boers won the election. In the Transvaal the English voters were split between two parties and the Het Volk was able to form a government in coalition with the Responsible Government Party. Botha became Premier with Smuts as his second in command. In the Orange River colony there were few English voters and the Orangia Unie Party won a clear majority. The government was led by Fischer with Herzog as his deputy. In February 1908 a similar development occurred in the Cape when Jameson and the Progressives were defeated at the polls by the South Africa Party,

CAUTION!

Thanks to the Tories, thousands of cheap Chinese are being imported into the Transvaal. If any one had said two years ago that they would do this, the Tories would have said it was

A SHAMELESS FALSEHOOD,

invented to catch your votes by the Liberals.

The Tories tell you that when they were last in power the Liberals sanctioned, in the case of British Guiana, a law

ALMOST EXACTLY THE SAME

as the Tory Chinese Ordinance for the Transvaal. But this, so far from being true, is

A SHAMELESS FALSEHOOD,

which could only come from people who had never read both Ordinances, which differ in almost every vital point that is essential to the charge of

SLAVERY,

which Liberals bring against the present Tory Ordinance.
[OVER.

An election poster issued by the Liberal Party of Great Britain

the political wing of the Afrikaner Bond. The Premier was an English-man, Merriman. Thus within six years of the end of a bitter war, the whole area was under Boer dominated governments, except for Natal.

The need for unity

The idea of a union of white southern African states had been de-veloping during this period and as soon as responsible government was restored, the political consequences of division became obvious. The economic interests of the Transvaal were in conflict with those of the southern states which was reflected most acutely in the problem of the railways. It was in Transvaal's interest to use the shorter and cheaper Delagoa Bay route but this would gravely hamper the economy of the Orange River colony, the Cape and Natal. Also, there were political problems arising from different native and Indian policies.

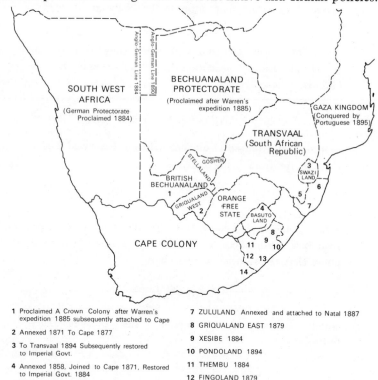

1 Proclaimed A Crown Colony after Warren's expedition 1885 subsequently attached to Cape

2 Annexed 1871 To Cape 1877

3 To Transvaal 1894 Subsequently restored to Imperial Govt.

4 Annexed 1858, Joined to Cape 1871, Restored to Imperial Govt. 1884

5 NEW REPUBLIC 1884

6 THONGA LAND 1895

7 ZULULAND Annexed and attached to Natal 1887

8 GRIQUALAND EAST 1879

9 XESIBE 1884

10 PONDOLAND 1894

11 THEMBU 1884

12 FINGOLAND 1879

13 GALEKA BOMVANA 1884

14 BRITISH KAFFRARIA (To Cape 1866)

The consolidation of white rule in South Africa

In the Cape, both Coloureds and Africans theoretically enjoyed the same legal rights as the Europeans; if they were able to meet certain economic requirements, they could vote. In Natal, Coloureds could vote and in theory the Africans could also do so but in practice the procedure for African registration was made so difficult as to be virtually impossible. In the two ex-republics there was no question of non-white voters. Colour discrimination existed at every social level throughout southern Africa, particularly more so in the ex-republics and Natal than in the Cape. With the development of the railways and mining industry, Africans were moving about the area in vast numbers and, indeed, the African population of southern Africa was becoming one immense labour pool. In these circumstances, the different laws and regulations in the various white states were bound to cause confusion and discontent.

The Bambata rebellion and the Indians in Natal

The Ndebele and Shona uprisings had proved that, although the Africans faced superior weapons and in some cases submitted to white rule with little resistance, their spirit was not crushed and they were far from acquiescing to the systems imposed upon them. In 1906, the Zulus rose in rebellion against the local whites. They had shown little resistance when their kingdom was annexed in 1887 but this was followed by the imposition of taxes to force them to work for the whites. Tension had developed until, inspired by a religious sect, they rebelled. The struggle to suppress them lasted six months and almost exhausted the resources of the colony.

Indian labour had been brought in to Natal in 1860 to help with the coastal sugar plantations. They had been promised permanent residency and full legal rights, including the right to own property, after ten years' service in southern Africa. A large and rapidly growing Indian community had developed in Natal. Many were still labourers, others took up market gardening to supply the vegetables and fruit needed in Durban and other urban areas, others became skilled craftsmen. Considerable numbers, however, took to trading and showed acute business acumen. They were satisfied with a lower profit than the whites could afford and, like all minority commercial groups in alien areas, they assisted each other in a way uncommon to the whites. Though many remained small traders, others acquired great fortunes and some sought commercial opportunities in other parts of southern Africa. They were particularly attracted to the Transvaal after the discovery of gold.

The Transvaal was, however, hostile to this group of non-Europeans and complex regulations limited their entry and their rights to trade and acquire property. In the Orange Free State they were banned altogether. Britain had used this discrimination in propaganda against Kruger during the war but afterwards they not only condoned the regulations but even extended them. The Indians in the area shared the growing political consciousness of their people in India and as Indians began to obtain a greater share in the government of their own country, the government of British India began to press for Indian rights in southern Africa. Obviously, from the point of view of white supremacy, a united policy on the Indian question was necessary for the whole region.

The Selbourne memorandum—Boers accept the idea of union

The movement towards unity was pioneered by British sections of the community. The main purpose of the Boer War had been to unite the region under the British flag. Milner had even considered suspending the Cape Constitution to force a Union on the country. The restoration of responsible governments meant the end of any idea of a British imposed Union and the British High Commissioner, Selbourne, set about persuading white southern Africans to unite on their own terms. He produced an impressive memorandum pointing out the effects of political and economic division and showing that settlement of vital questions concerning railways and customs was impossible. Because these differences were irreconcilable, Selbourne was inevitably called upon to arbitrate and the colonies were bound to accept the decisions of Conference or face a complete breakdown in communications and trade relations.

He thus argued that this inability to run their affairs was seriously affecting economic progress and he also pointed to the urgent need for a common policy towards the Africans and Indians. This memorandum convinced many people and Jameson introduced a motion in the Cape Parliament in favour of closer union while the Milner kindergarten formed closer union societies in many parts of the country.

The Boers had opposed union as long as it would have taken place on British terms but once they were in power in the two ex-republics, they began to favour the idea. However, they held back until Merriman had replaced Jameson in the Cape and then Smuts wrote almost immediately to Merriman suggesting that the time for taking steps towards unification had come. In the lengthy correspondence which took place between the two leaders many of the more involved problems were agreed upon in advance.

The National Convention

In July 1908 the parliaments of all the white states agreed to the formation of a National Convention to draw up a scheme for closer union and the delegates met at Durban from 12 October to 5 November 1908, transferring to Capetown from 23 November 1908 to 3 February 1909. When the convention was summoned there was still no clear picture of the form unification should take. At this stage the Afrikaners were in a dominant position and favoured a unitary system while the English preferred federation. However the majority at the Convention decided upon a unitary system; a national parliament of two chambers would have overriding power and the colonies were to be reduced to provinces with separate councils presided over by administrators appointed by the National government. All hope of preserving the different institutions and ways of life in the separate states was gone.

The Convention also spent a great deal of time on the questions of a national language and the site of a capital. English and Dutch were both made equal official languages and this could not be changed without a two-thirds majority of both Houses sitting together. The problem of a capital almost caused a breakdown of the Convention but a compromise was finally reached whereby Capetown became the

The delegates of the National Conference in Cape Town

233

legislative capital, Pretoria the administrative capital and Bloemfontein the legal capital where the Appeal courts would meet.

The struggle over the franchise

The most important problem at the Convention was that of the franchise. The conference was deeply divided between the Cape-type franchise allowing for some non-white representation and that of the rest of the region providing for only white voters. Again, the Convention agreed on a compromise; no non-white could seek election to the National Parliament. Non-Europeans would retain their voting rights in the Cape but these would not be extended to other provinces. Non-whites might also be elected to the Cape Provincial Council. Any reduction in these rights would require a two-thirds majority of both Houses. This clause and the other concerning the official language were known as the Entrenched Clauses.

Other decisions were taken at Conference about voting rights and the distribution of parliamentary seats. Provisions for seats favoured the Transvaal against the Cape. It was also agreed that white farming areas would have more representation than the towns which meant that the farmers, conservative and mainly Afrikaans-speaking, would have proportionately more political power than the townspeople, mainly English-speaking and relatively more progressive.

The decisions of Conference on voting rights reflected the past history of southern Africa. Racial prejudice had grown as a result of the economy and structure of the society, deepened by the series of frontier wars. The British attempt to destroy discrimination had led to the great Trek and the foundation of Boer republics on a basis of strict racial segregation. At the Convention, only a few of the Cape delegates supported limited political rights for non-whites. The delegates from the northern states refused to see such rights given to their areas and even sought their removal from the Cape. Within the Cape itself delegates from the eastern frontiers tended to side with the northern delegates.

White minority rule was confirmed just at a time when Africans were becoming increasingly politically conscious and when South Africa was undergoing economic changes which would heighten tension between the races. Thus decisions at Conference not only reflected the past but determined the pattern of future developments.

The Constitution drawn up by the National Convention met with general approval. A short second session was held to make minor amendments and in 1909 the Constitution was ratified by all the southern African states.

The next stage was to obtain British approval. A delegation was sent from South Africa to London but by this time opposition to the Constitution had had time to develop among Africans and a substantial group of liberal whites in the Cape. The African Peoples' Organisation, a party representing Coloured peoples and led by an outstanding Coloured politician, Abdurahman, also sent a delegation to Britain urging the extension of the Cape franchise to all of South Africa. The small political organisations of the African peoples joined together to form an organisation known as South African Native National Conference which sent two delegates, John T. Jabavu and Walter Rubusana, to London to press the same case as the African Peoples' Organisation. Finally, Schreiner organised a petition to the British Parliament against the Constitution and in particular the franchise arrangements.

These various groups received quite a sympathetic hearing in London and the Liberal government admitted that it would have preferred a franchise which did not involve racial discrimination. But the government also did not want to lose the chance of the peaceful unification of South Africa under the British flag. The international scene was growing more dangerous with the growth of German naval power and Britain did not want a divided South Africa with some areas anti-British. It was made clear by the South African delegates that a change in the franchise would destroy the Union. The Liberals capitulated excusing themselves by predicting that the superiority of the colour-blind system of the Cape would become obvious and would be voluntarily extended throughout South Africa. The South Africa Bill passed its third reading in Parliament by a huge majority and on 20 September 1909 it received Royal Assent.

Britain abandons her moral responsibilities

Thus Britain finally abandoned the responsibilities she had for so long recognised towards the non-whites in southern Africa. The way had been prepared by the Vereeniging Treaty and became final with the passing of the South Africa Act. Thereafter non-whites were left at the mercy of white settlers who made no secret of their prejudices. In only one respect did Britain draw back from relinquishing all responsibilities. This was in the areas of Basutoland, Swaziland and Bechuanaland. It was expected that these areas would join the Union before long but Britain insisted on certain conditions to safeguard the rights of African peoples. It was also laid down that the inhabitants of the three states be consulted before any handing over took place. Thus these three High Commission territories, as they came to be called, remained separate from the Union and have since become independent African states. At the same time, however, it was expected that the new white settlement in Rhodesia would soon join the Union of South Africa and provision was made to make this possible.

In this chapter we have been almost exclusively concerned with white politics. During the period the new weapons, communications, transport and new economic resources had put the whites in a dominant position in southern Africa.

Whereas in the past it had cost long years of expensive and bitter fighting to extend the frontiers of the Cape a few miles, at the time under review vast areas were occupied in the space of months, often with virtually no fighting. However, though it is true that the period was dominated by the activities of the whites, the significance of the events of the time lies in its effects on the peoples of southern Africa as a whole and on the kind of society which developed in the area. We shall return to these questions in the next chapter.

8 South Africa after the Union

In the last chapter we looked at the political forces which led to the rapid spread and consolidation of white rule in southern Africa and how unification was based on a constitution which reflected the racial attitudes of the white settlers and gave the conservative farmers a political advantage over the more progressive white townspeople. At the same time new economic and social changes were also underway, creating new tensions and releasing new political forces. It is time to look at these changes which have largely dictated the development of southern Africa since the Union.

The white farmlands

As we have seen, the white farmers' system entailed the snatching of vast areas of land from the Africans. Apart from the neighbourhood of the Cape, most of the land was used primarily for cattle rearing though the growing of wheat and maize was often a secondary activity. The farmers took advantage of cheap non-European labour. But with all these advantages the farmers were not rich and many lived only slightly above subsistence level. This was because the market for their products was very limited, their farming methods primitive and the soil and weather conditions poor. The farmers operated a system, half feudal and half capitalist. On most farms there was a permanent non-European population of farm labourers and their families as well as the white farmer and his family. The Africans were often allowed a small area of land to grow their own crops and keep some cattle, providing the manual labour and domestic service the farmer needed in return. Labourers were paid small wages in cash and kind. The farmer took responsibility not only for paying his labourers but also for looking after their health, resolving quarrels and even settling disputes over the payment of bride-price or disagreements between husband and wife. He decided whether they could hold a celebration and could intervene if it disturbed him. He could punish them by driving them off his land and those who displeased him could be beaten.

This relationship involved two important concerns of the white farmer. The farmer must maintain his status as a superior being whose authority could not be questioned. This was particularly important since he was heavily outnumbered by his non-European labourers. Also, because of the size of their farms, the settlers were isolated from one another and it would be difficult to get help quickly if there was an uprising. The second concern was to retain his labourers at the lowest possible wages. The non-Europeans resented this lack of freedom and the low wages offered and preferred to support themselves either by subsistence farming in the few areas left to Africans or by seeking employment in the towns. The farmers were thus deeply hostile to any suggestion of equality between the races and to any development in the towns which might undermine their authority on their farms or tempt their labourers to leave them.

The towns

Until the end of the nineteenth century, Capetown had been the only city in southern Africa which could be compared with the large towns of Europe and America. Durban, Port Elizabeth and East London were very much smaller. A few other centres, Grahamstown in the Eastern Cape, Bloemfontein in the Orange Free State, Pretoria in the Transvaal, were only administrative centres. The remainder of the region contained numerous small villages, or 'dorps' as they were called in Afrikaans. Urban centres, apart from the ports, were almost entirely commercial and administrative centres as well as marketing centres for farm produce. The towns also acted as educational and religious centres. There was virtually no industry in the towns apart from the minor crafts essential to the everyday living of farmers and townspeople. In most towns, white and non-white residential areas were separated though some rich Indian traders and Coloured craftsmen had shops and houses in the white quarter. The greater majority of non-Europeans lived in hovels and huts in separate settlements, called locations. These locations were often moved when the whites decided that they needed the land for their own buildings. A high proportion of the non-whites were migrant labourers who moved to the towns to work for a limited time in order to earn money and they intended to return home as soon as they had saved enough. They usually left their families in their villages but in time these men began to bring their families and settle in the locations. In spite of these conditions, urban employment was always more popular than agricultural work since the Africans enjoyed greater freedom in the locations than on the farms, the towns offered a more exciting and stimulating life and the level of wages was higher.

The reserves

Areas still occupied by African peasant farmers were known as 'reserves' and still exist today. The largest is in the Transkei occupied by the Xhosa, Tembu and Pondo. Another large area is the Zululand reserve and there are also reserves in the Transvaal. Politically outside the Union, but economically and geographically tied to it, were the High Commission territories of Basutoland, Bechuanaland and Swaziland. The first two were almost entirely occupied by African peasant farmers but Swaziland contained a substantial number of white farmers. The reserves were overcrowded and poor and, as the soil was inevitably exhausted, they steadily became poorer. Thus, the population was forced to leave the reserves and to work for the whites in order to supplement their meagre earnings. This was encouraged in the interest of white employers by the levying of taxes designed to force the people to go out to work.

The development of mines and industry

The discovery of diamonds began the increased demand for non-European labour and migrant workers were attracted from all over southern Africa including the independent kingdoms outside the Union. The building of railways and a more active commercial life increased employment opportunities and these developments were taken much further with the discovery of gold. Gold mining called for large numbers of skilled and unskilled workers. Skilled labourers were mainly recruited from Britain and other overseas countries and the unskilled labour was provided by African migrants who were housed in huge bachelor dormitories, known as compounds, on land owned by the mining companies. This pattern altered slightly just after the Boer war when, as we have seen, Chinese workers were brought in for the first time. However, as reconstruction came to an end Africans were released from other employment and the Chinese were sent home.

The pattern of racial division was natural at first since the African workers came straight from their villages and did not possess any skills appropriate to gold mining. It might have been expected that the division would break down as they learned more skills. The mine-owners favoured this since skilled African labourers would be cheaper

Early railways in South Africa

and in any case it was in their interests to employ the most efficient workers regardless of race. Such a development would be in conflict with the traditional structure of southern African society.

Even before the Union, some whites on the Rand (the goldmining area round Johannesburg), had realised that steps must be taken to prevent the Africans from acquiring skills necessary to perform jobs undertaken by whites. A mine manager, Cresswell, proposed that the mines be run entirely by white labour but this idea proved unworkable and was not supported by the majority of the mine-owners. Cresswell was later invited to lead the Labour Party, to fight against the advance of Africans and to protect white labour from non-white competition.

Cresswell's policy soon received growing support for after the Anglo-Boer war the composition of the white labour force began to change.

The Boers trek to the towns

As the pace of economic life increased, farming became more competitive and there were many more unsuccessful farmers as well as those ruined by the war. Those who failed with their own farms tended to live with relatives and were known as *by-woners* (someone who lives with me). But as circumstances deteriorated on the land, farmers were no longer prepared to tolerate these by-woners. Also, by the time of the Union, the whole of southern Africa had been brought under white rule. Boundaries had been drawn and the limits of white and non-white areas defined. Thus there was no longer any question of trekking to new areas of farming land and yet the white population continued to expand at a rapid rate. Farms therefore had to be divided and, since small farms could not generally pay their way, a new trek began, a trek of Boer farmers from the land to the towns. At the time of the Union, most whites were farmers. Today, the vast majority live in the towns. The Rand alone contains more than half the total population of white South Africans.

Competition for employment: the new frontier war

The whites who came to the towns were in a very weak position because they did not possess industrial or mining skills. On the other hand, they had grown up in a rigid social structure where the white man was always master. They would naturally struggle to preserve this superiority and higher standard of living that they had learnt to believe was the natural privilege of a white skin. Thus, they had to ensure that the more important and highly paid jobs in the mines were reserved for whites only. But the mineowners opposed this policy. Inevitably, the white workers sought political means of preserving the racialist structure with the backing of their relatives on the farms. As we have seen, it was in the farmers' interests to prevent any breakdown of white superiority in the towns. Thus the scene was set for a new frontier war, that between jobs open to non-whites and those reserved for whites only. It is this struggle with its widespread implications which has largely dominated the history of South Africa to the present day.

Origin of the Nationalist Party

The Het Volk Party of the Transvaal, the Orangia Unie Party of the Orange Free State and the South Africa Party of the Cape came together as a single party for the first election after the Union. It

Botha (on the left) and Smuts (on the right)

took the name South Africa Party but was led by the veterans Botha and Smuts of the Transvaal while Hertzog was the undisputed leader of the party in the Orange Free State. However, from the beginning the party contained mutually hostile elements.

The dominant spirit was that of Botha and Smuts, both men of broad views with no deep hatred for the British and British culture. They were reconciled to South Africa being part of the Empire provided that South Africans were free to manage their own affairs. They hoped, like Rhodes and Hofmeyer before them, to unite the two white groups in common fellowship. But those within the party with bitter memories of the war did not share this attitude and feared that the English language and culture would eventually swamp their own. They longed for the return of the old Boer republics and were particularly anxious about education policies. Hertzog and his followers felt that unless Afrikaner children were educated in their own language it would disappear and they gained wide support, especially in the rural areas.

Tension within the party grew steadily worse and in 1912 matters came to a head. Hertzog claimed that the two white groups should develop separately and that only true Afrikaners should be in power. His speeches were made at a time when Botha was campaigning in English-speaking areas. Botha was naturally furious and at the end of the year he dismissed Hertzog from the cabinet. The following year, Hertzog and others formed a Nationalist Party to oppose Botha.

The First World War and the rebellion

Only four years after the Union, the First World War broke out and South Africa had to decide whether to support Britain or Germany. Botha and Smuts, in accordance with their policies, took South Africa into the war and prepared to attack the German colony of South West Africa. But this imposed intolerable strains on the Afrikaners. To some of them Britain was still an enemy, Germany had supported the republics and German volunteers had fought alongside the Boers during their own war. A half-hearted and badly organised rebellion broke out but it was soon suppressed and Botha sent South African troops to invade and capture German South West Africa. South African troops also took part in the successful campaigns against German East Africa and fought in Europe as well. In these campaigns non-whites as well as whites took part though Africans were not permitted to bear arms and were restricted to non-combatant but often equally dangerous rôles. Nevertheless, travel abroad and the discovery of non-racialist societies opened the eyes of many non-white soldiers and aroused their political consciousness.

Though the rebellion had been suppressed with little effort, it was an important symptom of the underlying discontent with the pro-British policy of Botha and Smuts. This sentiment, defeated on the military front, expressed itself on the political front through the Nationalist Party which grew in strength in the rural areas of the Provinces. It remained bitterly hostile to South African participation in the war and afterwards it even petitioned the League of Nations for the return of the three republics.

The depression and the Rand revolution

The end of the war was marked by a period of economic boom which momentarily disguised the tension within South Africa. But the boom was soon followed by a world slump, the price of gold tumbled, export markets shrank, many business men became bankrupt and the weaker and less efficient farmers were forced to seek work in the towns just as opportunities for employment were contracting. The slump forced the capitalists to reorganise their labour in order to reduce costs and prevent the closure of some mines. But the colour bar made it impossible for non-whites to be employed in certain categories of employment and shortly after the war the white labour organisations in Johannesburg had forced the mine owners to agree to a standstill agreement in which this colour bar was preserved. Yet the most obvious way of reducing costs was to break down this agreement.

Many Africans who had by now acquired the new skills would work for much lower wages. The Chamber of Mines therefore decided to do away with the standstill agreement and this drove the white workers to desperation. A series of bitter strikes broke out and in 1922 the white workers in the Rand rose in open revolt. They succeeded in seizing and holding Johannesburg for a few days but Smuts rushed troops in and, after fighting in which about 200 people were killed, the revolt was suppressed.

The Labour-Nationalist alliance

This revolt was a turning point in South Africa's history because it brought into the open the struggle of the white worker to protect his rights and maintain his superior position over the non-whites. The white workers turned to political means to achieve their aims and the Labour Party was their political mouthpiece. The economic crisis had led to a natural alliance between the white farmers and the white industrial workers and the Labour Party thus allied with the National- ist Party to fight the coming election on a united front.

The Pact Government and its segregation policy

The political strength of the new alliance was proved in 1924 when the Pact won a majority in the elections and was able to form a government. The policies which South Africa has followed in recent years are for the most part simply a return to those of the Pact, pursued for essentially the same reasons. The main issue the Pact faced on being elected was the increasing pauperisation of a large section of the white population. Because of the traditional colour divisions in society, whites could not be employed as manual workers in the towns and the numbers of semi-skilled and skilled jobs was limited. South Africa was still mainly a primary producer with very little manufacturing industry. Moreover, whites from the rural areas were unskilled, poorly educated and unfamiliar with urban environment. The Afrikaners were the worst hit; they were the most conservative and least educated of the farming community, their language cut them off from access to education and technical advance in the world at large. They were thus the least capable of adaptation to new farming methods and were dominated in the towns by an alien language group and culture. The Afrikaner began to consider himself an outcast in his own country and this bred a fierce nationalist spirit and a deter- mination to use political power to save himself from his economic plight.

The Pact could ease the problem of employment in two ways; by increasing the size of the cake and by ensuring that the larger slice went to the whites. A policy of active industrialisation was undertaken. South Africa's second industrial revolution was begun with the open- ing of the national steel industry at Vereeniging. This was operated by a national corporation but private industry was also favoured by a deliberate policy of protecting home industries by customs charges on imported goods. The government supported and extended the policy of protecting the whites from non-white competition and in many cases non-whites were dismissed from jobs in order to give employment to poor whites. This was done on a large scale on the railways which were run as a government corporation. The policy was to keep the African population confined as far as possible to the Reserves which were slightly enlarged for the purpose, to limit migration by Africans to the towns, to abolish African voting rights in the Cape and to provide them with a separate and much reduced form of political representation.

The 'Black Peril' election

This last policy involved a change in the Entrenched Clause in the Constitution but the government was unable to obtain the necessary two-thirds majority in Parliament. In 1929 it appealed to the voters in a general election fought on the basis of the government's racial policies. It succeeded in winning a substantial majority. By this time, however, the composition of the Pact had changed considerably. Some of the leaders of the Labour Party, under the influence of Socialist ideas, were beginning to consider the non-Europeans not as a separate group but the victims of capitalist exploitation. But the voters were not convinced and the Labour Party thus declined as a political force and its representation dropped sharply as a result of the election.

The birth of the United Party

Soon after the Black Peril election, another world slump was triggered off by the Wall Street crash of 1930 and its effects were worsened by the government's attempt to stick to the gold standard. The Nationalists saw their popularity steadily shrinking. They were still unable to obtain the two-thirds majority to abolish African voters and they began to think of a coalition with the South Africa Party. The two parties were not divided on any deep matter of policy. The South Africa Party, though containing more liberal elements, fully supported the idea of white supremacy. The coalition was brought about in March, 1933 and, after a resounding election victory later that year, the two parties fused in 1934 to become the United Party. Hertzog, who remained Prime Minister, was then able to achieve his ambition of removing African voters from the register. In April, 1936, the Native Representation Act removed African voters from the common roll and provided for the separate representation of African interests by Native Representatives, who must be white.

The Purified Nationalist Party

The coalition was not acceptable to a small group of Afrikaner nationalists led by D. F. Malan. They felt that, by joining Smuts, Hertzog had sold out to British imperialism and capitalism. In July 1934 they broke away to form the Purified Nationalist Party, then widely known as the Nationalist Party, which became the spokesman of bitter nationalist feeling. As early as 1918, extremist Afrikaners had formed a secret society, known as the Broederbond (Brotherhood), which was pledged to fight for the Afrikaner language and culture and to seek to infiltrate all positions of influence within the country. Malan could count on the support of the Broederbond which was steadily growing more powerful. He was an initiated Broederbonder.

The rise of Nazi Germany and gathering tension in Europe imposed severe strains on the loyalties of the white South African population. They sympathised with the racialist spirit of Nazism and the belief in a master race was shared, even if in a rather different form, by the majority. There was, moreover, the traditional sympathy for Germany and hatred for Britain. Inevitably, Nazism exercised a considerable influence on the growing movement of extreme Afrikaner nationalism and greatly strengthened the upsurge of Afrikaner emotion which accompanied the Voortrekker centenary celebrations, held in 1938. Two new Afrikaner nationalist organisations were formed; the Reddingdaadsbond, an economic organisation dedicated to winning a position for Afrikaners in the ownership and control of industry, and the Ossewabrandwag (Oxwagon Sentinel), a semi-secret, para-military organisation dedicated to watching over the spirit of the Great Trek and winning political power for the true Afrikaners. This latter organisation was strongly influenced by Nazi ideas and methods. But the rise of Hitler and his demand for the return of German colonies posed a direct threat to South Africa who increasingly regarded South West Africa as part of their territory. The majority of whites there were now of South African descent. Thus, in spite of the attractions of Nazi philosophy, substantial support for Britain against Germany was growing.

The Second World War

The government was deeply divided at the outbreak of the Second World War in 1939. Hertzog and many of his followers from the old Nationalist Party favoured a policy of neutrality and gained the support of the Purified Nationalists. But Smuts, with the support of English-speaking members and moderate Afrikaners, wanted to join the British side. Smuts won by a small majority and the party split immediately. Hertzog resigned as Prime Minister to make way for Smuts and he joined with his supporters and the Purified Nationalists in opposing the war. One of them, Oswald Pirow, ex-Minister of Defence before the war, went further and formed an organisation, known as the New Order, to fight for an Afrikaner Republic on Nazi lines.

South African troops served on many fronts during the war and many non-Europeans also fought in the struggle against the Axis powers though they were again restricted to non-combatant rôles. This produced a slight shift in government attitudes towards racial policies for the interdependence of the South African peoples was clear. To maintain the production level required by the war effort, the industrial colour-bar had to be modified. The fact that non-whites served alongside whites in the battlefield, even if in humbler positions, made many feel that they could not be ignored once peace was restored. When the Japanese threatened to seize Madagascar, a natural position for launching an attack on South Africa, Smuts even went as far as to proclaim that he would arm the non-whites in a combined South African resistance. In this atmosphere Hofmeyer, nephew of 'Onze Jan' and leader of the liberal element of Smuts' party, was made deputy Prime Minister and long overdue measures of social improvement for non-whites were undertaken.

On the other hand, opposition became more extremist than ever. Helped by the government suppression of the Ossewabrandwag, the Purified Nationalists emerged as the undisputed leaders of extreme Afrikaner nationalism absorbing many of the Nazi principles of the other organisations in the process. During this time, they organised their racial attitudes in the form of a political philosophy called 'apartheid'.

At the end of the war Smuts and his party were in power with a huge majority and the next election was not due until 1948. The Allied victory seemed to have proved Smuts right and to have discredited the opponents of war. The United Party seemed assured of political power for the foreseeable future. But this appearance was deceptive, for the government had inevitably irritated a large section of the white population by the controls and regulations it had imposed during the war. The fact that many of these were continued after 1945 caused more discontent. Also, there was the anti-climax and disillusionment when the hard fought for peace did not produce the promised paradise. This was felt particularly among the ex-service-men. The situation was exploited by the Nationalists who had the advantage of the support of the rural areas which, in accordance with the Constitution, gave them a disproportionate number of seats in Parliament. The ruling party seriously underestimated this opposition and did nothing to preserve public support.

The apartheid election of 1948

The greatest issue of the 1948 election was racial policy. The United Party was split between a liberal wing, led by Hofmeyer, who looked forward to the ultimate disappearance of discrimination though over a very long period, and an extremist wing of United Party supporters whose prejudices were as strong as the Nationalists. Smuts seemed to be veering in the liberal direction but could never be decisive on racial matters. The great majority, like Smuts, were confused, recognising that racialism was wrong but not wanting dramatic changes in their own lifetime. The policy of the United Party was therefore one of 'wait and see', a policy allowing things to drift until a time when discrimination would eventually disappear.

In opposition to this, the Nationalist line was positive and definite, the theory of *apartheid*. This political creed had been worked out by Afrikaner thinkers, many of them University teachers during the period of the war. It was a mixture of traditional white South African attitudes, Nazi racialist thought, Calvanist Christianity and genuine, albeit misguided, humanitarianism. Apartheid simply means separateness. According to the theory, every race has a personality of its own and a culture distinctive of that personality. Its own separate destiny has been laid down for each race by God. Thus racial contact or mixture will contaminate the individual races and interfere with God's plan. Races should therefore develop along parallel lines but never meet. Apartheid supporters have always been muddled about their definition of a race. Sometimes they thought Europeans, Africans, Coloureds and Indians represented different races while others considered each African tribe as a separate entity. Similarly, some thought of all white South Africans as one race, others of English and Afrikaner as separate communities which should have their own uncontaminated cultures.

In accordance with the theory of apartheid, the traditional pattern of segregation in South Africa should be maintained and even extended. The infiltration of non-whites into white jobs must stop and

A segregated railway bridge

restrictions on Africans entering the towns increased. Social contact of any kind between the races should be eliminated. Separate facilities for the races should be provided in all public places and to avoid confusion the whole population should be carefully classified into racial groups each with its own residential area in the towns. Finally, there should be ultimate territorial separation. Africans should be encouraged to remain on the Reserves which would ultimately become independent states. Africans who chose to live in the white areas would have to put up with the restrictions imposed on them.

Apartheid offered the whites the opportunity of maintaining their supremacy while at the same time satisfying their consciences that their actions were reasonable and just according to God's will. In reality, of course, the theory contained a major contradiction. How could the Africans be free to develop independently on the Reserves which formed only 13 per cent of the land area when they formed the vast majority of the population? The reserves were already hopelessly overcrowded and to expand and develop them would cost enormous sums, a policy directly contrary to the interests of the whites. Also, where would the non-white labour come from for the industry in the white areas in order to maintain the economy? If the Africans on the Reserves did achieve full cultural and economic independence, what would prevent them from forming international alliances to redress the supression of their people in the white areas? There has always been a division among apartheid supporters between those who regard it merely as a pretext for maintaining white supremacy and justifying segregation to the outside world and those who seriously believe that non-Europeans should be given the opportunity to develop separately to the same level as the whites.

Apartheid was a powerful election weapon in 1948. The Nationalists retained their support in the rural areas and won over large numbers of white urban workers who had most to fear from non-white competition. This, together with their excessive share of rural seats, gave them victory in the election and they were able to form a government. From that time, they have been able to increase their hold and the politics of South Africa have been dominated by their attempts to put apartheid into practice.

The attempt to impose apartheid since 1948

It is impossible to set out here all the measures taken to impose apartheid and I will merely indicate some of the main lines which have been followed. In public places separate amenities have been provided for Europeans and non-Europeans. This has meant separate residential areas, entrances to public buildings and offices, buses, railway compartments, etc. Non-whites are now refused admission to public halls to watch plays, films, sport and to hear concerts and lectures. There have even been attempts to prevent different races from worshipping together in the same churches. Segregation in employment has been extended and where non-whites undertake the more remunerative and skilled jobs, the attempt is made to confine their activities to the service of their own race only. Thus, Coloured and African taxi drivers are forbidden to convey white passengers, African and Coloured doctors and nurses cannot attend white patients.

Vigorous attempts are made to preserve the towns for the whites and to prevent non-whites from acquiring permanent residence. An African needs a permit to travel to the towns and on entering he must register and obtain a work permit. If he fails to find employment he may be returned to the country and even if he does find a job, he can be deported from the town as soon as he loses his job. Africans are often forbidden to bring their families into the towns. The separation of residential areas is carried out under the Group Areas Act under which areas are marked out for occupation by one race only. Members of other races are forced to sell their property and move out. This measure has produced much hardship, particularly in the major towns like Capetown, Durban and Johannesburg where residential areas were not clearly defined and non-Europeans owned flourishing businesses in what have now been defined as white areas. The Indians are probably the chief sufferers under this particular policy since they have often been forced to sell their business and properties in the town centres at a price fixed by the whites and move out miles from town where business prospects are much bleaker.

The old, unified educational system has been destroyed and a

The main street of a shanty town near Johannesburg

separate system for Africans, known as Bantu Education, is offered in non-white schools which are kept under strict government control. The object is to prevent Africans from being trained for positions in white society which they will not be permitted to occupy. Africans are no longer admitted to the universities of Capetown, Witwatersrand, Natal and Rhodes and separate 'universities' are provided. There are even separate 'universities' for the African tribes. Members of staff are liable to dismissal for openly disagreeing with the policy of apartheid.

In return, Africans are offered eventual independent development in their Reserves but it is difficult to see how these areas can provide a reasonable livelihood for the inhabitants and even the most optimistic supporters of apartheid admit that a large proportion of the Africans will be needed to work in white areas for the foreseeable future. Apart from the Transkei and Zululand, the Reserves are small and scattered and talk of developing them as independent states is obviously absurd. The only area where the theory has been applied is in the Transkei, which received internal self-government in 1963, but it remains firmly under South African government supervision since by far the greatest portion of its budget is supplied by the Union. Thus, full independence in the Reserves would be a farce since they could not possibly accommodate and support more than a small part of the African population. These areas lack natural resources, are poor farming areas and are economically dependent on the Union. They are bound, therefore, to remain little more than labour reserves, where African workers can be sent when they are too old or feeble to be useful. They can then be supported without South Africa having to take responsibility for their welfare. Even if a policy of developing the reserves into independent Bantustans could provide a satisfactory solution to the problems concerning relations between Africans and Europeans, it would still leave the problems of the other non-white groups unsolved. The most that they have been promised is cultural autonomy in their own areas and a measure of independent local government.

The attempt to impose apartheid in South Africa has not only caused a great deal of upheaval and suffering but has also given rise to increased political tension. Hostility between the races has increased and many who would in normal circumstances support moderate constitutional progress have felt forced by the harsh extremes of government policy to adopt more extreme forms of opposition. Yet this increased tension has helped to strengthen the government. The basis for white support of apartheid is fear; physical fear and economic fear. The greater the tensions between the races and the greater the pressure from the outside world, the more the whites feel they must unite to defend their political position. Moreover, since 1948, South Africa has enjoyed an economic boom made possible by favourable world trading conditions. As the standard of living for the whites continues to rise, so they become more determined to protect their prosperity.

In 1948, the Nationalists won a majority of five in the election. Their victory was a surprise, even to themselves, and was made possible because of the distribution of Parliamentary seats. In the election, the United Party in fact won a substantial majority of the votes but not as many seats as the Nationalists. In the following general election in 1953, the Nationalists again won a majority of seats but was still a government of the minority. However, in the 1958 election, the Nationalists for the first time received a majority of the votes. Since then the substantial support of the whites for apartheid has not been doubted. In 1961, the Nationalists at last felt strong enough to achieve their long cherished dreams of making the Union a Republic in memory of the Boer Republics. A national referendum gave them a clear majority to do so but it meant a review of its position in the British Commonwealth and pressure from non-white Commonwealth states forced them to withdraw in 1961. Since then, South Africa is left in isolation to face almost universal hostility from the outside world. But this hostility has merely strengthened the fears of the whites and their determination to protect their interests. The Nationalist hold has been stronger since a Republic was declared than ever before.

The collapse of constitutional opposition

As the application of apartheid has become more and more extreme, so moderate opposition has become more impossible and more point-less. The traditional Cape liberalism has been destroyed as a political force. This development can be illustrated in the fate of the United Party. As we have seen, this party won a majority of the votes in 1948 but since then it has not been able to offer a convincing alternative to apartheid. It possessed a liberal wing of people genuinely opposed to apartheid but the vast majority within the party were basically in sympathy with it even if they did not like its extreme application. The only time when white political opposition looked like being effective was from 1951 to 1953 when the United Party was able to prevent the Nationalists from obtaining the necessary two-thirds majority to abolish Coloured voters in the Cape. In retaliation, the government proposed to effect the decision by a simple majority but this was declared unconstitutional by the Supreme Court. However, the government then set up a special court, the High Court of Parliament, with powers to override the Supreme Court. This blatant tampering with the Constitution evoked widespread opposition. The initiative was taken by a new organisation, the Torch Commando, organised by ex-servicemen of the Second World War who pledged themselves to defend the Constitution. This organisation grew rapidly into a national movement of massive proportion. A number of ugly incidents occurred at their meetings and there was even talk of civil war within the white community. But it soon became obvious that the Torch Commandos defended the Constitution but not the belief in Coloured voting rights. The government therefore dropped the idea of the High Court of Parliament and the Torch Commando speedily collapsed. In the 1953 elections, the United Party lost ground because their defence of Coloured voters alienated many more whites than it attracted. In 1956, the government was able to abolish non-white voters without violating the Constitution by inflating the Senate with its own supporters to obtain the two-thirds majority.

After the 1953 election, the United Party began to break up. Those genuinely opposed to apartheid formed two radical groups, the Liberal Party and the Progressive Party. Other former United Party supporters provide no real opposition but merely criticism in detail. In fact some opposition members have become even more extreme than government supporters in order to win over white support. At the present time, the only effective opposition in Parliament to the government's policies is provided by one member of the Progressive Party, Mrs Helen Suzman.

Growth of a police state

As opposition has been forced to become increasingly more extreme, so the government has steadily perfected the means of crushing it. Legal devices, such as the Suppression of Communism Act and more recently the Ninety-day Detention Act, have made it possible for people who oppose the system to be arrested and, without a trial, to be held in detention for long periods and forbidden from attending meetings or publishing their views. The political branch of the police, the Special Branch, has perfected its means of hunting down opponents to the regime until it has probably become the most efficient and effective political police force in the world. At the same time, ever-increasing sums have been devoted to military defence so that the Republic has a better military force than any other nation of comparable size. Opponents of the regime have been imprisoned, broken down psychologically, deported or forced to flee the country until, on the surface at least, all resistance has been broken.

Social and economic development of non-Europeans since the Union

The non-Europeans can be divided into three main groups, each with a separate legal and political status. The overwhelming majority are, of course, Africans. The Coloureds are a result of racial mixture, mainly between Europeans, Africans, Hottentots and Bushmen plus a small community of persons of Malay origin. The number of

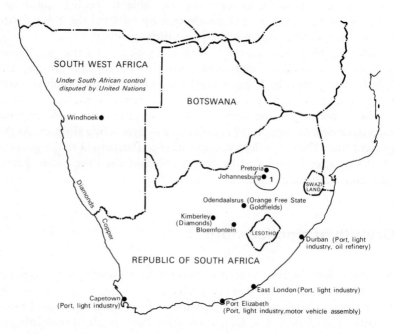

1 (Industrial hub of South Africa Gold, iron and steel, light industry)

The Republic of South Africa today, showing some of the main areas of economic activity

Coloureds amounts to about half that of the whites and they are most numerous in the Western Cape Province where Africans have only begun to establish themselves. The Indians were originally imported into Natal to work on the sugar plantations in the latter half of the nineteenth century but, having been in South Africa for several generations, have lost all but sentimental links with the land of their origin. They are most numerous in Natal. Many of them are still unskilled labourers but others are traders and some have become prosperous businessmen.

All these racial groups have been radically affected by the industrial revolution which has changed the face of South Africa. The process of industrialisation and urbanisation has affected them as much as the Europeans. With the continuous expansion of employment in urban centres, they have poured from the country into the towns until they now constitute the majority of the urban population. Like the Europeans, the non-whites suffered from the slump in the inter-war period and have benefited from the boom since 1945. Standards of living have risen, educational opportunities have expanded and, in spite of artificial barriers to stop them, the sheer pressure of demand for labour has enabled them to climb higher and higher up the employment ladder. On the other hand, the process of absorption of the non-European population into the increasingly urbanised and industrialised economy has been and still is gravely distorted. Wages for non-Europeans have been kept lower than those for whites and the majority of the population have benefited far less from the growth of the economy than it would have done in a freer system. Most of the non-Europeans still live in conditions of poverty and wretchedness and attempts to improve their positions in employment and opportunity are met with the stiffest opposition from the whites. Educational opportunities have been severely hampered because of apartheid policies. The Bantu Education Scheme and university education is deliberately intended to prevent non-Europeans from developing a sense of common identity with whites and even one non-European group with another. Financial resources for their education are pitifully inadequate and it is not surprising that the vast majority of non-white children still receive no education or too little to equip them for anything but the most menial tasks.

Worse than their deprived economic position is the deliberate insecurity of non-whites. Permission to undertake any skilled or semi-skilled work is given only in view of the absence of white men to do it and any slight fall in the economy will result in non-Europeans being removed in favour of white job-seekers. The establishing of their families in the towns is deliberately discouraged so as to maintain a migrant labour force, particularly of Africans. Africans are prevented from acquiring freehold property rights in urban areas and Indians and Coloureds are sometimes forced to abandon their homes and businesses under the Group Areas Act.

The hardest of all to bear however is the constant humiliation to which non-Europeans are subjected. In every sphere of life they are made to feel second class citizens. As we saw, living areas, public buildings, transport and entertainments are strictly segregated. They may not enter European areas after dark and must always carry a permit giving them permission to live in the towns. Their whole lives are subject to regulations from authorities they had no hand in electing and they suffer harsh and humiliating experiences in the hands of the police. Under these circumstances it is not surprising that demoralisation is widespread; drunkenness and drug addiction are rife and gangs of mentally unbalanced and anti-social hoodlums rob,

An African priest showing his pass. His photograph, name and number have been blacked out

rape and murder their own people adding to the misery and insecurity of life in the non-white locations. In reaction against their rejection by white society, some Africans have developed an extreme conservatism as a psychological defence. Though working in European areas, they cling as far as possible to a traditional pattern of dress. They hold fast to traditional cultures and ceremonies such as marriage and initiation rights and they consciously profess their rejection of European society and standards.

The development of non-European activity

Non-European political activity has to be considered separately for the three main groups. The Coloureds were in many ways in the most favourable position to develop political organisation. They adopted Afrikaans or English as their mother tongue and their culture was essentially European. The degree of Western education was higher amongst them than the other non-white groups and a considerable number of them were employed in skilled jobs from an early date. Many of them acquired the vote and participated in the politics of the Cape colony. In 1903, a political party, the African Peoples' Organisation, was formed and in 1905 Dr. Abdurahman, an outstanding Coloured politican, became its leader. In spite of his many efforts to cement an alliance between his party and the Africans, differences of culture and status long prevented this effective common front from being achieved.

The Indians, too, had an encouraging beginning. Many of them possessed high educational qualifications and substantial financial resources. In relation to the Africans they were a privileged group and the nationalism in their mother country inspired their opposition to the restrictions in South Africa. Indian political agitation began in 1894 when the Natal Indian Congress was founded under the leadership of a young Indian lawyer, Mahatma Gandhi. He perfected his policy of passive resistance as a weapon against white oppression before using it on a much larger scale in the struggle for the liberation of India. Gandhi's fight was aimed at the removal of restrictions governing the rights of Indians to move about the country and to purchase property. It won the respect of some white leaders and forced minor concessions.

Gandhi's policy had a great influence on African politics and the Africans later adopted it and employed it on a large scale. However, like the Coloureds, the Indians for a long time acted independently of the other non-European groups and a common front took a long time to develop.

In the Cape, where the wealthier Africans had voting rights under the 'colour-blind' constitution, African political consciousness was actively fostered by some of the more liberal white politicians who needed the support of the African voters. The Cape Native Voters' Association was founded in the 1880s and in 1884 J. T. Jabavu launched the first African newspaper, *Imvo Zabantsundu*. The C.N.V.A. naturally remained close to its white supporters hoping to achieve its aims with the help of white liberals. African organisations

Mahatma Gandhi as a young man in South Africa

were at first small and local but the threat to non-whites in the draft constitution for the Union made them realise that they must unite on a national scale. A South African Native National Conference was summoned which sent Jabavu and Walter Rubusana to London to petition against the proposed constitution.

The Ethiopian Movement

Political awareness among the mass of the African population first expressed itself in a religious form known as Ethiopianism. This was natural since most educated Africans had received their education from missionaries and were closely attached to the Churches. In the latter part of the nineteenth century, these Africans became increasingly aware of the contradiction between equality of men in God's eyes and the practice of white missionaries which was often as prejudiced as the ordinary white population. These missionaries failed to give responsibility in the churches to African members. Consequently, many Africans broke away to form churches free from European control. But struggles for leadership led to many divisions so that several hundred African churches came into existence. Though the Ethiopian movement was on the surface religious, it had a strong political element since it was an expression of African resentment at European dominance.

The Ethiopian movement had little immediate political effect but it did serve to awaken and encourage political opposition to European control. The churches, too, offered a training ground for organising, administering, public speaking, committee work, etc.

Founding of the African National Congress

The South African Native National Conference expired after what proved to be a hopeless delegation to London, but the idea of a national African political organisation remained alive. In 1912, delegates from all over the Union met to form the South African Native National Congress, later the African National Congress, and since then it has been the main platform for African political opinion in South Africa. Its membership is exclusively African but its ideals are non-racial and it has fought for political and economic equality for all the races. It founded and ran an important newspaper, *Abantu-Batho*, and popularised a number of songs and slogans which have become part of the fabric of African political life in southern Africa. The hymn, 'Nkosi Sikelele Afrika', has become the national anthem of Tanzania and Zambia. Like all non-European organisations in South Africa, the African National Congress has been in a cruel dilemma. With no effective voice in Parliament and faced with concerted resistance from the majority of whites, its attempts to obtain concessions are doomed to failure. Yet unconstitutional attempts at change had brought the full weight of the organised state machinery to bear on its supporters. Thus it has experienced periods of rapid growth and enthusiasm followed by periods of disillusionment and collapse.

Perhaps the highest point reached by the African National Congress before the Second World War was in the anti-pass movement of 1919–20 when masses of Africans destroyed their passes. But, though their action was strictly non-violent, their meetings were forcibly broken up, hundreds of arrests were made and the movement was effectively crushed.

Rise and fall of the Industrial and Commercial Union

Thereafter, the initiative in African political activity passed to the Industrial and Commercial Union, founded in 1919 by Clements Kadalie, a Malawian working in South Africa. Nominally a trade union, it was in fact a political organisation with an emphasis on economic issues. From small beginnings it grew rapidly until in 1928 it claimed about 200,000 members, by far the largest membership of any non-white organisation in South Africa. But it faced the same problems as the African National Congress; constitutional opposition was ineffective, unconstitutional activity was ruthlessly crushed. Trouble really began when the Communist members broke with Kadalie and his supporters. In 1926 they were expelled and finally they broke away to form an independent body. This triggered off more splits and the whole organisation rapidly collapsed.

The Defiance Campaign of 1952-1953

By far the largest and most impressive demonstration of non-European political activity began in 1953 by which time the repressive legislation of apartheid had brought hitherto divided groups together to face a common enemy. In April 1952, the African National Congress and the South Africa Indian Congress announced a massive campaign of passive resistance to unjust laws. The idea was that people of all races should refuse to obey the apartheid laws and allow themselves to

Women leaving jail after serving a term of imprisonment for taking part in the Defiance Campaign

be arrested *en masse* until the combination of moral pressure and physical breakdown should lead to their repeal. The campaign began on June 26 and rapidly assumed large proportions. It evoked tremendous enthusiasm and was conducted with admirable discipline and restraint. Many Coloureds joined in as did a number of white liberals. But government response was violent. Sentences of flogging were imposed. In October racial riots broke out in Port Elizabeth and East London. No connection between them and the Defiance Movement was ever proved and an enquiry was denied. It was easy for the government to use the riots as an excuse to crush the Movement altogether.

But the Defiance Movement had set an impressive beginning for co-operation between the different racial groups in the struggle against Apartheid. In 1954, the African National Congress, the South African Indian Congress, the Coloured Peoples' Political Organisation and the Congress of Democrats, a white political organisation founded in 1952 to struggle for racial equality, decided to hold a multi-racial 'congress of the people' to frame a 'Freedom Charter' for the future of South Africa. The Congress met in 1955 at Kliptown near Johannesburg and was attended by several thousand delegates. It drew up a lengthy charter outlining a blueprint for a fully democratic and non-racial society.

Treason trials and the birth of Pan-Africanist Congress

Government response to this demonstration of multi-racial solidarity was the arrest of 151 members of all races in December 1956. They were placed on trial and charged with treason. This trial dragged on until 1961 with the acquittal of all the accused but meanwhile the anti-apartheid organisations were deprived of their top leadership. This situation was responsible for the split in the A.N.C. in 1958. A number of its supporters broke away to form the Pan-Africanist Congress. Its policy was not, however, radically different from the African Nationalist Congress.

In March 1960 occurred one of the most horrifying and dramatic events in the whole history of the non-European struggle against apartheid. The Pan-Africanist Congress had called on Africans to surrender their passes *en masse* and seek arrest by the police. A large crowd including women and children collected round the police station at Sharpeville and, though unarmed and peaceful, the police,

Sharpeville. The crowd flees as the police open fire

admittedly frightened, suddenly opened fire. More than 200 Africans, men, women and children, were slaughtered. The Sharpville incident provoked a number of demonstrations throughout South Africa and roused violent protest all over the world. For the first time the horrors of apartheid were brought home to millions of people overseas.

Government reaction was to ban the A.N.C. and the P.A.C. and to end all constitutional political activity by non-Europeans. Since then non-European political leaders and their sympathisers have been imprisoned, arrested and forced into exile. Meeting in London, these exiles formed a United Freedom Front to carry on the underground struggle outside South Africa's borders.

The government's action in repressing constitutional opposition has convinced some non-European politicians that non-violent means have no hope of progress. They have been convinced, however reluctantly, that the liberation of South Africa can only be brought about by organised violence. In 1961, a new organisation, 'Unkhonto we sizwe', 'The Spear of the Nation', was formed dedicated to political change through sabotage of white property. A similar organisation, 'Poqo', was formed the following year. Since then, African parties have continued the struggle from outside South Africa's borders with the sympathy of the outside world and particularly the independent African states. Significant numbers of Africans have been smuggled abroad for training as guerilla fighters in Algeria, China and else-where. Much larger numbers of non-European and white opposers to apartheid are in permanent exile in Britain, independent Africa, America and other countries.

Future prospects

Though the Nationalist government remains firmly in power and apartheid is being applied ever more sternly, there are factors which give ground for hope. The rapidly expanding economy has largely solved the problem of the poor whites so that the deep feeling of economic insecurity is no longer an important factor. Not only has the balance of white population moved from the farms to the towns, but the farms themselves are being mechanised, a process which must eventually reduce the dependence of the farmer on cheap, unskilled labour.

The expansion of the economy has forced the whites to allow some non-Europeans to climb further up the employment ladder, and this is likely to be a continuing process. The spending power of the non-whites is now an important economic factor and increasing areas of the white business world depend on it. The very policy of apartheid has had paradoxical effects; Africans and other non-Europeans must be given training and responsibilities in their own areas and these trained individuals can no longer be considered as inferior. This situation has been made more extreme by the emergence of Lesotho and Botswana as independent states. The South African government wants to maintain good relations with them but this can only be done by treating their leaders as social equals.

South Africa's desire for friendly relations with African states makes it reach out beyond its borders. Intimate relations have been established with Malawi and a delegation from that country was entertained in South Africa's most exclusive hotel. Non-white states, such as Japan and Malaya and independent African countries, have come to take a larger part as trading partners with South Africa. The Republic has been forced to recognise Japanese as whites. These developments probably influenced the outcome of the 1970 election when a breakaway party—the Herstigte Nasionale Party—formed in protest against what it regarded as signs of excessive liberalism in racial matters in the Nationalist Party, was totally defeated at the polls. For the first time since 1948 the Nationalist Party lost a number of seats to the United Party. Mrs Suzman, the only member of the Progressive Party, was re-elected with a much increased majority and her party won votes in a number of other constituencies though it did not succeed in capturing any more parliamentary seats. The outside world is, moreover, growing impatient with South Africa's backward looking policies. The United Nations decreed that the Republic can no longer administer South West Africa and has been trying though without success to formulate a scheme for taking that area away from the Republic.

But it would be foolish to underrate the strength of deeply entrenched prejudice in South Africa where there are no signs of abandoning the policy of apartheid. Steps are being taken to limit non-white advance in industry by encouraging the immigration of poor white labour from countries like Greece and Italy. The government even seems prepared to risk damaging the economy by forcing firms to decentralise industry to the borders of African homelands to preserve apartheid. Even if economic change does eventually cause political and social change, bitterness between the races may have grown too strong for reconciliation to be possible.

International pressure could bring about a speedier change but South Africa's military strength and the heavy economic investment of Western powers in her industry are powerful deterrents to any really effective action of this kind. The future does not look bright.

9   Central Africa from the establishment of colonial rule

The establishment of colonial rule in Central Africa took place while the African peoples were experiencing great upheavals. The invasions of the Ngoni, Ndebele and Kololo and the expansion of the slave trade from the east coast had produced widespread disruption, misery and death. But it is easy to exaggerate the destruction of old societies and institutions. Even in Rhodesia after successive invasions and intrusions much of the old culture and even a sense of political unity lived on. The Ngoni and Ndebele invaders were actively building up new states embracing peoples of differing tribes and in the floodplains of the upper Zambesi, a Lozi counter-revolution drove out the Kololo and restored a traditional dynasty. The slave trade, too, brought some benefits. For example, the Bemba kingdom made use of firearms to strengthen itself internally and engage in steady expansion. A new balance was emerging but did not have time to establish itself before European intervention radically changed the situation.

The establishment of colonial rule in Rhodesia

In Rhodesia, colonial rule was introduced by the British South Africa Company of Cecil Rhodes. He used his vast financial resources and those of British capitalism to equip a column of South African whites who established themselves in the Shona-occupied areas in 1890. In 1893 a pretext was found for war with the Ndebele and Lobengula's regiments were mowed down with Maxim guns. The king fled to die in exile and, since the pioneer column was mainly made up of white settlers from the south, Rhodesia was from the outset very much an extension northwards of the South African system of white settler domination.

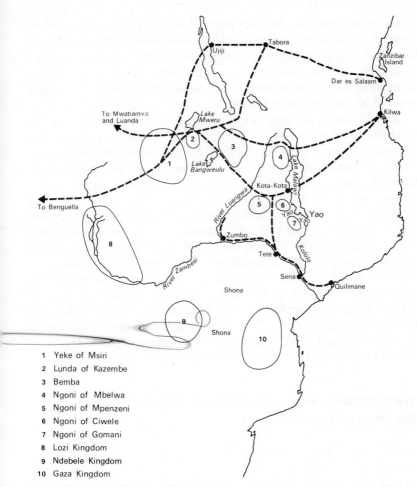

1 Yeke of Msiri
2 Lunda of Kazembe
3 Bemba
4 Ngoni of Mbelwa
5 Ngoni of Mpenzeni
6 Ngoni of Ciwele
7 Ngoni of Gomani
8 Lozi Kingdom
9 Ndebele Kingdom
10 Gaza Kingdom

Central Africa on the eve of the colonial period, showing the approximate position of some of the more powerful African States and the main trade-routes

The establishment of colonial rule in Malawi (Nyasaland)

In Malawi colonial rule was preceded by extensive missionary activity. The African Lakes Company, a partly humanitarian, partly commercial venture was set up to keep the missionaries supplied, to tap the trade of the area and to replace the slave trade with legitimate trade. In the disturbed conditions, the missions and the Company were bound to exercise considerable political power and mission stations tended to become little political states with quarrels, often leading to war, with Arab, Swahili and Yao traders. With few resources they pressed for British intervention, an important factor in the British government's decision to intervene in the area and exclude Portuguese hopes of occupying southern Malawi.

Colonial rule in the area of modern Malawi was established by Sir Harry Johnston acting as an official agent of the British government but partly financed by Rhodes in return for commercial concessions. Johnston's army was mainly made up of Indian troops lent to him by the British government of India. He met with strong resistance but by 1894 most of the area was occupied. In spite of Rhodes' assistance, the imperial government, under pressure from the missionaries and their supporters, refused to hand Malawi over to the British South Africa Company and it became the British Protectorate of Nyasaland, a name it retained until independence when it was called Malawi.

In Nyasaland Johnston made considerable grants to white settlers, especially in the south, in order, he hoped, to develop the economy and provide a revenue to meet the expenses of administration. But these settlers were not in a dominant position and the greater part of the land remained in African hands. The imperial government was firmly in control and the missions remained politically very important.

The establishment of colonial rule in Zambia (Northern Rhodesia)

In the area of modern Zambia, as in Nyasaland, colonial rule was preceded by considerable missionary activity. In the eastern half colonial rule was established by treaties through Johnston and his agents operating from Nyasaland under his agreement with Rhodes. Troops from Nyasaland helped to defeat resistance to the establishment of the British South Africa Company's rule. In the west colonial rule was established by agents of Rhodes operating from the south. The most important treaty was with the Lozi King Lowanika which stretched far beyond the borders of the Lozi kingdom.

Thus Zambia was initially divided into separate territories known as North Eastern and North Western Rhodesia. In 1911 they combined to become Northern Rhodesia, a name it retained until independence when it was called Zambia.

From the beginning, the British government insisted on its overriding authority in all areas occupied by the British South Africa

Company but the day-to-day administration was left in the hands of the Company under the distant supervision of the British High Commissioner for South Africa.

The development of Rhodesia—the rebellion of 1896-97

The white settlers in Southern Rhodesia brought with them the racialist attitudes of the south. They came attracted by rumours of rich mining prospects and abundant farming land. Though no vast gold deposits were found, there were numerous smaller deposits which could be worked by small-scale operators. Soon the whole of the central part of the Ndebele kingdom was staked out by white farmers. The resultant need for cheap labour meant that white farmers began to press the Africans to work for them, even against their will. Attitudes towards Africans, even chiefs, were often arrogant and insulting and the bitter hatred which built up began to spread. Older hatred between the Ndebele and Shona was submerged in the new opposition to their common white oppressors. The Shona Mwari-Mlimo cult which had been adopted by the Ndebele invaders provided a common link in bringing the two peoples together in common action.

In 1896, the Ndebele, who had the strongest political and military force and who had suffered most from the establishment of colonial rule, took advantage of the failure of the Jameson raid to rise in sudden rebellion killing all the whites they could lay hands on. Before the end of the year the Shona had joined them. Though unsuccessful, the rebellion's suppression was long and costly. Rhodes eventually negotiated for peace with the Ndebele leaders in the Matoppos mountains promising adequate land for their people, amnesty for their leaders and other concessions. Peace was restored with the Ndebele by the end of 1896 but the Shona fought on until late in 1897 before they were finally crushed.

The establishment of responsible government, 1923

These rebellions had greatly weakened the Company's position in Southern Rhodesia and it was more than ever dependent on the settlers who had been called upon to do much of the fighting. It was also in a weak position with the British government after its scandalous behaviour in the Transvaal and Southern Rhodesia. The best way of preventing Britain from cancelling the charter seemed to be to win the settlers, who were mainly of British stock, over to the Company's side. In 1898, therefore, it agreed to set up a Legislative Council with four elected representatives of the white settlers. The vote was available to adult male British subjects regardless of race, provided that they had an income of at least £50 per year and buildings worth £75. In practice this meant that only a few Africans could hope to gain the right to vote.

Once the white settlers had gained some political representation they began to press for more and in 1908 the Company allowed them to elect the majority in the Legislative Council. By 1923 when the Company finally laid down its administrative authority in Southern Rhodesia, the settlers were in virtual control. When the Company's rule ended the most important issue was whether Southern Rhodesia should join the Union of South Africa or become a separate country enjoying responsible government. At that time the whites were confident of maintaining their supremacy and saw little to fear from the African majority. They therefore had no desperate need to ally with the south for protection and they feared that by joining with South Africa they might be swamped by the Afrikaans-speaking majority among the whites there. They also feared that their economic interests would be neglected in favour of the south and that poor whites from the south would flock into the country to compete for the meagre opportunities of employment as skilled workers and craftsmen.

A plebiscite was held in 1922 and the majority voted in favour of separate development. Legally, it still remained under British authority and the British insisted that any legislation which discriminated against non-Europeans should be sent to London for approval, but this did not prove an effective safeguard. Economic qualifications for voting remained and were raised when the number of African voters showed any signs of increasing. The whites thus remained firmly in control.

Economic and political developments in Southern Rhodesia

Rhodes' dream of vast gold deposits in Southern Rhodesia never materialised and mining tended to be on a small scale though still playing an important part in the economy of the country. The country had to rely to a great extent on its agricultural resources. Maize was a

The first train to arrive at Salisbury

major crop from the beginning and tobacco rose to become the country's chief export. In accordance with Rhodes' plan to link Cairo by rail with the Cape, the line was brought up to Rhodesia from South Africa very soon after the establishment of the Company's authority. In time and with government support and protection a number of manufacturing industries, mainly for processing local raw materials, sprang up. Until the Federation, however, they remained on a small scale.

White politics in Southern Rhodesia

Farmers, traders, businessmen and small mineowners predominated among the white settlers. There was a relatively small Afrikaans-speaking minority, and a small band of white semi-skilled and skilled workers and craftsmen. Politics was dominated by the more prosperous farmers, businessmen and miners. The name of the ruling party changed several times but continued to represent the same groups and comprised the same people. The governing party usually held an overwhelming majority. There were two main opposition parties, one representing the poorer farmers, the Afrikaners and poorer traders, the other, the Rhodesia Labour Party, the special interests of white workers. Their main attack on the government was the failure to protect white supremacy. They were therefore important for ensuring that the government would make no concessions to reduce white dominance or give opportunities for the advance of non-whites.

The two-pyramids policy

The racial policy in Southern Rhodesia was similar to the policy, later called apartheid, of South Africa and in some ways it went further along the road to segregation. It was known as the 'two-pyramids policy'; in white areas the upper part of the pyramid was to be filled with whites and the African labourers formed the base, in the African reserves Africans occupied most of the pyramid but the small number of whites holding political power were at the top. The main pillars of this policy were the Land Apportionment Act of 1930 and the Industrial Conciliation Act of 1934. After the rebellions of 1896–97, the British South Africa Company had been forced to set aside reserves adequate for the support of the African population. Some reserves were set aside but many Africans continued to live outside them. In 1930 it was decided to introduce rigid territorial segregation and the land was definitely divided into areas for whites and Africans could no longer buy land outside their areas. More than half the land, the richer and most productive, went to the white minority. Under the Land Apportionment Act the division of land was to be final.

Since all the towns were in white areas, Africans could not acquire rights to permanent residence there. They could only live in segregated areas on the outskirts or in the servants' quarters attached to their masters' houses. Even in these places they needed official permission and had to be employed.

The Industrial Conciliation Act was designed to protect white workers from African competition. The act was framed in such a way as to make no mention of race but its intention was to deny Africans the right to join Trade Unions and to ensure that whites only had the higher paid work.

The 'two-pyramids policy' was thus designed to protect the interests of the white settlers. Africans were encouraged to remain on the land as farmers and the government supplied agricultural education for

Africans, but the whites were angry to find African competition for the limited market. By the Maize Control Act of 1935 measures were introduced to ensure that whites would receive better prices for their maize.

Though the Europeans talked of developing the African areas, they primarily thought of Africans as a source of labour for the white areas. Taxation was intended partly to raise revenue to pay for administrative costs but also to force the Africans to accept employment on white farms or in the mines. But the African labour supply could never meet the demand and Africans did retain sufficient land to support a considerable number of their people and even to provide for the payment of taxes. Moreover, Africans could travel to South Africa where wages were even higher. To prevent having to increase wages, Africans from outside Southern Rhodesia were encouraged to work in the country. As a result of this the real wages of African workers showed hardly any increase for 30 years after 1923.

Effects of the Second World War

During the war years 1939–45, Southern Rhodesians of all races saw military service in many parts of the world. Africans in particular returned with many new ideas and could not easily reconcile themselves to racial discrimination in their own country. Rhodesia enjoyed an economic boom during the war which continued afterwards and this was accompanied by a great increase in white immigration. White farmers now began to take over land not set aside for white farming. African squatters who had lived there were driven into the reserves where poverty and overcrowding were producing a disastrous situation.

After the war, the ferment of political activity heralded the collapse of the European colonial empires. The white settlers in Southern Rhodesia recognised the threat and began to seek ways of entrenching their position. As we have seen, in South Africa this took the form of adoption of apartheid but in Southern Rhodesia the reaction was more complex. There was a desire to conciliate African opposition and to win African support without radically altering the existing system. There was also the desire to protect white supremacy by consolidating the hold over the three new territories in Central Africa. We shall see that this led to active support of the idea of Federation between the three countries.

The Land Husbandry Act, 1951

By 1951 the continuing boom had produced a situation in which the supply of African labour through immigration was not sufficient and by this time, too, the economy of the country as a whole had greatly expanded. The market for agricultural goods was wider and European fear of African competition was not so great. It was feared that Africans might any day be a political force to contend with and it would be desirable to build up a substantial class with a strong interest in defending the existing situation. The Land Husbandry Act was perhaps the most revolutionary measure since the setting up of Southern Rhodesia. It provided for the abolition of the traditional system of land tenure in African areas. Instead of a share of tribal land, individuals could acquire the land they worked. These farms had to be a minimum size and could not be sub-divided. It was hoped that the individual farmers would feel they had a stake in the present political system. Those unable to acquire land would have to work in the towns and help the labour shortage. The result of the act was that large numbers of Africans found themselves in a desperate position without security in either the towns or country. Inevitably they turned to political activity and formed the basis for the development of African Nationalism as a mass movement.

Development of African political activity in Southern Rhodesia

The defeat of the rebellions left Africans disillusioned and it seemed clear that whites could not be driven out by force of arms. Thus there were no more serious uprisings and Africans accepted the need to adapt themselves to the new society and to direct their political activity into modern forms. The missions began to make converts on a large scale; the ever-increasing drive for western education had begun. In the mines, industries and homes of the whites they acquired new skills and experience of the modern world but also a sense of humiliation and frustration. They suffered indignities like the pass system and social segregation in buildings, offices and on transport similar to South Africa. At the same time, they made contact with Africans from other parts of southern Africa who were involved in political activity and, since many workers were migrants from outside Southern Rhodesia who worked for short periods only, the new experiences and ideas were carried into the rural areas and spread a growing consciousness of the nature of the new white settler-dominated world into even the most remote villages.

Since the Ndebele had been less severely crushed in the course of the rebellions than the Shona and their own political system had survived to a considerable extent, it was natural that they should be first to recover their political awareness and confidence. They also found themselves deprived of most of their traditional and best land. The first political activity was aimed at the restoration of the Ndebele Kingship and the return of sufficient of their lost land to give the Ndebele a definite national home in which they could develop a degree of Ndebele self-government. Its method of action was to present petitions to the British High Commissioner and King George V. Though it failed in its objectives, the movement continued to be popular among the Ndebele and in the 1920s the Ndebele Home Society was formed to press for the same concessions. Their political methods were modern and they enjoyed wide support but their ideas were very conservative. Apart from requesting more land than the whites would give, their ideas were much the same as the 'two-pyramids policy'.

The beginning of a different political organisation came in 1923 when the small number of African voters came together to form the Rhodesian Bantu Voters' Association. This association and a number of other societies known as Welfare Associations were thoroughly modern in outlook and concentrated on getting increased voting rights for Africans together with educational and social reforms. They were greatly influenced by the tactics of Jabavu and the Cape Voters' Association from which they gained much inspiration. Their weakness lay in the fact that they were confined to a small educated élite and were not very successful in communicating with the mass and gaining their support. At first, the leaders were South Africans and Nyasa-landers but by the 1930s educated Rhodesian Africans were beginning to take over the leadership of the Associations.

In 1934 an attempt was made to form a nationwide Nationalist Movement. In that year Aaron Jacha founded the Southern Rhodesian African Nationalist Congress, the first attempt in Central Africa at forming a truly national political movement. For a long time, however, it continued to act very cautiously and to have little appeal except to the educated élite.

African industrial organisation

The idea of industrial organisation was born in South Africa where Clemens Kadalie founded the Industrial and Commercial Union which rapidly grew into a political organisation in southern Africa. In the late 1920s Kadalie sent a fellow Nyasalander to Southern Rhodesia to found a local branch of his Union. He was deported but the idea caught on and branches were established in Bulawayo and Salisbury. Mass meetings of urban workers where their wrongs were denounced and unity called for attracted stronger mass support than the Welfare Associations but it also attracted the attention of the police. Its leaders were arrested and imprisoned in the 1930s and with the break up of the South Africa Industrial and Commercial Union, the Southern Rhodesian branch began to collapse. However, the idea lingered on and in 1945 the Reformed I.C.U. was an important African political organisation in Salisbury.

The religious experience of discontent

Before the war, African discontent had tended to express itself in religious rather than political form. The religious movement was really part of the Ethiopian Movement, described in Chapter 8. In the 1920s the African Watchtower movement which began in Nyasaland spread into the Shona areas of Southern Rhodesia and a host of other breakaway sects spread into the country from South Africa. By the '30s, religious independence had become a mass phenomenon among the Shona and since then Southern Rhodesia has become an important centre of the movement. These religious movements provided an outlet for African discontent and frustration, helped to keep their dignity alive and fostered the realisation that they were not inferior to their white overlords. This resistance and defiance could eventually be channelled in a political direction.

The Second World War was as much a turning point for the Africans as for the settlers. Ex-servicemen returned with experience of a world where a man's social standing did not necessarily depend on the colour of his skin. New white immigrants displaced African workers and as more and more Africans drifted to the towns, social problems and discontent there grew more and more intense. Uprisings in other colonial territories became known in Southern Rhodesia through the radio and newspapers. The Africans realised that they must learn the techniques of the modern world and the rush for Western education began. With this the development of potential political leaders was greatly increased and the masses became more able to understand the intricacies of modern politics. The new movement showed itself in the emergence of the Reformed I.C.U. and the revival of the Southern

Rhodesia Africans National Congress after 1945. That year the African railway workers staged a successful strike which led to official recognition of their Union. In 1948 the Africans joined in a nationwide strike which was joined by domestic servants. After the Land Husbandry Act of 1951 the S.R.A.N.C. became a real mass political party uniting almost all the streams of discontent behind the effort to win political advancement from the European minority.

Nyasaland in the colonial period

Nyasaland, unlike the other two Central African territories, never came under the authority of the British South Africa Company. It was an imperial Protectorate with a civil service recruited from Britain. The missions remained strong and Africans had a chance of attaining higher educational standards than in either Southern or Northern Rhodesia. Africans also had better opportunities for clerical and skilled work. Nevertheless, opportunities were still inadequate and educated Africans emigrated to the Rhodesias and South Africa. Because of their higher standards of education, they found it easier to absorb the techniques of political action in the modern world. Clements Kadalie was from Nyasaland and other Nyasalanders played important rôles in African political activity throughout southern Africa. White settlers did not play an important part in the establishment of colonial rule in Nyasaland but once British rule was established, considerable grants of land were made to them, particularly in southern Nyasaland. The coming of colonialism also brought with it a substantial immigration of Indians. Johnston held a high respect for Indian initiative and business acumen. He once said, 'Nyasaland should be ruled by whites, exploited by Indians and worked by blacks.' In time Indians came to dominate the internal trade and their stores were opened up in the remote areas of the country. Indians tended to form very tight communities and they did not easily allow Africans to acquire a share of their business and could easily eliminate African competitors. Like the whites, they tended to treat the African as inferior. Through their activities they played a vital rôle in the economy of the country. Unlike the Rhodesias, Nyasaland had no mineral deposits and it remained an agricultural country in which much of the land was poor. For a long time the main emphasis was on the development of European-owned plantations and the main exports were cotton, tobacco and tea. But Nyasaland remained a pitifully poor country and its economy depended on the export of

An Indian store in Nyasaland

African labour to the territories to the south. This had mixed results. The migration of large numbers of Nyasaland Africans meant the spread of modern techniques and discontent to the remotest areas of the land. The money sent home helped to pay for the maintenance of their families and pay their taxes. But this discouraged the government from recognising the need to develop the rural areas. Very little of the money sent home by migrant workers was spent on agricultural tools or fertilisers. Most of it went on paying taxes and buying imported goods at the Indians' stores. When the money was spent, the worker simply went back again to earn more. Thus Nyasaland became heavily dependent on South Africa and Southern Rhodesia.

White politics in Nyasaland

The white population of Nyasaland was always tiny compared to that of Southern Rhodesia. In 1907, two representatives of the white settlers were chosen by the Governor to sit on his Legislative Council and thereafter the settlers sought to improve their political position.

They joined to form the Association of Associations but there was never enough of them to win political control of the country which remained in the hands of the British government. The majority of the settlers therefore sought ways of linking with the larger body of settlers in Northern and Southern Rhodesia but these attempts failed until after the Second World War when the situation in Central Africa as a whole changed radically.

The development of African political activity in Nyasaland

Africans did not suffer such severe shocks from the establishment of white rule as in Southern Rhodesia. Most of the land remained in African hands and the number of settlers was small. Colonial rule, moreover, meant the end of the slave trade and brought a measure of peace and prosperity. Nevertheless, in the southern regions much of the land was taken over by white men and hunger became acute. Thousands of refugees from the harsh Portuguese rule in Mozambique added to the problem of overcrowding. The white settlers brought racial prejudices with them and in the towns Africans lived in separate locations and there were often separate counters in European and Indian stores. Even the missionaries who did so much for African education and who sometimes supported the Africans against the settlers were infected with the same spirit. Though they preached equality of men in God's eyes, they rarely gave full responsibility to their African preachers or mixed with them socially.

In Nyasaland as elsewhere opposition first took a religious form. The idea of religious protest was, in fact, first introduced by an Englishman, James Booth. His idea was to build up African religious communities which would be economically self-sufficient and in which Africans could prosper without Europeans. He was horrified by the racialist attitudes of most Europeans and in a long and troubled period during which he maintained his connections with Nyasaland he founded a whole series of different missions and gave help and encouragement to breakaway African church leaders, especially the Watchtower.

The rebellion of John Chilembwe

One of Booth's assistants at his first mission in Nyasaland was John Chilembwe. Booth took him to America where he was able to study at a Negro University. Chilembwe came back to Africa in 1906 and

Chilembwe's church being built

founded his own mission, called Providence Industrial Mission. He soon despaired of the treatment of his peoples and failed to see how the whites could reconcile this with sending Africans to fight European wars. As his letters and petitions were ignored he decided to lead a rebellion to prove that Africans could not be ignored. In 1915 his followers killed two Europeans but the rebellion was soon suppressed and he was killed while trying to escape. However, his memory remained as an inspiration to African leaders in later years.

The Watchtower and other independent African sects

The most important movement to express protest in a religious form was the Watchtower Church (Jehovah's Witnesses), founded in Nyasaland between 1908 and 1909 by Elliot Kenan Kamwana and entirely African controlled. It preached that the end of the world was at hand, that white rule would then be destroyed and the Africans would enjoy all the material goods and luxuries denied to them. The movement did not itself give rise to rebellion but rather served as a safety valve for African feelings of frustration and humiliation. The Nyasaland government was so alarmed by Kamwana's preaching that he was exiled towards the end of 1909 and not allowed to return until

1937. The movement, however, remained strong and spread into the Rhodesias. There were other independent African sects whose attitudes varied; some represented a direct protest against white domination, others an attempt to adopt the values of white society but without white control, others the preservation of traditional beliefs and customs, others the complete rejection of former African tradition.

The voluntary associations

African political activity of a modern type developed more rapidly and extensively in Nyasaland than in other parts of central Africa. As early as 1912, educated Africans in the north formed the North Nyasa Native Association which from 1919 began to press for direct African representation on the Legislative Council. In 1920 a similar association was formed in the south and after that a whole series of associations sprang up. By 1933 there were fifteen. These voluntary associations tended to have a rather narrow membership drawn from the educated Africans and their policies tended to be moderate and cautious. However, they did give Africans the experience of modern political action and social and political awareness could spread through the general African population. The government paid little attention to their petitions but the associations did express African feelings about the possible federation of Nyasaland with Southern and Northern Rhodesia and their representations to visiting commissions probably helped to frustrate the achievement of this idea before the Second World War.

In Nyasaland as elsewhere the war changed the whole of political life and Africans began to prepare for the struggle to decide the future pattern of society. In 1943 an attempt was made to unite the voluntary associations into a common organisation and in 1944 the Nyasaland African Congress was formed. It inherited the narrow membership of the bodies which made it up and expressed moderate policies. But it did mean that Nyasaland had a national African voice to focus African feeling in the struggles which lay ahead.

Northern Rhodesia before the Federation

Like Southern Rhodesia, Northern Rhodesia was first administered by the British South Africa Company but it remained predominantly a country of African peasant farmers. Throughout its history it has remained in this halfway position between the two extremes of white settler dominated Southern Rhodesia and the theoretically African country of Nyasaland. At first the number of white settlers was small. A certain amount of mining, especially round Broken Hill (Kabwe) was begun from the early years and by 1906 minerals had become the chief export. Until the discovery of the full potential wealth of the Copperbelt, however, mining remained on a relatively small scale. The most important economic development of the time was the extension of the railway. By 1906 the line had reached Broken Hill from Bulawayo and by 1909 had linked up with the railway system of the Belgian Congo. This helped the development of agriculture in the country as well as improving mining prospects. An increasing number of farmers set up farms on land alongside the rail line, others settled on the lands taken from the Ngoni of Mpezeni to the east and another smaller group settled in the north. But by far the greater number of whites settled near the railway. For the most part the line ran through sparse areas of African population so that European settlement was not as disruptive as in Southern Rhodesia. The settlers were generally a small community occupying a small fraction of the land and in the early days Northern Rhodesia, like Nyasaland, was mainly a supplier of African labour to the south. The effects were similar to those described for Nyasaland.

Northern Rhodesia becomes a British Protectorate

Though the white population in the country was small, their confidence was high and they had no doubt that the country would eventually become a white settler dominated country like Southern Rhodesia. They so seriously underestimated the potential political challenge of the African majority that they saw little cause to ally with their neighbours across the Zambesi. When in 1924 the British South Africa Company gave the country over to the white settlers, they opposed amalgamation with Southern Rhodesia. Northern Rhodesia thus came under direct British Administration.

The development of the Copperbelt

The existence of copper deposits was known to the outside world as early as 1895 but the surface deposits consisted of oxidised ores with

One of the towns which grew up round the copper mines

much lower copper content than those of neighbouring Katanga. However, in the 1920s it was discovered that vast deposits of sulphide ores lay under the oxidised layers. The so-called 'flotation' process had been discovered which made it profitable to mine the sulphide ores. Large capitalist companies were thus attracted to Northern Rhodesia and the result was an economic boom which revolutionised the country. After a brief initial setback, caused by the world-wide Depression, the Copperbelt mines have remained by far the main source of the wealth of the country. The growth of the copperbelt affected the life of the country in many ways. It attracted greatly increased white migration including large numbers of skilled and semi-skilled mine workers. Many of these came from South Africa and almost all of them shared a determination to protect their privileged financial position by preserving a white monopoly of the more highly paid jobs. The new wealth stimulated trade and brought considerable development not only to the Copperbelt towns but to the whole area along the line of rail. This area became an area of high economic development and white domination while the vast preponderance of the geographical area of the country remained poverty stricken but much less directly affected by white racialism.

The mines also attracted a huge African labour force. At first Africans sought employment for short periods only in accordance with the system of migrant labour. But in time they began to settle more or less permanently in the towns. The process of urbanisation, which still continues, had begun. The social attitudes in the towns were racialist but, since there were insufficient whites to do all the jobs, Africans had better opportunities in skilled and clerical work than to the south and there were better opportunities for Africans in government service and with the mining companies. Thus a small but important African élite grew up with the education to understand modern political methods and ready to take a lead in the development of modern African nationalism.

White politics in Northern Rhodesia

Like Southern Rhodesia, the white settlers fought for and won political representation under the administration of the British South Africa Company and in 1924 when the Company's rule ended they looked forward to a rapid advance to self-government. But the British attitude kept them in the minority on legislative and administrative councils. This made the settlers feel that they would not preserve their dominant position unless they joined with Southern Rhodesia. They began to press for amalgamation. The greatest blow to settler self-confidence was when in 1929 the British Colonial Secretary, Lord Passfield, pronounced that in Northern Rhodesia as in East Africa the interests of the Africans were to be regarded as paramount. Alarmed, the settlers eagerly sought union with their southern neighbour and in 1938 they met informally with representatives of Southern Rhodesia to discuss the amalgamation of the three central African territories. As a result of settler agitation the Bledisloe Commission was sent out to the area to investigate the possibility of unifying the three territories. White settlers in the whole region were enthusiastic but the Africans in the two northern territories expressed acute dislike for the idea of being handed over from the care of the imperial government to a settler dominated regime. As a result, the Commission was unable to recommend an immediate amalgamation.

The Second World War was a major turning point for Northern Rhodesia as elsewhere. It meant a great increase in the demand for copper from Britain, and the weakening of the imperial governments throughout the world and the upsurge of non-European rule caused the settlers to feel that their supremacy was by no means certain and that they must act swiftly to protect it.

During and immediately after the war, the white settlers in Northern Rhodesia pressed more vigorously for increased political power and a link with Southern Rhodesia. During the war, the war effort called for a united effort and a so-called National government was formed in the country. Then in 1945 the situation again altered radically when settlers gained majority rule in the Legislative Council. Led by Roy Welensky, originally a trade union leader of the white railway workers, the settlers were ready to make an all out effort to gain complete control of the country.

African political activity in Northern Rhodesia

As in other parts of central Africa, mass expression of political consciousness by Africans first took the form of religious movements. The Watchtower spread widely but was only one of a number of sects. Among them was a movement started by Tomo Nyirenda who taught that the country must be cleansed of witches and that he had an infallible method of detecting them. He was responsible for the death of a large number of people before he was finally arrested and hanged in 1925.

As in Nyasaland, modern political activity first took the form of voluntary welfare societies formed by the higher educated African élite. At first Africans from Nyasaland tended to lead these organisations but as the educational opportunities in Northern Rhodesia increased they fell into the background. By 1933 there were welfare associations in Abercorn, Kasama and Fort Jameson. Their policies were initially moderate; they pressed for minor reforms but did not question the general principle of white rule. However, the settlers' attempts at amalgamation forced Africans to unite their political opposition to the settler ambitions. Before the Second World War the settlers prevented African political unity but in 1946 the members of fourteen welfare associations joined to form the Federation of African Societies of Northern Rhodesia. It was a loose-knit but national organisation which could grow into a truly mass party.

Industrial unrest in Northern Rhodesia

The development of the Copperbelt gave Northern Rhodesia a larger scale of industry than anywhere else in central Africa with a huge concentration of African labour. Low wages, poor housing, racial discrimination and humiliation inevitably bred discontent. In 1935 there was a series of strikes accompanied in some cases by violent riots. Government troops were necessary to control the situation. In 1940 after the white mine workers had held a successful strike for improved pay and conditions, African workers went on strike for more pay and opportunities of advancement. These protests were spontaneous since the Africans did not possess a permanent trade union. After the war, however, provision was made for them to have a union and an Englishman, Ellwell, came out from England to establish a permanent organisation. Thereafter the African Mine Workers' Union and the African Railwaymen's Union became powerful organisations and were the main elements in the Federation of African Trade Unions. But for a long time African trade unions held back from committing themselves to an active political rôle.

The Northern Rhodesian government recognised the need to involve Africans in the government of their country but looked on the tribal chiefs rather than the African educated élite as true representatives. After 1930, the system of indirect rule was introduced through which chiefs were given a role in local administration. Thus just as traditional systems were being overtaken by the impact of European rule and economic activity the government tried to revive the old order. After the Copperbelt disturbances of 1935, Urban Advisory Councils were set up to enable the authorities to maintain contact with African workers. By 1943 the government realised the need for further increase in African consultation and the direct involvement of the educated élite. That year a series of African Provincial Councils were set up. Their members were largely drawn from traditional chiefs but a small element of elected representatives was permitted. In 1946 these measures were extended even further and an African Representative Council was formed consisting of twenty-five members selected by the Provincial Councils and four appointees of the paramount chief of Barotseland. Thus the government had set up a system for African consultation but mainly of the more conservative elements, traditional chiefs who had strong reasons for favouring the continuation of white rule. The African National Congress established in the same year was not regarded by the government as truly representative of the African peoples.

Struggles over the creation of the Federation

Immediately after the establishment of colonial rule in central Africa, the whites in the three territories were confident of maintaining their supremacy over their African populations and obtaining self-government. They thus saw no need to link up with South Africa or with each other. However, after the ending of the Company's administration this attitude changed. Northern Rhodesian settlers began to fear that they would not be able to entrench their position and settlers in Southern Rhodesia were anxious to extend their control northwards after the discovery of Northern Rhodesia's mineral resources. They felt it would be safer to unite the territories to protect the whites from the increasing African political activity. The small body of white settlers in Nyasaland was even more keen for unification and so the long campaign for amalgamation began. As early as 1929 the Hilton Young Commission was appointed to look into the possibility of uniting the three territories together or with the East African countries. The commission was unable to recommend immediate steps towards unification.

The Passfield Memorandum of 1930 was a great blow to settler confidence in the British government and they became convinced that their only hope was uniting together and eventually shaking off British control. Plans were laid at the informal Victoria Falls Conference of 1936 and in response the Bledisloe Commission visited central Africa in 1938. This commission noted the economic interdependence of the territories and recommended unification in principle. It could not make any firm recommendations because of its obligation to the African peoples in the Northern territories and their strong opposition to any link with the settler rule to the south.

During the war, the idea of unification was not allowed to die. An interterritorial council, the Central African Council, came into existence which in the years after the war launched a number of interterritorial services like the Central African Airways.

The end of the Second World War brought the whole situation to a head. The war had exhausted Britain and the break up of her empire was only a matter of time. Northern Rhodesian copper was more important to Britain than ever and the settlers were therefore in a position to exert strong pressure on the British government. At the same time non-European nationalist movements were growing all over the world and the settlers would have to move quickly. Moreover, racialism had been condemned by world opinion. The settlers would have to make some concessions to the Africans so that their policies would not be seen as openly racialist.

By 1948 the settlers seemed ready for a second attempt at achieving amalgamation. In Northern Rhodesia the settlers had gained virtual control of the government though at the same time admitting two

African representatives to the Legislative Council. In Southern Rhodesia the governing party under Huggins had won a resounding political victory. At the same time the Nationalists in South Africa had come to power with their open racialist philosophy of apartheid and their strong anti-British attitudes. The British would be in a weak position to oppose the settlers. At the second Victoria Falls Conference in 1949, the settlers felt that an outright demand for the amalgamation of the three territories would be too much for the British to accept and so they favoured the idea of a federation. And in order to make their plans appear non-racialist, they proclaimed a policy of multi-racial partnership and co-operation. But the British Labour government was not convinced and the alarmed Africans were assured by the Secretary of State for the Colonies that no move to join the three territories would be made until all the peoples had been consulted.

The settlers continued and increased their agitation and the Labour government saw itself in a perplexing position. There were strong arguments to prove that federation would increase the prosperity of all the peoples and would be most important to prevent the settlers in the Rhodesias from joining up with South Africa. The great copper companies saw the federation as the greatest hope for economic stability and progress and they put the weight of their influence behind the idea. The British government finally allowed British and Central African civil servants to meet in London to look at the technical aspects of the idea and by doing so were partially committed to federation.

The London Conference met in 1951, gave its approval to the federal scheme and drew up detailed proposals. At the same time a third conference was held at Victoria Falls to which, at British insistence, some Africans from Northern Rhodesia and Nyasaland were invited. They showed themselves totally opposed to federation. During the conference the British Secretary of State for the Colonies heard that the British government was about to be dissolved and he therefore brought the conference to an abrupt end but first encouraged the conference to vote in favour of the principle of federation in spite of African opposition.

The establishment of the Central African Federation

The new Conservative government in Britain announced its strong approval of the federal scheme for central Africa and in 1953, in spite

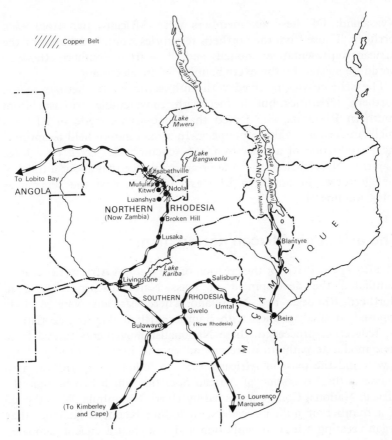

Copper Belt

To Lobito Bay

ANGOLA

Lake Tanganyika

Lake Mweru

Lake Bangweolu

Elisabethville
Mufulira
Kitwe Ndola
Luanshya

NORTHERN RHODESIA
(Now Zambia)

Broken Hill

Lusaka

NYASALAND (Now Malawi)

Lake Nyasa (L. Malawi)

Blantyre

Lake Kariba

Livingstone

Salisbury

SOUTHERN RHODESIA

Gwelo Umtal

Bulawayo (Now Rhodesia)

Beira

M O Z A M B I Q U E

(To Kimberley and Cape)

To Lourenço Marques

The Central African Federation

of African protest, the Central African Federation was born. Each
territory would continue to have its own government responsible for
local administration. In particular, these territorial governments would
be responsible for all aspects of native affairs within their territories.
In addition the British government would remain directly involved
in the administration of the two northern Protectorates. Finally,
there was to be an African Affairs Board to be a Standing Committee
of the Federal Parliament to intervene if any legislation was found to
be racialist. The legislation in question would have to be referred to
London for approval. The Federal Parliament would have powers
covering all matters involving more than one territory and was also
responsible for foreign affairs.

The Parliament consisted of thirty-five members, seventeen from
Southern Rhodesia, eleven from Northern Rhodesia and seven from

291

Nyasaland. Of these six members were Africans, two from each territory. Those from the northern territories would be chosen by the African Representative Councils and those from Southern Rhodesia would be elected by the overwhelming white electorate.

The scheme was received with enthusiasm by the settlers in the northern territories but it met with considerable criticism from Southern Rhodesia who feared that concessions made to Africans might undermine white supremacy. In a referendum held to approve the introduction of a federation, the scheme was elected by a huge majority. Nevertheless, it is important to notice that about a third of the electorate in Southern Rhodesia voted against the scheme as being too liberal.

The effect on African nationalism

The European drive for the creation of the Central African Federation stimulated the development of mass Nationalist movements in Northern Rhodesia and Nyasaland where Africans were strongly opposed to amalgamation with Southern Rhodesia. As negotiations for federation proceeded, these Nationalist movements turned from their moderate paths to more outspoken and radical attitudes. They now found the mass of Africans eager to follow them. In Northern Rhodesia the Federation of African Societies which had become the African National Congress was led by Harry Nkumbula. With the aid of a number of militant leaders, including Kenneth Kaunda, they began creating a mass organisation and launched a violent campaign against the Federation. Nkumbula called for African self-government and warned that if Federation was imposed by force life would become intolerable for the whites. Similar movements grew in Nyasaland and in Britain Dr Hastings Banda, a Nyasalander who had left his country early in youth for a long and successful career of study in Britain and America before settling in Britain as a doctor, gave the Congress movement his full support and tried to persuade British public opinion against the federal scheme.

But these attempts at opposition appeared in vain and the settlers seemed sure of victory.

White politics in the Federation

With the achievement of Federation, the settlers had gained the first major step on the way to consolidating their dominance in the area.

But final victory still lay ahead. It would only be secure when they established their control over the whole Federation and could win independence from Britain. It had been agreed that the status and constitution of the Federation would be reviewed in 1960 and the settlers were determined that they would then achieve independence. It was necessary, therefore, both to strengthen white control and to make such concessions to the Africans that would convince Britain and the world at large of their good intentions. Perhaps the most important concession, apart from African representation in Parliament, was the establishment of a multi-racial University for the Federation in Salisbury. Unfortunately, due to the limited educational opportunities for Africans, the student population was predominantly European and the increase in secondary education for Africans was not considered a high priority.

Open racial discrimination in public places was illegal and a campaign was launched to break down the traditional colour bar. Even in Salisbury, swimming baths were finally declared open to all races. The main direction of policy under the Federation was, however, directed to strengthening the settler position. The Federation resulted

The Kariba Dam

in an economic boom, particularly for Southern Rhodesia. The price of copper stayed high and profits increased in industries in Southern Rhodesia, which could now rely on an assured market in the two northern territories. Salisbury blossomed into a modern town of skyscrapers and the huge Kariba dam was built to provide power for the growing industries, creating the largest man-made lake in the world.

While Southern Rhodesia profited from federation and Nyasaland made some gains, Northern Rhodesia was the greatest loser. It saw the money earned from its mines drawn away to Salisbury and enjoyed relatively little development. Southern Rhodesia continued to encourage the immigration of new white settlers on an unprecedented scale.

Politically, the main settler advances took place in 1957 and 1958 when the Federal Parliament passed the Constitution Amendment Act and a Franchise Act to ensure that African representatives were elected by a predominantly European electorate instead of by Africans only, as was the case of the four representatives from Nyasaland and Northern Rhodesia. The African Affairs Board queried both measures but its protests were overruled by the British. The settlers now looked forward to complete victory in 1960.

The destruction of the Federation

But just as the settlers saw victory ahead the tide was turning against them. To a great extent this was the result of events outside central Africa. The emergence of independent non-European nations after the War proved that they could be just as valuable trading partners with Britain as countries controlled by white settlers. Also, British experience of the Mau Mau in Kenya and French experiences in Indo-China and Algeria showed that attempts to suppress the political ambitions of the majority in colonial countries could lead to expensive and futile struggles. In Africa, Ghana was granted independence in 1957 and Nigeria and other colonies were clearly moving along the same road. Britain, conscious of her world image, increasingly criticised for policies in central Africa and anxious to avoid another costly war of colonial repression, needed only to be convinced that the African majority in Nyasaland and Northern Rhodesia were likely to offer serious resistance to continued Federal rule and were capable of forming viable governments which would not be too harmful to British interests. This the African leaders succeeded in proving.

The situation in Nyasaland offered the most favourable opportunities for African Nationalism where there were relatively fewer white settlers. Its people had experience of working in South Africa and Southern Rhodesia and had no doubts of the dangers of allowing their country to fall permanently under settler rule. Furthermore, there was little European investment in the country and the protagonists of Federation would not be too upset to see Nyasaland leave the Federation as long as the two Rhodesias remained firmly joined together. The introduction of the Federation sparked off violent riots in the south of the territory and, though put down, showed the depth of African antipathy. The Nyasaland African Congress spread throughout the country and the young leaders sought a man who could command world respect and bring the struggle to a climax. Their thoughts turned to Dr Hastings Kamuzu Banda who had taken an active interest from the beginning. At first he was reluctant to come but in July 1958 at last accepted their invitation and arrived in Nyasaland. Mass meetings listened to him denounce the 'stupid so-called federation'. By early 1959 it was clear that the vast majority of the people were behind him and the authorities felt that unless drastic action was taken they would lose control of the situation altogether.

By this time African Nationalism was growing into a powerful movement in Southern Rhodesia as well. The upsurge of the movement to the north acted as a powerful stimulus. The effects of the Land Husbandry Act of 1951 were beginning to be widely felt and the African National Congress, under Joshua Nkomo, was growing rapidly into a formidable mass organisation. The situation in Nyasaland was so serious that it was felt that the situation could only be brought under control by troops from Southern Rhodesia but it was feared that this might trigger off an uprising in the south. A state of emergency was thus declared in Rhodesia though no violence had occurred. The African National Congress was banned and its leaders arrested. Then an emergency was declared in Nyasaland, troops flown in from Southern Rhodesia and Banda and many other leaders arrested. In Northern Rhodesia no state of emergency was declared but Kaunda and his followers were arrested and the new Zambia African Congress was banned.

These measures were intended to demonstrate the strength of the settlers but they had the opposite effect. The British government became convinced that Banda had the masses behind him and that an attempt to stop the Nationalist movement would only lead to a bitter armed struggle. It decided to come to terms with Banda, a relatively moderate leader, rather than allow more extreme elements to come to the fore. While Banda was in jail, a new movement, the Malawi Congress Party, was formed and by the time Banda was released in 1960 the British government had already decided to negotiate with him as the effective political leader of the majority of the people of Nyasaland. In June 1960, in London a constitution was agreed which put the country well on the way to majority rule. It was clear that the Federation could not possibly gain independence under settler rule in 1960 and that the Federal review would have to be postponed.

In spite of upheavals elsewhere, the settlers still appeared firmly in control of Northern Rhodesia. Events after the formation of the Federation took a downward path. The African National Congress was badly demoralised by its failure to prevent the imposition of federation. Its organisation was poor and tended to drift. There was a successful boycott of butchers who discriminated against African buyers but little progress was made at the political level. In 1955 Nkumbula and Kaunda were arrested and imprisoned for two months on a charge of distributing a banned publication, called 'Africa and the Colonial World'. Kaunda came out determined to break the settler domination and Nkumbula decided on a more moderate policy in co-operation with white rule.

Nkumbula's moderate policy aroused considerable opposition from Kaunda and other radical leaders and they also opposed Nkumbula's way of running party affairs. Matters came to a head in October 1958 when the Governor, Benson, proposed a new constitution giving Africans a greater voice in the affairs of the territory but keeping effective power in European hands. Arrangements were designed to result in a Legislative Council of twenty-two members, fourteen of whom would be Europeans. The settlers hoped that this would weaken the force of African opposition to white rule but Kaunda recognised that if Africans accepted the new constitution they would be playing into the settlers' hands. He demanded that the African National Congress call for a ban of the elections but Nkumbula decided to co-operate. Kaunda therefore walked out of the Congress with a number of other radical leaders to form the Zambia African National Congress.

With little time at its disposal, the new party threw itself into building up its organisation and calling for a boycott of the elections. The swing towards them grew steadily and at the All-African Peoples' Conference in Ghana in December Kaunda made a much better impression than Nkumbula. His prestige and that of his party was

Dr. Hastings Banda

Dr. Kenneth Kaunda, first President of Zambia, at the Independence celebrations

greatly increased. The government felt that unless drastic action was taken, the Zambia Congress would establish a firm hold on the masses. In March 1959 Kaunda and other leaders were arrested and restricted to remote rural areas and the Z.A.N.C. declared illegal. In the elections the settlers had a greater advantage and the African National Congress suffered a severe setback. But the arrest of the Z.A.N.C. leaders, like the emergency in Nyasaland, proved the beginning of the end of settler power in Northern Rhodesia. The arrested leaders became political martyrs and two new parties were formed to carry on the radical tradition of the banned Z.A.N.C. On 1 August 1959 they joined to become the United National Independence Party and leaders broke from Nkumbula's A.N.C. to join them. The new party spread like wildfire and on his release Kaunda was able to take the leadership of a party clearly establishing itself as the main political movement for the masses.

1960 was a decisive year for the history of the Federation when settler leaders, under Roy Welensky, Prime Minister of the Federation, still hoped to gain independence at the review conference.

Everything depended on Northern Rhodesia where the settlers still seemed to be in a commanding position. But the U.N.I.P. convinced the British that there could be no peaceful solution to the problem of Northern Rhodesia without giving Africans a far greater say in the territorial government and winning Kaunda's support. The need for movement towards majority rule was recognised. The settlers were now on the defensive. In this situation, at the Federal Review Conference in London the British would allow no major changes in the status of the Federation until the constitutions of the territories had been modified.

In Nyasaland the progress to majority rule was now straightforward but in Northern Rhodesia the settlers were still determined to fight for their supremacy and the salvation of the Federation. Early in 1961, the British Colonial Secretary, Ian Macleod, proposed a complex constitution for Northern Rhodesia which would ensure African majority rule in the Legislative Council but Welensky and others brought pressure to bear so that it was modified to give the settlers continued dominance. This change brought widespread alarm and frustration. Kaunda announced that unless the new proposals were withdrawn he would 'paralyse' the government. Though Kaunda insisted on peaceful protest violent upheavals took place over wide areas. These were suppressed by troops but the British government was now convinced that African Nationalism was too deep seated to be repressed without severe bloodshed. The constitutional proposals were again altered to give Africans a small majority.

The election of 1962

Faced with the final constitutional change, the settlers fell back on one last hope; to accept the inevitability of an African led government for Northern Rhodesia and to work for an alliance with the A.N.C. in the hopes that this would still be controlled by whites and would agree to remain in the Federation. This idea seemed hopeful because of the role which Tshombe played in Katanga. As a result of the elections held in 1962, the two African parties between them held a slight majority of seats but the settler party remained the largest single group. If Nkumbula had fallen in with the settlers' plan, the settlers might have succeeded but his loyalty to African Nationalism and pressure from within his own party led him to enter a coalition with the U.N.I.P. The triumph of African Nationalism in Northern Rhodesia was assured and the Federation was doomed.

On 31 January 1963 the Central African Federation, which had been established ten years earlier to consolidate settler rule in Central Africa, was dissolved. On 6 July 1964 Nyasaland become the Commonwealth of Malawi and on 24 October Northern Rhodesia became the Republic of Zambia.

Development of (Southern) Rhodesia: 1961 Constitution

The development of African Nationalism in the two northern territories was paralleled by a similar growth in Southern Rhodesia. The African National Congress in Southern Rhodesia expanded under Joshua Nkomo into a mass nationalist party. The declaration of a state of emergency in 1959 was in fact a recognition of the power of the movement. The banning of the party and the arrest of its leaders led to the emergence of a new party, the National Democratic Party in January 1960. Thus the development of African Nationalism seemed to follow a path similar to the other two central African territories.

Joshua Nkomo

But the situation to the south was very different. Southern Rhodesia was in many ways a small South Africa. Above all, the settlers were self-governing and had their own military forces. African Nationalism therefore did not face a British government concerned with trade and disinclined to enter upon an expensive war of colonial repression but a government of settlers determined to preserve their supremacy and racial privileges. Thus in the Constitutional conferences of 1961, the territory gained a new constitution which provided for African representation but which was aimed at maintaining settler control for the foreseeable future.

Nkomo first agreed to accept this new constitution and then changed his mind. This proved an important turning point in Rhodesia's history for Whitehead's United Federal Party, deprived of the support of African voters to ensure victory over the more racialist Rhodesian Front, was defeated. The traditional opposition with its strong racial conservatism came into power. The National Democratic Party was banned but once again emerged in a new form as the Zimbabwe African Peoples' Union. But just as the other two territories moved towards independence under African rule, Southern Rhodesia was controlled by the more extreme supporters of white dominance. These frustrations led to a split in the African Nationalist opposition in 1963 and as the two African parties struggled with each other for the allegiance of the African peoples, they lost any chance they might have had of influencing the course of political development which was still under settler control.

Triumph of the Rhodesian Front

The settlers in Southern Rhodesia had been attracted to the idea of federalism partly because of access to the mineral wealth of Northern Rhodesia but still more to effect the best means of continuing white supremacy. For these objectives, they had been prepared to make some minor concessions to the African majority but even at the time of the Federation a substantial body of whites opposed these concessions. This group doubted the wisdom of linking with the north and tended to look to closer relations with South Africa. With the loss of the northern territories by the settlers, it was inevitable that the Southern Rhodesian whites should turn their political direction to the south and it was thus not suprising that the ruling United Federal Party was defeated by the Rhodesian Front with its strong racialist attitudes and pro-South African bias.

The Unilateral Declaration of Independence

The direction of British policy north of the Zambesi proved to the white Rhodesians that any connection with Britain, however slight, was a dangerous lever which might be used in favour of African political advancement. They decided that full independence was the only way of entrenching white supremacy for ever. The British government insisted on six principles which would have to be met before independence was granted. One of these was unimpeded progress to majority rule.

But the whole point of independence was to prevent such a political direction and, since an agreement was clearly impossible, the party began to think of declaring independence unilaterally. The first Rhodesian Front Prime Minister, Winston Field, drew back from such action and was replaced by Ian Smith. Smith waited for the outcome of the British General Election in 1965. The result was a victory for the Labour Party which would certainly not give the Rhodesian settlers what the Conservatives had refused. But its majority was very small and it was therefore in too weak a position to take very strong measures against any action by the settlers. As the crisis came to a head, Prime Minister Wilson warned Rhodesia of the

A Rhodesian newspaper the day after UDI

tragic consequences of a unilateral declaration of independence but at the same time assured them that force would not be used. This was all Smith needed and on 11 November 1965 independence was declared and precipitated a crisis in which not only the countries of southern and central Africa but the rest of the continent and the world at large are still involved.

Part **four**

Middle Africa

10 Middle Africa 1880-1930

Years of turmoil, exploitation and despair

The fifty years after 1880 represent perhaps the darkest period in the history of the peoples of Middle Africa. As described in the last chapter of Volume I, storm clouds had been gathering before the European invasion. The growth of military states and Arab power and the increasing devastation which they produced had created much uncertainty. The marauding bands of the European invading powers added to the disorder until peace was finally established. But with peace came the destruction of those African states which might eventually have reached stability under African rule. While peace was maintained by the overwhelming power of European arms, the agents of the Colonial governments were active throughout the area forcing men to abandon their fields and villages to work for European economic ventures. A series of plagues and famines struck further at men and cattle and by 1930 the population of the area was, if anything, less than it had been in 1880. The period was punctuated by revolts against Colonial rule but these revolts were the desperate and despairing rebellion of men who preferred death itself to the living death of harsh exploitation and little resembled the self-confident thrusts of later nationalists. Each revolt was put down with great severity by the Colonial governments and yet these governments themselves did not provide a very stable framework for society during much of this period. They were all short of money and unable to devote much attention to what they called 'native administration' as they were often driven from expedient to expedient in their efforts to survive financially. Towards the end of the period a great war occurred between the colonial powers which affected Middle Africa more than any other part of the continent and increased the confusion. This was a period of revolution, but a revolution which for many in Middle Africa must have seemed directionless, contradictory and generally depressing.

The invading powers

Four European powers—Portugal, Britain, Germany and King Leopold of the Belgians' so called 'Congo Free State'—took part in the invasion of Middle Africa. Portugal had possessed establishments on the coast of Angola since the sixteenth century. During the seventeenth and eighteenth centuries these possessions had prospered considerably from the slave trade but had then declined and during most of the nineteenth century were poor settlements struggling to change from the slave trade to a trade in palm oil, beeswax and ivory. The Portuguese garrisons were small and ill-paid and seldom ventured beyond the ports. The few Portuguese traders in the hinterland depended upon the security of African political and trading systems, notably that of the Ovimbundu people, to carry on their trade. Although deriving little profit from Angola and their other colony, Mozambique, the Portuguese were very jealous of these possessions because, together with their imperial possessions in China and India, they represented Portugal's main claim to distinction and importance among its larger and stronger European neighbours. Portugal was anxious to retain and, if possible, extend them. In 1884 an opportunity to do this came when Britain offered to recognise Portugal's claim to the mouth of the River Congo. Up to that date, Britain had been against any extension of Portugal's claim to the coastline because the Portuguese taxed trade heavily and antagonised British merchants.

In 1882 the British government became worried that the French, who were exploring the area of the Ogooe river, might claim the mouth of the Congo and close the basin of that river to British trade. The Portuguese and British governments negotiated an agreement by which Britain would have recognised Portuguese claims to the Congo's mouth in return for trade concessions. However, before the agreement was ratified France and Germany protested and the whole matter was referred to a conference of the European Powers and the United States which met at Berlin in October 1884.

The Berlin West Africa Conference 1884-5

The main business of the Berlin West Africa Conference was to decide the fate of the Congo Basin. The Conference itself did not deal with claims to territory but dealt mainly with the facilities which occupying powers should offer traders or missionaries of other nations. While the Conference was going on, the various European governments negotiated their territorial claims in Middle Africa. King Leopold of the Belgians put forward the claims of the International African Association, a semi-private body working under his Presidency which was interested in exploration and development and which had sent a number of expeditions to the Congo area. When first formed in 1877 it had no territorial ambitions, but when Portugal, Britain and France quarrelled about claims to the mouth of the Congo River Leopold suggested that his organisation, later to be called the 'Congo Free State', should be given it so that the Congo would be neutral. He promised that the Congo Free State government would collect low duties on exports from the area and thus satisfy traders of all nations. The United States and Germany supported this idea and, with assurances that Leopold would protect their interests, France and Britain also agreed. Thus, by the end of the Conference in February 1885 the Congo Free State had emerged as a new government recognised by the European Powers with a claim to most of the Congo Basin together with agreed boundaries near the coast separating its territory from a French colony north of the River Congo and Portuguese Angola to the south.

Germany also acquired a colony in Middle Africa. In February 1885 the German government gave a charter to the Society for German Colonisation permitting it to hold territory on Germany's behalf in East Africa. The British government gave a similar charter to the Imperial British East Africa Company. Neither government intended at first to remove the control which the Sultan of Zanzibar exercised over the coastline. The Companies were supposed to work in the area behind a ten mile strip along the coast belonging to the Sultan. However, there was constant friction between the Germans and the Sultan's people and in 1890 Germany and Britain combined to force the Sultan to renounce his claim to the Tanganyikan coastline. The Sultan still had a claim to the coastline of Kenya further north and the British East Africa Company continued to act as the Sultan's agent until the Company handed its possessions to the British government in 1895. But in fact the administration of the coastline there had effectively slipped from the Sultan's hands by 1890.

European penetration 1885-1890

By the end of 1885 therefore the Colonial Powers were prepared to move in and take possession of the several territories that had been assigned to them. The Portuguese were anxious to advance from their positions along the coast of Angola. King Leopold sent off expeditions to push out along the lower Congo River up to Stanley Pool. The Imperial British East Africa Company was examining the resources of the domain it had acquired. But claims were different from realities. Before 1890 the agents of colonisation made little impact on the life of Middle Africa and were able to secure a position of command in only a few places. The period of exploration continued but Europeans did not penetrate far beyond the main routes. The caravans of the European missionaries, merchants and political agents were scarcely distinguishable from African, Arab or Indian trading caravans. The men who staffed them were from the international but mainly Swahili speaking communities of coastal men: Wanyamwezi, Ovimbundu, men from Maniema and others who congregated around the main trading centres on the coast and in the interior waiting for employment. A caravan was, in many respects, a law unto itself. It had to eat, and in areas of food shortage it ate village supplies. It was powerfully armed and would steal cattle and crush the villages which tried to block its path. It sought fixed points along its routes where foodstuffs and ivory and other trading goods were stored in quantity and consequently favoured the growth of centralised states, fortified cities and depots like Tabora or Ujija. The advent of Europeans increased the number of caravans and they built their own 'bomas' (stone built forts) to add to those already along the trade routes. Europeans seldom ventured beyond the trade routes or the capitals of the major states in this early period. The politics they engaged in was the politics of the trade routes and of the great states. It was in the trade centres and the cities, not in the rural areas, that the political agents of the colonial powers first began to intrigue and manoeuvre towards positions of power.

The establishment of European power on the coast.

In the east the Germans and British first pushed themselves into a commanding position in areas directly under the Sultan of Zanzibar's control. The Sultan's rule itself was of fairly recent origin. Sayyid Barghash had begun, from the middle of the 1870s, to establish a regular administration over the peoples of the coastal districts where his predecessors had only exercised informal control. A small disciplined army backed up the rule of Jumbes or chiefs whom he appointed to rule over groups of villages. His administration was still pushing

Sayyid Barghash, Sultan of Zanzibar

inland along the trade routes when the German and British companies arrived. The Sultan's capital on the island of Zanzibar lay open to blockade or the threat of bombardment by European fleets and both methods were used to extort concessions from Sayyid Barghash and his successor. His administration in the coastal areas depended on European goodwill. An Englishman commanded his army and British advice and support had helped him establish his administration. But after conflicts between the Sultan's officials and agents of the German Colonising Company, the German government insisted on limiting and finally removing his jurisdiction and, although Britain would have preferred that the Sultan retain control over the coastline, she was not prepared to challenge Germany on this issue. But while the Sultan made diplomatic concessions, his Arab and Swahili subjects and fellow countrymen were less conciliatory. They resented the high-handed actions of European officers and when the Sultan conceded to the Germans the right to raise their flag and collect customs taxes in August 1888 they rose in revolt. The 'Bushiri rebellion', which affected the coastal districts under British as well as those under German rule, caused the German government to take over the East African colony as the German Colonisation Society was unable to cope with the situation that developed. During 1889, the German and British governments blockaded the coast to prevent the import of modern arms and in May 1889 a German government officer arrived with a thousand well-equipped soldiers recruited in other parts of Africa. By the end of 1889 Bushiri, the principal leader of the rebellion, had been executed and German forces were fastening their rule on the coastal districts until by the end of 1891 they had control of the entire Tanganyikan coast. To the north the British, operating from Mombasa, also suppressed opposition to their rule but were not firmly in control until 1895. On the other side of the continent, the starting points of interior routes were already in European hands by 1885. The Portuguese had garrisons in Angolan ports; King Leopold's agent, Stanley, had pushed his way along the lower reaches of the Congo and established stations that secured access to the navigable stretches of the river. By 1890 the Europeans were ready to begin securing control of the interior. In 1890 and 1891 they made agreements in Brussels ensuring that they alone received the most modern weapons and having control over the African coastline they were able to enforce these agreements.

The establishment of European power in the interior

Between 1885 and 1890, many European expeditions travelled over middle Africa negotiating their passage for the most part with the African or Arab authorities in power. But during the 1890s this situation rapidly changed. In 1890 the Portuguese moved inland, defeated Chief Ndunduma, one of the most important leaders of the Ovimbundu, and won a commanding position on the Bihe Plateau at the centre of the largest trading system in the interior of Angola. In 1891 the Katanga Company (under King Leopold's control)

A LITTLE PARTY IN EAST AFRICA ONLY GOING TO COLLECT A FEW BUTTERFLIES AND FLOWERS FOR THE DEAR KAISER, THAT IS ALL!!

"We came very near to having Kilima-Njaro attached to the British Empire, only the German Emperor said he would very much like it, because he was so fond of the *flora* and *fauna* of the place . . . Would the English have expected to get any territory on account of their great interest in the *flora* and *fauna* here."—*Stanley speaking at Chamber of Commerce, May 21.*

A cartoon depicting the Germans in East Africa

sent a force to Msiri's capital at Bunkeya in the Katanga. Msiri refused to put his government under the Congo Free State's control and was killed. His already crumbling empire quickly disintegrated. The uneasy alliance between Tippu Tip's Arabs and Swahilis and the Congo Free State broke down completely in 1892 resulting in a full scale war in the area of the Lomami and Lualaba Rivers. The Arab rulers had superiority in numbers but the Free State forces had better arms. In a series of bloody campaigns the Free State defeated its principal Arab enemies and then turned round in September 1893 and arrested and executed its principal ally, Ngongo Lutete. By 1894 the Free State was unquestionably the most powerful force in the eastern basin of

the Congo. Meanwhile, to the east, the Germans had suffered two defeats: one by Chief Mkwakwa's Hehe warriors in August 1891 and the
second in June 1892 by the Chaggas at Moshi. But then the tide
turned. In January 1893 the Germans defeated Siki, the leader of the
Wanyamwezi, and secured control of the caravan routes in Central
Tanzania. In August 1893 they won a decisive battle against the
Chagga and secured control of the Kilimanjaro region. In October
1894 they stormed the Hehe capital and, although Mkwakwa continued to fight a guerrilla battle until 1898, the Germans were free of
the threat of attack by the armies of a compact Hehe state from 1894
onward. After a brief but dramatic clash, the British made an agreement with the powerful Masai Laibon giving the British free use of a
large part of the principal route through Kenya. The Masai's neighbours, the Nandi, however, were not so easily won over and a battle
between them and the British in 1895 ended indecisively. Nandi
warriors continued to attack British traffic until they were finally
defeated in 1906. In Uganda the British advance was greatly facilitated
by an alliance made by missionaries with a faction at the Kabaka's
court. The agents of the Imperial East Africa Company came as
allies of the Ganda. The British victories were the victories also of the
Ganda warriors who provided the main body of the armies that
marched against Bunyoro in 1891 and 1893. Individual Ganda also
helped in the establishment of British rule in Usoga, in Ankole and in
northern Uganda. In the early stages the establishment of British rule
in Uganda was hardly more than an extension of the Ganda political
system over the neighbouring peoples. Meanwhile, with careful
diplomacy and by exploiting the rivalries of the different factions at
the Kabaka's court, the British gradually changed their position from
that of helpful allies to that of arbiters of Buganda politics. 1897 to
1900 were the decisive years. The Kabaka Mwanga was deposed, his
party defeated and the faction favoured by the British installed in
power and the 1900 Uganda agreement signed. As a result the principal Ganda chiefs recognised British sovereignty over Buganda and
the rest of the area described as the Uganda Protectorate.

The extent of European control

By 1900 the European Colonial governments were in commanding
positions throughout most of Middle Africa with the exception of
north and south Angola. The Cuanhama warriors in the south
remained self-confidently independent of the Portuguese until 1915,

while in the north the Dembos and other peoples held out until the painful advance of the Portuguese between 1907 and 1909. However the European Colonial Powers had not fastened their system of government upon all the peoples in the territories they claimed. Nor had they established peace and order. For many the Colonial governments' victories brought freedom from former masters but few were able to use that freedom in so positive a way as the Ganda chiefs after the destruction of the Kabaka's power. In most cases freedom quickly turned to confusion and uncertainly, followed by the exactions of the Colonial government as it set up its taxation system. The Colonial governments extended their rule gradually and unevenly during the first two decades of the twentieth century. Even by 1920 the process was by no means complete. The fact that Colonial rule was not imposed at once on all the peoples of Middle Africa is worth noting for it accounts for much of the uneven development and its later serious repercussions. The Colonial governments tended to adopt and extend the use of existing languages and political systems. In Tanzania and Kenya, Swahili was much used in both administration and education far beyond the coastal area where it was habitually spoken. The Free State government made the Kongo, Lingala and Luba languages play a similar rôle. The Germans took up the system of ruling through Akidas or appointed Chiefs which they had met in their first years of activity when confined to the coast and trade routes. The British also had a trade routes mentality in their first years in Kenya and they forced the Kikuyu and other peoples to accept men they described as chiefs but who were in fact merely former caravan leaders or trading administrators. In Uganda this tendency to extend existing political systems and personnel was even more marked. Not only did the British extend the boundaries of the Ganda kingdom, Ganda officials, clerks and teachers were given posts in all the surrounding areas and Ganda dominance in the Colonial Administration continued well into the twentieth century.

Disease and famine

While the Colonial governments were reaching out from the coast, rivers and trade routes, the greater part of Middle Africa was shaken by a series of plagues and famines that undermined the people's power to offer much more than brief despairing bouts of resistance. In 1889 the first recorded outbreak of rinderpest in Africa outside Egypt was noted in Somalia. Within a year it spread to Kenya, then crossed East Africa and reached Lake Nyasa by 1892. Thereafter it swept back and forth across the whole of Middle Africa during the 1890s attacking the herds of most cattle-keeping peoples. When the plague struck severely it could kill every animal a community possessed. Communities like the Hima or the Masai who knew no other life but herding were devastated by these visitations. Many starved to death; others fought over the few remaining cows. Other peoples who kept cattle as a store of wealth or as a sign of social status found their riches obliterated overnight. Less dramatic but more prolonged and debilitating was the spread of new diseases. Jiggers appeared in the Angolan interior in the 1870s and gradually spread through the population. Outbreaks of smallpox occurred in the Congo Basin in the wake of the European invasion. Sleeping sickness also came seeping into the western Congo and a serious epidemic killed tens of thousands of the population of Busoga and Buganda. Venereal diseases also became more virulent during and after the period of the invasion. The last two diseases not only killed the living but also reduced the birthrate. Local famines were not uncommon since the rainfall over a large part of the area was unreliable. During this period, however, there were some particularly severe famines. The most notable occurred in Kenya where famine, together with disease, severely reduced the Kikuyu and Kamba populations leaving wide areas of formerly inhabited land vacant. There was a famine also at a crucial moment in Katanga when the troops of the Congo Free State arrived in 1891. The famine continued after Msiri's death killing large numbers of the population. From 1906 to 1907 after the Maji Maji rising in south eastern Tanzania widespread famine destroyed entire villages and left the whole area in a depressed state for many years. Communities suffering such calamities were in no fit state to offer serious resistance to the impositions of a foreign government.

The first railways: the Congo

The Colonial Powers had established their rule in Middle Africa to develop and exploit its resources and consequently found it necessary to improve the existing transport system for only the most valuable products could be economically transported by headloading. Only by building railways could transport costs be reduced sufficiently to bring European manufactures into the heart of the continent and to bring out African products on a large scale for export. In the Congo Free

Building a railway in the Congo

State a comparatively short stretch of railway between Matadi and Kinshasa, where the river was unsuitable for steamers, promised to link a vast natural communications system with the sea. The building of this line, which began in 1889, placed a heavy burden on the Kongo people. Although the Free State was not slow to force all those who could to work, there were still not sufficient men available since they were already heavily involved in the porterage business and in the construction of the Free State's administrative centre at Boma. Shiploads of labourers were brought in from Sierra Leone and Nigeria on contract. The work was hard and widespread disease brought death to a substantial proportion of the workmen. Many fled before their contracts expired and few renewed their contracts. Men were imported from China but the Kongo people had to bear the greater part of the work. When in 1898 the line was complete thousands of men were suddenly released from employment. New burdens were soon to be imposed but the railway construction had abruptly changed the life of the peoples of the lower Congo river and drawn them forcefully into the colonial economy.

The first railways: East Africa

The British government, anxious to have a better line of communication with the Upper Nile, started construction of the much longer Mombasa to Uganda railway in 1895. Whereas the Congo line passed through fairly populous districts, the Uganda line, after the first twenty-five miles inland, went through country which was almost uninhabited. Large numbers of Indian labourers were brought in and few Africans were employed. The railway construction teams crawled slowly across the Kenyan plains and mountains almost in isolation until the last year when they descended toward Lake Victoria and entered the populous Kavirondo districts before reaching the line's terminus on the Lake in 1901. Apart from creating some demand for domestic servants and providing a new market for the foodstuffs produced by the Kamba and Kikuyu peoples, the railway building had little direct impact on the lives of the Kenyan peoples. Once complete the line made possible the development of a cotton exporting industry and the British Colonial administration began to look around for additional goods to transport in order to make the railway pay its way.

The Germans took twelve years (1893–1905) to build their first line from Tanga to Usumbara which was only about eighty miles long. Consequently, it had less effect on African life and on trade than did the British or Free State lines. Their next venture, however, was more ambitious and made a serious impact on African life both during and after construction. In 1905 the Central Railway set off from Dar es Salaam and by 1907 it had reached Morogoro. In 1912 it entered Tabora and by 1914 it had reached its terminus on Lake Tanganyika. Between 1906 and 1912 the northern railway was extended from Usumbara to Mount Kilimanjaro, more than doubling its former length. These large and quickly constructed railways placed a substantial burden on the resources of the colony. Several years before the idea of building a Central line was approved by the German government, the Colonial administration in Tanzania tried to show that such a railway would be feasible by forcing an increase in the colony's revenue and exports. They raised taxation and compelled people to grow cash crops. The people of Tanzania therefore began to pay the price of the Central railway long before the first line was laid.

The rubber boom

Finance was a continual problem to all the Colonial governments in Middle Africa for, unlike the governments in many parts of West Africa, most were unable to benefit from and build up existing trade but had to start almost from scratch. By 1890 all the Colonial administrations were in severe financial difficulties. The German Colonisation Society and the Imperial British East Africa Company sank under their debts and had to be rescued by their respective governments. The Congo Free State saved itself by persuading the European Powers at the Brussels Conference in 1890 to 1891 to allow it to collect import duties. Thereafter it improved its financial position by establishing what amounted to a commercial monopoly within its territory. Had it not been for the sudden and dramatic rise in rubber exports all the governments, but most particularly the Angolan and the Congo Free State governments, would have been in an even more difficult position. Angola had exported rubber from the mid-1870s onward. But the trade increased extremely rapidly from 1886. By 1893 the port of Benguela was exporting almost nothing but rubber and the new product compensated for the decline of the ivory trade. But after 1900 the price of rubber began to fall. Exports had to be increased to maintain the previous level of income. The rubber itself became more difficult to obtain as the more accessible sources were worked out. A decline set in and although prices recovered somewhat before the First World War, the Angolan export had almost dried up by 1912. The Congo Free State went through a similar cycle. King Leopold, whose organisation was almost bankrupt in 1894, was a rich man by 1900 and was using money made from the Congo to build palaces and finance public works in Belgium. The rubber export grew from two tons in 1891 to six thousand tons in 1901. When prices began to fall the Free State tried to save itself by making it difficult for producers to sell to anyone but government agents. People were forced to collect rubber and deliver it as taxes to government stations. Prices to the producer were artifically lowered in 1901 so that the Free State and its subsidiary companies could maintain their profits. These abuses had existed before but they became harsher and more obvious after 1900. Finally, after a storm of protest in Europe in 1908, the Belgian State assumed control of the Congo Free State from King Leopold. East Africa was less affected by the rubber boom. Rubber production contributed to the revenue of the colonies of Tanzania, Uganda and Kenya in the first decade of the twentieth century but it never played such a dominant rôle as in Angola and the Congo.

Another form of discontinuity

The rubber boom was another event, like the construction of the railways, which disrupted the life of the people without producing any clear cut new historical movement. Hundreds of thousands of men were mobilised all over Middle Africa for rubber collection. The 1880s and 1890s were a golden age for the Ovimbundu people in Angola but with the decline in 1900 they, who had formerly employed others, had to sell their labour. In Tanzania, Morogoro became an important rubber collecting centre but by 1907 there was no more rubber there. This cycle was repeated all over the Congo basin, in western Uganda and along the coastal strip of East Africa. Between 1906 and 1912 many European companies hired men to clear land and plant trees to establish regular rubber plantations but most of these proved unprofitable and many went bankrupt. The growth of the colonial economy, like the early industrialisation of Europe, proceeded by fits and starts with frequent failures for which Africans often had to pay. The rubber boom and collapse was an outstanding example of this.

The revolts

As the Colonial governments extended their rule they constantly encountered resistance: robbery of caravans, refusal to pay taxes, refusal to provide compulsory labour. Sizable forces were maintained to deal with such situations. The Congo Free State's 'Force Publique' numbered 16,000 men in 1905. The German security force in East Africa was some 2,300 strong and the British military force about 2,000 excluding police. These men were quick to shoot

Beating rubber in the Congo

and burn villages at the first sign of opposition. Away from the main
centres their annual tax-gathering expeditions closely resembled the
old marauding raids and their columns came back to base with herds of
cattle or crowds of conscripted labourers. These military activities

led to many small incidents but there were few major military engagements. There were two battles between the British and the Nandi in 1900 and 1905. Some 200 men were killed in a serious struggle between the Chagga and the tax gathering Germans in 1900. There was more serious fighting between the Portuguese and the peoples to the north of southern Angola between 1904 and 1915. These were isolated incidents. But the Bailunda rising on the Bihé Plateau in Angola in 1902 presented a rather different form of opposition. It arose from widespread economic grievances among people severely affected by falling rubber prices and governmental exactions and was not the struggle of a tribe trying to maintain its sovereignty. For several months battle flared across the Plateau until the weight of Portuguese arms brought it to an end. In 1904 in the Sankuru district of Kasai several formerly distinct and often mutually hostile communities among the Bashilele, Bakuba and Bangende united in a politico-religious movement and rose against the Free State regime. The rising was suppressed with heavy bloodshed as was another rising in the Lulonga district in 1905, but not before 145 agents of the hated 'Abir' rubber trading company had been killed between January and July.

Maji Maji

In 1905 in southern Tanzania, the most widespread revolt of all broke out in an area where German administration had been particularly harsh in its tax collection and most active in carrying through its compulsory cotton growing schemes to provide a substantial cash crop export and prove the viability of railway projects. Artificially low prices were paid for the crop when harvested. A portion of the proceeds was taken by the government to finance the administration of the scheme and another portion was assigned to local authorities. Consequently many of the men who had actually produced the crop received nothing for their labour. This fraud drove men to despair and a movement arose to rid the country of colonial rule. Native doctors spread the word from village to village that deliverance was at hand. They claimed to have found a medicine which would turn the bullets of the colonial forces to water—hence the name of the movement, Maji, meaning 'water'. Claims of this sort were not uncommon in Africa at this time and even later. What was remarkable was that the movement crossed tribal and other boundaries. So strong was the solidarity against colonial rule that the German administration in southern Tanzania collapsed between July and September 1905. The revolt reached as far as Morogoro and spread to the outskirts of the colonial capital at Dar es Salaam. Then the Germans rushed in reinforcements and took the offensive. Resistance was bitter but ineffective. By the end of 1905 the Colonial administration was again in control of most of the areas where the revolt had broken out. Fighting continued up to 1907 in the Songea area until the Germans finally defeated the once powerful Angoni warriors. The failure of the rising left the whole of south Tanzania in a depressed state. War and famine had undermined the self confidence of the people. Much wealth and trade were destroyed and the tsetse fly made the devastated areas unfit for future settlement.

Years of reappraisal

During the years between 1905 and 1909 most of the Colonial governments, their bitter rivalry and mutual suspicion having by then largely died away, were anxiously re-assembling and reconsidering their achievements, aims and methods. The crude frontiers of colonial states had been replaced during the last years of the nineteenth and during the first years of the twentieth centuries by more realistic boundaries which took account of African political systems removing possible causes of misunderstanding and friction between the colonisers and producing more co-operative attitudes among their officials. The era of competitive grasping at territory was not over but adjustment of boundaries was now once more a matter for high diplomacy in Europe and no longer preoccupied officials in the colonies. At the same time the high hopes of the early colonialists had suffered some severe shocks. All the colonial governments were more or less insolvent and dependent on inflows of money from metropolitan governments or loans from financiers. The railways often had insufficient traffic even to pay running costs; the rubber boom was fading away; the revolts had shaken the colonial edifice and produced serious debate on colonial policy in Europe. Among colonial officials there was serious discussion as to whether better results could be obtained by waiting for African producers to develop cash crops or by encouraging the development of European plantations, for of the few European plantations which had been set up many had failed. The British decided to stimulate African cotton growing in Kenya in 1906. The Belgians, determined upon reform, reduced the number and size of the large concessions that had been made to private interests, notably the private domain of King

Leopold in the central Congo, and in 1910 restored the right of producers to sell their crops freely and suppressed the system of paying
taxes in products of the soil. In Tanzania, Governor Rechenburg (1906–
1912) favoured African agriculture and having removed planters from
the Legislative Council, went ahead with the Central railway which
aimed at opening up the large centres of African population in the
northwest to trade rather than building a line in the northeast where
the European planters had their plantations.

The growth of the plantation economy

At this time Middle Africa was still hesitating between becoming a
society of free cash crop producing farmers as was much of West
Africa or becoming a society dominated by great European controlled estates where Africans worked as labourers. Nevertheless,
although colonial policy seemed to be moving in the direction of the
former solution, the period between 1908 and the first world war was
one during which the plantation economy grew in a strong and sustained fashion. Plantations, mines and railway projects got under way
in the Congo and put increasing pressure on the labour supply.
In 1910 the first of many labour recruiting agencies—the Bourse du
Travail—was set up in Katanga to bring men from distant places to
work in the mines. The work of these agencies was backed up by the
action of the administrations. By 1916 46,000 labourers were working
in mines and plantations in the Congo. In Tanzania the number of
wage earners rose from 70,000 in 1909 to 172,000 in 1912–13. A large
proportion of these labourers, who were engaged on comparatively
short one or two year contracts, had to trek long distances on foot to
reach their places of employment. Many spent several months going
to and from work. Although the Colonial governments considered it
their duty to ensure that every man was fully employed there was a
constant shortage of labour in many European enterprises. Consequently the growth of the plantation agriculture stifled the development of African cash crop production. It is possible that the
labour shortage produced by the forcible diversion of men from the
Kavirondo district of Kenya to settlers' farms on the Highlands
caused the disastrous failure of the African cotton growing experiment
there in 1907. The rise in the prices of agricultural products in the
1920s enabled the planters and plantation companies to push forward
towards a dominating position in the field of export production and
despite their policy declarations the Colonial governments were unable

to stand up to the forces of expanding European capitalism. Big companies could offer impoverished Colonial governments and their servants immediate financial and other benefits. King Leopold had been lavish in granting concessions for immediate financial gain to such companies as the Abir rubber company and the Société Anversoise. In 1907 the Société Minière was formed to exploit the resources of Katanga and a vast concession was handed over to the Lever company to establish oil palm estates in the northern Congo Basin. The demands of these organisations for labour and other favours soon resulted in a twisting and a whittling down of the Belgian reform measures both in theory and in practice. Governor Rechenberg fought his private war against the planters in Tanzania but they were able to exert pressure on the German government at home and the Colonial government was soon spending money on railways to serve their interests. In Kenya the settlers were already well organised by 1908 and successfully put pressure on the government to force low cost labour to work on their estates.

The impact of the First World War

Middle Africa was more heavily affected by the First World War than any other part of the continent. Elsewhere the campaigns were fairly brief. In Middle Africa German forces continued to resist until armistice day in November 1918. The vortex of the struggle lay in Tanzania although there was war also between Portuguese and Germans in southern Angola. Once more East Africa saw voracious bands of fighting men scouring the land, burning, destroying and eating up the small food supplies of impoverished villages. Throughout the whole of Middle Africa recruiting agents were out in strength seeking men to act as carriers for the warring forces. The Colonial Powers were at war and no moral scruples about forced labour deterred them from raising every man they could. The main battles were fought close to the railways but whenever the armies left the railways enormous numbers of carriers were required. At the beginning of the war the comparatively small German force operating in northeast Tanzania where there were many railways had 8,000 carriers constantly engaged in bringing up supplies. The British and Belgians counted their carriers in hundreds of thousands. Thousands died of disease and exhaustion and had to be replaced. Thus the war produced yet another meaningless bout of frenetic activity in Middle Africa; four years of energetic struggle which for Africans led nowhere. The war was followed by a wave of famine and disease. Spanish 'flu swept across Middle Africa in 1918–19 carrying off an estimated 25,000 people in Uganda alone and severely affecting Tanzania, the Congo and Kenya. Finally, there was a further outbreak of rinderpest which reached catastrophic proportions in some parts of Uganda.

A wave of unrest

In the early 1920s there were a number of political protests in different parts of Middle Africa. The general background conditions for these outbreaks were similar to those behind the revolts of the early years of the century. At the end of the war the prices of African exports rose sharply but then suffered an equally sharp fall in 1920–21. In British East Africa rapid changes in the value of currency added to the dislocation. Again people were baffled by the confusing colonial economic system and again Africans were called upon to pay the cost of economic upset through lower prices for their products and, in Kenya, through sharp reductions in the wages of plantation employees. But this time there were no concerted armed risings. A significant change had taken place in people's thinking and reactions and the strength and weaknesses of the colonial regime were better understood. In the Lower Congo popular discontent found its leader in Simon Kimbangu who first demonstrated his power by healing the sick and dying and then set out to lead the people into a new society. Polygamy, idols, even dancing were rejected, schools were set up, a new day of rest was proclaimed, the end of the colonial regime was prophesied and an organisation was set up to provide food for those who came to be cured. The Colonial government was not attacked but ignored by the tens of thousands who came to hear Kimbangu. He was arrested but later escaped and remained in hiding for several months before giving himself up. He was tried and deported to Lumumbashi but his movement went on and was to reappear strongly later in the century in a modified form as the 'Church of Jesus Christ as revealed to Simon Kimbangu'. In 1921 the moral power of Kimbangu's teaching was such that it not only won over those who had been working with the colonial regime but it also shook the self-confidence of the colonial rulers themselves for they were uncomfortably aware that his arrest and trial were without legal or moral justification. Kimbangu's boycott of colonialism was not the only protest against Belgian rule in this period. Another movement spread from Sankuru to Equateur and the Kwango. In Kenya Harry Thuku, organiser of the Young Kikuyu Association, led a movement which demanded the abolition of the newly introduced pass system, the reduction of the poll tax and the return of Kikuyu lands. His programme appealed to both workers whose wages were threatened and to squatter farmers on European owned lands who were being forced to give their labour instead of paying rents for the land they occupied. His method of forming 'Associations' with the object of influencing government policy was similar to that used by the settlers themselves. Between 1920 and 1922 Thuku placed his demands before the authorities and held great meetings in Nairobi and elsewhere. In March 1922 he was arrested and a demonstration in Nairobi broken up by police firing on the crowd. After these events unrest died down but Thuku's movement was also to reappear later in modified form. There was trouble too in Uganda but there the pattern was rather different. In Uganda the control of export production was largely in the hands of the Saza chiefs who had secured property rights by the 1900 Uganda agreement and the 1907 land settlement. In 1918 the traditional Bataka chiefs, the guardians of old clan rituals, came forward as spokesmen of the people, agitating for a revision of the land settlement in their favour. The Bataka Association they formed in 1920 also drew attention to the increasing exactions (the 'envuju' payments in produce and the 'busulu' periods of compulsory labour) which the chiefs were imposing on those in Saza lands. The Bataka chiefs had much popular support, including that of the young Kabaka. Their agitation failed to alter the land settlement but in 1927 a limit was imposed on the exactions which chiefs could demand of the people.

More railway building

The 1920s saw a very notable improvement in the communications of middle Africa. By 1928 the Benguela railway in Angola had been extended to the minefields of Katanga and a new port of Lobito which was constructed next to Benguela became the most prosperous commercial centre in Angola. Work was continued on lines bypassing the unnavigable sections of the Congo river and on lines from Katanga to the Angolan border and to the Kasai river at Port Franqui. Eight and a half million pounds were spent on improving communications in Kenya and Uganda by building lines round Lake Victoria to Kampala and in the Kenya Highlands. In Tanzania, too, by 1929 the extension of the railway system was complete from Moshi to Arusha and the Central line was being extended from Tabora to Mwanza on Lake Victoria.

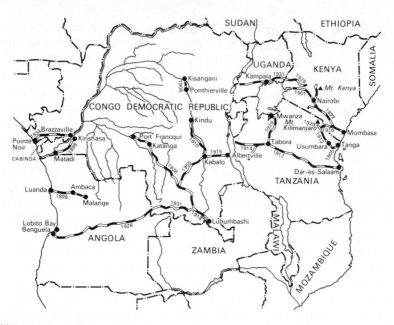

Middle Africa: railways and the dates of their completion

Railway politics

As a result of pressure exerted by the white settler politicians the railway systems were deliberately designed to serve the interests of European controlled economic enterprises in Middle Africa. Rather than integrating the country they greatly improved the amenities in certain favoured areas while leaving others quite unserved. In the Congo the several networks were not even linked with one another. The railways were not designed to draw the countries together but to link the centres of production with the outside world by the most direct routes. This gave an impetus toward a lopsided development with a few prosperous modern centres being served with foodstuffs and with migrant labour from neglected and backward hinterlands.

Road construction

This situation was somewhat improved by extensive road building programmes during the decade following the First World War. Up to 1920 there was little road construction. In the Congo the total network of what were classed as roads amounted to only 1,400 miles. By 1947 there were over 62,000 miles of road most of which had been constructed before 1937. The period of rapid road construction began in 1921. The 875 miles of road which existed in Orientale Province in 1922 grew to 10,000 miles by 1929. This sudden increase in road construction was due to the great wave of motor vehicle imports during the period 1925–30 making possible a more flexible transportation system than that provided by the railways. In Angola the Portuguese were quick to see the advantages of motor transport and started an intensive road building programme in the 1920s. In Uganda the old pre-war road tracks and ox-wagon trails were replaced during the 1920s by a reasonably satisfactory system of dirt roads and by the end of the decade most of the more populous districts were accessible by road. Kenya and Tanzania with overall vast distances and low population density were less well served but even so there was a great deal of road building during this period. The importance of the road building and the increasing use of motor vehicles during this period for the history of the people of Middle Africa can hardly be over-estimated. It brought a revolution in the life of countless communities as social, economic and cultural transformation became possible in concert with other communities. At first road building was simply another colonial imposition. The roads were constructed with local labour, usually unpaid and forcibly recruited. But once open to motor transport they greatly diminished the necessity for head porterage of goods. Men were now able to return to more rewarding activities. In Tanzania by 1938 hardly anyone could be found who was willing to trek by foot over anything but short distances. The long journeys on foot from south to north were a thing of the past. People now went by lorry. The lorries could also penetrate to villages away from the main centres and collect their cash crops for export. The reduced cost of transporting foodstuffs put an end to the age-old fear of local famine in this part of Africa where the rainfall was inadequate and undependable over the greater part of the land. The roads opened up new horizons for men in formerly isolated communities. Some villages moved or, as in the Congo, were moved by administrators up to the road to form new communities which could take advantage of the new facility. The neglected countryside and rural areas slowly began to make progress.

The plantation economy in power

It was one of the misfortunes of Middle Africa, in the short term at least, that large scale European controlled enterprises secured a dominating position in society just before the road and motor transport revolution began to open up new prospects. Mines and plantations in Angola and the Congo and white settler agriculture in Kenya moved into a period of comparative prosperity in the early '20s when, after the sharp boom and slump of 1920–21, the world demand and prices for primary products rose once more. In the Congo the great Katanga copper mines got into their stride. Tin and diamond mining got under way. The great plantation companies such as Lever could now depend entirely on the production of their large, European managed plantations for supplies of palm oil, rubber and other goods. In Angola diamond mining began and soon became one of the colony's major exports, together with sisal, sugar and coffee from European-run estates. In Kenya the white settlers in the Highlands finally mastered the problems of farming and plantation-produced coffee and sisal became the main exports backed by the settler-produced maize. The settlers, planters and companies were consequently able to wield an even greater influence than before over the Colonial governments during these years. In Kenya the white settlers were bent on nothing less than complete control over the colony. They demanded the right to elect their own government to rule the two and a half million or more people in the country and when this was refused in 1922 they planned to seize the railway and kidnap the Governor. The British government, anxious to avoid a repetition of the Boer War situation, was conciliatory. However, the government of India, affronted by the settlers' attacks on the rights of Indians in Kenya, exerted pressure on the Colonial Office in London and the path to settler rule was blocked and the policy of 'paramountcy of native interest' promulgated in London. However, the Legislative Council, which had existed since 1906, was now given European and Indian elected representatives and in effect became dominated by settlers. This was reflected in the strongly pro-settler bias in most of its policies. For a while it seemed as if Uganda might go the same way. In 1920 the British Colonial Office veered toward a policy of permitting more land purchase by Europeans and labour legislation favourable to their interests. In 1920 the establishment of a Legislative Council with members chosen exclusively from among planters and representatives of large companies formed part of a movement towards a settler and company controlled regime. But this movement was arrested by London in 1923 when it became clear that African productive enterprise was more successfully strengthening the country's economy than the weak and unsuccessful efforts at plantation agriculture. In Tanzania, where, before the war, the settlers and companies had become almost as strong as their Kenyan counterparts, the situation was radically changed by the destruction of the estates during the war and the removal of their German owners. The settlers, many of whom were non-British, had difficulty in recovering their position after the war. But the press supported their interests, settlers in neighbouring Kenya sought to bring pressure to bear and the weak Governors who ruled the country up to 1926 were often swayed by their arguments. In many ways the early 1920s represented the heyday of settler power and what defence of African interests there was within the colonial system was conducted by the missionaries and humanitarian opinion in Europe.

The proletarisation of African labour

As European enterprise forged ahead in the early 1920s it put an increasing demand on African manpower. In the Congo the number of men employed by European firms, construction schemes and plantations rose from 147,000 in 1922 to over 400,000 in 1925. An additional 40,000 men were engaged on government public works and in the ranks of the Force Publique. Nevertheless the labour supply still fell short of demand and government officials were ordered to ensure that every able-bodied man was working for either the government or some European employer. Forced labour became the order of the day. By the middle of the decade the government were talking in terms of the 'total mobilisation of labour' to meet the incessant demand. But upon investigation it was found that the point of 'total mobilisation' (estimated at 15%–16% of the total population in wartime Europe) had practically been reached. Much has been written about the exploitation of the Congo during King Leopold's reign. The exploitation was more comprehensive and systematic during the 1920s, but being better organised and less violent it gave rise to less criticism in Europe. The burden placed on the African community in Kenya was, if anything, greater than in the Congo. There too the government forced men to work on European farms. In 1919 Governor Northey issued his famous circulars to administrative officers telling them to 'encourage' men to work on European estates. After missionary criticism the circulars were eventually withdrawn but much courage on the part of the administrators was needed to resist the demands of the settlers who were in such a strong position in the 1920s. In Uganda also, where African chiefs were the main landowners there was a heavy demand for labour as production rose and migrant workers came in from Rwanda and elsewhere. At the same time, in the Congo and in Kenya especially, measures were taken to prevent Africans from earning money by gathering and producing cash crops on their own farms. In Kenya they were forbidden to produce the most valuable crop, coffee; it was said that African production of coffee would encourage the spread of diseases affecting the crop. The discouragement of African cash crop production was a method of keeping wages down for wages were so low that a man could earn in a few days gathering crops what he would be paid for a month's work on a European plantation. Africans were being made into a proletariat without property and without control over the means of production. This was already true of trade and commerce. In Angola Africans were forced out of trade by a system of licencing of traders. In the Congo the large firms controlled the purchase of cash crops and much of the distribution of imported goods. In East Africa, Indian traders were able to beat the small African traders out of business because of the financial support and trading connections they maintained with the big Indian trading companies which themselves were linked with the commercial power of western India and the wider world of business and finance. During the 1920s the situation began to change. Whereas the majority of workers had been casual labourers whose energies were used for short periods in the main centres after which they returned to their villages, now urban communities began to grow up in the new centres. Balubas began to reside permanently in towns like Luluabourg and Lumumbashi. Bakongo were taking up permanent residence in Kinshasa. This movement marked the beginning of greater continuity in the life of Middle Africa.

The exceptional Ganda

As has already been noted African society suffered from the colonial regime up to the middle 1920s but it was not transformed by it. Inter-state warfare was stopped, but inter-village warfare still went on in many areas. The growth of states was stopped but the few colonial administrators made only occasional, though disruptive, political interventions. Colonial-appointed chiefs wielded petty dictatorships over many villages which had been autonomous but states like Bakavu or Rwanda continued much as before. One state which *was* transformed and which played an active rôle throughout this period was Buganda. The chiefly oligarchy which came to power there in the late nineteenth century regarded itself as the partner of the British administration—not as its subordinate agent. The chiefs, who were either Christian or Muslim, were mainly educated men, prosperous from their cotton estates and anxious to modernise. The corporate strength of the oligarchy was most clearly expressed in the new Lukiko or Parliament and the self confidence of the Ganda ruling class epitomised in the burly figure of Sir Apolo Kagwa, Katikiro or Chief Minister until 1926. Kagwa, who left behind him a mass of correspondence equal to any contemporary European statesman, was at once a reformer and a stout defender of his state against colonial encroachment. While gladly accepting advice and technical assistance he was not prepared to tolerate uninformed or unwanted interference. A stickler for legality, he took his stand on the Uganda agreement which defined the relationship between the Baganda state and the British government. When in 1910 the British interfered in the

Sir Apolo Kagwa
(right) in 1902

333

delicate question of chiefs' property rights he engaged a solicitor to fight the Ganda case. From the 1890s to the 1920s the British were careful not to offend him. Buganda was the heart of the British Protectorate in Uganda and although the British administration was secure there elsewhere it was not firmly established. But after the First World War, as other districts were organised under British administration and officials grew accustomed to more high-handed dealings with weaker states, so the British wanted closer control of Buganda. Kagwa insisted that the Provincial Commissioner should deal only with him and the other Ministers of the Ganda State and not give directions on his own account to local authorities. But by then Kagwa was old and unwell; his relations with the young Kabaka were uneasy and his political position weakened. In 1926 he resigned and an era in Ganda affairs came to an end. Buganda began to look more like other colonial administered states.

The economic slump

The middle 1920s marked the highwater mark of the post war economic expansion. In 1927 and 1928 prices began once more to fall and by the end of the decade the economic slump occurred. The whole colonial economy stopped expanding and goverments reduced their activity to a minimum. It was the final discontinuity in a period filled with false starts of various kinds. It principally affected European and government activity and by slowing them down it gave Africans a much needed breathing space and allowed them to take stock of their position and set about recovering control of the destiny of their country. Export industry may have suffered a devastating blow but the African economy could move forward making use of the new road facilities. Education expanded rapidly in the 1930s. New administrative and social organisations began to blossom. Middle Africa began to lay the foundations of a new society.

11 Building a new society in Middle Africa

The years around 1930 can in many senses be regarded as a turning point in the history of Middle Africa. It was then that the balance began to swing away from the thrusting forces of colonialist imperialism toward resurgent African enterprise. After the confusions and turmoil of the previous period, new dynamic forces began to emerge which were progressively to transform Middle Africa and create a new society. This is not to say that from 1930 onward the colonial regime began to falter or fade away. In many respects it was to become more active than before. But its activity was increasingly outweighed by the constructive forces of a modernising, progressive African society which finally engulfed and threw off colonial control during the early 1960s.

Demographic dynamism

In 1926 many of those concerned with the administration of the Congo felt that a crisis was at hand. There was a general belief that under the impact of the colonial regime the population of the country was declining and would continue to decline unless serious measures were taken. It is debatable whether the population had indeed declined but certainly some areas of the country had been depopulated since the 1880s and the population generally speaking was not rising. In East Africa, although there was not the same alarm, the picture was not very different. Large areas such as southern Tanzania had been depopulated and most of the evidence pointed to a stagnant or declining population. But from the middle 1920s the picture began to change. Although we have no very reliable figures, there is every indication that the population began to rise and in some areas rose fast. For example, it is estimated that in Kenya the Kikuyu population was expanding at the rate of 1·5 per cent every year between 1925 and 1935 and the population of Tanzania nearly doubled between 1921 and 1950. All the evidence points to the period just before and just after 1930 as being that when the 'population explosion' which is now such a marked feature of African life in Middle Africa, began. There were many reasons for this development. As the colonial regime, having secured a monopoly of the use of force, established more peaceful conditions there was a substantial extension of farms in many areas. The Sukuma people moved out into Zinza Province to take up new land. In eastern Tanzania men came down from the mountains and out of palisaded villages to cultivate fields which were formerly abandoned. In Kenya Kamba had been coming down from the hills into the plain since the first decade of the century. Kikuyu cut into the defensive forest fringes of their territory. People in Nyanza Province spread out from their villages. In the Congo also, Baluba and other peoples began to move into lands along the line of the Port Franqui–Katanga railway. Road building and the increasing trade in foodstuffs also permitted a more rapid and efficient development of agriculture. Farming extended rapidly, more food was produced and a growing population could be sustained. At the same time a more determined effort was made to stamp out the recurrent famines and epidemics which had in former years decimated the population. In 1918–19 the Uganda government, alarmed at the onset of famine, distributed 800 tons of food in Busoga. Its efforts were not entirely successful but thereafter it was able to act with greater effect to prevent sudden droughts from ruining communities which lived on the border of subsistence. In 1925 the Congo government became alarmed in a more general way about the living conditions of the people. The Colonial government took up the question of public health more vigorously and began to build up a network of dispensaries and health centres throughout the country. These, together with the efforts of the missions and the companies in the same field, soon provided the Congo with one of the best medical services in Africa. In East Africa also the governments turned more actively to the fight against disease. The Uganda government's expenditure on its medical department expanded four-fold in the years between 1919 and 1928. In 1928 there were fifty-nine dispensaries in Uganda; by 1938 there were 108. In Tanzania there were 310 dispensaries by 1934 most of which had been set up during the previous ten years. These services gradually improved general health and above all guarded against the spread of the major epidemic diseases. Inevitably the rapid growth in population radically changed its composition. The proportion of children and youths in relation to the rest of the community began to grow. The young men who were to fight for independence in the 1940s and 1950s were born around this time and these, together with growing families brought optimism and self confidence to replace the frustration and depression of the previous period.

Educational progress

It was in this optimistic atmosphere that an extensive movement towards new schools took place in many parts of Middle Africa. The movement was uneven since mass demand for the new education occurred among different peoples at different times. Whereas in Buganda many thousands of schools set up before the First World War continued to expand, the education system established before the war in Tanzania was severely disrupted during the war and by 1930 was only reaching the position it had attained in 1914. On the other hand, by 1945, education had still not started to spread on any substantial scale among the Masai. In many parts of the Congo, Tanzania and Kenya in the late 1920s and early 1930s schools began to spring up in large numbers in villages at a distance from the main mission stations. Up to 1910 in the Congo the Catholic missionaries especially had followed the *ferme chapelle* system of gathering together small communities of ex-slaves and social outcasts around a few missionary centres apart from and usually in opposition to the rest of society. Since the missions were the main organisers of education and the chief suppliers of teachers, education tended to be narrowly focused rather than widely spread. By 1930 this situation had profoundly changed. The central mission stations still provided the bulk of the teachers, but among whole peoples the acquisition of literacy and the new ideas that went with it had become a popular movement. It was no longer necessary to bribe children to go to school. Villages built their own schools and engaged their own teachers, sometimes with the aid of whatever missionary organisation they preferred, or with the aid of the African churches and educational organisations that began to appear. In Kenya where there had been forty schools in 1912 there were 2,000 in 1930. Many of these schools were condemned as 'bush schools' by the educational departments of the Colonial governments who measured them against the yardstick of formal European education and found them wanting. But these schools cannot be judged by the range of their very limited and often heavily religious curricula for this overlooks the important movement of the human spirit that they represented. The teachers were men of vision who opened up new perspectives, created new aspirations and indulged in serious social criticism at a local level. The rapid growth of these schools was part of the hungry search after a better order of society which was so

Congo children at a mission school

characteristic of this period. The years between 1920 and 1940 were rich in movements of this kind. In the Lower Congo, Simon Kimbangu and his disciples provoked a widespread popular movement which extended beyond the boundaries of the Congo to the French held territories to the north. In Buganda the Abamaliki movement working outside the missionary organisations satisfied the widespread demand for baptism which appeared among the lower classes of Ganda in the early 1920s. In 1929 a revivalist movement within the Christian church affected Rwanda, Uganda and Kenya. In 1933 the primate of the African Orthodox Church of South Africa, Archbishop Alexander was invited to Kenya and baptised large numbers of Kikuyu. Throughout this period, the Wata wa Mungu—the people of God—were also at work among the Kikuyu. These movements went hand in hand with the rapid development of education and when the first surges of energy had passed they left behind them a larger number of more vigorous schools. While the proliferation of schools, religious revivals and baptisms changed the outlook of village communities there was another aspect of the movements which was concerned with social criticism on a broader plane. Simon Kimbangu was concerned not only with changing local customs but with removing the colonial burden from the shoulders of the whole Kongo people. Archbishop Alexander was brought to Kenya to found an independent African Orthodox Church which would organise and gather together many local communities under solely African control. The initiative to do this had been taken by a number of teachers who, impatient with the missions' unsympathetic attitude and failure to understand Kikuyu customs, had set up their own schools organisations—the Kikuyu Independent Schools Association and the Kikuyu Karinga Educational Association. These movements and the ideas behind them produced a growing solidarity among the Kikuyu people as a whole just as the Kimbanguist movement produced a sense of unity among the people of the Lower Congo. The slow development of secondary education played a similar rôle within the framework of the established educational system. Whereas village and elementary schools mainly produced local change, secondary schools produced an élite which could seriously challenge the colonial order. Consequently the Colonial governments mostly discouraged the growth of secondary schools and preferred to provide agricultural training or trade schools and attempted to restrict higher instruction to their own requirements for medical assistants or public works engineers. But the Colonial governments were not always able to exercise firm control over the educational system. The bulk of education was in the hands of the missions who themselves had to be responsive to African demands since so many of their schools were the result of African enterprise. In Uganda the attempt between 1925 and 1934 to stifle the growth of secondary education and create purely vocational schools was blocked by missionary and African resistance. Makerere College emerged in 1933 as a fully fledged secondary school and by 1939 there were 1,335 secondary schools in Uganda. Since the missions in the Congo were more dependent on government finance they conformed more closely to what the government required. But there, as elsewhere, the missions were anxious to produce priests and pastors and the seminaries provided another avenue to higher education. But generally speaking between 1920 and 1940 the number who received higher education was small. Primary education was dominant and secondary education still something for the future. The educated élites had not yet emerged as a significant force and such bodies as the Tanganyika African Association formed in 1929 had a very restricted membership. In Angola education had scarcely reached the village level. There were schools in the coastal cities and some Ovimbundu districts but discouragement by the colonial government and the constant activity of labour recruiting agents severely limited the possibility of educational development.

The consequences of the economic slump

From 1928 to 1938 the demand for products exported from Middle Africa and the prices paid for them fell to an unprecedented low level. For example, from 1929 to 1933 the price of cloves—Zanzibar's principal export—fell from twenty-four rupees a frasilah to six rupees and prices remained low until the Second World War. This dramatic fall, while striking a severe blow at the major industry in Zanzibar also hastened a social revolution. The Arab planters who had dominated the island were ruined and many Indian capitalists suffered a severe setback. Many estates had to be sold and were bought by Swahilis who could work on smaller profit margins. This shift in economic power was reflected in the increasing involvement of Africans in the administration and in 1934, when local government was reorganised, more power was placed in the hands of local, mainly African, communities. Elsewhere in Middle Africa the economic depression had a similar effect. It hit hardest at foreign planters who spent heavily on imported goods to maintain a high standard of living and affected least the African farmers who were engaged in subsistence farming. Although these farmers earned less from their export products they also paid less for cotton textiles, their main import, as large quantities of cheap Japanese cloth was appearing on the markets. However, whereas in Zanzibar the administration did little to save the Arab planter aristocracy, elsewhere the Colonial governments took measures to ease the foreign settlers' and companies' difficulties and continued policies which reduced the benefits Africans might have derived from the new situation.

The plantation economy in danger

In Kenya the effects of the economic depression were worsened by attacks of locusts and droughts between 1931 and 1934. But the government assisted the settlers with loans and a Land Bank was set up in 1931 with a capital of £500,000. The settlers turned increasingly to the production of wheat and dairy produce which could be sold profitably behind the tariff barrier. Africans still had to pay the same taxes as before even though their wages were reduced from fourteen shillings to eight shillings a month and the price of their export articles such as hides and ghee had fallen further than the prices of other exports. However, after some initial losses the African farmers began to profit from the situation by taking over the production of crops such as maize which the settlers were no longer able to produce profitably. The old distinction between African 'subsistence' farming and settler cash crop production began to disappear. In Tanzania in the early 1930s as the area of plantation land was reduced, coffee growing by the Chagga people and in Bukoba continued to develop. Cotton production extended especially on the southern shore of Lake Victoria and tea planting began in the southern Highlands. As the Chagga farmers became comparatively wealthy better systems of organisation such as the Chagga co-operative society were set up and education extended rapidly. In central Tanzania, however, where the soil was poorer, there was not the same progress. Many communities found their cash incomes severely reduced and being unable to find the money to buy cotton textiles began to clothe themselves in bark-cloth once more. In 1939 they were still struggling against the age-old enemy of periodic famine. Uganda, mainly because the cash economy was almost entirely African based, suffered less from the depression. Despite falling prices, coffee production increased without a break. Cotton production fell between 1929 and 1932 but then rose faster than before as farmers in more remote areas began to see the advantages of securing a cash income in this way. Better houses were built, co-operative societies were formed and schools were set up. In the Congo and Angola the slump checked the vigorous growth of the plantation economy. The completion of the major railway projects just before the slump reduced the demand for construction labour and carriers. More men were able to return to their villages to develop their own farms although taxes remained high and forced labour was still exacted for road construction and government service. Like governments in East Africa, the Congo administration began to encourage African cash crop production. In 1933 the *paysannat indigène* policy was adopted by the Belgians. African farmers were to form the backbone of society and the Congo was not to be a place for large scale European settlement. In the ensuing years the Colonial governments paid considerable attention to the development of African production and their efforts resulted in a substantial extension of cotton cultivation by African farmers. In areas where the soil was suitable for cotton the farmers became quite wealthy even though the price was kept artificially low. In other areas, such as the central Congo where yields were less, the crop was hardly worth growing and forced cotton cultivation became a major grievance against the colonial regime.

The age of indirect rule

Between 1925 and 1940 there was much anxious discussion by the colonial rulers about systems of 'native administration'. There was a major controversy about the relative advantages of 'indirect' and 'direct' rule. Sir Donald Cameron, Governor of Tanzania between 1925 and 1931, claimed by gradual reforms to have introduced indirect rule in Tanzania. After considerable argument a law was introduced into the Congo which was designed to have the same effect. Local government areas, based on traditional African groupings and headed by a chief with some traditional sanction, were established. In the Congo these chiefs had some autonomy as they had their own treasuries from which the local officials were paid. However, no single law could produce a uniform type of administration throughout such wide areas with so many diverse forms of social organisation. In Tanzania the Chagga people fitted fairly well into the system of indirect rule. But in the coastal areas it was difficult to find a better authority than that of the nominated chiefs, whom the Germans and the Arabs before them had appointed. Indirect rule worked well in

Buganda where there was an existing state system in pre-colonial times. It could not so easily be imposed on the small Kikuyu communities where there was no single African authority which could exercise accepted rule over any substantial number of villages.

Local government becomes more African

Whether colonial rule was direct or indirect, however, there was one feature common to most of Middle Africa during this period—except Angola. A more meaningful dialogue was begun between the Colonial government and African society. During the 1920s and 1930s administrators began to make serious studies of the organisation of African societies and began to take African political and legal institutions into account more seriously, asking Africans how they thought local government should be organised. Europeans now became more conscious than ever before of the richness of African culture. Here and there administrators and missionaries turned from breaking down African customs to the preservation and development of the traditional institutions. The 1920s and 1930s saw an increase in work such as that of the Reverend Van Wing who in 1921 produced his 'Bakongo Studies' and contributed much to the development of Bakongo self-consciousness through his studies of the history and institutions of the Bakongo people. Much of this kind of work was done for practical reasons to produce information for Colonial governments. But, whatever the motivation, Africans found that they were being more frequently consulted. As the Colonial governments began to pay more attention to the problem of establishing an effective system of local government its doings became more comprehensible. It began to look less like an agency for exploitation and more like a government for the people. Communities began to identify themselves with the administrative areas to which they were assigned and for those who had formerly lived within the narrow bounds of closed village societies this often meant the opening up of wider perspectives. In other cases, pre-colonial systems which had been broken down in the early colonial period were now resuscitated and pre-colonial tendencies toward the creation of wider unities were given new scope. The Hehe people were able to unite again under their paramount chief. The Sukuma and Nyamwezi peoples were drawn together into federations in 1927 and 1928 and although internal disputes led to the breakdown of the central councils in 1930 the two federations remained as judicial and administrative units. In Kenya the system of rule through appointed chiefs was gradually brought to an end from 1924 onward and Local Native Councils were established whose members were to some extent determined by popular choice. Although Colonial administrators supervised the working of these new bodies there was now more opportunity for the people to discuss how administration should be run and to decide how the growing funds at the disposal of local government treasuries should be used. After the political paralysis and petty tyrannies of the previous period, this represented some considerable advance.

Looking backward and looking forward

The development of local government and the restoration of old political structures had certain inherent dangers. There was the possibility of old pre-colonial divisions being restored. The re-establishment of the traditional ruling families often meant that power was placed in the hands of old men with old ideas leaving few opportunities for progressive, younger men. Indeed, some Colonial governments saw this as a means of restricting the activities of nationalistically inclined young people. At the same time the constant search for the oldest institutions gave the new system a conservative if not a reactionary character. For example, Buganda could be regarded as having been successful in retaining some autonomy while remaining under colonial control. Or it could be seen as a society where an established ruling class of chiefs were anxiously preserving their own power and social and political inequality. Nevertheless these conservative features were mainly superficial and must be weighed against the fact that the people were at last securing a more meaningful grip upon the administrative system. Furthermore indirect rule did not really restore the pre-colonial political structures of Middle Africa. As well as basing local administration on traditional institutions, the Colonial governments were also trying to create administrative areas of fairly equal and manageable size. While some former states like that of the Hehe were reunited, others were broken up as was the old Lunda Empire. The Buganda kingdom remained intact but the areas adjacent to it, such as Busoga and Toro which Buganda had been about to take over before the British invasion, now became more markedly autonomous as the Colonial government of Uganda in the late '20s made the administrative boundaries of the various native authorities more rigid. On the other hand new unities emerged as the Colonial government gathered small communities with similar institutions into new administrative districts, as was the case with the Tetela people in the central Congo, the small separate Bakongo communities, the Sukuma communities and the Chagga chiefdoms. A number of communities along the northern stretch of the Congo river traced their descent back to a common ancestor, Mongo, and as administrators collected their several histories they began to acquire a solidarity which was based on tradition but was nevertheless not traditional. Loyalty towards these broader communities made co-operation easier in building roads and schools, in marketing cash crops and also provided a framework in which African culture could flourish and develop more vigorously. In the early stages they represented an opening up of men's minds. If the tribal lines began to harden later that was the response of another generation to the trials of other times.

The colonial superstructure

Many of the disputes and discussions that went on in the centres of Colonial government before and during the Second World War were still nearly as remote from the life of the people as had been the discussions at the Berlin Conference of 1885. Africans seldom participated in the debates and they had no say in determining the shape of government as a whole. There were Legislative Councils in each of the East African territories after 1926 but they had no African members before 1945. Selected missionaries and Secretaries of Native Affairs were expected to protect African interests. In the Congo unofficial members were added to the Councils in 1933 but, until 1947 when two Africans were admitted to the central government council, the unofficial members were all European.

Closer union in East Africa

One of the major issues discussed by the governments of East Africa during this period was the question of closer union. From 1924 onward the British Colonial Office pressed for the establishment of some form of co-ordinating authority which would lead ultimately to the amalgamation of the East African territories into a single federation, hoping in this way to make possible economies in defence, customs administration, railway development, postal services and other such matters. There was much opposition to the scheme in Zanzibar,

Uganda and Tanzania. In Kenya the settlers at first resisted the idea but in 1926 began to support closer union provided that it would be accompanied by the concession of an elected European majority on the Legislative Council. Their enthusiasm, however, made Indians and Africans more suspicious of the scheme than before and when Sir Hilton Young's commission investigated the question in 1928 it reached the conclusion that the climate of opinion was not in favour of any major change. In 1931 a Select Committee of Parliament, after hearing Indian and African objections, again decided that the time was not opportune. The three states, four including Zanzibar, continued to co-operate in running various common services but no political step was taken to bring them together until after the war. By then the states were too firmly fixed and the East African High Commission, set up in 1948, was too weak and too settler-dominated to attract the loyalty of rising nationalist opinion.

German colonial ambitions

The Colonial governments in Middle Africa were also troubled in the last years before the war by Germany's demands for compensation for the colonies she had lost in 1919. Germany was particularly interested in Middle Africa where there were German settlers in the former German colony of Tanzania. In 1938 the fates of Tanzania and the Congo were the subject of diplomatic discussions between Germany and Britain and there was much uneasiness in colonial circles but the onset of war put an end to all uncertainty.

The impact of the Second World War

Although the Second World War did not have the same disastrous effect on Middle Africa as the first world struggle and no military campaigns were fought there, apart from the British and Italian troops' battles on the north Kenyan frontier, preliminary to the Italian defeat in Ethiopia, the war had a great impact on the life of the people and the war years were a period of crucial change throughout most of the area. Kenya became the base for military operations and later a rest centre for troops engaged in the Middle East. This created a large demand for foodstuffs and the settler farms were more profitably active than ever before. The Congo and Middle Africa provided supplies in a more general way but on an equally large scale to the allied nations as a whole. With the Japanese invasion of South East Asia in 1942 came a serious reduction in the supply of certain tropical products and Zanzibar cloves were now in great demand. Formerly unprofitable rubber plantations could now sell all they produced and rubber was even gathered in the forests again. There was an enormous demand for copra, sisal, cotton, palm oil and minerals which were of direct military value. The period between 1940 and 1945 was reminiscent of the early 1920s. There was a scramble for labour and the government intervened to force people to work more. In the Congo compulsory cultivation, mainly of cotton, was increased to 120 days of a man's working year. Rubber collection and food growing was speeded up by forced labour and emergency powers were taken to deal with the problem of labour shortage. Labour legislation was used to prevent absenteeism and to keep wages low. In East Africa, government action was less harsh but there was a return to compulsory labour after May 1940 to increase the production of maize and other food crops. In Uganda some 77,000 men were recruited for military service. In Kenya the figure reached 75,000, about 20 per cent of the adult male population. Nevertheless, despite this outflow of men, export production was stepped up and the production of food crops maintained. The Second World War put a strain on Middle Africa's resources which was probably equal to if not greater than anything previously experienced.

Middle Africa's vigorous response

The effect of the Second World War was rather different from previous plunderings by the Colonial governments of Middle Africa's manpower resources. This was a more mechanised war than the First World War. The army did not want carriers and other totally unskilled labourers. Many soldiers received some form of technical training—if only as drivers. They saw other societies in other parts of the world where the supremacy of the white man was not an accepted fact as at home. In Middle Africa itself there was a great increase in the demand for skilled and semi-skilled labour. Many secured jobs as clerks or mechanics with government or private enterprise. Even for those who went to do unskilled tasks in the mining centres there was the challenge of entering a new society— the society of the big city. The Congo copper mines were already an established industry when war broke out. But the war effort extended their production from 122,000 tons in 1939 to 165,000 tons in 1944.

Tin production, already well established before the war, was doubled. The mining towns no longer resembled the depressing chaos, the semi-slave camps of early days. Since 1928, in an effort to stabilise their labour force, the Congo mining companies had been providing more attractive social conditions, proper accommodation and medical services and a new urban society was emerging. People began to regard a working visit to these new cities less as an imposition and more as an interesting and exciting experience and, within a few years of the outbreak of war, the Colonial administrators began to be worried by the beginnings of a rural exodus. Men were now going to work in the cities by choice and not by force. No doubt the enforced collection of rubber and cultivation of cotton in rural areas was partly responsible for the exodus but the attraction of the cities played an important rôle. The jump from 536,000 wage earners in the Congo in 1940 to over 700,000 in 1945 did not involve the same amount of human misery as the increase from 125,000 to 421,000 between 1920 and 1926. This growing African preference for town life started the rapid growth of cities in Middle Africa which was to continue throughout the next two decades. Between 1940 and 1945 the population of Kinshasa rose from 47,000 to 96,000 and that of Lumubashi from 27,000 to 65,000. The pattern of protest against colonial rule also changed significantly. Revolts now began to occur in the cities rather than in the rural areas. There was a dock strike in Mombasa in 1939, a strike by Union Minière workers in Lumumbashi in 1941, a mutiny of the Congolese Force Publique at Luluabourg in 1944 and a dock strike at Matadi in 1945. These were not peaceful strikes and the Colonial governments regarded them as a serious challenge to their authority. They were accompanied by bloodshed and stirred the whole populations of the affected towns. Trade unions were still very weak and were not even allowed in the Congo. The strikes represented real economic grievances for, although the prices of Middle Africa's products were rising on the world market, the real income of the people did not rise appreciably. Economic controls had been set up to limit the consumption of the people. Africa was producing more but the industrialised nations now involved in war production had not the manufactured goods to send in return. Also, the supply of cheap textiles was cut off from Japan when that country entered the war in 1941. Consequently, higher wages and higher prices for export crops would merely have led to inflation and the Colonial governments kept down wages as much as possible and limited the producer price of crops through the operation of marketing boards and other controls. Nevertheless, the cost of living rose rapidly, foodstuffs were often in short supply and Tanzania had to import substantial quantities of maize to avert famine. Although Portugal was not involved in the war, Angola was also affected by the increased demand for her export products. African coffee farmers were able to sell their crops at a better price and the diamond mines and the port of Lobito were more active than ever before. But Angola was now lagging behind its neighbours in many respects and there was a flow of labour away from Angola towards the neighbouring Congo and even towards distant South Africa.

The post-war boom

After the period of post-war reconstruction, the Korean war gave a further boost to world consumption of minerals which Middle Africa produced. The Colonial governments now had substantial sums of money, accumulated marketing board surpluses and loans from the controlling states in Europe, which could be invested in economic development. In the 1940s and 1950s many major projects were undertaken, some of which, like the groundnuts scheme in Tanzania, failed miserably, but most of which were successful. Railway networks were improved, many roads were tarred, hydro-electric schemes were carried through, notably the Owen Falls dam in Uganda and those in the Katanga area of the Congo. Secondary industries such as brewing, textile manufacture and shoe making, were established—especially in the Congo, where by 1950, less than half the population was engaged in agriculture. Kinshasa became a sizable city with a population exceeding 100,000. Although the other countries of Middle Africa still remained primarily agricultural the city of Nairobi rivalled Kinshasa in size and industrial activity, and the populations of the major cities continued to grow rapidly throughout the whole area, including Angola, despite the economic recession after 1957 in the Congo and the troubled period of the early 1960s. The excitement and adventure of the city had taken hold of the popular imagination and a new urban culture was emerging.

The gap between city and village in terms of amenities and opportunities steadily widened during these years. The best job opportunities were in the towns. In 1946 the minimum workers' wage was raised in the Congo and in the ensuing years the Union Minière gave a series of wage increases to its employees. In the 1950s the proportion of the population in clerical employment increased rapidly as clerks could earn substantial wages compared with other workers. The shops and

Building houses for workers at the Owens Falls scheme

warehouses were now filled with a wider range of desirable goods. Imported radios, bicycles, motor vehicles, sewing machines and other goods found their way through retail channels to the villages. Social links between town and village remained strong as town associations often had branches or connections in the villages. The rapid extension of national education systems tended to produce a common set of values across the land. The most remote areas were drawn into the cash economy. Money became the principal measure of a man's worth and money seemed easier to make in the town than in the village. The change in social values was made easier by the fact that the population was predominantly youthful. The birthrate continued to rise and the deathrate fell due mainly to the improvements in public health. The development of medical services was by no means even throughout the area for whereas the Congo had a medical assistant for every 3,000 inhabitants the Angolan health service was very weak. It was out of this thrusting, changing and vigorously expanding society that the nationalist movement grew during the eventful decades of the '40s and '50s. The winning of independence was part of a wider historical movement among the mass of the people which continued in motion after political power had been transferred to African hands.

The colonial system begins to crack

While this rapid social and economic development was in progress the system of colonial rule was beginning to crumble. The Second World War altered the shape of world politics. Russia and the United States emerged as the major world powers and both were opposed to the continuance of European colonial rule. Britain had more or less lost control of politics in India before and during the war and had little alternative but to grant independence to India and Pakistan in 1947. Thereafter, the dissolution of the British Imperial system was merely a matter of time. In 1946 Governor Ryckmans of the Congo had declared 'The days of colonialism are past', indicating a very remarkable change of mind among the colonial rulers.

Imperialism was now on the defensive. It felt it had to justify its existence and begin reforms leading ultimately to the emancipation of the peoples subjected to its rule. However, the first concessions made were quite paltry. In 1945 the first Africans were admitted to the Ugandan Legislative Council and in 1950 they secured parity of representation with Europeans and Indians on that body: eight Africans balanced four Europeans and four Asians. But none of these were elected and on the other side of the table were sixteen official members. The government had not begun to transfer power; it had merely provided an official channel through which people could make petitions and question what was done. Tanzania, being a mandate, was more affected by the changing climate of world opinion for it was open to inspection by the United Nations. The United Nations had a broad membership and was more critical of colonial administration than the League of Nations had been. It was anxious to see that mandates advanced towards independence. United Nations missions visited Tanzania periodically and provided emerging nationalist opinion with a platform for expressing its views for self expression. But, until 1955, African unofficials on the Legislative Council still numbered only three and these were chosen by the Governor from chiefs who were regarded as 'loyal' by the administration. In the Congo reform took much longer to materialise. Under the cumbrous system of government, reform legislation passed from Provincial Councils to the Government Council in the Congo and from there to the Ministerial Council and Consultative Council in Belgium and from there back to the Congo and so on for nearly ten years. And then, the central piece of reform legislation entailed the introduction of representative government at the local level only. Nationalist opinion had to put strong pressure on the Colonial government before any real political concessions were made. In Kenya there were two Africans on the Legislative Council by 1946 but this was less significant than the changes in the Ugandan or Tanzanian Councils for in Kenya independence meant independence not only from the colonial power but also from the ambitious white settlers in Kenya itself. Since before the First World War the political associations of the settler group had maintained constant pressure on the administration. Their elected representatives on the Legislative Council spoke frequently and forcefully. During the war settler members had acted as semi-official Ministers. In 1945 one was made Minister of Agriculture. Although the settlers had no formal control of the instruments of government, they were so strong that the Colonial government felt obliged to negotiate with them before deciding any significant change in the country's constitution. They represented a serious obstacle to African advance.

Nationalist politics in Kenya

African nationalist movements were stronger and more active in Kenya than anywhere else in Middle Africa. The Kikuyu Central Association which was so active in the 1920s extended its activity to bring in an Ukamba Members' Association in 1938. It was backed up by other movements with similar aims. In the religious field there were the African Independent Pentecostal Church and the African Orthodox Church and a number of sects such as the Dini ya Yesu Kristo. In the field of education were the Kikuyu Independent Schools and the Kikuyu Karinga Educational Associations. The very existence of these movements, committed to African control in religion and education, represented a protest against the colonial regime. There were also some less militant political groups centred on the Kikuyu Association and, after, 1934, the Kikuyu Provincial Association founded by Harry Thuku. The growth of membership of the Kikuyu Central Association from 300 in May 1938 to 2,000 in March

1939 was symptomatic of the spread of popular discontent. The expanding population was suffering increasingly from land shortage. Overcropping was resulting in soil erosion in the more heavily populated areas. Increasing cattle herds were destroying the pastures they fed on. From 1930 onwards European settlers began to turn Africans out of rented farms on their estates which they had tilled for many years and had come to regard as their own. The Europeans were now using the land themselves and wanted labour rather than rents. The fate of these farmers created anxiety even among those living outside the settler areas. The Carter Land Commission of 1932 attracted attention to the problem and its limited consultation of the people raised some hope that there would be an improvement. But it ended with a firmer demarcation of the boundaries of the settler areas, parts of which were claimed by African families as their ancestral lands. The atmosphere of suspicion of government intentions thickened. In the late 1930s the government began to reduce cattle herds with a view to making the cattle industry more productive. The final object was worthwhile but the immediate result was the slaughter of a proportion of the people's animals. As a result there were violent demonstrations, petitions to government and riots during the late 1930s and 1940s. Government schemes for soil conservation also placed a burden on the people, and added to the general unrest. The demobilisation of soldiers at the end of the war added a new group of determined men to the number of dissatisfied for many former soldiers were unable to get jobs and others were frustrated by the limitations the colonial regime placed on African enterprise.

Jomo Kenyatta and the Kenya African Union

In 1946 a man appeared who could unite almost all the anti-colonial elements and direct them in a purposeful fashion toward nationalist objectives. Jomo Kenyatta was born at the end of the nineteenth century and had been involved in the nationalist movement from its beginnings in the 1920s. He was a well educated and forward looking man who maintained contact with and respect for the traditional customs of the Kikuyu people to which he belonged. He remained a radical nationalist and never lost contact with the rising new generations. He had followed Harry Thuku in 1921, was general secretary of the Kikuyu Central Association in 1929 and editor of its newspaper. He then went to Britain to put the people's grievances before the British government and public. He visited Moscow and also wrote a study of Kikuyu life. In 1946 he was hailed as the leader of Kenyan nationalism and became the unchallenged President of the newly formed Kenya African Union in 1947. From his headquarters at the Githunguri Training College he directed the dissemination of nationalist ideas through the independent schools organisation, through trade unions and through public meetings. The strength of the nationalist movement steadily grew but few important political gains were made. In 1951, when the British Colonial Secretary visited Kenya, the Kenya African Union submitted a document calling for an increase in African membership of the Legislative Council from four to twelve, that these men should be elected, that the number of Africans on the Legislative Council should equal that of Europeans and Asians, that racial discrimination be abolished and that the way be opened for Africans to reach the higher grades in the civil service. These demands aimed principally at replacing white settler power with African power and the decision of the government to give additional seats on the Legislative Council to Europeans enabling them to maintain parity with the combined strength of other races was a defeat for the K.A.U. The number of African appointed members was raised from four to six. The settlers were on the whole pleased by the decision but for this very reason African nationalist opinion was incensed.

The Mau Mau rising

While Kenyatta was organising public opinion in conventional fashion another movement, Mau Mau, was also at work. Its connections with the K.A.U. remain obscure because Mau Mau worked in secret and was proscribed by the government. But both movements worked for the same ends and there was personal contact between the two organisations. From 1950 Mau Mau began administering oaths to persons requiring them to support the organisation and to fight the government until independence was achieved. In 1951 Mau Mau's activity became sufficiently marked for the government to declare it an unlawful society but by 20 October 1952 the situation was so serious that a State of Emergency was declared. British troops were called in and strenuous measures were taken to arrest the Mau Mau leaders and destroy the movement. By this time Mau Mau was a powerful organisation. It had members in nearly all the Kenya tribes but its main area of activity was in Kikuyu districts. It was committed to violence as a means to independence and the oaths symbolised this

Kikuyu soldiers with old arms during the Mau Mau uprising

violence. Several thousand people were killed as a result of assisting the government. But the bulk of the population sympathised with the Mau Mau aims. War camps in the mountains were supplied with food from villages by willing helpers and with arms and ammunition purchased or stolen from the security forces themselves. In Nairobi hidden arms factories manufactured weapons. In spite of the State of Emergency the oathing ceremonies were increased. The government's action in closing the independent African schools drove more men into Mau Mau's ranks. Many unemployed and even criminal elements from the towns went out to join them in search of adventure. The Colonial government used armoured vehicles and artillery; war camps in the hills were bombed; whole villages were uprooted and moved to cut off food supplies from the fighting bands. The government forces killed some 7,800 people and lost some 500 of their own men. The Mau Mau fought a mainly defensive battle, only attacking to secure supplies of arms. Few settler farms were attacked and only thirty European civilians were killed. Mau Mau's offensive was carried out mainly on the political front through the oathing ceremonies which struck at the people's psychological acceptance of the dominance of colonial power. The government forces took three years to isolate the fighting men in the hills and after that sporadic guerrilla warfare continued until 1960 when the State of Emergency ended. Nevertheless, the Mau Mau rising had important political consequences. The settlers realised how great was their dependence on British arms and the presence of British troops put real power back into the hands of the Colonial government. The campaign cost the British some £50,000,000 and tied down a large number of British troops that were needed elsewhere. It was a heavy burden which the Colonial government was anxious to lose and unwilling to repeat. The days of one-sided, small concessions were now ended. The days of negotiations with nationalist leaders with force behind their words were about to begin.

Kenya moves toward independence

When the Emergency was declared in Kenya in 1952 Jomo Kenyatta was arrested, together with nearly 200 other political leaders. He was tried, convicted of managing Mau Mau and imprisoned. All political activity was paralysed and between 1953 and 1955 African political parties were banned. But the Colonial government knew it had to tread carefully and seek to conciliate the African people. It attempted to produce a multi-racial constitution which no one group would be able to dominate. Pressure was exerted first of all on the settlers to make them give up the idea of seeking ultimate control of the country. Their ranks were split into two factions by the decision to appoint an African Minister in 1954; one faction led by the leader of the European elected members favoured the move; the other led by Briggs opposed it. Although Briggs's group won eight seats to Blundell's six in the 1956 elections, Blundell, with the backing of the administration, remained Minister and the two groups worked together in the European Elected Members' Organisation. But in 1959 when the administration were planning further constitutional reforms Blundell again broke away and formed the New Kenya Group (later Party) and the European members of the Legislative Council were roughly equally divided between the moderate multiracialist New Kenya Party and Briggs' extremists.

The Asian community was already split into Indians and Pakistanis and in 1951 this split was recognised by the creation of separate constituencies and the allocation of seats to each faction. The African community was also divided by a number of government measures. First, all those connected in any way with Mau Mau were removed from power. A campaign emphasising the negative aspects of Mau Mau was mounted while all those who had fought against Mau Mau were accorded favours and rewards. A myth was created that the Kikuyu alone were principally, if not wholly, responsible for the movement and the government encouraged anti-Kikuyu feeling among the other tribes. In 1954 when appointing the first African Minister, the government passed over the moderate and longest standing African member of the Legislative Council, Eliud Mathu, a Kikuyu, and gave the post to a Luo. When, in 1955, the ban on African political parties was lifted their activity was restricted to the district level, thus encouraging a number of competing organisations each more or less identified with a tribal group. In the mainly Kikuyu Central Province, politics were not permitted. When, in 1957, the first elections for African members of the Legislative Council were arranged they were run on the basis of the so-called 'fancy franchises'. Apart from educational and property qualifications, those who were accounted to be disloyal to the government were not given the vote while others were able to secure up to three votes. The result was an election run almost entirely on tribal lines. In the Central Province the administration helped a man from the Meru minority into the seat against a strong Kikuyu candidate. Meanwhile, the promotion of some Africans to higher places in the administration, the police and the army, caused a certain amount of dissension amongst those who felt they were being left behind. It is surprising that any political unity survived this period of careful government diplomacy.

The revival of nationalist politics

However, despite divisions over personalities and group interests, the African political parties were united on the crucial issues connected with progress towards independence. All those elected in 1957 campaigned against the constitution which provided for only two African Ministerial posts compared with the four held by European unofficial members. They joined the Legislative Council but refused to accept office as ministers. As the time for the Lancaster House Conference of 1960 approached the two major African groupings — the moderate, multi-racialist Kenya National Party, which represented the mainly smaller tribes, and the Kenya Independence Movement — drew together to form the African Elected Members' Organisation in November 1959. Once the constitution was radically changed and completed at the Conference they again drew apart. Meanwhile in the cities a powerful movement had emerged which largely avoided the dangers of inter-tribal factionalism. With the ban on political parties in 1953 the Kenya Federation of Labour became the spokesman for popular grievances. Its connection with international labour organisations enabled it to survive attacks from the administration. Its ability to organise and secure better conditions for its members secured it widespread support among the workers. Two major strikes, one in Mombasa, the other in Nairobi in 1955, showed its bargaining power. The careful policies of Tom Mboya, its General Secretary, ensured that it did not become identified with any one tribal group. The trade unions represented a unifying force at a time when the political parties were in disarray. The other major unifying force was Jomo Kenyatta, whose imprisonment, if anything, had enhanced his stature. A Luo politician, Oginga Odinga, was the first to call for his release and soon Kenyatta's return became the main slogan for all parties in the 1961 election. Even Blundell, whose liberalism amounted to little more than an attempt to maintain contact between the settler community and the reforming Colonial government, began to speak in favour of Kenyatta's release. It soon became clear that Kenyatta alone could head a government which could claim anything like general African support. His release in August 1961 caused general rejoicing. He immediately became the centre of political discussion and by the end of the year he was a member of the Legislative Council taking the seat of a sitting member who had made way for him.

The last step to freedom in Kenya

A very complex situation faced Kenyatta on his return. The Lancaster House Conference had brought substantial changes in the constitution and Kenya was already halfway along the road to independence. There was now a wholly elected Legislative Council and a Ministerial Council with four official and eight unofficial members, four of which were Africans. Of the Legislature members thirty-three were elected in the ordinary way to 'open seats', ten seats were reserved for

Europeans, eight reserved for Asians and two for Arabs. The Legislative Council then elected twelve 'national' members: four African, four European and four Asian. Finally the Governor had the power to nominate additional members if need be to produce a government majority. A united African front could have had control but unfortunately there was no unity. In early 1960 the Kenya African National Union was founded as a successor to the Kenya African Union, with Kenyatta as President although he was still a detainee. Another man held the post pending Kenyatta's return. Tom Mboya was General Secretary and Oginga Odinga Vice-President. The minority tribes, fearing the K.A.N.U. would be Kikuyu–Luo biased and neglect their interests, set up a rival body, the Kenya African Democratic Union. In the 1961 elections the K.A.D.U.. benefiting from a delimitation of constituency boundaries favourable to the minority tribes won eleven seats with 150,000 votes. The K.A.N.U. won nineteen seats with just under 600,000 votes. At first both parties refused to take office until Kenyatta was released. But finally K.A.D.U. agreed to form a government with Blundell's party and a few other specially elected members. Even then the K.A.D.U. could not secure a majority in the Legislative Council and the Governor used his power to add eleven more members. Thus when Kenyatta returned a minority party was in power and the African members of the Legislative Council were split. The question of minority rights had been raised and with it the more dangerous question of regionalism, for K.A.D.U. was encouraged by Blundell and others to seek ultimate security from Kikuyu–Luo domination through a regionalist constitution. Within K.A.N.U. itself there were bitter personal rivalries, notably between Tom Mboya and Oginga Odinga. The problem still remained of the continued exclusion of former Mau Mau sympathisers. In the cities there was serious unemployment and in rural areas continuing land hunger. Meanwhile, the settlers, although no longer representing a serious political danger, from 1960 onwards had begun to realise their assets and send them out of the country, presenting a serious threat to the economy. Kenya needed more, not less capital investment to create more profitable employment for its people.

Kenyatta's first attempts to unite the rival groups failed. However, by making concessions to K.A.D.U.'s regionalism at a further constitutional conference in London in 1962 he was able to draw K.A.D.U. into an uneasy coalition. A general election in May 1963 gave K.A.N.U. a majority in the Legislative Council and in June Kenyatta became Kenya's first Prime Minister. He distributed ministerial offices to most of the different tribes and factions; feelers were sent out to the

Mau Mau men in the hills; even the settlers were conciliated through social contacts and were soon acclaiming the man they had formerly condemned. Discussions were begun with a view to establishing a wider East African Federation. By the end of the year Kenya had become entirely independent. Kenyatta had produced an impressive measure of national unity out of an extremely confused situation. His dominating personality enabled the people of Kenya to call for freedom with a single voice and to replace colonial rule with an African government to which all but a very few on the Somali border were prepared to give their loyalty.

Kenyatta and Mboya leaving for London to take part in independence talks

Politics in Uganda

The situation in Uganda was very different from that in Kenya for the major problem was not settler domination but rather what form independence and African rule should take. Some parts of Uganda had already secured virtual self government by 1945. The lack of British administrative staff and the policies pursued by Sir Charles Dundas, Governor during the wartime period, had enabled the kingdom of Buganda to secure a position of virtual autonomy. Dundas had pursued a policy of non-interference with the result that Buganda was practically ruled by its Kabaka and Lukiko. The kingdoms of Toro, Ankole and Bunyoro, although less free from colonial interference, were moving in a similar direction. The landowning chiefs who held power in Buganda were mostly well-educated and modern-minded men who made full use in their administration of the rising educated élite. The way forward politically seemed to many to consist in protecting Bugandan institutions from outside interference and securing control of the foreign dominated economy. After the war, more Ugandan shops and commercial enterprises began to appear and co-operative societies were rapidly organised. However, while Buganda insisted on confining its ambitions to securing and maintaining its own autonomy the problem remained as to the fate of the other interlacustrine kingdoms, and the smaller groups in northern Uganda and the idea of building a broader national unity could make little headway. However, in the context of the 1940s and early 1950s the proponents of Bugandan autonomy could claim they were being realistic for the central government of the Protectorate was wholly alien. The addition of one African member to a Legislative Council the rest of whose members were either European or Asian could change little. Furthermore there was the ever present danger that Uganda would be incorporated in a larger East African Federation under settler control. The neighbouring presence of settler dominated Kenya made leaders of opinion in Buganda concentrate on conserving and extending what independence they had rather than joining in the struggle of all the peoples of Africa for independence.

Conflict between Buganda and the Colonial government

From 1945 onward the policy of the Colonial government altered. Concessions were stopped and there was renewed colonial interference

in Bugandan internal affairs. The Protectorate administration introduced policies of economic and social development designed to benefit
the lower Bugandan classes and the neglected northern areas. Consequently a new educated élite began to emerge which was more
interested in broader nationalist ideas. But Buganda resented the
Colonial government's interference. Relations steadily deteriorated
until in 1953 there was a complete rupture, occasioned by a statement
by the British Colonial Secretary which suggested that the principle
which had led to the establishment of the settler dominated Federation
in Central Africa might be extended to East Africa. The reaction was
immediate. The Lukiko demanded that Buganda be transferred from
the Colonial Office to the Foreign Office—a method of securing a
status similar to that of Middle Eastern countries which had treaty
relations with the British government. The request was refused and
the Colonial government deposed the Kabaka. All factions in Uganda
rallied to the Kabaka's defence. In 1955 the Colonial government had
to admit defeat and the Kabaka was restored. Loyalty to the Kabaka
became the most powerful political force in Buganda and the possibility of Ganda co-operation with nationalists elsewhere in Uganda was
greatly hampered. After this, paradoxically, constitutional advance
became the Colonial government's main weapon, for their easiest
means of recovering control was to offer a more Africanised central
government which would be more attractive than Bugandan autonomy.
At the same time the Bugandan leaders, while blocking the path of
constitutional progress at the centre, made increasing attacks on alien,
especially Asian, businesses.

Uganda moves towards independence

Political parties had begun to emerge in other parts of Uganda. The
nationalist Uganda National Congress, founded in 1952 and mainly
Ganda based, identified with the 'out' groups in Buganda politics and
was supported by the lower classes of Ganda society, young intel-
lectuals and others who were dissatisfied with the existing system. The
U.N.C. was gravely weakened by the Kabaka crisis, losing many
supporters as the ranks closed behind the Kabaka. The Democratic
Party, urged into existence in 1956 by the Catholic bishops as a counter
to the allegedly Communist ideas of some U.N.C. members, benefited
from the existence of Catholic action organisations within and beyond
the Buganda kingdom and sought to identify itself with the under-
privileged. The U.N.C. began to increase its support by recruiting

members outside Buganda and by 1958 was largely a non-Ganda party. A general political awakening was beginning throughout Uganda. Buganda's gains through defiance of the Colonial government stimulated others to realise that the Colonial government was not invincible. In 1957 a demand was made that the system of direct election to the Legislative Council, already conceded to Ganda, should be extended to all. The government agreed and in 1958 the first elections were held.

Out of these elections emerged a new organisation—the Uganda People's Union—which was anti-Ganda in outlook, channelling the old grievances against the formerly powerful Buganda state and the new resentment against Ganda obstruction of constitutional progress. The Colonial government then determined upon a new measure of political advance and a new constitution was promulgated in 1960. At last something like a truly representative Legislature was provided for in place of the previous multi-racial bodies with their large representation of European and Asian interests. The way to independence now lay open but it was not the sort of independence that was wanted by Buganda. The Lukiko replied to the announcement of the constitutional changes with a unilateral declaration of Bugandan independence and an order to all Ganda citizens to boycott the subsequent elections. The Democratic Party, with its leader, Benedict Kiwanuka, won the 1961 election. Only 30,000 of the million Buganda voters participated in the election and all but one of the Buganda seats went to the Democratic Party. Meanwhile, Milton Obote became leader of the opposition. Obote had been the leader of the non-Ganda wing of the Uganda National Congress, but prior to the elections of 1961 he had amalgamated with the Uganda People's Union to form the Uganda People's Congress, whose membership and outlook was generally anti-Ganda. Observing from the 1961 elections that a party with no support in Buganda was doomed to perpetual opposition Obote reached an agreement with the Buganda political organisation, the *Kabaka Yekka* (Kabaka only) to work together against the Democratic Party. This collaboration secured for Buganda substantial concessions at the 1961 constitutional conference in return for which Buganda would co-operate with the Uganda state. Buganda was allowed greater autonomy than any other administrative region and the members of the central legislature were to be selected by the Lukiko and not elected. The result of these arrangements was that the U.P.C. emerged the victor from the 1962 elections. In alliance with Kabaka Yekka it beat the Democratic Party at the polls in the elections to the Lukiko and the Lukiko selected members for the central Legislature who supported the U.P.C. government. On this basis Uganda secured its independence in October 1962 and Milton Obote became Prime Minister. The alliance of non-Ganda, nationalist U.P.C. and Buganda loyalists was an uneasy one and did not stand the test of time. But future arrangements for the running of Uganda political affairs were to be worked out in entirely Ugandan terms without the intervention of any colonial power.

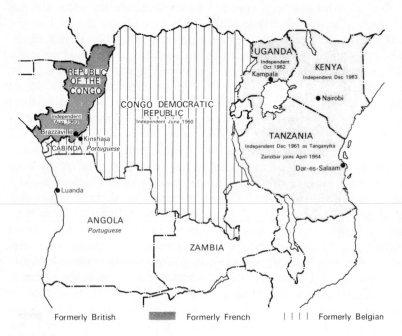

Middle Africa today

Tanzania secures independence

Tanzania's path to freedom was comparatively smoother and less disturbed by internal dissension for the Colonial government, anxious to avoid crises like the Mau Mau rising or the Kabaka affair, co-operated in the end with nationalists. And the United Nations exerted pressure to speed up political progress. The two main issues were whether the constitution should be a British or African creation and whether independence should come in the 1960s or some time after 1970. That independence came early and through African initiative was largely due to the efforts of Julius Nyerere and the Tanganyika African National Union. T.A.N.U., established in 1954, aimed at creating a spirit of national unity by breaking down local and sectional feelings and mobilising opinion in favour of independence. It took up local grievances against colonial rule and people were encouraged to look on T.A.N.U. as their protector against injustice. It was regarded by the government as subversive and banned in many areas. In 1956 the unofficial members of the Legislative Council united to form a rival organisation—the United Tanganyika Party. Nyerere persistently pursued moderate policies and sought above all international support for his nationalist cause. T.A.N.U. forged close links with the rapidly growing trade unions and by 1958 had secured 250,000 members. The government recognised its political force in that year by nominating Nyerere and Rashidi Kawawa, the General Secretary of the Tanganyikan Federation of Labour, as members of the Legislative Council. The Colonial government then decided to allow elections of the official members of the Council but stipulated that each constituency should elect one member for each racial group. Nyerere, although at first opposed to this multi-racial system in a country with a 98 per cent African population, persuaded T.A.N.U. to make use of this arrangement and select its own European and Asian member for each constituency.

The result was a sweeping victory for T.A.N.U. No U.T.P. candidates were returned and the U.T.P. quickly disintegrated. The number of T.A.N.U. branches increased rapidly as the public realised that the party now had real power. Prolonged strikes during the next two years on the railways and the sisal plantations made the government aware of the necessity of negotiating with T.A.N.U. and brought about discussions concerning future advance between Governor Turnbull and Nyerere. In 1960 a new round of elections for a legislature which was to be mainly African once more proved T.A.N.U.'s strength. All but thirteen T.A.N.U. candidates were returned unopposed. A one-party state virtually existed *de facto* in Tanganyika. Independence came almost as a matter of course in December 1961.

The union between Zanzibar and Tanganyika

Politics were brought to life amongst the 300,000 or so inhabitants of Zanzibar and Pemba with a new constitution in 1956 which provided for the election of six members to the Legislative Council. The radical Zanzibar National Party which grew out of the old Arab Association had links with Egyptian nationalism and Communist China. The Afro-Shirazi Party, an amalgamation of former African and Shirazi Associations, was almost prompted into existence by the administration and by T.A.N.U. on the mainland. However, racial politics

President Nyerere announcing the union between Tanganyika and Zanzibar

and personalities played a major rôle in the election campaign of 1957 and in the end Afro-Shirazi numbers won the day. As a result, inter-racial bitterness and strife were greatly increased. Further elections were held in 1961 to choose a legislative Council from which a Council of Ministers and Chief Minister would be drawn to replace the old Executive Council. The elections, accompanied by much inter-racial violence and bloodshed, resulted in a draw between the Z.N.P. and A.S.P. producing constitutional deadlock. For two years Zanzibar had a caretaker government until further elections in 1963 paved the way for independence. This time the Z.N.P. won twelve seats, the A.S.P. thirteen and the Z.P.P.P. (a party which broke away from the A.S.P. before the 1961 elections) six. A coalition was formed between the Z.N.P. and the Z.P.P.P. and Zanzibar became inde-pendent in December 1963 with the leader of the Z.P.P.P., Muham-mad Shamte, as Prime Minister. In January 1964 a police mutiny led by John Okello deposed the Sultan and a republic was proclaimed with the leader of the A.S.P. as President and a former leader of the Z.N.P. as Foreign Minister. Much rioting followed the revolution. Large clove estates were confiscated and large businesses were taken under government control. These policies alienated the Western powers and the new regime sought support from Eastern Europe, Russia and China. This successful revolt triggered off other mutinies in the armies of Tanzania, Uganda and Kenya and British forces had to be called in. Nyerere, realising the dangers which the Zanzibar revolution could create for East African governments, entered into an agreement with the government of Zanzibar effecting a union between the two states. Thus in April 1964 Tanzania came into being. However, for most purposes Zanzibar maintained its autonomy and the revolu-tionary government remained master in its own house.

Political dissension in the Congo

The transfer of authority from the colonial power to an independent African government took place more suddenly in the Congo than in any of the East African countries. Up to the middle 1950s the colonial administration was still vigorously in control. Enlightened paternalism was the order of the day. Government, missions and companies concentrated on improving social conditions while resisting African attempts to rise beyond subordinate positions. In 1954, however, the explosive schools issue, which so seriously divided opinion in Belgium itself, was transferred to the Congo. The Belgian Colonial Minister, a

Liberal, ordered the establishment of state schools in the Congo to break the missions' virtual monopoly of education. Much bitterness was aroused between the mainly clerical Flemings and the largely anti-clerical Walloons and each side turned to the Congolese for assistance. The previously stifled voice of Congolese opinion was now encouraged to speak. The development of higher education which had lagged behind that of African countries of comparable size, was hastened forward by the dispute as each group created new institutions. The Catholic church, long a supporter of the colonial regime, began to speak of political reform. From 1957 onward an economic recession producing unemployment and popular discontent further weakened the colonial regime.

The Congo moves towards independence

In 1956 the Kinshasa journal 'Conscience Africaine' which represented the views of one of the rapidly expanding groups of educated men (*cercles des évolués*) produced a manifesto demanding progressive advance towards independent African government. A few weeks later the Abako organisation produced a counter manifesto calling, in a more radical fashion, for advance towards Congolese independence. There were many cultural and ethnic organisations like the Abako in the towns which claimed to represent and defend the interests of a particular tribe or linguistic group. The Abako represented the Bakongo people of the lower Congo as well as those living in neighbouring Angola and Congo-Brazzaville. Originally it aimed at developing the Kikongo language and Kikongo cultural institutions but its 1956 manifesto gave it the leadership of the nationalist movement. In 1957, after the long deliberations over local government reform in Belgium and the Congo, pilot elections for a new form of municipal government were held in Kinshasa and Jadotville. In Kinshasa the Abako won the election and its leader, Joseph Kasavubu, became the Burgomaster (Mayor) of one ward in Kinshasa. His inauguration speech in April 1958 in which he declared that democracy would not be complete until the Congo secured at least autonomy made a considerable impression. More people were drawn into political discussion as further elections were held in other large cities during 1958. The first elections were also held under a law passed in 1957 for the reform and democratisation of local government in rural areas. Public political debate was further activated by a government working party sent to the Congo to consult public opinion about the pace and direc-

A poster in a Leopoldville market announcing the date of independence

tion of political advance. Also many Congolese represented their country at the Brussels Exhibition in 1958 where they were able to exchange ideas and hear all kinds of nationalist opinions. After the virtual political silence of the previous period 1958 was a year of most vigorous political discussion at all levels of society in the Congo. The turning point in Congolese political development was 4–6 January 1959. On the fourth a riot broke out in Kinshasa after an Abako meeting had been banned. Disorder reigned for two days, European shops were broken into and burned and over forty people were killed. The administration was faced with the alternatives of repression or political concession. They chose the latter. On 13 January a statement was issued that the Congo would now move toward independence. The nationalist leaders, observing that the formerly dictatorial Colonial government was losing its nerve, clamoured for an early date for independence. In April 1959 at Luluabourg a congress of political parties dominated by the recently reorganised Mouvement National Congolais under the dynamic leadership of Patrice Lumumba, demanded independence by 1961. The Abako demanded independence by March 1960. From then on events moved with increasing rapidity. Political parties sprang up all

369

over the country. The government began to lose control of rural areas, especially the crucial Kinshasa–Matadi area where the main transport systems converged. Farmers began to pay dues to the parties instead of paying taxes to the government. The Belgian government was obliged to negotiate independence with the nationalist leaders and at a round table conference in January 1960, faced with the combined front of the hitherto divided nationalist parties, the Belgian government set 30 June 1960 as independence day, after elections for a national assembly in May. From this point onward the Colonial government faded out of the picture and events were largely, though by no means entirely, determined by internal Congolese forces.

What form of state ?

There was considerable difference of opinion among the nationalist leaders as to the form of the new constitution. The Movement National Congolais stood for a unitary state, for its supporters came from the smaller tribes in the centre of the country who would benefit from a national union. They had no important economic resources and had suffered much from compulsory cotton cultivation and consequently tended to be politically and socially radical in outlook. In contrast the Katanga Province held the greater part of the economic wealth of the country. But although the mine workers enjoyed a comparatively high standard of living the inhabitants of the Katanga region felt they had not adequately benefited from the wealth around them. A large proportion of the cities' inhabitants were stranger Balubas from Kasai and it was they who had dominated the 1958 municipal elections. In reply the tribes of Katanga Province organised themselves into the Conakat party to push Kasaians out of city government. At the same time, the white European residents, who were already hostile to the Kinshasa government, formed an alliance with Conakat in the hope that by detaching Katanga from the rest of the Congo they would be able to maintain their privileged position and preserve some measure of white supremacy. Under their influence Conakat began to demand a Federalist constitution giving Katanga virtual autonomy. The Abako party stood roughly midway between the M.N.C. and Conakat. Abako had always been a movement of the Bakongo people, and it wanted some degree of local autonomy to enable it to develop Kongo culture—especially with the Kongo people across the frontiers. The unitarism versus federalism debate, begun in 1959, was the main subject of discussion at the

1960 conference. No clear-cut decisions were made and the matter was left for final determination after independence. At the May elections no party emerged with a clear majority. Lumumba's party had the largest number of seats, thirty-three out of a total of 137. A coalition was formed by the M.N.C. and the Abako together with the Parti Solidaire Africaine and other small groups. Lumumba became Prime Minister and Kasavubu, the Abako leader, President.

Political crisis

Within a week of independence the Force Publique mutinied. A large proportion of the panicking European population left the country. At the same time the Conakat government in Katanga Province seceded. Belgian troops were sent to stop the mutiny and Belgian technical assistance strengthened the Katanga regime. Katanga held on to the receipts from its exports which continued to flow out through Angola and the Conakat leader Tshombe commanded a powerful, rich and effective government while Lumumba's central government was virtually paralysed. In response to Lumumba's call the United Nations sent advisers and later military forces to his assistance but the situation continued to deteriorate. On 5 September Kasavubu dismissed Lumumba from office and called on Joseph Ileo to form a government. On 12 September the army commander, Joseph Mobutu, announced that he was neutralising both President and Prime Minister and the Government was placed in the hands of a body of Commissioners chosen from among university students. In November Antoine Gizenga, a supporter of Lumumba and ex-Vice Premier, set up a provisional government in Stanleyville where he received the support of the provincial government and declared that his government would stand for Lumumbist principles. In January 1961 Lumumba was assassinated in the Katanga where he was flown by accident as a Government prisoner. The Gizenga government continued to stand by their dead leader's principles of a unitary state and a more radical outlook in internal and external affairs. Thus by the beginning of 1961 there were three governments in the Congo—the secessionist regime in Katanga, Mobutu's commissioners in Kinshasa and Gizenga's Government in Stanleyville. Gradually the Kinshasa Government got the upper hand as it remained the only internationally recognised Government. By 1963 the Katanga had been brought back within the Congolese Republic by force. A Lumumbist rising which broke out in the east in 1964 was suppressed

Members of the U.N. force in the Congo.

by 1966. Meanwhile the administrative basis for secessionist movements was greatly undermined by the subdivision of the former six provinces to form twenty-two. The swollen cities became the focuses of public life as more migrants poured in from the rural areas. Politicians were discredited owing to their corruption and their failure to control the political situation. The police organisation, the army command and the civil servants became of key importance. In 1965 Mobutu overthrew President Kasavubu and the Congo fell under military rule.

Colonial rule and revolt in Angola

In 1954, when the Abako organisation was beginning to emerge in the Congo, the Union of Angolan Peoples under Holden Roberto was established in north Angola. Shortly afterwards the more radical 'Popular Movement for the Liberation of Angola' (M.P.L.A.) was clandestinely organised with closer connections with the peoples in the east. Political activity grew steadily and culminated in an explosion of revolt in early 1961. There were severe riots in the capital Luanda and a major rising in the coffee growing areas of the north. The Portuguese, firmly against any form of independence for Angola, answered these risings with violent repression, arresting many people in Luanda and bringing in Portuguese troops to re-establish Portuguese rule in the north. A feature of the rising was the evident hostility which existed between Portuguese settlers and the African population. The government had pursued a policy of encouraging Portuguese immigration into Angola and the white population had grown from 79,000 in 1950 to 170,000 in 1959. In a country with limited resources such as Angola the newcomers competed with Africans for what employment there was and racial friction was constantly severe. Although some 25,000 Portuguese troops were stationed in Angola the very violence of their methods, the burning and bombing of villages, swelled the forces of resistance and the Colonial government eventually found it necessary to offer some economic and social reforms. Compulsory cotton cultivation was abolished together with some of the marketing agencies concerned with keeping down prices for African-produced crops. Portuguese citizenship was accorded to all, thus removing the legal basis for some of the former administrative oppression. Plans were made to introduce a more representative form of local government. However, there was no abatement of nationalist activity. In 1963, with the backing of the Organisation of African Unity, a government of the Republic of Angola in exile was organised in the Congo. Arms passed through the Congo to resistance forces and a large part of northern and eastern Angola became a battlefield. By

M.P.L.A. units fighting under difficult conditions

1963 there were 43,000 Portuguese troops engaged in action and in the ensuing years these were expanded still further. With its other commitments in Guinea and Mozambique the Portuguese government came under increasingly heavy strain and increasingly isolated internationally. It relied for support on the government of South Africa. By the middle of the 1960s it had become clear that Angola had been drawn into the vortex of the struggle between independent Africa and the white supremacist regime in the south.

Conclusion
Africa since independence

The attainment of political independence by the bulk of the African continent within the last twelve years is a major event for both Africa and the world. With speed comparable to that with which the European powers had partitioned the continent in the last decades of the nineteenth century, Britain, France and Belgium transferred sovereignty to their African subjects almost overnight. Between 1957 and 1969 no less than forty-two countries became independent, constituting a good third of the total membership of the United Nations Organisation. The status and stature of independent African countries were suddenly transformed: in international bodies and on the diplomatic scene they became the equals of their former colonial masters. Only a brief explanation of this event can be offered here. Although the political withdrawal by the ex-colonial powers was prompted partly by the agitation of Africans for independence and partly by the disastrous effect of the Second World War on the image of the Western European imperial powers, it should be remarked that world ethical opinion, which became progressively hostile to possession of colonies in the last quarter of a century, played no small part in the decision of imperial rulers in Africa to decolonise. Pressure is still being brought to bear on Portugal, the only colonial power in Africa, to grant independence to Angola and Mozambique, territories which up to date are regarded as mere projections of metropolitan Portugal.

Some benefits of colonial rule

Although the colonial era in Africa was very short—in most places not exceeding sixty years—two major benefits conferred upon the continent by the ex-colonial rulers should not be overlooked. First

Independent States

1 MOROCCO			
2 ALGERIA			
3 TUNISIA			
4 LIBYA			
5 UNITED ARAB REP			
6 MAURITANIA	23 NIGERIA		
7 MALI	24 CAMEROON		
8 NIGER	25 CENTRAL AFRICAN REP.		
9 CHAD			
10 SUDAN	26 GABON		
11 ETHIOPIA	27 CONGO		
12 SOMALIA	28 DEM. REP. OF CONGO		45 CABINDA (POR.)
13 SENEGAL			46 ANGOLA (POR.)
14 GAMBIA	29 UGANDA		47 SOUTH-WEST AFRICA
15 GUINEA	30 KENYA	38 LESOTHO	
16 SIERRA LEONE	31 RWANDA	39 MADAGASCAR	48 RHODESIA (BR.) U.D.I. declared 1965
17 LIBERIA	32 BURUNDI	40 EQUATORIAL GUINEA	
18 IVORY COAST	33 UTD. REP. TANZANIA	41 SWAZILAND	49 MOZAMBIQUE (POR.)
19 UPPER VOLTA	34 ZAMBIA	42 MAURITIUS	50 IFNI (SP.)
20 GHANA	35 MALAWI	States not yet independent	51 REUNION (FR.)
21 TOGO	36 BOTSWANA	43 PORTUGUESE GUINEA	52 FRENCH SOMALILAND
22 DAHOMEY	37 SOUTH AFRICA	44 SPANISH SAHARA	53 COMORO ISLANDS (FR.)

Modern Africa

is the fact that the colonial rulers were the architects of the present-day political map—that of nation-states recognised and respected by the world. By and large the boundaries drawn up by the Europeans during the scramble—boundaries which, as is often stressed, cut

376

across ethnic groups in some areas—have come to stay. In this regard the important point is not the inter-state bitterness or warfare encouraged by colonial boundaries in some parts of independent Africa, but the fact that the majority of independent states have accepted these boundaries as fixed and worthy of being defended. Worth emphasising is the fact that before colonial rule the boundaries of present-day nation-states encompassed large numbers of kingdoms, states and empires quite often at war with one another. It is the peoples of such small and warring kingdoms and states that the ex-colonial powers administered under one political umbrella, thereby creating the nation-states of today.

Second, the colonial rulers implanted the ideas of modernisation to which every independent African nation-state is inexorably committed. Though in varying degrees, every colonial power demonstrated the technological superiority of Europe by building roads and railways, harbours and airports; by introducing mechanical transportation, more durable types of houses and an endless list of manufactured articles, which create new tastes and seek to improve the physical comfort of their subjects. Every colonial power helped to develop the natural resources of its territories, and show the best way to utilise them; they maintained a new kind of law and order with the aid of a standing army and police force, law enforcement agencies upon which the new nation-states have had to depend to keep the peace; every colonial power established a new kind of administrative system which emphasised literacy as the oil greasing the machine and directly or indirectly encouraged education, thereby sowing the idea of a nation-state run on modern lines.

All these ideas of modernisation constitute the colonial heritage which the educated élite, to whom the ex-colonial powers transferred power and authority, cherish most. Schools and hospitals, roads and railways, motor cars and lorries, newspapers and radio, skyscrapers and tastefully designed brick or concrete houses, the English and French languages, the civil service, efficient police, a well-trained and well-equipped standing army, a rationalised and diversified economy, mutually beneficial commercial relations with the outside world, and government with the techniques of the advanced world— all are parts of the colonial heritage which Africans have accepted and would not wish to see disappear with the white man's political withdrawal. The acceptance of modernisation by the bulk of the African population is evidenced by the terrific growth and importance of towns all over the continent and the invasion of the continent by the emblems of superior European technology.

In one sense the impact of modernisation on African society has been quite terrific: it has put an end to isolationism. Gone are the days when the horizon of the African was limited to his town, his own people or his continent. Technologically, economically, socially and ideologically Africa has become exposed to, and become part of, the rest of the world; the course of the African's history has ceased to be entirely fashioned by him. Nevertheless, the effects of modernisation on African mores and culture should not be exaggerated. Much as Africans are eager to acquire technological know-how and literary skills, the attachment of the majority of the population to their cultural heritage remains strong. Only a minority, the relatively very small group of educated élite, who in many ways have become Europeanised, really admire the alien culture of Europeans—their language, manners, dress, religion, mental orientation, style of life, moral and social values in addition to their political thinking and aspirations. By far the majority are still adherents of indigenous religion or of Islam, with all the values associated with these religions. Unlettered, they live largely in villages, farming by traditional methods and leading a life very little different from their ancestors'. Chiefs and kings, priests and charm-makers, folklore-retailing, wit-learning and wit-exchanges in the evening, belief in and fear of witchcraft and spirits—all remain essentials in the lives of the majority of Africans today.

However, the importance of the educated élite in independent Africa far exceeds their number. Invariably they are the leaders of government, the policy-makers in matters of modernisation, the leaders of public opinion, monopolists of the departments of government, including the police and the army, and the spokesmen for their countries in the rest of the world. In a sense the educated élite constitute an oligarchy which has merely stepped into the white man's shoes and is running the new nation-states in their own interest. Even more than before in Africa, knowledge means power and the major events in independent Africa have been determined by, or centred on, the educated minority.

Pan-Africanism

One major event in post-independence Africa is the development of Pan-African feelings which have been institutionalised in the Organisation of African Unity. Pan-Africanism, it should be stressed, is nothing new or peculiar to the twentieth century. For many years it was widely held that the origin of the Pan-African concept was to be found in the New World, from among West Indians and American Negroes, and that it was only after the educated Africans had had contact with Negroes like Marcus Garvey and W. E. B. Du Bois that the Pan-African idea began to be imbibed and expressed by the educated élite in Africa. However, Pan-Africanism was also conceived in Africa independently, quite early in the nineteenth century through the Ethiopian movement. This sought to express Pan-African nationalism through the medium of Christianity and the Christian Church. It had nothing to do with the territory of Abyssinia, better known as Ethiopia. The movement conceived the word 'Ethiopia' in its alleged ancient meaning, according to which Ethiopia meant Africa and Ethiopians Africans. Basing their belief and hope on Psalm 68:31, 'and Ethiopia shall soon stretch forth her hands unto God', by the second half of the nineteenth century the Ethiopians of West Africa affected to believe that the days of glory and ascendancy of Africa and the Africans were at hand. According to the vision of the Ethiopians, not only would all Africa be emancipated politically but the African continent would give leadership and inspiration to the other continents in science and technology, in the literary arts and in the worship of Jehovah. A clear assumption of the West African Ethiopians was that all Africans would be Christians.

Possibly the earliest exponent of the Pan-African ideal was an African born on African soil and moulded by the African environment at a time when the concept had not begun to be expressed in the New World. He was James Johnson, who was duly honoured for his Pan-African activities in London in 1900 by the first Pan-African Congress. James Johnson was born in the small village of Benguema in the British colony of Sierra Leone around 1835. His parents were Yoruba recaptives. Educated in the West African Methodist and Anglican Primary Schools he attended the C.M.S. Grammar School where he graduated in 1854. For the next four years he was at Fourah Bay College where he tutored from 1860 to 1863.

From 1863 to his death in 1917 James Johnson advocated African nationalism in church and state. For him there was no separation, and there could be no separation, between religion and politics. As an ardent Christian he dreamed of seeing the entire continent of Africa Christianised in such a way that all the rulers would be Christian leaders as well. His ideal of a theocratic Pan-African State would, he hoped, solve all the Africans' problems. Firstly, it would wipe away all sectionalism and tribalism: it would make all Africans one people. Johnson denounced sectarianism, according to which the church in Africa was divided into innumerable denominations, as a European invention that was creating unnecessary divisions among Africans. Ideally he wanted the emergence of an African Church for the whole of Africa. This African Church was to be manned entirely by Africans; the theology, hymns, orientation, liturgy and modes of worship were all to be African. For Africa he wanted the Christianity of the Bible divested of the European cultural accretions which the church had acquired through centuries in the European environment.

Parallel with this African Church was the African State. James Johnson deplored the sectional and tribal feelings that existed in his day and he looked forward to the day when there would be only one state of Africa. In other words he was a Pan-Africanist *par excellence*, anticipating the one-state doctrine for all Africa of Kwame Nkrumah. Indeed the cosmopolitanism of James Johnson extended to the Negroes of the New World, whom he described as 'Africans in exile'. He felt that they should return to Africa to escape the oppression they were suffering from the white Americans and he made some effort to encourage the 'Africans in exile' to settle in some parts of Yorubaland.

An aspect of the ideology of African nationality to which independent Africa attaches importance is the 'African Personality'. It is largely a cultural phenomenon by which the values and virtues of the African cultural heritage are expressed and projected by African writers and statesmen. James Johnson was also an exponent of the doctrine of African Personality. Throughout his life he stressed time and again that the church in Africa must wear the African complexion and that Africans must retain the best in their culture and institutions. It was his conviction that Africans were a distinct people endowed with a cultural heritage of which they should be proud; that for Africans their customs and institutions were in their best interests and that contact with Europeans should not mean the death of healthy African customs and institutions.

The ideas and ideals of James Johnson have been described so as to show that well before Du Bois and Marcus Garvey of the New World began to formulate the Pan-Negro ideology, Africans in Africa had anticipated their ideas. Nor was James Johnson alone in the fertility of his mind and the Pan-African vision. In West Africa there was E. W. Blyden, who used his pen and tongue advocating the Ethiopian programme and projecting in the literary world the African Personality; there was also John Chilembwe in Nyasaland who spoke for all Africans about their exploitation by the colonial powers in the First World War.

The Pan-African Conferences

At the same time it must not be suggested that the Pan-African movement owed nothing to the 'Africans in exile'. They should be remembered as the convenors and the chief actors of five of the six Pan-African Congresses which met between 1900 and 1945. At these the most energetic individual was Dr. W. E. B. du Bois, the well known Negro scholar who died in 1965 at the age of ninety-three. However, the convenor of the first Pan-African Congress was H. Sylvester Williams, a West Indian barrister. In a memorial to Queen Victoria the delegates protested against the ill-treatment of Africans by the white rulers of South Africa and Rhodesia. The second Pan-African Congress was held in Paris in 1919, at a time when efforts were being made by European rulers to settle problems resulting from the First World War. One important delegate from French West Africa was Blaise Diagne, then the foremost nationalist in French West Africa. The point to emphasise about this Congress is that it advocated eventual self-government for colonial Africa and African participation in governments 'as fast as their development permits'.

The third Pan-African Congress met in 1921 at three centres— London, Paris and Brussels: the fourth in 1923 in London and Lisbon: the fifth in 1927 in New York. These Congresses had little impact, all merely reiterating and re-affirming the principle of African participation in the administration of colonial Africa.

Undoubtedly the most important of the Pan-African Congresses was the sixth and last of the series, which met in Manchester in October 1945. This Congress took place in a much healthier climate than its predecessors. The principle of self-determination which the American President, Woodrow Wilson, had announced in 1919 was echoed in the Atlantic Charter of 1941. Nationalist movements had become more aggressive in several parts of colonial Africa and several Labour Party spokesmen in Britain had begun to advocate self-government for colonial peoples. In a series of lectures delivered in the United States in February 1943, Lord Hailey, already a protagonist of the interests of colonial peoples, declared that the issue of ultimate independence for colonial peoples was no longer a matter for debate. 'Independence itself is a consummation which must necessarily commend itself to democratic thought', he said. Efforts should be made by colonial powers to prepare their subjects by 'a graded political education which will enable them to manage their own affairs without external control'.

It was in such a climate that the educated Africans, who for the first time dominated the Congress, demanded that the principles enunciated in the Atlantic Charter should be applied to Africa. The African delegates included several who were to play a leading rôle in the struggle for independence. There was Kwame Nkrumah whose zeal in the Congress exceeded that of any other individual; there were H. O. Davies, S. L. Akintola and Magnus Williams, lawyers-in-training from Nigeria; there was Wallace Johnson, a redoubtable trade union leader from Sierra Leone. Jomo Kenyatta of Kenya was there, as well as Peter Abrahams, the famous novelist from South Africa. This Congress was far more radical in tone than the previous ones. Independence was demanded for colonial Africa and it was emphasised that, should all other methods fail, force should be used to achieve the desired goal. Parts of the resolutions of the Congress read as follows: 'Congress expressed the hope that before long the peoples of Asia and Africa would have broken their centuries-old chains of colonialism. Then, as free nations, they would stand united to consolidate and safeguard their liberties and independence from the restorations of Western imperialism as well as the dangers of Communism.'

The All Africa Peoples' Conference

Important as the Pan-African Congresses are, it should be stressed that the Pan-African concept did not become popular and widely accepted all over the continent until after 1957 when Ghana gained independence and the wind of change began to sweep through the continent with a velocity that drove the ex-colonial powers to grant independence to states which were not yet fully prepared for it. At the head of the Ghana government was a man bent on militant agitation for the Pan-African movement. From Accra, capital of Ghana, Kwame Nkrumah made pronouncements that inspired nationalist leaders in former Nyasaland (Malawi), Belgian Congo, and Northern Rhodesia (Zambia), and which progressively dismayed the ex-colonial powers. In April 1958 all the independent African states to date—Ethiopia, Liberia, Libya, Egypt, Morocco, Tunisia and Ghana— met as the All Africa Peoples' Conference. They were to meet again at Tunis in January 1960. This conference is significant for two reasons. Firstly, representatives of non-independent African countries were there as observers and in the light of what they saw there returned to their respective countries to hasten the exit of their colonial masters. Secondly, many of the resolutions of the conference anticipated those of the Organisation of African Unity formed five years later. The member states declared that they would observe a policy of 'positive neutrality'; they pledged themselves to observe one another's political and territorial integrity and to settle their differences by conciliation and mediation within the African community. Finally, the conference established a permanent Secretariat in Accra.

The Organisation of African Unity

By May 1963, when the Organisation of African Unity was born in Addis Ababa, the desirability of the independent states coming together had become obvious. The Pan-African concept, which binds together all African peoples and states, had taken firm root. One of the things that persuaded them to come together and become Pan-Africanist was the colour of their skin—white inhabitants of Kenya, Rhodesia, Portugese Africa and the Republic of South Africa, who also regard the African continent as their home, were excluded. All the members, except Ethiopia and Liberia, had at one time or another suffered under the colonial régime. Consequently they were suspicious of the ex-colonial powers, whose economic grip upon their former colonies had not been relaxed.

As embodied in the O.A.U., and as African writers emphasise, Pan-Africanism stands for the dignity of Africa and of Africans on the world stage; it rejects the idea that Africans are in any way biologically inferior to other races and it fosters race-consciousness; it inspires African peoples with a belief and confidence in themselves as a people. Pan-Africanism rejects subservience to ex-foreign masters in any form. Consequently, Pan-Africanists advocate a policy of positive neutrality in the ideological warfare between the Western and the Communist worlds. Popular slogans of Pan-Africanists include 'Africa for the Africans' and 'African Personality'.

The O.A.U. is a league of sovereign African states. At its inception its declared purposes included the desire 'to promote the unity and solidarity of the African state', 'to co-ordinate and intensify their co-operation and efforts to achieve a better life for the peoples of Africa' and the hope to eradicate all forms of colonialism from the continent. The supreme organ of the body is the Assembly of Heads of State and Government which meets at least once a year. Then there is a Council of Ministers comprising the Foreign Ministers of member states. However, much of the work is done by the General Secretariat

383

which is located in Addis Ababa and has since 1963 been run by Diallo Telli, a Guinean, as General Secretary.

The aims of the founders of the O.A.U. are very grand. To effect quick modernisation of the continent, various commissions were set up to deal with the social, economic, educational, health and nutritional problems of African society. There was as well a Defence Commission, the precise functions of which are not clear. However, a Committee for Liberation with its headquarters in Tanzania does exist, giving aid and granting arms to freedom-fighters in Portugese Africa, Rhodesia and the Union of South Africa, one of the objects of the O.A.U. being 'absolute dedication to the total emancipation of the African territories which are still dependent'.

The O.A.U. has survived six turbulent years, and although its critics have often concentrated on the internal divisions and rivalries that plague it, its achievements must not be under-rated. On several issues at the United Nations, African states have been able to speak with one voice, particularly where the oppressive measures of the racist rulers of Rhodesia, Portugese Africa and the Republic of South Africa are concerned. Also the efforts of the Committee for Liberation which encourage guerrilla warfare in these white-controlled territories should not be minimised. Border disputes have been settled through the O.A.U. Perhaps its greatest achievement to date is that through its Special Committee on the Nigerian crisis the big power blocs, whose ideological interests are inimical to the interests of Africa, were not able to intervene. In fact all the major powers found it difficult to intervene aggressively because the O.A.U. presented itself as best qualified to settle this essentially African dispute, demanding an African solution in the African way.

This is not to say that the O.A.U. is united on all issues and it is important to underline its major problems. There are differences of opinion among member states as to the methods to adopt in the implementation of the ideals to which the founders pledged themselves. One major division is in respect of the attitude towards the ex-colonial powers, all of whom happen to be part of the Western bloc. The radicals—Ghana, Guinea, Mali, Algeria, Egypt and Morocco—forming the Casablanca group who advocated a militant programme involving mortal blows at imperialism and neo-colonialism, were led by Kwame Nkrumah and were supposed to be anti-West. Then there was the more patently pro-West Monrovia Group consisting of Sierra Leone, Liberia, Nigeria, Togo, Ethiopia and Libya, among others. Although none of these groups pursued a concerted or co-ordinated policy the divisions into which they crystallised was a crack that undermined the solidarity of the O.A.U.

A greater point of difference arose over whether there should be only one government and one head of state for Africa. According to Kwame Nkrumah, the prominent protagonist of this continental federal state, the surrender of its sovereignty by each state was the only effective way to crush imperialism and neo-colonialism in Africa. Clearly such a proposal would reduce the new nation-states to mere provinces of the continental state. Each member is naturally jealous of its newly won sovereignty: what most member states would appear to want is functional co-operation rather than integration. Not surprisingly, then, Kwame Nkrumah's pleas for his proposals in 1963 were coldly received by member states. There can be no doubt that the concept of a continental federal state for Africa is still a far-off ideal. For apart from the centrifugal forces that threaten the solidarity and cohesion of each nation-state, a phenomenon that will be examined presently, all attempts at union at the regional level have ended up in words rather than in action.

Take, for instance, the gestures made in West Africa by two or more states to form a union. In November 1958 Ghana and Guinea formed a 'political entity' which, it was hoped, would be the basis for a broad union of West African states. However, the plan failed when it came to putting it into practice. Consider also the fate that befell the Mali-Senegal Union of 1959 which, in the words of a Mali legislator, was expected 'to create a single federation which may extend— why not—from Dakar to Brazzaville'. Within a very short time the union ceased to exist. In spite of the geographical and cultural unity of the Maghreb a union of the Maghrebian states, the desirability of which has been expressed time after time by Maghrebian leaders, has remained a dream. The ease with which the Unity of the Nile Valley movement of some Egyptian and Sudanese sponsors collapsed will also be recalled. In East Africa, where Kenya, Uganda and Tanganyika inherited common services, the tendency since independence has been for each country to pull out, establish separate institutions and adopt independent policies. The University of East Africa has broken up, the University Colleges of Nairobi, Makerere and Dar es Salaam becoming full-fledged universities.

The point must be made that within the O.A.U. leadership the ambitions and aspirations of the personalities are very difficult to reconcile. Until he was overthrown in February 1966, Kwame Nkrumah was regarded by all Ghana's neighbours as an over-ambitious man suffering from an incurable megalomania and Ghana was regarded as the breeding ground for undesirable elements being trained to overthrow the legitimate governments of their countries. In eastern Africa, relations have been somewhat strained between the governments of Malawi and of Tanzania and Zambia owing, among other things, to differences resulting from the policies of these countries towards the Republic of South Africa.

Apart from differences in language—English, French and Arabic—several groups of states owe allegiance to other non-African organisations, allegiance which can hardly be reconciled with the purpose and tenet of the O.A.U. For instance the north African states are members of the Arab League which is consumed with the desire to fight a conclusive war with Israel. Not only is the confrontation with Israel their main preoccupation but some of the states, particularly Egypt, have tried to introduce the Israeli issue at the O.A.U. forum. Also Egypt is a member of the Afro-Asian Solidarity Committee which has its offices in Cairo and which propagates anti-Israeli views. Then there is the question of the ex-British colonies being members of the Commonwealth, while the former French colonies are more or less oriented towards Paris and have a special relationship with the European Economic Community.

Disputes resulting in fighting have arisen between member states over borders, for instance Morocco against Algeria and Somalia against Kenya and Ethiopia. It was a setback for the O.A.U. when, over the Nigerian crisis, four states—Ivory Coast, Tanzania, Zambia and Gabon—recognised the secessionist regime in Nigeria, in spite of Article III (3) of the O.A.U. Charter concerning 'respect for the sovereignty and territorial integrity of each Member State and for its inalienable right to independent existence'. However, the vast majority of the body observed this pledge and adopted a policy of trying to reconcile the two parties in the civil war within the framework of Nigerian unity.

Despite setbacks, an encouraging start

However, despite the teething problems of the O.A.U., its merits and achievements should not be played down. Judging by the difficulty that the European countries who claim that they are advanced in political matters have been finding in having an organisation of European unity, the surprising thing about the O.A.U. is not that it is plagued by enormous problems but rather that it has survived at all; that it is taking practical steps to see that independent African states are pooling their efforts on the continental level in certain matters; that it still maintains the symbolic unity of Africa.

Political instability

While the educated élite were achieving a measure of success in the O.A.U., the political systems inherited by them from the ex-colonial rulers became increasingly unsuitable. In a manner and with a speed that bewildered the rest of the world one government after another collapsed between 1963 and 1969. One clique of the educated élite, sometimes with the support of the army, replaced another without any formal consultation with the illiterate masses. In Dahomey alone there were five violent changes of government between 1963 and 1969. In states like Guinea, Zambia, Malawi and Tunisia—to name a few—where no coups have yet occurred, and where leaders of the independence movements continue to rule, the stability of the governments has been threatened either by plots or secessionist tendencies. Apart from Liberia, there is no country in Africa whose head of state or government does not have big problems on his hands. For instance, in December 1962 President Habib Bourguiba of Tunisia barely escaped death from the hand of an assassin; in January 1963 Sylvanus Olympio, President of Togo, was killed; in August 1963 President Fulbert Youlou of Congo (Brazzaville) was overthrown; in January 1964 President Julius Nyerere of Tanganyika trembled as a mutiny threatened his regime; towards the end of the year four members of the banned Sawaba Opposition party of the Republic of Niger were publicly executed; early in 1965 the Premier of Burundi was assassinated, and in June President Ben Bella of Algeria was overthrown in a military coup. Two months later President Nasser announced the discovery in Egypt of a large-scale plot against his regime. In January 1966 Nigeria, which used to be regarded as the bastion of political stability in Africa had a coup in which several political leaders lost their lives; a month later 'Osagyfo' Nkrumah, who had considered himself coup-proof, was dramatically toppled from power. The army took over in Libya in September 1969, deposing King Idris, and in Uganda in February 1971, deposing Milton Obote.

Some reasons for this instability

The obvious question is why this chronic political instability, and why within a decade of attainment of independence have these political convulsions occurred? Several explanations have been offered and two of them are worth considering. One explanation is that the ex-colonial powers withdrew too quickly, too soon, before Africans were fully prepared for self-government. The other explanation is that the political systems and organs of government left behind by the ex-colonial powers are really unsuitable for, and unworkable in Africa. The first explanation is patently invalid: it assumes that all along the ex-colonial powers consciously set out to train Africans to assume the management of their affairs; an assumption entirely without foundation. As late as 1958 the French government expected its colonies to vote for a common destiny with Metropolitan France, while in the ex-British territories the British rulers consciously kept the educated élite from power and authority until after the Second World War when agitation for independence became increasingly stronger and the British decided to withdraw, partly in response to mounting anti-colonial world opinion. It is true that in the ex-British territories like Nigeria, Ghana, Sierra Leone and Uganda, the educated élite had more than a decade of apprenticeship in administration under British surveillance—a situation much better than that of Congo Kinshasha which was offered independence suddenly. However, not much should be made of a situation of this kind. For in spite of the long tutelage which Ghana, Nigeria and Sierra Leone had under the British, coups have occurred in all of them and a secession similar to that of Katanga threatened Nigeria. On the other hand, the state of Guinea which obtained independence in the most dramatic fashion, literally overnight, without trained personnel and with retaliation by France, has remained politically stable.

The second explanation is certainly to some extent valid and it cannot be denied that one of the major causes of political instability in Africa is the unsuitability of the political systems left behind by the ex-colonial powers. The administrative system at the local level and the civil service for which the educated élite provide the literary skill have come to stay. It is where political directorship is concerned that the élite leadership splits into cliques. In ex-British colonies the parliamentary democracy left behind is of the 'Westminster' type which can best flourish when there are two or more political parties built upon ideology-based policies and which seek a mandate every five years or thereabouts from an enlightened and literate electorate. In the ex-French colonies the system inherited from Metropolitan France is basically similar. However, in Africa not only is the percentage of illiteracy staggeringly high but the electorate is untrained. Therefore whether one looks at Egypt from 1923 to 1952 or the Sudan after independence or Nigeria since 1964 the Westminster model never operated in the way and with the success it does in Britain. Once in power political parties desire for the most part to stay in power indefinitely and often take strong steps to eliminate opposition.

The rôle of the opposition party

Indeed in many states political leaders have claimed that the concept of an opposition party is alien to the African; that members of such an opposition must be bent on subversion and that instead of being rational and constructive critics of government they must be working for the overthrow, by any means, of the party in power. It is argued that Africa cannot afford to waste any skilled people in political opposition, and that all resourceful and talented citizens should work together within one party in the interest of the state. Leaders such as Nkrumah, Houphouet-Boigny, Keita, Sekou Touré and Nyerere all, in varying degrees, converted their countries into one-party states. Before they were overthrown, the Abbé Youlou of Congo (Brazzaville) and Léon M'ba of Gabon contemplated similar action. Recently Zambia, Kenya and Uganda have shown indications that opposition parties might be more closely controlled. In Egypt the only political party allowed to exist has been in power since its inception in 1956. Even in Liberia where there is no official ban on the formation of opposition parties, the True Whig Party, which has been ruling the country continuously for more than a century, monopolises the political scene.

Obviously opposition parties do not accept these arguments as sufficient to justify their being paralysed and their leaders exiled. Rather they contend that the ruling political parties are adopting policies which they, the opposition parties, could not endorse and that the heads of governments have become dictators. While there is no doubt that differences in matters of policy exist between the leaders in power and those out of government there are equally differences arising from conflicting personal ambition, seen in the use to which heads of governments have put their power in reducing the opposition. It is sad indeed that such bitterness has developed within the ranks of the élite leadership in independent African states which was united in the days of agitation for independence. One of the bitterer aspects of this was seen in Ghana where Kwame Nkrumah, who was proclaimed Osagyefo or 'Messiah', oppressed his erstwhile colleagues to an extent that horrified the rest of the world. The elderly Dr. J. B. Danquah, to whom Nkrumah owed his return to the Gold Coast in 1948 as General Secretary of the United Gold Coast Convention, died in detention where he was held under the Preventive Detention Act for his opposition to Nkrumah's dictatorship. In Malawi, two of Dr. Hastings Kamuzu Banda's supporters, who were among those who invited him to take power, became his opponents within a few months of the attainment of Malawian independence.

However, the political instability of independent Africa cannot be wholly explained by the failure of the parliamentary system of government. In some countries the ethnic or tribal factor has been decisive, while in others soldiers have decided to sweep aside civilian rulers who had become discredited in the eyes of the masses. In this chapter there is space to discuss only these two elements—tribalism and the military take-overs—but the causes and circumstances of coups in independent Africa are very complex and vary from country to country.

The dangers of tribalism

Very few African states are free from tribalism. One of the achievements of the ex-colonial powers was that they created multi-ethnic nation-states; people who had fought bitterly against one another in the pre-colonial era and would never have contemplated living together within the same boundaries were forced to accept one central and unified administration. For instance, Gabon with a population of just half a million has forty languages, Ethiopia over seventy languages and Nigeria over 250 tribes; Tanzania has over 120 tribes, Zambia about seventy-three, Togo fourteen and Liberia about twenty. Although in no part of Africa did the ex-colonial powers make any conscious effort to examine the causes of political and economic friction between tribes and provide remedies, ethnic loyalties and memories of past inter-tribal warfare seemed driven underground. However, it has been shown that they were, in fact, neither dead nor buried despite the intermingling of ethnic groups and growth of multi-ethnic urban areas. Consequently at independence it was nation-states and not nations that were created by the ex-colonial powers. Therefore as soon as, or even before the colonial rulers had withdrawn their suzerainty, ethnic loyalties and pre-colonial intertribal bitterness began to reappear, gathering strength and threatening the solidarity of the new nation-states.

Although few countries have been unaffected politically by the tribal factor only a few examples can be cited here. Though the religious element is present in the situation in the Sudan the civil war that has been going on there since 1955 is largely inter-ethnic—between the Arabs of the north and the Negroes of the south. In Uganda one source of perennial danger to the state has related to the position of the kingdom of Buganda. This was the source of conflict between the late Kabaka, King Edward Mutesa, and the ex-President, Milton Obote, who comes from a small tribe in the north of the state. In Congo (Kinshasa) the Lunda and the Tshekwe have still to live down the bitterness of pre-colonial times. In Kenya there is potentially dangerous tension and it is to be hoped that this will not represent a threat to the eventual succession to the presidency. In West Africa also the inherent tension between tribal groupings has resulted in violence and disruption. However, the differences in West Africa go beyond simple tribal rivalry. While the coastal people are relatively literate, adaptable and Christian, the peoples of the interior are relatively less literate, are more traditionalist in outlook and, in many areas, Muslims. A further difference in Sierra Leone and Liberia is also noteworthy. The Creoles of Sierra Leone are descendants of tribes from all over West Africa released in Sierra Leone by the British in the nineteenth century; their ancestral roots then are not in the hinterland. In the same manner the Afro-American rulers of Liberia are descendants of Negroes who migrated to the coastal areas of Liberia from the United States in the nineteenth century.

In other parts of Africa evidence of the danger of tribalism to political stability is to be found in almost every state, but the danger has been greater in some than in others and has resulted in civil war. It was in Congo (Kinshasa) that the first secession in independent Africa occurred. Moise Tshombe led the Baluba, Lunda and Bayala tribes of Katanga into secession in 1960. Then, in 1967, the Ibo of Eastern Nigeria declared secession from Nigeria, provoking the civil war that continued into 1970. In other countries the existence of a well-equipped and well-trained army, loyal to the nationalist cause, has prevented such threats from becoming a reality. At this point, the rôle of the army in independent Africa is worth examining, for it is the army under the control of the central government that has guaranteed the continued solidarity and territorial integrity of all the states that have so far been rocked by secessions.

The rôle of the army

It will be remembered that in July 1952 the army toppled King Faruk from his throne, and since that time has imposed a unified administration on the Egyptians under the leadership of Colonel Nasser. In 1958 the army struck in the Sudan and again in 1969 to prevent the state splitting up. In 1962 the Algerian army, under Colonel Houari Boumedienne, removed Ben Bella, and made

Boumedienne himself President of Algeria. On 25 November 1965 General Mobutu, who had been in charge of the central government that had been used so much to keep Congo (Kinshasa) together, seized power and became President. In Uganda, ex-President Obote used the army to integrate Buganda with the rest of the country.

While the reasons and circumstances of the various military take-overs in independent Africa varied from place to place, the overall effect of the coups is clear: the military rulers have in every case been the preservers of national unity, the destroyers of secessionist movements and defenders of the territorial integrity of the state. Armed with modern weapons to intimidate would-be secessionists the military rulers seem to enjoy the support of the people who have all too often lost respect for their civilian rulers.

Communism and capitalism

Despite its political instability, independent Africa has many achievements to its credit in foreign policy, economic development and education. Hardly had African countries become independent before they had to deal with two problems of international scale. On the one hand neo-colonialism and on the other the ideological conflict between the capitalist and Communist worlds. Neo-colonialism is found in the continuing influence of the ex-colonial or imperial powers in the domestic and foreign policies of the newly independent states and is particularly obvious in the economic field where the colonial-type economic relations are not only retained but strengthened. In some ways independent African states have exercised their sovereignty in their relations with other non-African states and powers in a manner and to an extent that their ex-colonial masters find unpalatable. At the United Nations, for instance, African states vote in favour of the admission of Communist China to the world body in spite of opposition from some of the world powers. Over colonial questions like South West Africa, Rhodesia and Portuguese Africa on which Britain, France and Belgium equivocate, African countries register their votes in favour of complete independence for these countries.

Also worth mentioning is that some African states have provoked the hostility of western countries by extending contact and relations to the Communist world—a part of the globe which the former colonial powers would not wish African states to be exposed to.

On the international front, something of an ideological scramble for

Africa between the Communist and capitalist worlds began as the colonial era came to an end. Both sides hoped to see African states supporting their own bloc. So, to strengthen their influence and promote their interests, each bloc has provided 'aid' which is expected among other things to endear the recipient African state to the givers. Thus states like Liberia, Sierra Leone, Nigeria, Malawi and Kenya are labelled as 'pro-west' and Guinea, Egypt, the Sudan, Algeria, Tanzania and the Congo (Brazzaville) as 'pro-Communist'.

Such a classification is entirely wrong. None of the African states sees itself as a pawn on the ideological and diplomatic chessboard of the great powers. In fact the course of action pursued by each state is dictated by what African rulers regard as being in the interests of their respective countries. They are not basically interested in the ideologies and cold war politics of non-Africans and have nearly all adopted a policy of 'positive neutrality' or 'non-alignment'. Under this policy African states exercise freedom of action to deal with whatever countries they like all over the world, irrespective of their political system or philosophy of life. African states deal with all countries in the light of their own needs. For example, when in the early '50s, the United States refused to finance the Aswan Dam project, the Egyptians turned to Russia, a Communist power willing to ensure the carrying out and success of the project. Subsequently President Nasser continued to make use of Russian assistance in other spheres without in any way committing himself to remodelling Egypt on Russian Communist lines.

That the African states are not the lackeys of the outside powers is repeatedly demonstrated from the fact that all of them maintain diplomatic links with both blocs and welcome 'aid' from many directions. Independence of outlook in Africa is shown clearly in their interpretation of socialist doctrines. Thus although as with the Russians, the socialist ideas of African statesmen derive from Karl Marx, none of them has applied Marxist ideology unmodified. Rather they have all contended that the African milieu is different from that of Europe and that socialism in Africa must therefore necessarily be different from its European counterpart. Consequently in Ghana under Nkrumah and in Tanzania, socialism has meant, for the most part, an attempt to achieve social justice by limiting the amount of wealth of the individual. In Tanzania it has meant as well a philosophy of self-support and of development in rural areas. In the Muslim countries of Egypt, the Sudan and Algeria, where socialism is proclaimed, it is without any prejudice to Islam, a religion that ought not to be tolerated or respected according to the Marxist analysis.

393

Economic progress

In economic matters Africa has widely asserted its independence and has thereby made substantial progress. After independence, initiative for the direction, pattern and pace of commercial and economic development became the responsibility of educated African nationals who have attempted to break the white man's monopoly in banking, insurance, shipping and civil aviation.

Encouragement was given to Africans by African governments to enter into these enterprises and in many states governments have established enterprises of their own. While in some countries the wholesale trade is still in the hands of foreign companies, laws are being made in several states to alter this and already the retail trade is moving into the hands of African businessmen. In the mining industry, governments encourage mining companies to increase royalties and, when possible, to allow state participation as partners. One other prominent feature of economic development is industrial-isation. Not only does the establishment of industry provide employment for a large number of Africans but the economy becomes diversi-fied. For throughout the colonial era Africans were encouraged to produce raw materials for export only; little effort was made to establish factories that would produce such manufactured goods as were imported in large quantities.

Of course, in economic matters independent African states cannot afford to be as assertive or independent as they are in political matters, because they lack the capital and technological skill indispensable to the development of the resources of the continent. To enjoy economic growth and thereby swell the much-needed revenue of the state, African rulers have had to bend a great deal to foreign traders and investors. Therefore very generous terms are offered to European and American investors who bring in managerial and technical staff. As far as the establishment of industries is concerned the best that most African governments has been able to do is to participate with foreign investors in industrial enterprises. It should be stressed that indepen-dent Africa's economy is very vulnerable. Should investors—almost exclusively from entrenched ex-colonial countries—decide to withdraw their investments and services, continuing modernisation would be slowed down.

Furthermore, should the developed parts of the world decide not to purchase the raw materials of independent Africa (which they buy at prices fixed in London, Paris and New York) the continent would tend to revert to the peasant economy of the pre-colonial period.

Education

Realising that the means of social, political and economic change in which they should invest is education, independent African states have been spending large sums on the schools. Never in the history of education has so much faith and hope been reposed in it as in Africa today. The knowledge imparted by education constitutes power, making mere birth irrelevant to the social and political aspirations of modern Africa. Literary education is the lever to ever higher status in society; its higher form is the pass-key to leadership in politics, business and the professions. Hence the allocation of upwards of 50 per cent of their budget to formal education by some of the African states. Hence the readiness of the ex-French colonies to accept French money and personnel for education on a very large scale, at the price of further promoting French culture in Africa. By 1965 there were no less than 7,500 French teachers in primary and secondary schools in former French Africa.

Before the Second World War, schools, particularly secondary schools, were few and far between in Africa. Left largely in the hands of Christian missions, the distribution of educational facilities was uneven, depending on the size and policy of missions. Facilities were concentrated more on the lower half of West Africa than anywhere else on the continent outside the Republic of South Africa. Of course, in Muslim countries there has been some form of literacy for centuries, but the *khuttabs* and *madrasas,* as these schools are called, are still to be studied historically and their quality assessed.

This is not the place to go into the history of western education in Africa. It suffices to say that the thirst for it at every level and in every state is unquenchable. Every village wants to have its school, every district its secondary school and every country its university. At university level the only institution where university education was available in Black Africa in the last quarter of the nineteenth century was Fourah Bay College, affiliated to the University of Durham in 1876. At the end of the Second World War university institutions numbered five only, but between 1946 and 1965 twenty-three universities were opened. There is no better index to the determination of independent Africa to catch up with the rest of the world in the raising of the quality and standard of life of its peoples.

Questions

Introduction

1 Describe briefly the industrial situation in nineteenth century Europe. How did it lead to an interest in Africa?
2 Why do you think that commercial companies played such an important role in occupying Africa?
3 Show how the Europeans' task of occupying Africa was made easier by the divisions within African society.
4 In what way did the anti-slave-trade crusade provide a rationalisation for colonialisation?
5 Give some of the reasons for the popular revolts which occurred between 1895 and 1907. How successful were these revolts?

Chapter one

1 Do you think Lord Cromer's policy in Egypt was successful or not? Give reasons for your answer.
2 What were the reasons for the surges of nationalism in Egypt at the close of the nineteenth century?
3 Discuss the state of Anglo-Egyptian relations in the early twentieth century. How did the Dinshawai incident and World War One contribute to this state?
4 What was Sad Zaghlul's contribution to the nationalist movement in Egypt?
5 Describe some of the major reforms initiated by Nasser.

Chapter two

1 Was the Condominium Agreement strictly upheld by the British? What were some of the advantages and disadvantages to Egypt and the Sudan of the Agreement?
2 Trace the rise of nationalism in the Sudan.

3 What factors caused the civil war in the Sudan?
4 Describe the rise of Dejazmatch Tafari (Haile Selassie) to the throne of Ethiopia.
5 Why was the Wal Wal incident so significant?
6 What major reforms has Haile Selassie made in Ethiopia?

Chapter three

1 Explain Hubert Lyautey's policy of indirect rule.
2 What contribution did the Berbers make towards nationalism in the Maghreb?
3 Why do you think that religion played such an important role in the nationalist movements in the Maghreb?
4 Write brief notes on the following: Habib Bourguiba, Ben Bella, Mohammed V, Hadj Messali, Ferhat Abbas.
5 Imagine that you are a member of the F.L.N. in Algeria. Put forward your case for independence.
6 Compare and contrast the achievement of independence in Libya with that in Algeria, Morocco and Tunisia.

Chapter four

1 How did the French and British methods of acquiring territory in West Africa differ?
2 Give some of the reasons why the European powers were able to take over West Africa with so little difficulty.
3 'European rule was imposed on West Africa by "diplomacy" and war.' Discuss this statement, explaining what is meant by 'diplomacy'.
4 Discuss briefly the divisions of West Africa amongst the European powers after the scramble. Illustrate your answer with a sketch map.

Chapter five

1 How did France's policy of *assimilation* come to be replaced by the *association* policy? How do these two policies differ?
2 Outline some of the advantages and disadvantages of the British policy of Indirect Rule in West Africa.
3 What were the basic differences between the British and French administrative policies? Which do you think was the most successful?
4 'French and British economic policies in West Africa were designed to benefit mainly the colonial powers.' Do you think this is true? Give reasons for your answer.

5 Describe the attempts of the educated élite to fight colonial rule before 1939.

Chapter six
1 How did external factors influence the nationalist struggle in West Africa after Word War Two?
2 Trace the constitutional development of Nigeria and the Gold Coast leading to independence.
3 'French colonies achieved independence more peacefully than British.' Do you agree with this statement?
4 In what way did the rise of political parties create dissension in pre-independence colonies?
5 What problems do the independent West African countries face in bringing about an economic revolution?

Chapter seven
1 What effect did the industrial revolution and the discovery of minerals have on southern Africa?
2 What does the story of the Ndebele indicate of the way in which white settlers obtained influence and land?
3 Describe the relationship between Cecil Rhodes and the British Government.
4 What were the results of the collapse of the Jameson Raid?
5 Write brief notes on the following: the second Anglo-Boer War, the Treaty of Vereeniging, Alfred Milner, the society for Christelike Nasionale Onderwys.
6 How did decisions at the National Convention determine the pattern of future events in South Africa?

Chapter eight
1 How did the development of mines and industries affect relationships between Africans and whites?
2 What was the cause and significance of the Rand revolt?
3 The election of 1948 was won by the Nationalist Party largely on their theory of apartheid. Explain this theory, showing how it has been developed since 1948, and pointing out the obvious contradictions in its nature.
4 'The policies which South Africa has followed in recent years are for the most part simply a return to those of the Pact Government, persued for essentially the same reasons.' Discuss this statement, showing how the Government seeks to enforce its policies and to overcome any opposition to them.

5 What was the significance of the Defiance Campaign of 1952–1953?

Chapter nine
1 How did the establishment of Colonial rule differ in Malawi and Rhodesia?
2 What part did Rhodes and his Company play in establishing Colonial rule in Malawi, Rhodesia and Zambia?
3 Write brief notes on the following: the Land Husbandry Act of 1951, the Reformed Industrial and Commercial Union, the Watchtower Movement.
4 Explain the two-pyramids policy.
5 What were the causes of Chilembwe's rebellion in Nyasaland?
6 What social effects were produced by the development of the Copperbelt?
7 Discuss the factors leading up to the establishment of the Central African Federation, and the main forces behind its destruction.

Chapter ten
1 What were the main problems the European powers had to overcome in establishing their control of the interior?
2 What effects did the building of railways and roads have on the Congo and East Africa?
3 'The growth of the colonial economy, like the early industrialisation of Europe, proceeded by fits and starts with frequent failures for which Africans often had to pay.' Discuss this statement with reference to the rubber boom and collapse in Middle Africa.
4 How did the growth of the plantation economy affect the Africans and the white settlers?
5 Write brief notes on the following: the Maji Maji rebellion, Simon Kimbangu, Harry Thuku.
6 What was the position of the Ganda State before 1926?

Chapter eleven
1 'The rapid growth of schools in Middle Africa was part of the hungry search after a better order of society which was so characteristic of the period 1920–1940.' Discuss this statement.
2 During the 1920s and 1930s the colonial administrators in Middle Africa began to consult the Africans on how they thought local government should be organised. What were some of the results of this policy?

3 What effects did the Second World War have on Middle Africa?
4 To what extent is it true to say that by 1946 the days of colonialism in Middle Africa were past?
5 What was Jomo Kenyatta's main contribution to nationalist politics? Trace his progress from President of the Kenya African Union in 1947 to Prime Minister of Kenya in 1963.
6 Trace the rise of political parties in Uganda leading up to the U.P.C. victory in the 1962 elections.
7 Why was the transition to independence in Tanzania smoother than in Kenya?
8 Describe the roles of Lumumba, Kasavubu and Mobutu in the Congo.

Conclusion
1 What are the aims and ideals of Pan-Africanism?
2 Describe the main achievements and failures of the Organisation of African Unity.
3 Put forward reasoned arguments for both sides of the view that there should be only one government and one head of state for Africa.
4 Suggest some reasons for the political instability in post-independent Africa.

There is a wide list of books published suitable for additional reading in connection with this course, and the following selection will be found useful but should not be considered definitive.

General

J. Anene and G. Brown (eds), *Africa in the Nineteenth and Twentieth Centuries,* Ibadan University Press and Nelson, 1966

R. Oliver and A. Atmore, *Africa since 1800,* Cambridge University Press, 1967

R. Oliver and J. D. Fage, *A Short History of Africa,* Penguin, 1962

Tarikh, a journal of African history for schools and colleges published twice yearly by Longman for the Historical Society of Nigeria

Kenneth Kaunda, *Zambia Shall be Free,* Heinemann, 1962

Jomo Kenyatta, *Facing Mount Kenya,* Secker and Warburg, 1938

A. J. Luthuli, *Let my People Go,* Collins, 1962

Tom Mboya, *Freedom and After,* Deutsch, 1963

Kwame Nkrumah, *Africa Must Unite,* Heinemann, 1963

Kwame Nkrumah, *I Speak of Freedom,* Heinemann, 1961

Northern Africa

A. A. Boahen, *Britain, the Sahara and the Western Sudan, 1788–1953,* Oxford University Press, 1964

P. M. Holt, *A Modern History of the Sudan,* Weidenfeld and Nicholson, 1961

P. M. Holt, *Egypt and the Fertile Crescent,* Longman, 1966

A. H. M. Jones and E. Munroe, *A History of Ethiopia,* Oxford University Press, 1955

West Africa

J. F. A. Ajayi and I. Espie (eds), *A Thousand Years of West African History,* Ibadan University Press and Nelson, 1965

A. A. Boahen, *Topics in West African History,* Longman, 1966

M. Crowder and R. Akpofure, *Nigeria: A Modern History for Schools,* Faber, 1966 (students)

M. Crowder, *Story of Nigeria,* Faber, 1966 (teachers)

B. Davidson, *A History of West Africa 1000–1800,* New Edition, Longman, 1967

J. D. Fage, *A History of West Africa,* 4th edition, Cambridge University Press, 1969

C. Fyfe, *A Short History of Sierra Leone,* Longman, 1962

J. D. Hargreaves, *Prelude to the Partitition of West Africa,* Macmillan, 1963

W. E. F. Ward, *A History of Ghana,* 2nd edition, Allen and Unwin, 1958 (teachers)

W. E. F. Ward, *Short History of Ghana,* Longman, 1957 (Students)

J. B. Webster and A. A. Boahen, *The Revolutionary Years : West Africa since 1800,* Longman, 1967

Southern and Central Africa

B. M. Fagan (ed), *A Short History of Zambia,* Oxford University Press, 1961

A. J. Hanna, *The Story of the Rhodesias and Nyasaland,* Faber, 1960

C. W. de Kiewiet, *A History of South Africa, Social and Economic,* Oxford University Press, 1951

J. D. Omer-Cooper, *The Zulu Aftermath,* Longman, 1966

T. O. Ranger (ed) *Aspects of Central African History,* Heinemann, 1968

P. E. N. Tindall, *History of Central Africa,* Longman, 1968

E. A. Walker, *A History of Southern Africa,* Longman, 1957

A. J. Wills, *An Introduction to the History of Central Africa,* 2nd edition, Oxford University Press, 1967

Middle Africa

B. Davidson, *East and Central Africa to the late Nineteenth Century,* Longman, 1967

K. Ingham, *A History of East Africa,* Longman, 1962

B. A. Ogot and J. A. Kieran (eds) *Zamani : A Survey of East African History,* East African Publishing House and Longman, 1968

The Oxford History of East Africa, three volumes, Oxford University Press

Index

Hilton Young commission, 289, 346
Houphouet-Boigny, Félix, 188, 189–90, 389

Ibadan, 19, 173
Ibo, 145, 187, 391
Idris, King, 123, 125–6, 387
Ijebu Kingdom, 31, 145
Imperial British East Africa Company, 12, 24, 309, 310, 314, 319
Indépendants d'Outre-Mer, 189
India, 44, 206, 259, 307, 351
Indians, in Kenya, 318, 330, 346, 357; in Nyasaland, 279; in South Africa, 231–2, 238, 249, 252, 256–7, 259; troops in Africa, 13, 14, 270
Industrial and Commercial Union, 262, 278
International Suez Company, 50, 65–6
International African Association, 309
Isandhlwana, battle of, 15
Islam, 35, 45, 82, 102, 105, 106, 107, 110, 112, 393
Ismail Pasha, 44, 46, 47, 86
Israel, 60, 386
Istiqlal Party, 111, 114
Ivory Coast, French occupation, 8, 134, 136, 145, 147–8, 161, 163, 188–90; independence, 190; post-independence, 192, 193, 194, 386

Jaja, King, 144
Jabavu, John T., 235, 259–60
Jameson raid, 218–19, 271
Jews, 60, 67, 110; see also Israel

Kadalie, Clements, 262, 278, 279
Kagwa, Sir Apolo, 333–4
Kasavubu, Joseph, 368, 371, 372
Katanga, Belgian control, 210, 313, 316, 324–5, 327, 349, 370; secession, 371
Kaunda, Kenneth, 292, 295–9
Kenya, British occupation, 28, 93, 309, 320; communications, 28, 318, 329; economy, 323, 324, 326–7, 330, 336, 341, 346; Egypt and, 23; independence, 360; nationalist struggle, 352–60; population, 335–6; post-independence, 83, 309, 383, 385, 386, 389, 393
Kenya African Democratic Union, 359
Kenya African National Union, 359
Kenya African Union, 353–4
Kenya Federation of Labour, 358
Kenya National Party, 358

Kenyatta, Jomo, 353–4, 358–60, 382
Khatmiyya tariqa, 75, 76–7, 79–80
Kikuyu, 315, 316, 318, 326, 333–6, 339, 353–4, 357
Kikuyu Central Association, 352–3
Kikuyu Independent Schools Association, 339, 352
Kikuyu Karinga Educational Association, 339, 352
Kinshasa, 317, 332, 348, 349, 368, 369; see also Congo (Kinshasa)
Kittaniya brotherhood, 113
Kiriji wars, 31
Kitchener, Lord, 49, 50–1, 223
Kongo people, 316, 318, 370
Kruger, President, 205–6, 212, 216, 220, 221, 222, 223, 232
Kumasi, 14, 141, 161, 187

Lagos, British administration from, 154, 158, 159, 170; British occupation, 8, 10, 31, 131; communications, 33; nationalism, 39, 171, 173
Lancaster House Conference, 358
League of Nations, 59, 91, 94–5, 147, 157, 244, 351
Liberal Constitutional Party, 109
Liberal Party (South Africa), 255
Liberia, 134, 141, 382, 383, 384, 387, 389, 390, 391, 393
Libya, 100–1, 122, 123, 125–6, 187, 384
Lij Iyasu, Emperor, 83–4
Lobengula, King, 208, 211, 213, 214, 268
Lobito, 327, 349
London Conference, 1951, 290
London 'Convention', 200
Lourenço Marques, 213
Lowanika, King, 270
Lozi Kingdom, 268, 270
Luluabourg, 332, 348, 369
Lugard, Lord Frederick, 24, 101, 137, 154–7, 158, 159
Lumumba, Patrice, 369, 371
Lunda Empire, 344, 391
Luo people, 357, 358
Lyautey, Hubert, 101–2, 103

Macpherson Constitution, 187
Maghreb, 73, 101, 103–5, 123–5, 385; see also North Africa
Mahdist movement, 18, 23, 75, 77
Maji Maji revolt, 35, 316, 322–3
Malawi, 199, 210, 266, 300, 382, 386, 387, 393; see also Nyasaland